Mental Wellness Made Easy

The Smart Way™ to Manage Stress

Emotion Regulation and Stress Management for Everyone

*Maintain and Restore Mental Well-Being
Develop Healthy Habits of Thought*

Also by ♥ Jeanine Joy, Ph.D.

Harness the Power of Resilience: Be Ready for Life

Burnout: Prevention and Recovery, Resilience and Retention, Evidence-based, experience-informed, root cause solutions

Prevent Suicide: The Smart Way, Transformative Empowering Processes Provide A Better Way to Prevent Suicide

Empowered Employees become Engaged Employees: Using Science to Solve the Employee Engagement Crisis, *The Smart Way: Applied Positive Psychology in Action*

Rescue Our Children from the War Zone: Teach Social and Emotional Skills to Improve Their Lives: *Applied Positive Psychology 2.1*

True Prevention--Optimum Health: Remember Galileo

Is Punishment Ethical? The Fallacy of Good and Evil

"Trusting One's Emotional Guidance Builds Resilience", Perspectives on Coping and Resilience. Ed. Venkat Pulla, Shane Warren, and Andrew Shatté. Laxmi Nagar: Authors Press, 2013. 254-279

Other books in the works by Jeanine Joy:
Diversity Appreciation: Using Science to Transform the Paradigm
An Apple a Day Keeps the Doctor Away: Positive Thinking
Beyond Inspirational
Schizophrenia: Reconstructed in a new Paradigm: Recovery, Voices, Hallucinations, Emotions
Burnout Relief: Stress Reduction for Teachers
Responding to the Emergency: Burnout Relief for First Responders
A Reprieve from Burnout for Attorneys: Mitigating the effects of Chronic Stress
Beyond Mindfulness and Work/Life Balance: The Smart Way to Lower Stress

Thrive More, Now Publishing

Mental Wellness Made Easy
Maintain and Restore Mental Well-Being
Develop Health Habits of Thought
The Smart Way to Permanently Reduce Stress

A Thrive More, Now Book / 2018

Published by
Thrive More, Now Publishing
Charlotte, North Carolina

ISBN-13: 978-1-64370-434-0

All rights reserved
Copyright © Jeanine Joy, 2018
All rights reserved, including the right to reproduce this book or portions thereof in any form whatsoever. For information: Thrive More Now Publishing, Rights Department, P.O. Box 6888, Concord NC 28078
For information about discounts for bulk purchases, training programs, or speaking engagements, please contact Thrive More, Now Publishing.
www.ThriveMoreNow.US

She was beautiful, for the way she thought. She was beautiful, for the sparkle in her eyes when she talked about something she loved. She was beautiful, for her ability to make other people smile, even if she was sad.
No, she wasn't beautiful for something as temporary as her looks. She was beautiful, deep down to her soul. She is beautiful.
F. Scott Fitzgerald

Everyone has this beauty inside themselves. Good mental health releases it for all to see.

The most beautiful people we have known are those who have known defeat, known suffering, known struggle, known loss, and have found their way out of the depths. These persons have an appreciation, a sensitivity, and an understanding of life that fills them with compassion, gentleness, and a deep loving concern. Beautiful people do not just happen.
Elisabeth Kubler-Ross

Contents

Contents v
Reviews: IX
Testimonials: X
Dedication XII
Acknowledgements XII
Forward 1
    Medical Care 4
    How to Approach This Material 4
Prologue 7
Why is mental health important? 8
What is Your Current Status? 9
What is Good Mental Health? 9
Mental Illness Pathway Illustration 12
    Introduction 13
If you have a diagnosis... 14
Mental Illness 15
Risk Factors for Mental Illnesses 15
Symptoms of Stress 16
Depression Characteristics 17
Bi-Polar Disorder (BPD) 17
Depression, Anxiety, Bi-Polar Disorder, PTSD, OCD, and Anger Notes 18
Relationships: Stress, Energy, Emotion, Biochemistry, Thoughts, and Cellular Communication 18
Brain Chemistry 19
The Funnel and Emotion Diagram 23
    What Humans Do and Why They Do It 24
    New Definition of the Purpose and Use of Emotions 25
Is Using Emotional Guidance Selfish? 31
Lean Toward Satisfying Perspectives 36
Satisfying Process 40
Validation 43
Teaching Children Emotional Guidance 43
Be Realistic 45
Long-term, Short-term 46
Hope 48
Source of Emotional Guidance 48
Emotional State 49
Emotional Guidance Process 51
Topics 51
History of the Definition of Emotion 55
    Energy 57
Comparison: Old Way and New Way to Use Emotions 59
    Back Stories 63
        Understand how Your Brain Processes Data 64
    Individual Perception 67
        Emotion Regulation: Automatic and Conscious 67
Expectations 70
Define Yourself: Don't allow Other People to Define Who You Are or What You Can Be 70
Focus 71
Beliefs: Example 73

- Rational Thought 76
- Confabulation 77
  - Unhealthy Habits of Thought Path to Depression 79
- Biochemical Path to Depression 79
- Prevention and Recovery Strategies 79
- What Causes Chronic Stress? 80
- Build a Strong Foundation 80
  - Factors Associated with Healthy Habits of Thought (Overview) 82
  - High-Level Factors That Contribute to Positive Outcomes 83
    - Happiness 84
    - Resilience 85
    - Explanatory Style 88
    - Psychological Flexibility 91
    - Mental First 91
  - Stress Management Coping Strategies 93
    - Coping vs Thriving 94
  - Develop Healthy Perspectives 99
    - Your Purpose 99
    - Autonomy 100
  - Emotion Regulation Process: Overview 101
  - Transformational and Advanced Coping Skills 103
  - Transformational Strategies 105
  - **Develop Healthy Habits of Thought (Transformational)** 107
    - Supportive, Empowering Beliefs (Transformational) 110
  - Healthy self-esteem (Transformational) 115
- Comparison of Self to Others 122
- A Sense of Entitlement 123
- Fear of Being Judged 124
- How Can We Not Care What They Think When What They Think Matters? 124
- Optimism (Transformational Coping) 126
- Internal Locus of Control (Transformational) 126
- Growth Mindset (Transformational) 127
- Emotion Regulation Beliefs (Transformational) 127
- Re-define Your Best (Advanced and Transformational) (Resources) 128
- Self-Compassion (Advanced to Transformational) 132
- Perfectionism 133
- Self-love or Self-respect (Transformational) 133
- Open to New Experiences (Transformational) 134
- Positive Thinking (Advanced to Transformational) 135
- Make Happiness a Priority (Transformational) 137
- Human Dignity (Transformational) 138
- Appreciation (Palliative to Transformational) 139
- Visioning (Advanced to Transformational) 141
- Diversity Appreciation (Adaptive to Transformational) 141
- Poor Guidance about Priorities: Change Unsupportive Beliefs (Transformational) 144
- Develop Healthy Attitudes (Transformational) 144
- Forgiveness (Transformational) 146
- Easily Offended 149
  - Advanced Stress Management Coping Strategies 153
- Metacognition (Advanced Strategy) 153
- Metacognitive Processes (Advanced) 154
- Respond Proactively to Emotions (Advanced) 155
- Cognitive Restructuring/Reappraisal (Advanced Coping) 156
- It's Bogus (Advanced Coping) 159
- Use Science and Experience to Support Yourself (Adaptive Coping) 159

If Everyone . . .	159
Words Matter	160
Death – Plan Ahead	160
Power of Thoughts/Words: Quantum Physics	161
Be Flexible (Advanced)	169
Trust Your Guidance (Advanced and/or Transformational)	169
Adjust Your Focus (Advanced Coping)	169
Give Yourself Credit Where it is Due (Advanced and Transformational)	169
Labels (Advanced)	170
Reframing (Advanced)	170
Positive Affirmations (Advanced)	174
Expectant Questions (Advanced)	176
Positive Reframing (Advanced)	178
Look for Silver Lining (Advanced and Transformational)	179
Savoring (Advanced)	180
Strengths (Adaptive)	182
Adaptive Coping	183
Curiosity	183
Planning (Adaptive Coping)	183
Social Support (Adaptive)	184
Set Limits: Say No (Adaptive)	185
Sleep (Adaptive)	187
Meditation (Palliative to Transformational)	187
Religion/Spirituality	188
Unhealthy Habits of Thought (Identify and Change)	189
Anxiety	190
Habits of Thought	191
OCD	192
Anger	194
Catastrophizing/Awfulizing	194
Worry	197
Pessimism	198
Suppressing Emotions	201
Negative rumination	203
Co-rumination	203
Self-Abuse	206
Self-Criticism	206
Self-Harm	211
Self-Sacrifice	212
Making others happy	213
Low Self-esteem	213
Can I feel better about myself?	218
Low Self-Efficacy	218
Willingness to seek support	219
Denial	219
Cautious (overly)	220
Avoidance	220
Insisting on Control	220
Cynicism	221
Addictions	223
Surface-Thinking	223
Final Thoughts about Unhealthy Habits of Thought	223
Why is The Smart Way the Best Way?	225
The Smart Way is:	225
Compare CBT to The Smart Way	226

- Compare Mindfulness to The Smart Way 231
- Work/Life Balance 237
- Communication 238
  - Advice Q & A 239
    - Heartache 239
    - Feeling Lost and Unable to love 240
    - Loss of a child (grief) 240
    - Depression 241
  - Primary Prevention 243
  - The Benefits of using The Smart Way 245
- Outcomes You Can Expect 245
  - Reviews 248
  - Cultural Differences 248
  - Dr. Joy's Books ii
  - About the Author: Jeanine Joy, Ph.D. iii
  - Appendix I – Emotional Guidance Scale (EGSc) iv
  - Appendix II: Zones and Outcomes Chart v
  - Appendix III - The Smart Way Training for Groups vi
  - Appendix IV– Religious Passages that Support Emotional Guidance XVIII
  - Appendix V- Effects of a Positive Mindset XVIII
  - Appendix VI - Suicide Prevention XXII
- Emergency Numbers XXII
- Suicide Risk Factors and Warning Signs XXIII
  - Appendix VII - Public Health and Mental Health XVIII
- Bi-Polar XX
  - Appendix VIII – Emotional Words XVIII
  - Works Cited XIX
    - Citations XXXI

Reviews:

Book: Empowered Employees Become Engaged Employees
Title of Review: <u>Actually Achieving Employee Engagement</u>
By William McPeck on September 28, 2016

As a student of employee engagement, I was naturally attracted by this book's title. The issue of employee engagement has emerged as one of the key issues in today's workplace.

The employee engagement literature suggests that attempts to address employee engagement up to now have met with little significant success. Despite the efforts, according to Gallup's employee engagement surveys, the level of employee engagement has held steady at approximately 30%.

In this book, Dr. Joy makes the argument that little has changed in employee engagement because efforts to date have failed to target the root cause of the problem – the emotional state of employees. The book is based on the premise that employees can learn how to feel better on purpose and therefore be in a position to better tap into their own personal intrinsic motivation and make better use of skill based empowerment techniques.

In the Introduction, Dr. Joy states the book's purpose is to "help managers understand how to improve employee engagement." Each chapter of the book specifically addresses an area researchers have identified as being important to employee engagement. The chapters include such important areas as:

• Perception
• Cognitive Processes
• Resilience
• Psychological Flexibility
• Happiness

As a student of employee engagement, this is the first book I have read devoted exclusively to linking employee emotional state to employee engagement. I believe this book makes a significant contribution to the literature on employee engagement.

The book reflects a combination of the published research literature, exercises, self-help tests, an extensive bibliography and, of course, Dr. Joy's own ideas, perspectives and experiences as well. Despite the book's containing a heavy dose of the research science, I found the book to be engaging and easy to read.

This book certainly achieved its stated purpose and has greatly contributed to my knowledge of and thinking about employee engagement. I am sure it will do the same for you. If you have any interest in the subject of employee engagement, this book should be on your "Must Read" list.

Book: Empowered Employees Become Engaged Employees
By RGB on November 13, 2016

This book is an excellent examination of a critical factor in the success of any business or organization. As any knowledgeable business owner/leader knows, the commitment of employees/workers is a critical factor in customer satisfaction which in turn is the primary driver of market share.

The book can be somewhat technical in some sections, and is clearly written for the human resource professional. However, I believe it is worthwhile for anyone who is interested in motivating a workforce.

I recommend it highly.

Book: *Our Children Live in the War Zone: Teach Them Resilience to Improve Their Lives, Applied Positive Psychology 2.1*

Title of Review: A FAVORITE ALL TIME BOOK

By Rhapsody on November 2, 2016

This is a positive MUST read book. It can help anyone in any stage of life in any circumstance. I'm going to get a copy for my children and grandchildren for Christmas!!

Testimonials:

Jeanine Joy, PhD is not only a well-respected and published author; she is also a fantastic facilitator and speaker. Her style is both trusting and inspirational and provides audiences with the knowledge and practical applications needed to move organizations to the next level. If you are looking to someone who has the experience and the energy to lead, Jeanine is definitely the person you want on your team. You will not be disappointed, and your bottom line will be better for it.

John Metcalf
President, Workforce Systems Associates

I find Jeanine to be extremely insightful into all aspects of human behavior. She is passionate about what she does and about helping others. Her ability to breakdown behavior into the most fundamental elements, understand what motivates and creates behaviors and provide feedback that can help align, alter and/or fully change behaviors is astonishing. She understands the human condition as it relates to professional and personal relationships and at a level you can understand. In my business - working with medical professionals - she has an in depth understanding of the stressors and burnout associated with the profession and she is outstanding at helping individuals cope and find balance in their lives. She is an outstanding speaker and I would recommend any organization, medical practice, hospital or group to explore her services for the benefit of their staff and ultimately their patients.

Michael Tekely, AAI
Regional Vice President at MedMal Direct Insurance Company

If you are looking for a motivational, insightful speaker, who can provide practical techniques for understanding people and changing behaviors, contact Dr. Joy. I have heard Jeanine give presentations at the Contingency Planning Association of the Carolinas and the Charlotte South Park Lions Club. Her insights on gauging what motivates, and how to influence groups and individuals may be applied in a variety of situations from raising awareness about corporate preparedness to ways of attracting volunteers for civic activities. Contact Dr. Joy, you won't regret it.

David Shimberg, MBCI, CBCP
Business Continuity Consultant

Dedication

This book is dedicated to everyone I've taught how to reduce stress and feel better that ever expressed appreciation to me for helping them. Whether it was a stranger I stood next to in line at the bank who shared a tidbit of their day that I helped see from a lighter perspective or someone who worked hard in one of my classes to move past abuse that had plagued them for decades, this book is dedicated to you.

Your feedback fed my soul and kept me energized to continue finding answers the best way to explain what I learned so it is easily understood and implemented. Your suffering, large or small, stirred me to action. I am pleased with the results and hope you are, too.

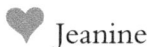 Jeanine

Acknowledgements

A new idea is first condemned as ridiculous and then dismissed as trivial, until finally, it becomes what everybody knows.
William James

The work of thousands of researcher has contributed to my expertise in understanding how to develop healthy habits of thought. I greatly appreciate the work they put into conducting the research and the often arduous task of getting it through peer review.

I also feel especially warm appreciation for William James, the father of modern psychology, whose quotes are frequently found in these pages.

More personally, the value of the feedback from those I have taught skills that increase their resilience and sense of empowerment cannot be quantified. They have helped me refine the explanations and methods presented here, allowing me to communicate more effectively with you.

Forward

He who mixes the pleasant with the useful gains everyone's approval.
Horace (BC 65-8)[p]

I tend to write in a very matter of fact way that is sometimes interpreted as not caring or compassionate. That is far from the case. I write in a matter of fact way to communicate information that will help people who are suffering and to prevent people from suffering in the future because writing that way provides greater clarity. If I could gather everyone who is hurting in my arms and hug them to wellness, I would. As you read these words, know that you are not alone. There are others who have been where you now are who have found a way to feel better. If they can do it, so can you. Be patient with yourself.

Mental illnesses are beyond epidemic levels. In the United States, 1 out of every 5 people experience mental illness every year. It may seem that we have an epidemic of mental illness but what we have is a widespread lack of coping skills. Mental illness is a symptom of having inadequate and inaccurate information, the absence of which allows chronic stress to push people down the path to mental illness.

The scientific understanding of the path to mental illness is growing quickly but distribution of that information to the people has been slow. This book fills that gap. We now know that common habits of thought lead to anxiety, depression, and other mental illnesses. Healthy habits of thought maintain mental well-being even when someone faces adversities. This book helps you identify your own habits of thought and provides tools that help you change your habits of thoughts so they support mental well-being and reduce the stress you experience.

Cultures around the world teach children to develop unhealthy habits of thought because we didn't know what we were doing. It is no wonder that we have high rates of mental illness.

Why choose this book?

Dr. Joy studied a single big question for decades, "What makes some people thrive in spite of adversity?" Human thriving begins with the thoughts you choose to think. You may feel as if you have no control over which thoughts you think but by the time you apply the strategies presented here you will change your mind.

You will understand how long it takes to notice real differences and what you will see as early indicators that your efforts are making a difference. You'll understand the process so you won't give up when you're on the brink of success.

These solutions are evidence-based and experience-informed and have already helped thousands of people. I first began teaching early versions of the information you'll learn in *Mental Wellness Made Easy (MWME)* in 2001.

You will understand why the Advanced and Transformational Strategies presented are current best practices that take humanity beyond mindfulness and work/life balance to true happiness and better health.

This book is written for the average person. These strategies help people from all walks of life and all ages. The teenager dealing with a broken heart or loneliness, the young career person or parent who is overwhelmed, frustrated, or frightened, and the senior citizen who wonders whether they are still relevant in a fast-changing world will learn valuable strategies in these pages. Individuals diagnosed with a variety of mental illnesses have found relief using these strategies. The primary purpose of this book is to help you develop skills that prevent mental illnesses and help people who are already suffering improve their lives.

Mental health professionals will find new tools to help themselves and their clients but this book is written for the layperson. The science that supports this work was documented in four earlier books. If it hasn't already helped other people, it is not included here.

If you experience frequent stress (chronic stress), it is an indicator that you do not have the coping skills necessary to be as good as you could in your current situation. It is an early indicator that if you don't change something your mental well-being is at risk. Applying what you learn in *MWME* will put you back in control and allow you to fulfill more of your potential.

The vast majority of stress coping skills that are promoted are Palliative or Adaptive.* Until recently, those were best practices. But science is marching forward and they are no longer the best we can do. Advanced and Transformational Stress Coping Strategies have the ability to permanently reduce stress. *MWME* teaches you state-of-the-art best practices.

The examples and scenarios are designed to be flexible. A scenario that describes the end of a relationship can be applied to the end of a job. When you begin thinking in terms of everything as a relationship it is surprising how much our relationships with people can resemble relationships with jobs, homes, and hobbies and vice versa. By knowing why a strategy works, you will know when it can be used effectively in different situations.

A book that contained solutions for every possible stressful situation would be too heavy to carry. Viewing stressful situations as relationships (with people, jobs, money, electronics, health, body, academics, etc.) provides the flexibility to see that a solution that helps with a relationship with their job can also help you with a relationship with an in-law.

Stigma about mental illness has been a persistent issue. Stigma originated during an era when no one understood why some people became mentally ill and we didn't know how to cure mental illnesses. Today we know both cause and in many instances, cure. We know how to prevent mental illnesses before they occur by increasing healthy habits of thought.

---

* Palliative practices temporarily reduce stress but do not change the situation causing stress. Adaptive practices increase practical skills like budgeting, time management, etc.

In this book you'll learn:
- To identify whether your usual habits of thought are healthy or unhealthy.
- How to change your automatic thoughts (habits of thought) so that they support outcomes you want.
- To determine whether your current thought is healthy or unhealthy.
- To change unhealthy thoughts to healthier thoughts.
- To identify what types of coping skills you are using and choose the one that will benefit you the most.

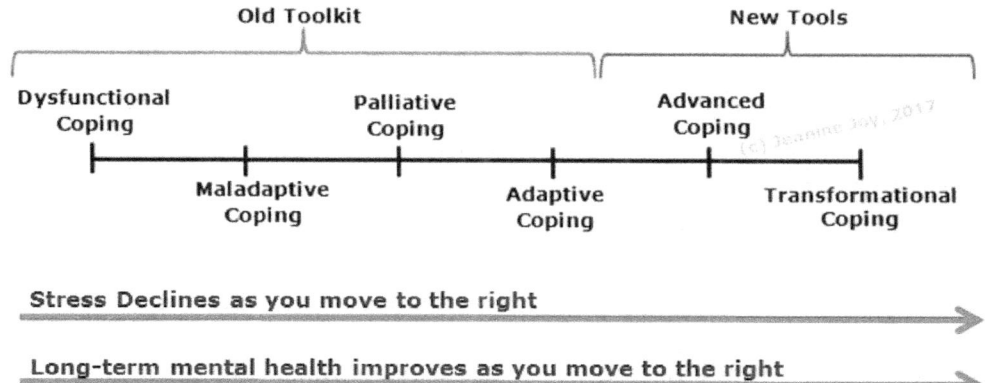

1. To develop Advanced and Transformational Stress Coping Strategies that permanently reduce the amount of stress you experience every day.
2. Why life so often felt like you were running around on a hamster wheel and how to make real progress.

MWME is designed to help you learn about your own psychology and provide strategies that help you develop healthy habits of thought. There is nothing stigmatizing about reading it or about applying the strategies. This book is not therapy. You do not have to tell anyone what you are doing. Most of the work can be done in the privacy of your own mind.

Strategies presented in *MWME* have been successful in curing chronic, life-long depression. Some of hery earliest clients have been depression-free for ten years after decades of serious depression. Individuals with PTSD, Bi-polar disorder, anxiety, schizophrenia, multiple diagnoses, anger problems, and other mental illnesses have been helped with these strategies. No guarantees can be made that using these methods will cure you because there are many variables but the most significant variable is within your control. That variable is whether or not you apply the skills.

Medical Care

If you are under a medical professional's care, do not stop treatment without consulting your mental health care provider. Do not discontinue any medications without supervision. Stopping your medication without supervision can lead to unintended consequences including life threatening problems.

You can learn and apply these techniques if you are in therapy. If you believe you need professional care you should consult a mental health professional. The information provided is intended to help you thrive. This book is not medical advice and is not a substitute for medical advice. It is not a diagnosis.

If you believe you are in danger of harming yourself or someone else, please call your local emergency number or visit the emergency department of your local hospital, call your local police department and ask for a Crisis Intervention Trained Officer (CIT Officer), or call the suicide hotline. You can also call the National Suicide Prevention Lifeline now at 1-800-273-TALK (1-800-273-8255); TTY: 1-800-799-4TTY (4889) to talk to a trained counselor. You can also call your doctor.

International Emergency Numbers

Australia	000	Switzerland	112	UAE	112
New Zealand	111	India	102	Brazil	192
Fiji	000 or 911	Hong Kong	999	Costa Rica	911
United Kingdom	112 or 999	Israel	101 or 112	S. Africa	112, 10 177
Ireland	112 or 999	Japan	119	China	120
Turkey	112	Nepal	102	Philippines	117 or 112

How to Approach This Material

Readers should not accept what I tell them in these pages as the truth simply because it is written. Try it out in your own life and see how it works for you. Use this book to learn skills that will help you maintain or restore your mental health, and to develop critical thinking skills.

The ability to decide for yourself is better for you than just accepting it as true because an expert told you it is true. It will increase you confidence that you understand what you read in these pages. Every strategy is designed to help you feel less stress and emotionally better.

Key to Symbols

When the number for a citation is followed by a "p", it indicates that the quote has been paraphrased. For example, [33p] indicates a paraphrased quote whereas [45] indicates an exact quote.

This symbol indicates that a strategy you can use to develop Advanced Coping Strategies to reduce stress or a Transformational Strategy to change a belief is presented near the symbol.

This symbol indicates that information about how long the process usually takes to create desired changes is provided near the symbol. Time is important because when someone fails to achieve the desired results it is most often because they gave up too soon.

Rituals you may want to adopt are mentioned at various points in the text. This symbol indicates recommended rituals that can help you experience less stress on a daily basis.

Prologue

Let us think of education as the means of developing our greatest abilities, because in each of us there is a private hope and dream which, fulfilled, can be translated into benefit for everyone and greater strength for our nation.

John F. Kennedy (1917-1963) Thirty-fifth 35th President of the USA

Since 1995, I've spent about 50,000 hours studying and teaching "What makes some humans thrive in spite of adversity?" The subject has consumed me because the answer has the potential to improve the quality of life for everyone.

If you're trying to figure out life, how you feel, or how to feel different than you feel, it can be like trying to figure out a 1,000 piece jig saw puzzle that is solid white. When you understand the information provided in *MWME*, it feels as if a vivid picture suddenly appeared on the jig saw puzzle, making it easy to put everything in its proper place.

I encourage you to adopt a risk management approach to life which means doing what you can to reduce your risk of undesired outcomes. It also means not worrying about things you cannot control or about things that have a very low probability of happening.

Stress is one of the most important things to manage. The reason stress management is so important is that chronic stress is a leading indicator for nearly all physical and mental illnesses. That means that when you are experiencing chronic stress the damage has begun. That doesn't mean you have to stop doing what you are doing. It means you need better stress management strategies.

The benefits of lowering stress and the detriments of living with high stress are provided in the Benefits Chapter (pg. 245).

Our society tolerates way more stress than it is healthy to tolerate.

When we do something that causes physical pain we don't keep doing it. With mental pain, many people continue doing the thing that caused pain again and again. The physical equivalent would be running your hand over a board and getting splinters and then doing it again and again and again.

Most Americans are chronically stressed. We have become so accustomed to being stressed that it feels normal to us. But normal does not mean healthy. Many of us brag about how much stress we can experience as if it is a badge of honor. Doctors treat stress symptoms, but are helpless against the root cause because the root is in the mind. Corporate wellness programs are designed to address symptoms, not the root cause. It's time for change. Many people believe they can ignore mild signs of stress such as headaches and stomach acid, but it's easier to fix before it becomes mental illness, hypertension, obesity, diabetes, or heart disease. Life is much better with good stress management strategies.

One reason people keep repeating actions that lead to mental and emotional pain is they did not know how to stop doing it. Mental and emotional pain are indicators (symptoms) of chronic stress. You will learn how to manage your emotions in healthy ways using Advanced and Transformational Stress Management Coping Styles. When you learn how to stop chronic stress, life feels good.

- Advanced Stress Management Coping Strategies change your current stress level without requiring you to change the circumstances first.
- Transformational Strategies change the amount of stress you feel on a daily basis as the result of your automatic responses.

If you feel stressed, you are not alone, 54% of employees report that they are chronically stressed.[1] Remember, that number is people who are employed. The number is higher for people who are unemployed.

People use the best coping methods available to them even if those choices will make things worse in the long run. Significant advances in the science of human thriving (what helps humans thrive in spite of adversity) improve the available options. We can now optimize our mind to increase our ability to fulfill our potential and maintain mental well-being. Until very recently, the continuum of strategies for coping with stress stopped at adaptive coping strategies. Recent advances expanded the spectrum of coping skills to include Advanced and Transformational Strategies.

These brief descriptions highlight the importance of this shift.

- ***Dysfunctional Coping:*** Makes the situation worse, fast.
- ***Maladaptive Coping:*** Increases stress, allows problem to fester, situation gets worse slowly.
- ***Palliative Coping:*** Decreases stress temporarily but does not solve the problem.
- ***Adaptive Coping:*** Changes the situation in ways that reduce stress.

New Tools:

- ***Advanced Coping:*** Quickly reduces stress without requiring the source of the stress to change first.
- ***Transformational Coping:*** Permanently reduces stress experienced every day.

Why is mental wellness important?

- Your mental health affects every important area of your life including physical health, relationships, and academic, career, and sports success.
- Mental illness affects 1 in 5 people each year (20%).
- A little more than half the people with a substance use disorder have a diagnosable mental illness.[2]
- Mental illness affects 70% of youth in state and local juvenile justice systems.[3]
- 37% of children age 14 or above who have a mental illness drop out of school.[4]

- 90% of completed suicides have an underlying mental illness
- Mental illness is the cause of disability in 4 out of 10 cases.[5]

What is Your Current Status?

Questionnaires you can use to see how you are doing are available on my website, Happiness1st.com. The questionnaires cover numerous topics including:
- Depression (PHQ-9) Questionnaire
- General Anxiety Questionnaire
- Stress Symptoms Questionnaire
- Burnout Questionnaire
- Burnout Questionnaire (clinical subtypes)
- Self-esteem questionnaire
- Brief Coping Skills Questionnaire
- Longer Coping Skills Questionnaire
- Thriving Questionnaire

Using the questionnaires before you begin the book and again after you apply the strategies will allow you to see your progress. You do not have to provide information to me in order to use the Questionnaires. (Link: http://www.happiness1st.com/mental_health_questionnaires/)

What is Good Mental Health?

Good mental health is much more than the absence of a diagnosis of a mental illness. Being mentally healthy is best understood by how it impacts our life. Mental well-being means we are able to function at high levels in a wide variety of situations. People who have good mental health:
- Can face adversity without experiencing high levels of stress.
- Bounce back quickly from adversity.
- Are able to create and sustain healthy relationships at home, work, and with friends and teammates.
- Aren't always happy.
  - It would be accurate to say they lean toward the positive but they are authentic. If they are sad, they don't pretend to be happy.
- Have skills that allow them to feel better even when things don't work out as planned.
- Spend more time feeling good, which means they experience less stress.

Sweet Zone	Hopeful Zone	Blah Zone	Drama Zone ↓↑↓↑↓	Give Away Zone	Red (Hot) Zone	Powerless Zone
Joy	Hope	Contentment	Ornery	Blame	Anger	Hatred
Appreciation	Gratitude	Boredom	Irritation	Resentful	Revenge	Powerless
Enthusiasm	Upbeat	Pessimism	Frustration	Doubt	Rage	Jealous
Happiness		Apathy	Impatience	Guilt	Provoked	Grief
Optimism		Uninspired	Impatient	Worry	Outraged	Fear
Belief			Disappointment	Discouraged	Furious	Despair
Freedom			Overwhelmed			Hopeless
Eager						Lethargic
Love						Depressed

The Zones represent emotional states separated by how empowered and stressed people experiencing those emotions feel. There are more than a thousand emotional words. The Zones shown do not illustrate every emotion that would be in that Zone. The right Zone for an emotion can be identified by finding an emotion in the Emotional Guidance Scale (EGSc) in Appendix I that feels a similar degree of empowerment/disempowerment or stress.

Experiencing emotions in Zones below Hopeful and Sweet does not mean you have poor mental health. Chronically (consistently) spending time in lower Zones is:

- An indicator that you are experiencing chronic stress which is a serious risk factor for developing mental illness, and
- An indicator that you would benefit from learning strategies to manage your emotional state so you experience less stress.

None of my work tells anyone how they should feel. You feel how you feel. I do not encourage anyone to always feel happy. I encourage everyone to learn skills that allow them to experience better-feeling emotional states when they want to feel better.

Strategies that help you change your level of stress and emotional state are provided throughout the material in MWME. The emotional state you are experiencing dictates which strategy will be of the most benefit to you in reducing stress. Using the right process is important. If a process makes you feel worse, it is not the right process to use at that time.

Attempting to jump from depressed to happy doesn't work. Smaller steps create a successful journey. The small steps can be taken in quick succession so an individual who has practiced skills that allow them to feel better can move quickly from Zone-to-Zone. For example, before I understood these skills it took six months or more to recover from heartbreak. After learning these skills, I was able to move through the Zones from Powerless to the Sweet Zone at the end of a relationship in less than a weekend.

This is not through suppressing emotions which is a Dysfunctional Stress Coping Strategy. It is important to understand that when someone shifts in this way the new emotional state is stable with respect to the situation that originally caused the low emotional state. The way the situation is perceived has changed so it no longer feels disempowering or stressful.

Mental illness is at epidemic rates. The percentage of people experiencing chronic stress indicates the situation will become worse, not better. The goal of this book is to reverse this trend by empowering people with knowledge about how their minds process information and how to optimize the programming their mind uses to process data. The Mental Illness Pathway Illustration on the next page provides a big picture view. Negative emotions indicate you are experiencing stress. Chronic stress is the most significant indicator that mental wellness is declining.

Low emotional states indicate the mind and body are stressed.

The Mental Illness Pathway Illustration shows the relationships between emotional states and developing mental illness. There are important relationships between emotional state, stress, and energy that you must understand to know why skills that help you manage your emotional state can prevent mental illnesses from developing and speed recovery from existing mental illnesses.

Emotions indicate:

How much stress we are experiencing
- Positive emotions = low stress
- Negative emotions = increasing degrees of high stress

How much energy we have available to do what we are planning to do
- Positive emotions indicate we have more energy
- Negative emotions indicate we have less energy
  - There is an exception. Rage and anger can be bottled up energy exploding and exhibit more energy than almost anything other than passion and eagerness.

Biochemical changes in our mind are associated with some mental illnesses. Biochemical changes are a symptom of mental illness; not the cause. This is discussed in more detail in the Relationships: Stress, Energy. . . section of the Introductory chapter.

Negative emotions do not cause harm. Emotions are indicators that your mind and/or body are experiencing stress. Just as the low battery light on your phone or the check engine light in your car are not the problem, emotions are not the problem. Failure to notice the emotion and take appropriate action(s) in response to the indicator is what causes damage to the mind and body.

Mental Illness Pathway Illustration

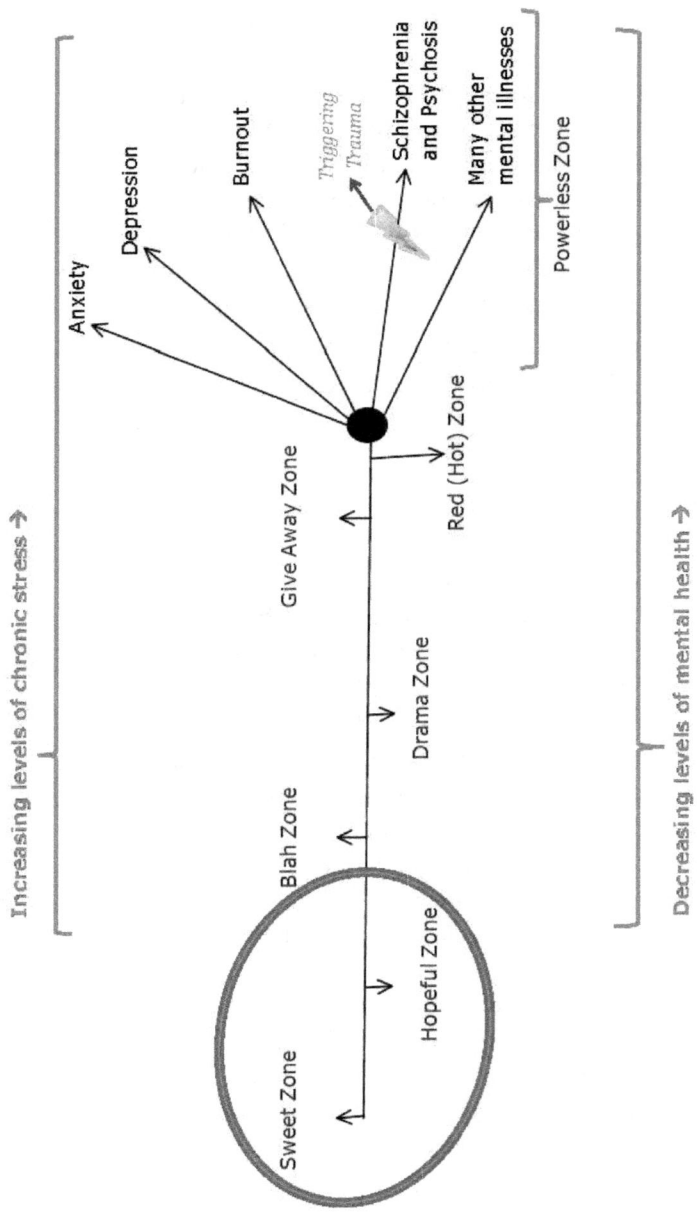

Introduction

One of the prevailing sources of misery is in the generally accepted assumption, that because things have been wrong a long time, it is impossible they will ever be right.
John Ruskin (1819-1900)

The knowledge and skills provided herein are provided in a format that does not require a scientific background. I've worked very hard over the years to simplify the concepts. These strategies have helped teens to CEO's, Individuals who are illiterate, and individuals with advanced degrees, including medical doctors, have reduced their daily stress with the strategies presented in this book. While the book is written for adults, the concepts are simple enough for parents and teachers to share with children.

The reason I've been able to see mental health and illness through a lens that perceives mental illness as both preventable and curable is because I did not take the traditional route to building the foundation of the knowledge I'm sharing. Our society tends to look at what isn't working (in mental and physical health) and try to fix it instead of looking at what works well and applying concepts and skills that maintain wellness to improve health.

Think of it this way. If you'd never seen a car and someone was going to give you a car and you had to understand how it worked, would you choose?:

A. A car that was functioning well, or
B. A broken car

Our medical model took option B a long time ago and continues to view health (mental and physical) from the viewpoint of fixing something that is broken. I studied what worked well and then applied what I observed to situations where improvements were desired. When someone who is suffering from mental illness begins using their mind differently, their mental health improves.

Traditional methods divide our bodies into parts and study them as if they are separate. Our mind and body are a system that won't work well without all the important parts.

When we study healthy minds and bodies and compare what they do to what those who have unhealthy outcomes do, we find that the difference begins with how we think. We can focus on beliefs, attitudes, mindset, or habits of thought and find the same outcome. Disempowered thoughts lead to poor outcomes. Empowered thoughts lead to better outcomes.

Over a period of more than a decade, I discovered that habits of thought can be changed deliberately and that when they are, all areas of our life become less stressful. As our habits of thought become more empowering our habitual emotional state improves to one that feels better. Our automatic behavior improves as our emotional state improves.

You'll learn how to change habits of thoughts that lead to poor outcomes to habits that lead to better results. This is not about teaching you what to think. You will understand the results of thinking in a variety of different ways and make informed choices about which habits of thought you decide to develop.

You'll learn about new research that shows us how to accurately interpret our emotions so that they make sense. When our emotions begin to make sense, life feels less chaotic and we feel like we have more control.

In order to benefit from this book it must be used as a workbook, not just something you understand intellectually. You must use the strategies and feel the improvements in your mood and stress levels.

Historically, mental health was viewed as the absence of a diagnosable mental illness. *MWME* views both physical and mental welness as a person who is thriving, which is a more positive situation than the absence of mental or physical illness.

If you have a diagnosis

A mental illness diagnosis can feel like this:

Imagine taking a car trip. Someone else drives while you read, sleep, or play on a Game Boy. When you arrive at your destination, you don't know how you got there. When you decide you don't like being there you have no idea how to get away from the place you don't like because you don't know how you got there. It's a little like trying to find your way while you are blindfolded.

This scenario describes how it often feels when someone is diagnosed with a mental illness. They didn't pay attention to how they got there. In all fairness, our society doesn't encourage us to pay attention to the markers along the way that let us know we're heading to a destination we won't enjoy. Once a diagnosis is made, you are in a windowless room with no visible door. A diagnosis tells you where you are but nothing about how you got there in the first place.

A diagnosis tells you: This is where you are.

Yes, there is a lot of research that informs mental health professionals what drugs or types of therapy help some people with the same diagnosis. The problem is that the same strategy doesn't work for everyone. The reason is those drugs and therapies were developed based on where the person is; not on how they arrived where they are. They are in a windowless room, too.

When a broader view is taken, the path out of the situation becomes clear.

After reading *MWME*, you will never again be oblivious about how to get where you'd rather be or fail to notice the signs that you're heading to a place you don't want to be. You'll know how to make adjustments to your path before you go where you don't want to go.

Mental Illness

"A mental illness can be defined as a health condition that changes a person's thinking, feelings, or behavior (or all three) and that causes the person distress and difficulty in functioning." [6]

Indications of mental illnesses can include:
- Significant personality change
- Inability to cope with problems and daily activities
- Strange or grandiose ideas (this could also be an indication of genius)
- Excessive anxieties
- Prolonged depression and apathy
- Marked changes in eating or sleeping patterns
- Thinking or talking about suicide or harming yourself
- Extreme mood swings—high or low
- Abuse of alcohol or drugs, and
- Excessive anger, hostility, or violent behavior.

A person who shows any of these signs should seek help from a qualified health professional. [7]

Every person is different and mental illness does not show up the same way in everyone. That being said, some warning signs that indicate consulting a professional for an assessment to determine if you would benefit from assistance can be generalized. It is very important to remember that most mental illnesses can be treated and the sooner help is obtained the better the prognosis usually is. That is not to say that someone who has suffered for decades is beyond help. That simply isn't true but it is usually easier the earlier a person seeks help. That being said, someone who resists help is better off waiting until they are ready to accept assistance and the best thing they may be able to do is work on being receptive.

Risk Factors for Mental Illnesses

Chronic stress is the most common indicator that an individual is at risk of developing mental illness. Chronic stress indicates the individual does not have the level of coping skills needed to thrive under those circumstances. Other factors are environmental, some are genetic, and some are social. All these factors combine to influence whether someone becomes mentally ill. The ability to successfully manage stress to low levels, regardless of conditions, protects against mental illness even when environmental, social, or genetic risks are higher.

Social factors that increase the risk of developing mental illness include:

- Chronic Stress
- Severe parental discord
- Economic hardship
- Physical Abuse
- Verbal Abuse
- Sexual Abuse
- Neglect
- Unhealthy habits of thought*
- Attention disorders
- Learning disorders
- Parent's criminality
- Overcrowding
- Exposure to violence
- Parent's substance use disorder
- Mentally ill parent
- Severely restrictive parenting
- Low self-esteem
- Heartbreak
- Death of a family member or close friend (especially unexpected and sudden or if the child perceives herself to be at fault)
- Caregiver such as a grandparent, especially one who *should* love the child, who treats the child poorly (verbal abuse, unfairly harsh compared to other children, blames the child for the parents' failure to achieve success, etc.)
- Experiencing a traumatic event

Symptoms of Stress

When stress is not well-managed, your physical and mental well-being declines. Appendix VII details the long-term outcomes of unmanaged stress.

Our society promotes some *false premises* about stress that contribute to the increasing levels of both mental illness and chronic illnesses. Some of those false premises include:

- Powering through stressful situations means you are strong.
- You can't do anything about stress.
- Stress is required to be motivated.
- Stress improves performance.
  - This is sometimes true just like it is true that sometimes people who bottom out make drastic positive changes in their lives. It's not the best way to manage stress.
- You have to just power through, like the Energizer bunny, if you want to be successful.
- If you can take it, stress won't hurt you.

Warning signs of stress can come in the form of physical, mental, cognitive, emotional, energetic, or psychological and/or behavioral symptoms including: [8, 9]

---

* Unhealthy habits of thought are explained later

Warning Signs (Indicators of) Stress

Physical

Muscle tension
Headaches
Exhaustion/fatigue
Weight changes
Sleep disturbances
Teeth grinding
Frequent illnesses
Stomach aches
Hypertension
Sweating or trembling hands
Sexual dysfunction
Diarrhea or constipation
Back pain
Restlessness
Indigestion
Increased pain
Dizziness
Racing heart
Ringing in the ears
Immune function decreases
Digestive function worsens
Central Nervous System issues
More accidents
Increased risk of pre-term births
Increased risk of adverse epigenetic changes
Increased risk of adverse behavior and health outcomes in offspring

Behavioral

Hurrying
Increased accidents
Decreased productivity
Increased use of drugs
Increased use of alcohol
Unhealthy eating patterns
Isolation
Cigarette smoking
Procrastination
Conflicts with others
Restricted breathing
More sedentary
Bossiness
Compulsive gum chewing
Inability to get things done
Increased relationship conflict
Engage in riskier behaviors

Cognitive

Trouble thinking clearly
Lack of creativity
Forgetfulness
Memory Loss
Inability to make decisions
Poor concentration

Emotional

Emotions below the Hopeful and Sweet Zones on the Emotional Guidance Scale (EGSc)

Psychological

Irritability
Less emotional control
Often worried
Feeling overwhelmed
Easily frustrated
Thoughts of running away
Loss of sense of humor
Difficulty making decisions
Crying spells
Intense bouts of anger
Attitude critical of others
Restlessness
Nervousness
Anxiety
Boredom, no meaning
Edginess, ready to explode
Feeling powerless
Loneliness
Unhappy for no reason
Easily upset
Burnout
Depression
Anxiety
Suicidal Thoughts
Suicide

Energetic

Energy level declines in response to thoughts (as opposed to because of hunger or fatigue)

Depression Characteristics

- A sad mood
- Energy loss or low energy
- Feeling worthless
- Sleeping too much
- Difficulty sleeping
- Irritability
- Trouble concentrating
- Self-criticism
- A change in appetite or weight
- Recurrent thoughts of death or suicide
- Feeling hopeless about the future
- Loss of interest in activities that one used to enjoy
- Difficulty concentrating
- Inappropriate guilt
- Physical slowing
- Less coherent thinking
- Easily agitated
- Feeling unloved
- Indecisiveness

Bi-Polar Disorder (BPD)

Bipolar disorder is also called manic-depression. It is called bi-polar because it alternates between depression and elevated moods. The symptoms during the depressive periods are the same as other types of depression.

Behaviors when the mood is elevated are not the same as behaviors associated with positive moods in mentally healthy people and include three of the following (to be diagnosed):
- Overly inflated self-esteem
- Increased talkativeness
- Decreased need for sleep
- Increased goal-directed activity
- Seek pleasurable activities regardless of associated risks
- More likely to be involved in risky behaviors [10]
- Racing thoughts
- Easily distracted
- Increased agitation

Depression, Anxiety, Bi-Polar Disorder, PTSD, OCD, and Anger Notes

- The path out of depression travels through anger and rage.
- Anxiety is a tendency to spend time in the Drama, Give Away, and Powerless Zones which is caused by the habits of thought the person has developed.
- Bi-polar Disorder can be characterized by someone who finds themselves in the Powerless Zone who attempts to jump to the Sweet Zone. Visualize someone leaping from one building to the next and not making it all the way, clinging to the side until they can't cling anymore and then falling back to the Powerless Zone. Step-by-step journeys are more successful than huge jumps.
- PTSD and OCD are the result of chronic habits of thought that aren't beneficial. Building different neuro-pathways will help your mind automatically travel healthier pathways.
- Anger issues and being quick to violence is the result of developing neuro-pathways in the Hot Zone and beliefs that increase stress when challenged.

Relationships: Stress, Energy, Emotion, Biochemistry, Thoughts, and Cellular Communication

This book reframes mental health and mental illness as existing along a continuum that spans great mental health to debilitating mental illness. Viewing emotional states as existing along a continuum allows you to see which emotion to reach for as the next step. It removes the blindfold created by a diagnosis. It becomes easy to see which direction to lean towards. Viewing mental illnesses along a continuum that contains mental wellness makes it possible to understand the direction and behaviors required to prevent mental illness and in many cases, cure mental illnesses. Chronic, long-term mental illnesses including depression, anxiety, and PTSD have been cured* by changing habits of thought to healthier ones.

---

* Defined as 10-years symptom-free.

When the big picture is visible you can see where you want to go, know how to get there and measure your progress so you don't give up when you're about to be free.

In 2007, researchers concluded that emotions are a sensory feedback system like our sight, sound, sense of touch, taste, and smell. The new definition of emotions and the relationships between stress, energy, emotion, biochemistry, thoughts, and cellular communication have significant roles in preventing, and recovering from, mental illness.

The top of the funnel in the diagram indicates the energy everyone has the potential to receive and the clarity of cellular communication that is possible in their body. Notice that it is the same size for everyone.

Brain Chemistry

Low emotional states indicate you are experiencing stress. Stress also means the biochemistry of your body is being negatively impacted. Consistent or chronic low emotional states can lead to changes in the biochemistry of the brain that are then studied in an effort to determine the cause. It's like running off the road and hitting a tree because your tire blew out because of a nail and studying the tree to determine why you hit it. The answer is not there.

One problem is that there isn't an ethical way to study the process because it would require identifying people at risk for depression and monitoring of their brain chemistry but not providing relief so that the changes in the brain can be observed. Once an individual is identified as needing treatment, not providing it is not ethical.

The level of stress indicates whether the valve that determines the clarity of cellular communication and the energy available to the person is open or closed. Stress makes the valve opening narrower. When stress interferes with cellular communication, biochemical and epigenetic changes can occur in the body.

Our thoughts determine our level of stress. We receive immediate feedback about how stressful each thought we think is from our emotions and energy level.

The dark area at the bottom of the funnel reflects how much well-being is being blocked by stress. Another way to look at this is being similar to static on the line during a phone call that makes clear communication difficult.

The amount of energy that you feel is determined by how freely it can flow to you. The one exception is explosive emotions where the accumulation of blocked energy can explode into anger or rage. The light area at the bottom of the funnel reflects how much well-being is being allowed to flow.

For this illustration, well-being is defined as the root of well-being, the clarity of communication between your cells and the amount of energy flowing through you. Well-being encompasses much more than this, but these two factors determine all the other factors.

If cellular communication is not clear it can lead to all sorts of problems. Likewise, if you do not feel energetic, it can lead to all sorts of problems. For example, when cellular communication is unclear your cognitive abilities decline.*

When your cellular communication is not clear, the biochemistry of your body does not function at optimum levels. Over time this can lead to biochemical imbalances that are often associated with depression. Biochemical imbalances are an indicator of depression (a symptom). Biochemical imbalances and depression are indicators; not the cause.

Drugs address the biochemical imbalance but not the cause. If drugs fixed the cause they could cure, not just provide dose-dependent relief.

Stress causes the lack of clear communication. Your body is very resilient. If you learn to reduce the stress you experience on a daily basis your body will work to restore the biochemical balance your mind and body requires for optimal functioning.

I'm going into detail about these relationships because many people insist that depression is a biochemical imbalance. Emotional depression is often accompanied by a biochemical imbalance. Both are symptoms of chronic stress overloading your body to the point where a lack of clear cellular communication led to depression and to a biochemical imbalance.

Our senses are designed with redundancies. We have two eyes. We have two ears. Emotion indicates the level of stress being experienced in a particular moment. Like our other senses, how much stress we are experiencing has redundant methods of letting us know how stressed we are feeling. How much energy we feel is the second indicator of how much stress we are experiencing.

A diagnosis is a label. Labels are good indicators of where you are but they obscure where you began and where you can go from where you are.

Think of this picture of a river as the sum total of emotional and mental health states you could possibly experience.

---

* More technical, evidence-based information about this in in Appendix VII.

Later you will learn how to navigate down river toward better feeling emotions and the things you may be doing that are causing you to navigate upstream, toward worse feeling emotions. For now I just want to make a point about the label we call a diagnosis.

Diagnoses do not tell us how we arrived where we are or how to get where we'd rather be. They are simply indicators of where we are. Think of a diagnosis as putting a steel pipe in the river and getting inside it. You can't see where you are in relationship to the river. You can only see where you are from inside that pipe. You can't see how close you are to things that look and feel better when you're stuck inside a diagnosis.

If you have a diagnosis, do not stop any treatment but do stop thinking about your diagnosis as who you are. A diagnosis is simply where you are. Don't say "I am depressed" or "I am anxious" or "I am schizophrenic."

Instead say, "Right now I am in the river at depression or anxiety or schizophrenia. I am learning how to navigate to other places in the river."

This is the first step in getting the blinders that a diagnosis creates off. It doesn't mean you're cured or you can stop any treatment. It just means you have a better idea of how to be where you would rather be as far as your stress level and emotional state are concerned

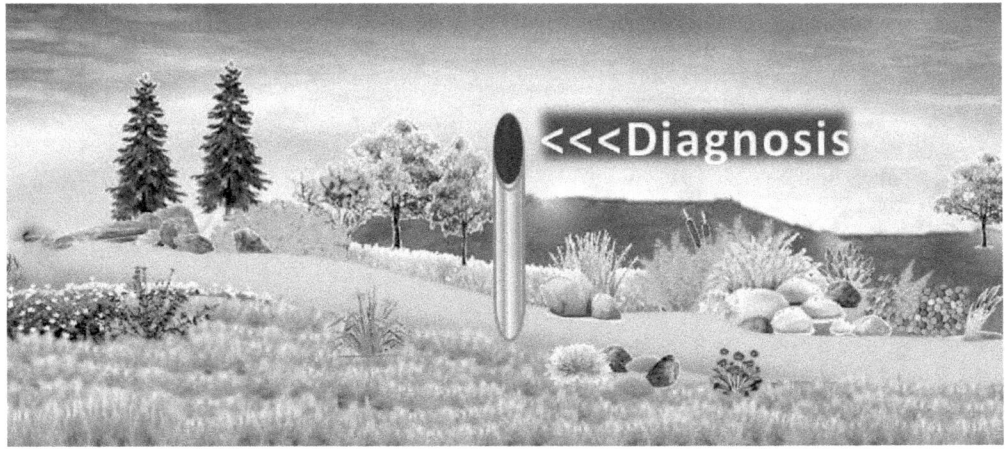

Another analogy that helps to understand this concept is imagining you are inside a car. It is not a self-driving car. All of the windows have been

painted black. You can't see anything through the windows and the doors are locked. How far are you going to drive that car when you can't see anything outside the car?

Now imagine that the windows are clean and you can see everything around you. There are places you can see where you would like being more. Perhaps you'll decide to move to a spot in the shade where it isn't so hot. Or, if it is a cool day, you may decide to move to a spot in the sun where it feels warmer. If you are on the edge of a cliff you may decide to back away from the cliff. If there is a pretty view that you could see better from another location you may move to see the better view.

Diagnoses are good for helping you understand where you are. But when you allow a diagnosis to define you, it paints the windows of the car black so you can't see how to get where you want to go.

You can know how much stress you are experiencing two ways. By how you feel emotionally and how you feel energetically. In my work I use seven categories (Zones) of emotions that are separated by how empowered or disempowered a person feels when they are experiencing the emotions in those Zones.

Any emotion you feel can be accurately placed into the correct Zone on the EGSc (See Appendix I) by paying attention to how empowered or disempowered you feel when you feel the emotion and then finding the Zone for emotions that have a similar level of empowerment. The Sweet Zone is the most empowered and the Powerless Zone is obviously the least empowered.

Let's go back to the funnels. The Funnel and Emotion Diagram connects the emotional state to the amount of interference the level of stress indicated by the emotions is causing.

Every outcome of stress can be explained with this simple illustration. Positive emotions lead to better outcomes in relationships, health, and success in academics, career, and sports.

Emotions indicate the level of stress you are experiencing. Stress means cellular communication is not as clear as it needs to be for optimal functioning.

The Funnel and Emotion Diagram

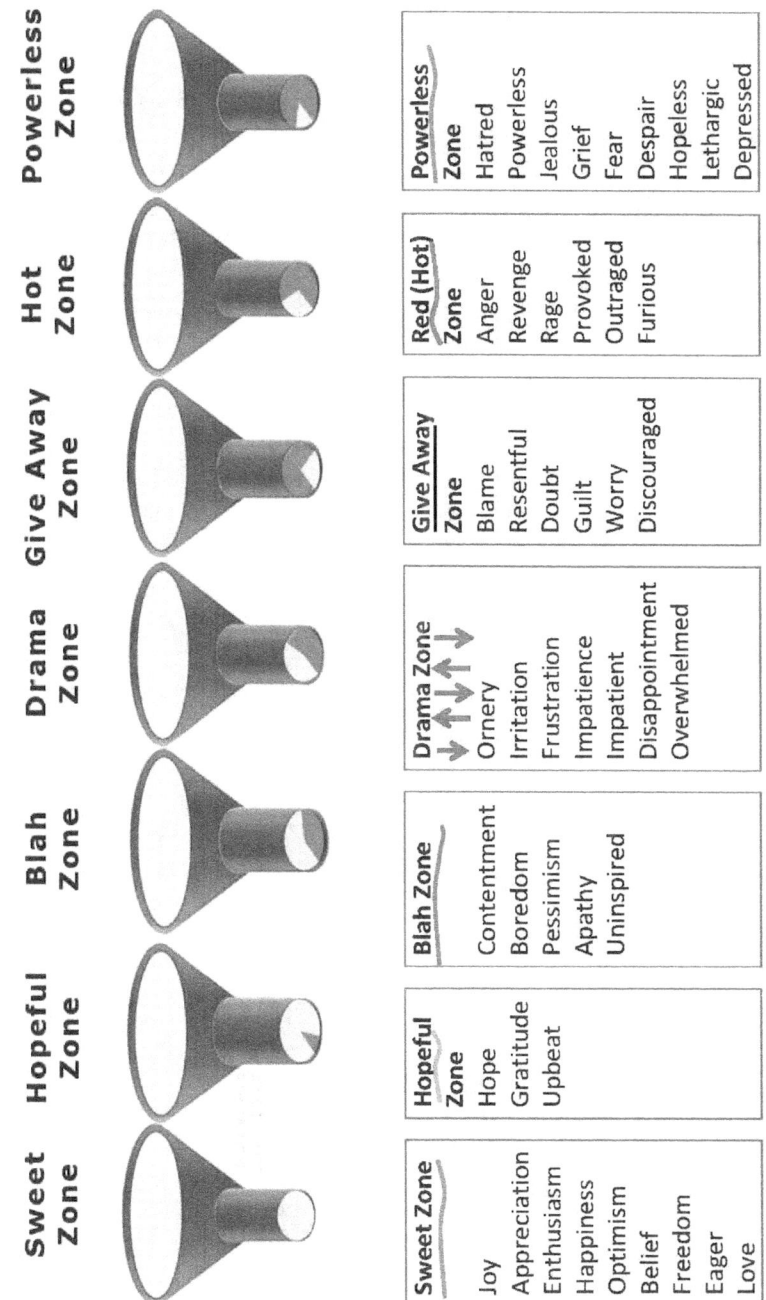

Sweet Zone	Hopeful Zone	Blah Zone	Drama Zone →←→	Give Away Zone	Red (Hot) Zone	Powerless Zone
Joy	Hope	Contentment	Ornery	Blame	Anger	Hatred
Appreciation	Gratitude	Boredom	Irritation	Resentful	Revenge	Powerless
Enthusiasm	Upbeat	Pessimism	Frustration	Doubt	Rage	Jealous
Happiness		Apathy	Impatience	Guilt	Provoked	Grief
Optimism		Uninspired	Impatient	Worry	Outraged	Fear
Belief			Disappointment	Discouraged	Furious	Despair
Freedom			Overwhelmed			Hopeless
Eager						Lethargic
Love						Depressed

What Humans Do and Why They Do It
Happiness depends upon ourselves.
Aristotle (384 BC-322 BC) Greek philosopher

The answer to this question is short and sweet:
We do what we believe will make us feel best. [11, 12, 13]

Examples of how this plays out in our lives are endless. Sometimes we avoid things because we believe they will make us feel worse. At other times, we do things because we believe they will make us feel better.

We do things we don't want to do because they serve the purpose of something we do want. We may go to a job we no longer enjoy because we want to provide for our family. We are civil to in-laws we don't like because we want a good relationship with our spouse. We treat our boss with respect even if we don't respect him because we want to keep our job.

We do things we want to do because we believe doing them will feel better than not doing them. If we love a particular sport it is because of how that sport makes us feel. We look forward to spending time with certain people because we feel better when we are around them.

It often doesn't look like feeling better is the reason we do things but if you dig deeper into the motivations, the belief that we will feel better if we do something (or better if we do not do something) is always at the root.

We are often not consciously aware of our motivation to feel better. Increasing our awareness of this goal gives us more control over our choices and our emotions.

New Definition of the Purpose and Use of Emotions

If you shut up truth and bury it under the ground, it will but grow, and gather to itself such explosive power that the day it bursts through it will blow up everything in its way.
Émile Zola (1840-1902)

Imagine that you have never cooked anything. You have also never seen a cooked chicken. You decide to have company over for dinner and cook a chicken for your guests. You look up a recipe for baked chicken in your cookbook and follow the instructions precisely, including cooking the chicken to 120°. When your guests arrive you proudly serve a nearly raw chicken. The cookbook had a misprint that told you to cook the chicken to 120° when 160° is the right temperature to cook a chicken. You wouldn't blame your oven for the raw chicken once you knew the cookbook was wrong. You served raw chicken because chicken isn't cooked until it reaches 165° degrees, but it doesn't mean the thermometer is broken. It was the instructions you were using that led to the undercooked chicken.

The scientific understanding of the purpose and use of emotions took a quantum leap forward and overturned the earlier understanding of emotions in 2007. Until you learn the new definition, you risk using the wrong instructions to respond to every thought you think.

Humans have an emotional feedback system that works perfectly but when we have the wrong instruction manual to interpret and respond to the feedback they receive, we don't benefit from the feedback and emotions can seem unreliable.

Emotions have been scientifically re-defined as a sense. The closest other sense is our sense of touch. If we treated emotions more like we do our sense of touch and made no other changes most people would be far better off than they are right now.

When we touch something and it feels good we tend to continue touching it. When we touch something and it hurts, we pull back from it.

It's easy to be clear that we don't want to touch things that cause discomfort or pain.

When it comes to emotions, society has created many convoluted concepts that misguide us. One way this plays out in people's lives is when someone else tells someone how to live their life.

We can feel strongly that we want to do something, such as major in a certain field but because someone else wants us to do something else with our life, we question our decision. Even when the thought of doing the thing that someone else wants us to do causes emotional discomfort, many people do it anyway.

If that same person were telling you to repeatedly rub your fingers across sandpaper you wouldn't keep doing it. Pursuing a career that causes you to feel negative emotion is no different. No, it won't make your fingers bleed. But over time it will do far worse. Negative emotion is an indicator that your body is experiencing stress. Chronic stress makes everything in your life worse and, if it continues, your life will continue to get worse. Your relationships, health, career, and ability to enjoy life will not be anywhere near what they could be if you are chronically stressed.

There are two ways to reduce stress:
- Change your thoughts
- Change your actions

When we put our fingers on a hot engine we withdraw them immediately. We recognize that the pain we are experiencing is not what we want and that it indicates the situation is not healthy for us. Emotional pain means the same thing. Your perspective about the topic you're thinking about is not healthy. Yet, many people will tolerate strong emotional pain for long periods of time. Emotional pain is not a reflection of how much you care. Emotional pain is an indicator that the way you're perceiving a situation is not the best way for you to look at the situation. What does best mean? It means your perception of the situation is not the healthiest and most supportive perception that is available to you.

Emotions are road signs in life's journey. In *MWME*, you'll learn what the signs mean and healthy ways to react to them. Historically, emotions were viewed as:
- Confirmation of our judgments about the rightness or wrongness of what we were thinking about when we felt the emotion.
- Negative emotion about a loss is often viewed as evidence of how deeply we cared.
- The beginning of a cascade of biochemical responses in our body that prepare us to fight, flight, or freeze.

There is a distinct difference between fear that makes the hair stand up on the back of our neck and the fear we experience when we allow the nightly news to pump stories designed to scare us into our home.

Fear defeats more people than any other one thing in the world.
Ralph Waldo Emerson (1803-1882)

The hair standing up on the back of the neck type of fear indicates we may need to fight, flight, freeze, or take evasive action to avoid a dangerous situation.

The new definition of the purpose and use of emotions overturns the earlier view of emotions as it relates to the majority of fear and other negative emotions.

The new definition of the purpose and use of emotion states: [14, 15, 16, 17, 18]

1. The purpose of positive emotion is to guide us toward *self-actualization.**
2. Emotions are responses to thoughts.[19]
3. Each thought elicits an emotional response.[20, 21 & 22]
4. Thoughts create meaning for events in life.[23]
5. The most productive response to negative emotion in modern life is a Right Response (RR), which is:

Mentally reach for a different perspective about the situation, one that feels better, and adopt that perspective as your own because it serves your highest good to do so. [24]

In the paper where Katherine Peil Kauffman coined the phrase Right Response (RR) she elaborates and clarifies the difference between a RR and suppressing emotions:

"There is a vast difference between a RR and suppressive emotion regulation, as the corrective action itself is informed by the specific emotional message, is consciously undertaken and it self-preserves through open, approach behavior, adaptive development and social cooperation. In short, the RR is a self-developmental response more indicative of the neurally well-endowed, culturally creative human being."[25]

Advanced Stress Management Strategies help you apply Right Responses. The new definition of Emotional Guidance is simple to understand. Children tend to master it faster than adults because we are born using it. Modern society trains us to ignore it in favor of our irrational minds † and the preferences of others.

When we see something, we tend to believe it. When we hear something, we tend to believe we heard it. When we touch something, we tend to believe what our sense of touch tells us about it. When we smell something, we believe it smells the way our nose interprets it. Those senses are providing sensory feedback.

Emotions are sensory feedback from our oldest sense. The only reason we do not trust them as much as our eyes, ears, nose and touch is that we have been trained not to trust them. When interpreted accurately, emotional feedback is the most accurate sense.

Remember, we perceive and interpret reality. We do not experience a fixed actual reality. Everyone perceives a different reality.

The myth that negative emotion means something outside ourselves is bad is commonly believed. This myth is responsible for significant amounts

---

* Self-actualization is the realization or fulfillment of one's talents and potentialities, considered a drive or need present in everyone.

† In the next chapter, you'll learn that our minds aren't as rational as we are taught. Cognitive biases distort our thinking and because we are unaware of those biases, we believe we are perceiving facts that are frequently just opinions.

of unnecessary stress every day. Negative emotion means we are looking at something from a perspective that is less than ideal for us.

Let's look at a difficult situation for an example of alternative ways to perceive an event. Imagine a law enforcement officer working a murder investigation. If the job required the officer to focus on the loss felt by loved ones or the experiences the victim will miss in the future, negative emotion would quickly depress the officer.*

The law enforcement officer's job requires a problem-solving attitude. When gruesome details are the focus, the perspective is in relationship to answering the question, "What will this tell me that will help solve this case?" Focusing on future action feels better than focusing on an unchangeable past event. Focusing on solving the case feels better than focusing on a life ended too soon. Focusing on providing answers to the family feels better than thinking about all the times the family will miss their loved one in the future.

In the last episode of Season 6 of CSI Miami, Horatio Caine's death is faked. When his co-workers learn he is dead they are overcome with grief but in under less than a minute they turn their attention to solving the case and they are able to function. Art is imitating life in this episode.

Negative emotion is not saying the situation is bad. Nor is it saying it is good. Negative emotion is communicating that there is a way to perceive the situation that is more in alignment with our personal goals. A law enforcement officer choosing to focus on the aspects of a case that feel the worse will not be able to achieve the goal of solving the case. Her cognitive function will be impaired. Her immune system will be depressed. Choosing the worse feeling perception will not advance the goal of solving the case.

A mental stance of hopefulness that the case will be solved reduces stress. Lower stress supports better cognitive function which is required to accomplish the task—and is accompanied by better feeling emotional responses. This is one reason working on cases that are personal (for a police officer or treatments on family (for doctors)) are discouraged. The personal nature makes it more difficult to focus on aspects that feel the best.

We have the ability to choose the way we perceive any event. Our Emotional Guidance guides us to the viewpoint that gives us the best chance of achieving our goals.

With practice, we can learn to trust our Emotional Guidance as much as, or more than, our other senses. Once that level of trust develops, life improves immeasurably. This is because our emotions take into consideration information available on the quantum level that our other senses do not consider.

For example, our Emotional Guidance considers others' intentions. While our eyes might catch a glimmer of intent through body language, accurately interpreting body language is a science that few have mastered.

---

* I am not saying officers do not think about these things, I am saying their job does not require them to focus on these aspects.

Our ears might sense something in the tone of voice, but unless we are experts, we may not trust our interpretation. Interpreting and trusting our Emotional Guidance is far easier than becoming an expert in body language or the nuances contained in tones of voice.

Hope and faith protect us against depression. Without an understanding of your guidance, it can be extremely hard to have enough faith in things that do not make sense and that you cannot see clearly.

A major contributor to the epidemic of mental illnesses is that people believe they know how to understand and respond to their emotions. They've been doing it since they were young so the idea that they've been doing it incorrectly, even when they learn the way they were taught was based on a flawed premise, is a radical change. What is radical is clinging to an idea that prevents you from living your best possible life.

Self-actualization is becoming more of the best possible version of you. Self-actualization is not a finished product. When you learn a new skill, the person you have the potential to become expands. Self-actualization is about becoming your best self. It is a journey, not a destination.

The minute a man ceases to grow, no matter what his years, that minute he begins to be old.
William James

Can you see how William James quote reflects that when we stop moving toward self-actualization we begin to be old? When you get to the next chapter on Energy think about this and how blocking the flow of energy accelerates the aging process.

Let's define emotion.

Emotions are guidance.[26, 27, 28, 29, 30, and 31]

Positive emotions are telling us that our thoughts, words, and actions are moving us toward self-actualization.

It breaks down in this way:
1. If what we are thinking, saying, or doing feels good it is leading us toward self-actualization. However,
    A. Even if what we are thinking, saying, or doing feels good, if it feels even slightly worse than our prior thought, the lower level of positive emotion indicates that our momentum is being slowed by our thoughts. It might be easier to understand with a car analogy: you are still pressing on the gas pedal but you are not giving it as much gas, or, you are giving it a consistent amount of gas but now you're traveling uphill. In either case, your progress is slower if your emotional state does not feel as good (even when it still feels good).
    B. If our emotion feels bad but our thought feels better than the thought we had immediately before the one we are now thinking, we are turning toward self-actualization. In the car analogy, the negative emotion indicates we were heading away from our desired destination and the improvement in emotion indicates we have turned in a direction that is not heading as far away from our desired destination.

a) When someone who has been heading away from self-actualization begins heading toward self-actualization there is a sense of relief, even if they are still in a bad emotional state. For example, being frustrated feels better than being enraged. Boredom feels better than frustration, etc. You'll feel more satisfied when you think a thought that feels better and less satisfied when you think a thought that feels worse.

2. Negative emotions are an indicator that the thought we are thinking is not the best perspective we could take about the specific situation we are thinking about. The vast majority of fear experienced in modern life is self-induced by the perspectives we take about the subject.

We are more often frightened than hurt; and we suffer more from imagination than from reality.
Seneca (4 BC-65) Roman philosopher

- To begin moving toward self-actualization, find a more empowered thought.
- Negative emotions are good because they provide guidance. We are not intended to stay in negative emotions any more than we would continue rubbing our hand on a redwood plank that is giving us splinters.
- If the hair on the back of your neck is standing up, you should be afraid and take appropriate action. Your body feels different when fear is because of a real danger.
- Many people spend a large percentage of their time being unnecessarily afraid or worried. Remember that worrying and being afraid are indicators that your mind and body are experiencing stress.

You can change your habits of thought to get rid of common fears and worries by using Advanced and Transformational Stress Management Strategies. This list represents a small sample of common unnecessary worries.

- Crime
- Of not being loved
- Air plane crashes
- That we will not be respected
- Of being alone
- Of our inner thoughts
- Of wrinkles
- Of being a loser
- Of being fired
- Of being laid-off
- Of making a mistake
- We will miss *Game of Thrones*
- Being afraid our mate will leave us
- That we will fail at _____
- Of bugs/bees/rats/dirt/etc. etc. etc.
- Not being smart enough
- Not being good looking enough
- Not having a perfect body
- Of what others think about us
- Of a partner's infidelity
- Of being "not good enough"
- Of meeting new people
- Of not having enough money
- Loved ones being in an accident or a victim of a crime
- That George R. Martin will die before he finishes the next book

- Being afraid the person we like doesn't like us
- That we will not be accepted into or by _____
- That it will rain on our wedding day
- That our credit isn't good enough to _____
- Of powerful people whose only influence in our lives is derived from our spending time thinking about them
- Of being offended by someone else's words
- Being afraid we will resume an addiction
- Being afraid we will not find our soulmate
- Of people who look different than we do
- That we will not achieve our dreams
- Of how we compare to other people

Eliminating fear and worry does not mean you will become oblivious. You will take appropriate actions to reduce the risk but you will not spend time feeling worse than you could feel. Risk management includes activities such as wearing seat belts, locking your doors, paying attention to your intuition, having faith in yourself and others (but not when it contradicts your intuition), and other strategies that reduce the risk that what you don't want will happen.

Is Using Emotional Guidance Selfish?

One of the first arguments people make against following Emotional Guidance is that it seems selfish to do what feels best to us regardless of what others want. It does sound selfish if you don't dig deeper. When you look deeper, you find that people selfishly want a lot of things that counteract this objection including:

- We want good relationships with others,
- If we're happy, we want others around us to be happy and we're far more likely to be happy if we follow our Emotional Guidance,
- We enjoy doing nice things for other people, even strangers, when we feel good, and
- When we feel good we are far more likely to behave in socially acceptable ways.
- People who behave badly (intentional rudeness to violence) didn't feel good before they behaved in undesired ways. Bad behavior is the result of attempts to feel better by someone who lacks stress management skills. [32, 33, 34]

Emotional Guidance considers everything we want and is excellent at finding ways that allow us to maintain great relationships without having to give up things that are important to us. Our guidance tells us that it is not our job to attempt to control others' behaviors so we stop trying to make others behave the way we want them to so that we will be happy. We choose to be happy even when those around us do not do what we would prefer they do.

Setting goals that include being loving and respectful and having good relationships means your Emotional Guidance will consider these goals when it provides the guidance you receive.

Hot Cold

The way Emotional Guidance works bears a strong resemblance to the children's game where an object is hidden and the child is given clues such as *You're getting warmer* or *hot* or *You're getting colder* or *cold* to help the child find the hidden object. Positive emotions mean you're moving toward self-actualization and negative emotions mean you're moving in opposition to self-actualization.

While it does feel different to move from despair to anger than from anger to frustration, or from hope to passion, each of these is a step in the right direction, each is *getting warmer*. The common element of each step in the better-feeing direction is a feeling of relief (a releasing of tension or stress). The emotion that is in the *warmer* direction always feels better than emotions that are *getting colder*.

When individuals know they have guidance and have practiced using it, they know that no matter how bad their current circumstances may seem, they can find ways to feel better.

Emotional Guidance and Stress Management Strategies

Once the purpose and use of emotions is understood, the value of developing Advanced Stress Coping Skills that help you find perspectives that feel better becomes evident. Eventually, individuals can use Transformational Stress Management Strategies to train their minds so that their initial, automatic thoughts about situations are less stressful than they were in the past. Using Transformational Strategies retrains your brain at the level of subconscious thought so that the first thought you think is more supportive of self-actualization.

When something happens, a subconscious appraisal of the situation, occurs that leads to a conscious thought about the situation. The conscious thought is based on subconscious appraisals that vary significantly from person to person, and even in the same person, depending on the individual's current emotional state.

Factors that affect the subconscious appraisal include our beliefs about:
- Our locus of control
    - Whether we believe our thoughts, words, and actions have an effect on the outcomes we achieve
- Core Self-evaluations
    - Self-esteem
    - Self-efficacy
- Our value and worth (deservedness)
- Expectations about the future
    - Positive – optimistic
    - Negative - pessimistic

- Our current emotional state
- Our focus
    - Short-term goals
    - Long-term goals

Your subconscious appraisal (our first thoughts about something) is only one of many potential perspectives you could take about the situation. Multiple people experiencing the same circumstances will not arrive at the same subconscious appraisal. Our beliefs lead directly to our automatic thoughts[35] and directly affect the way we appraise every situation.

An automatic process compares our appraisal of the situation (thought) to our self-actualized self to determine the emotional response we reeive. Two factors contribute to the emotion we experience.
1. Our unique preferences, and
2. Our best potential future self.

An example of different emotional responses follows. Someone who wants to go to college to become a teacher feels ecstatic when she is accepted by a college that will give her reduced tuition because of her chosen profession. Someone else who only applied to college reluctantly to please her parents will not be ecstatic to be accepted.

Our responses differ because we appraise the situation differently.[36] Our Emotional Guidance considers our unique goals.

Parents often pressure children to study a subject the parent wants them to study instead of what the child wants to learn. This does not turn out well because the motivation to do well comes from the emotions we feel and if we are pressured to pursue someone else's goals we do not have intrinsic motivation* to be successful in that field.

The subconscious appraisal of a situation is not the only possible appraisal. Most situations have many ways to accurately perceive them. Emotional Guidance helps us evaluate alternate appraisals.

The High Stress/Low Stress illustration (page 34)demonstrates how emotional state and stress level are related to our perceptions and focus. There are three places we can focus on:
- Where we are
- Where we want to be
- Where we don't want to be

There are three important aspects of our relationship with where we want to be and where we don't want to be:
- How far we perceive ourselves to be (near or far)
- Our perception of the possibility of achieving the desired or undesired state (achievable vs. not achievable)
- The speed at which we believe we will arrive at the desired or undesired state and how long we think it should take

---

*An intrinsic reward is an internal reward, such as positive emotions we feel in response to actions that move us toward self-actualization.

For example, at the beginning of medical school, a student who believes he or she will graduate will feel positive emotion even though graduation is a lot of work and years in the future. In this example, the student perceives the possibility of achieving the desired state as achievable and believes it will take a reasonable amount of time.

A similarly situated student who fears he or she will flunk out of medical school will feel negative emotion and be more anxious. This student is focused on where he or she doesn't want to go instead of the desired destination. Instead of working towards what is desired, the student's focus is to fight against failure. This student will experience a higher level of stress. Higher stress reduces cognitive capabilities and increases the likelihood of failure.

Use the High Stress/Low Stress illustration (below) to help you identify how you perceive situations and events that are of concern to you.

Potential examples could include:

- A divorce or custody battle
- Unexpected obstacles
- Work success or failure
- The government
- Increased expenses
- Reduced income
- Leisure time available to you
- Relationship difficulties
- Ability to keep up with new information or technology

What is your pattern? Do you tend to focus on what you want or what you don't want? Deliberately shift your focus between what you want and what you don't want and feel the emotional difference that occurs. Do you doubt yourself or your skills? Do you accept responsibility for outcomes? Do you worry about things you cannot control?

High Stress/Low Stress Illustration

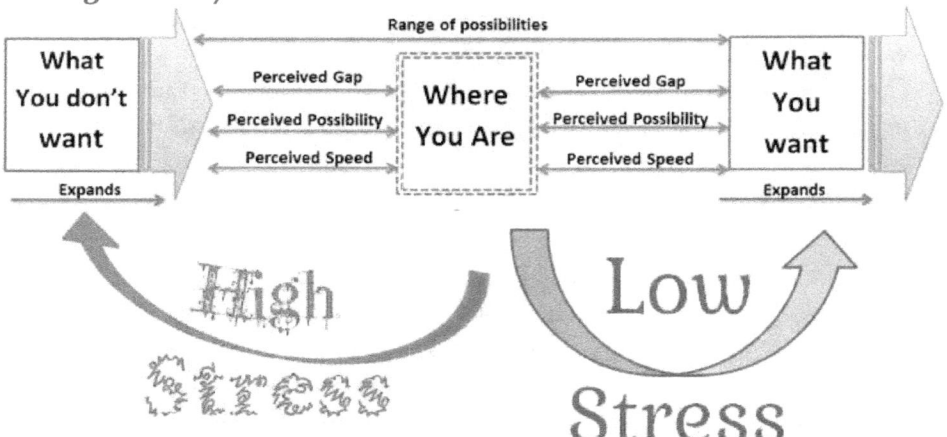

As we move through time, the three categories of what is desired, not desired, and where we are, change. As we accomplish more, our desired accomplishments increase. Things that were once wanted can become unwanted things. My first apartment is a perfect example. I was thrilled to move into that small apartment with no dishwasher and a wonky air conditioner when I was 18 years-old. I would be decidedly unhappy to find myself back there today when my desired home has shifted dramatically. What did you once want that you would not be happy with receiving now?

The illustration makes it easy to see that we can be in the same situation and, depending on our perceptions, feel very different levels of stress. Learning to change our perspectives to ones that are less stressful provides many advantages.*

Pay attention to how your thoughts feel. When you notice you are feeling negative emotion, ask yourself if:

- You are expecting things you do not want, or
- Expecting it to take too long to get what you want, or
- You are pushing against things you do not want instead of focusing on what you do want, or
- You do not believe things can turn out well.

There are opportunities to practice Advanced Stress Management Strategies in many situations. For example, during a time-constrained 2,000 mile automobile journey, our vehicle broke down. We could have focused on the inconvenience of the situation, on concerns that we might not be able to finish the trip within the required time frame, or even paint the situation with a broader brush and link the situation to a *why me* attitude about life in general not going well. Or, we could focus on the helpful people we encountered who went beyond expectations to help us at the Gwinnett Place Ford dealership that kept their service team past quitting time on a Friday night so they could fix our vehicle when the part arrived from Atlanta.

All the above thoughts reflect aspects of the reality that existed. A deliberate choice to focus on the thoughts that feel best made the experience part of a fun adventure. Less appealing thoughts would have made the journey seem frightening and unpredictable.

Do you think they would have stayed after their closing time on Friday to finish before they quit for the weekend if we had been irritable and complained the whole time? Compare the outcome we experienced with what would have happened if they hadn't done that for us. I was driving my daughter to Sedona to begin attending school. I had a flight booked home that would get me home the day before I left for a 3-week vacation in Europe. Our options were limited. We would have either had to rent a car and drive it to Sedona and then pick up my vehicle four hours from home after my trip to Europe or put my daughter on a plane. Both choices would have left her without transportation from her living quarters to school.

Nearly every day we experience situations with many different possible outcomes. Healthy habits of thought help us achieve preferred outcomes. Every time a situation turns out a little better than it could or would have, if we had unhealthy habits of thought, our life is better. Over time, those small (and sometimes not so small) differences add up to significant differences.

---

* The Benefits Chapter and diagrams in Appendix V illustrate many of the benefits of lower stress and improved emotional states.

Lean Toward Satisfying Perspectives

Healthy habits of thought feel better than unhealthy habits of thought. In the following examples, choices of more and less satisfying thoughts demonstrate a few of the possible perspectives you could choose about a situation, emotional state, or diagnosis. If you've ever been encouraged to *think positive* but didn't know how, these examples <u>begin the process</u> of showing you potential thoughts you can gravitate toward that will be more positive than unhealthy habits of thought.

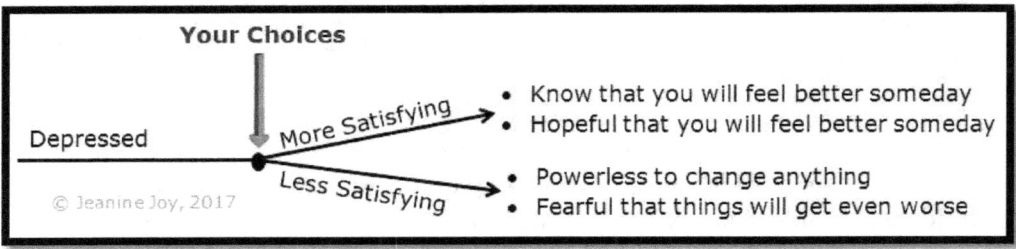

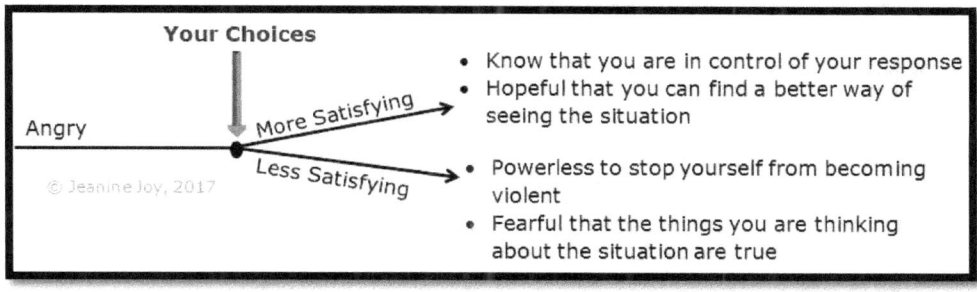

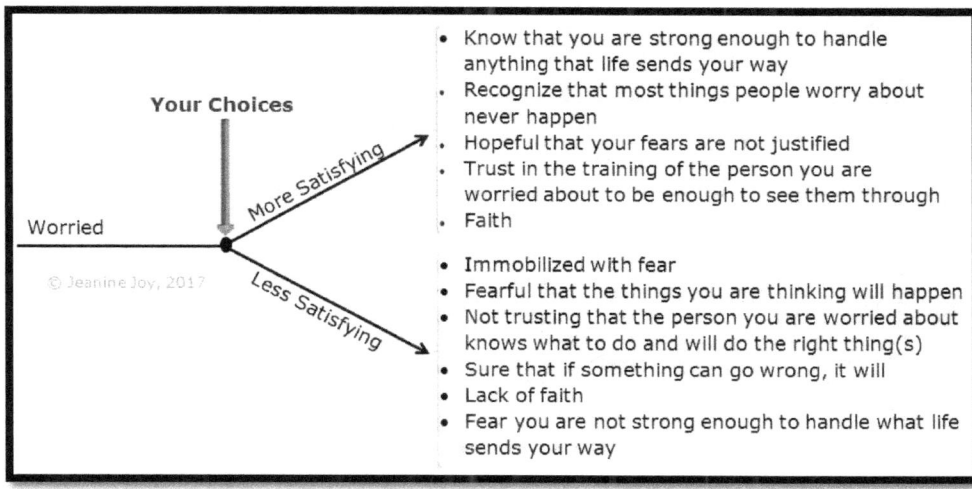

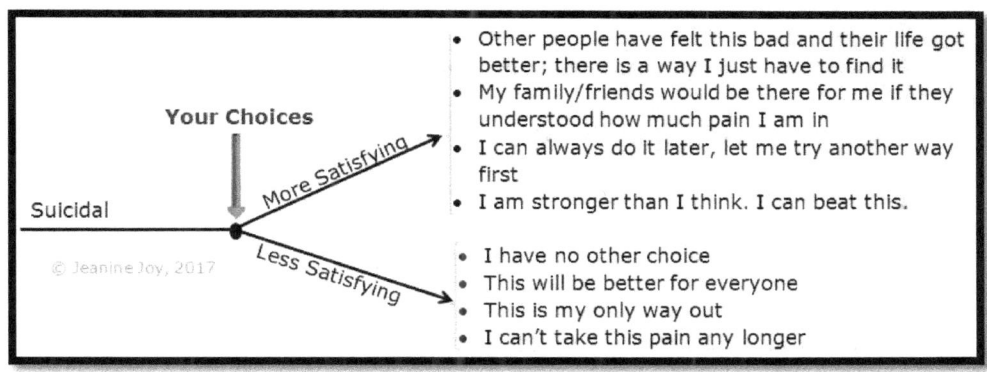

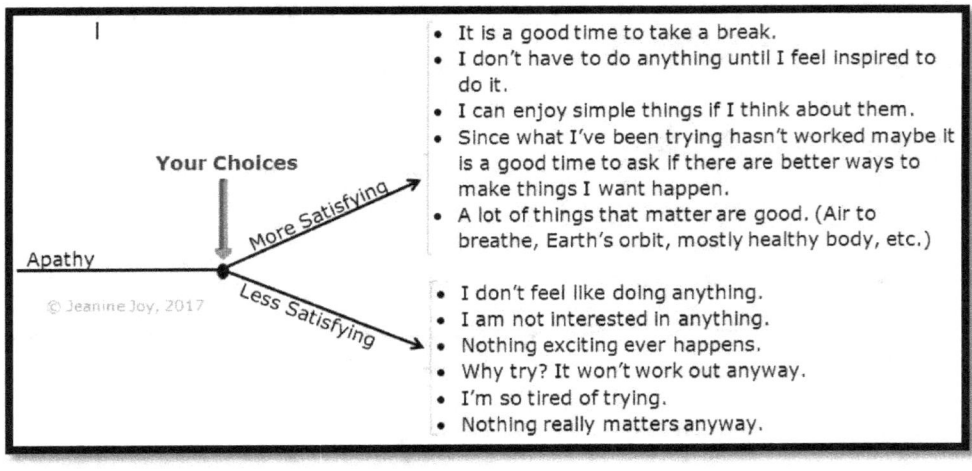

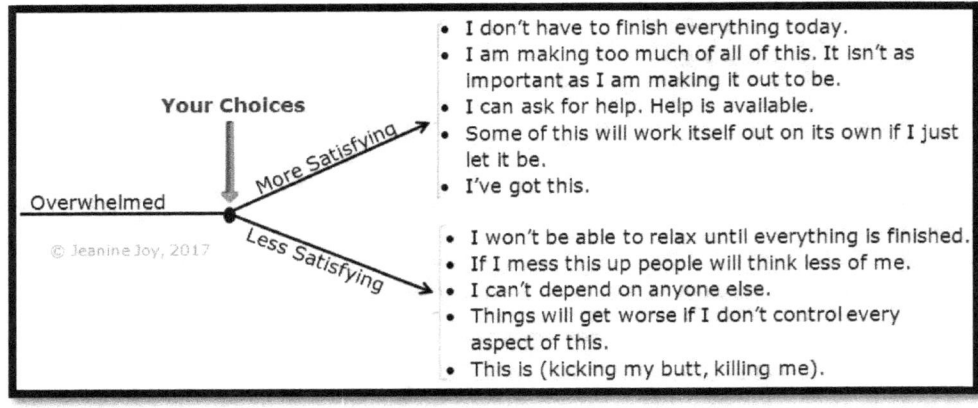

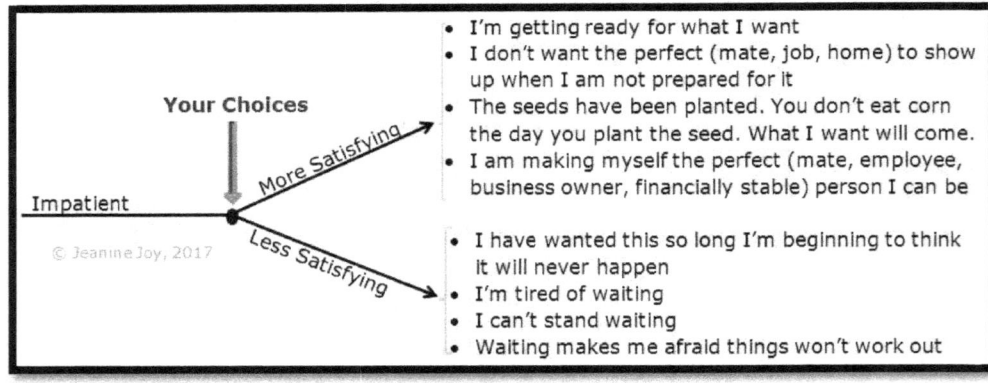

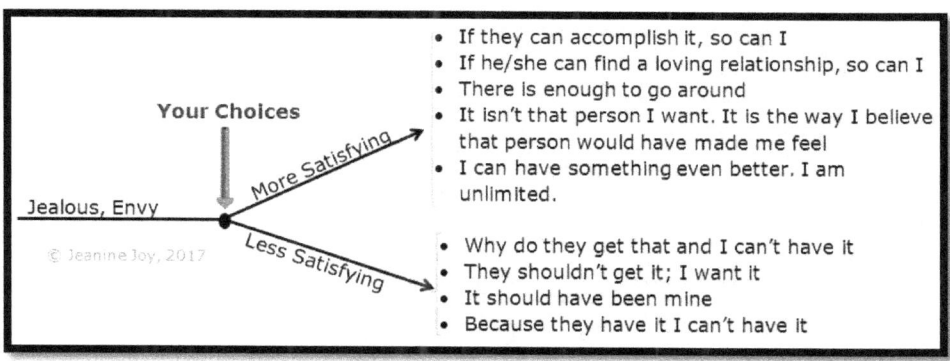

Once your emotional state is in the Sweet or Hopeful Zones you have three choices. You can choose thoughts that:
- Are more satisfying
- Maintain your current emotional state
- Are less satisfying (unhealthy direction)

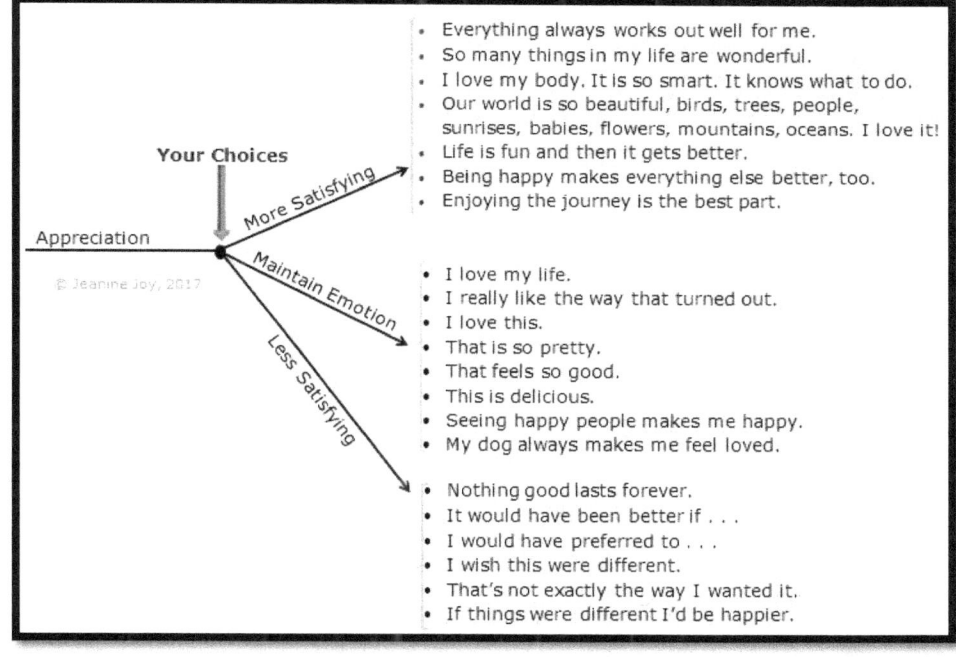

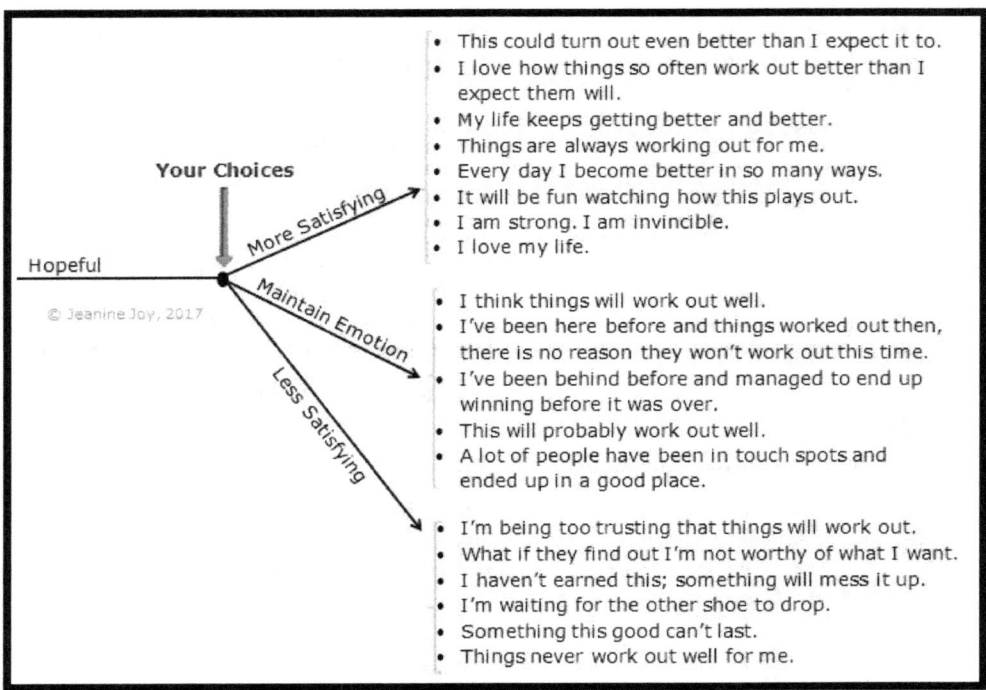

Satisfying Process

Use the following diagrams to identify possible thoughts you could choose about situations in your life that you would like to feel better.

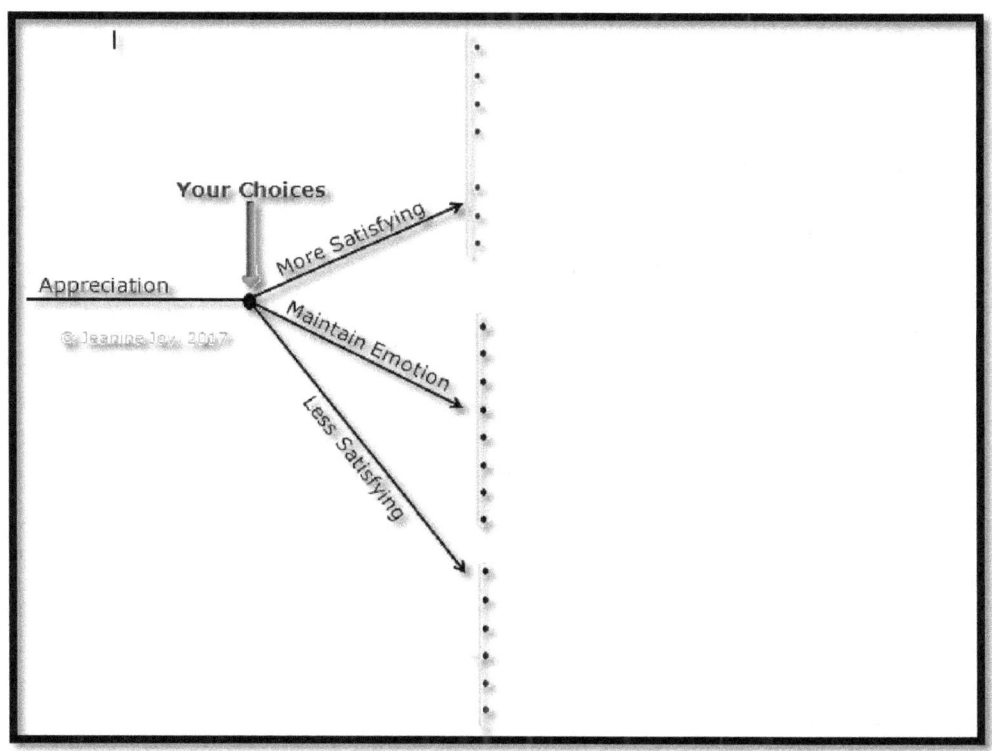

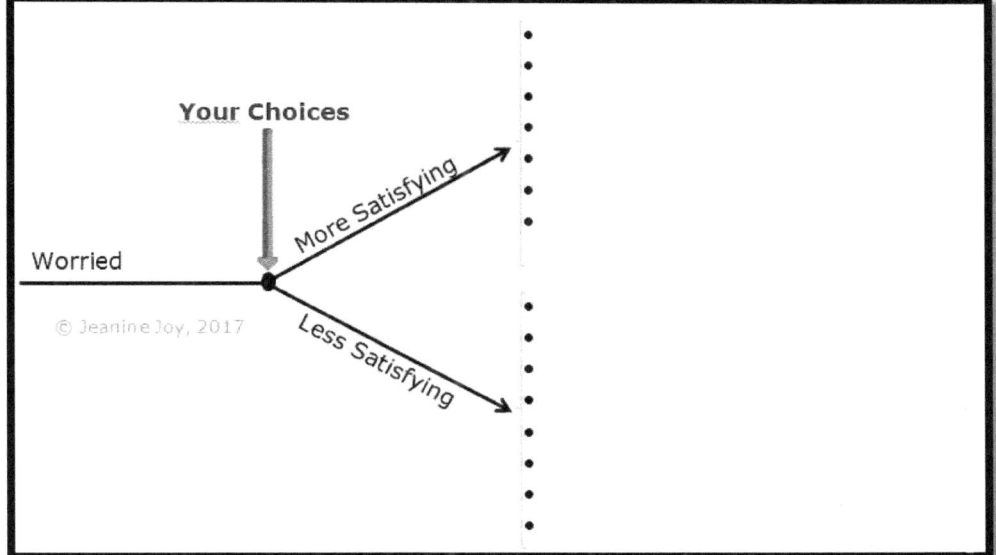

Emotional Guidance considers information available on the quantum level of physicality. Emotional Guidance bypass filters that distort information our conscious mind receives. You'll learn more about this in later chapters. The only reason humanity is not thriving is because we have been taught to misinterpret the feedback from our Emotional Guidance. I do mean the *only* reason. Everything else anyone might point to as a reason is a symptom of this root cause.

The job of the rational mind is to prove our personal beliefs to us and create meaning from our experiences. This would work exceptionally well if the beliefs we have were deliberately crafted in a society that understands the impact of beliefs and nurtures beliefs that lead to thriving. We do not yet have that luxury. Many common beliefs diminish thriving yet our rational minds trap us into lives that repeatedly prove those beliefs to us by interpreting reality as if they are true.

One of the first questions people ask when they hear we have guidance is why the world is not thriving if we have this guidance. The answer is that society teaches us to misinterpret our guidance and to trust other information more than our guidance.

People gain no benefit by ignoring the output from their emotions. Ignoring negative emotions is no different than ignoring pain from your sense of touch. Emotional pain is an indicator that a different perspective would be advantageous to you. When emotional pain is ignored, or suppressed, it is harmful to our well-being. Imagine rubbing sandpaper across your thigh, noticing that it is uncomfortable or even painful and just continuing to rub the sandpaper across your thigh. You don't ignore hunger or thirst because you know the discomfort is providing you with information you need to remain healthy. Negative emotion is providing you with information you need to remain healthy.

Negative emotion tells you that you are experiencing psychological stress. When we feel psychological stress it quickly sets in motion biochemical and cellular changes that, if ignored, compromise our physical and mental well-being. We no longer need to ask someone if they feel stressed to know they are stressed if we have access to their saliva, blood, or urine because we understand how psychological stress changes the body's biochemistry. In time, chronic stress can cause changes at the genetic level of our and our offspring's cellular DNA. Basic human functions (immune, digestive, cognitive, and central nervous system) are all affected by psychological stress.

All emotions are good because they are providing guidance. The question is whether the receiver understands the message or the appropriate response to the message. With practice you can develop trust in your Emotional Guidance.

Within a year of beginning to use my guidance I trusted it even without being able to identify a reason. Sometimes you figure out why you received the guidance and other times you never figure it out. One example of not knowing the reason and finding out later happened in 2011-12. My fiancée and I were booked for a cruise and months before the trip we both began feeling we should not take the trip. We cancelled our plans. My Fiancée's father died when we would have been on a portion of the trip where we were at sea sailing between San Diego and Hawaii. I enjoy several vacations each year and that is the only one I have ever cancelled after it was booked.

Validation

The desire people have for validation of their choices often leads to disagreements.

Regardless of the choices you make, there are people who disagree with your choice. Examples of divided opinions are all around us. Having choices is good, but expecting everyone else to make the choice we make creates conflict.

At the root of it all is a defensiveness born of insecurity. Because people do not understand their guidance, they feel an unsatisfied desire to have their decisions validated. The desire for validation is natural. We are born with guidance that provides validation. When we have a *Hell Yes* experience, we are receiving loud and clear validation from our Emotional Guidance. When we do not receive validation, we can become upset—because we inherently feel that our choices should be validated. We have been looking for validation in the wrong place. Our guidance is where our need for validation should be satisfied. Our guidance validates our choices when they are correct for us and lets us know when they differ from our best path by providing negative emotion. When we are on the way to self-actualization, our Emotional Guidance cheers us on (positive emotions). When we veer away from self-actualization, our Emotional Guidance gives us a sign using negative emotions.

When we do not recognize Emotional Guidance for what it is we do not feel validated. Once you trust your Emotional Guidance, your level of confidence increases as the result of the validation provided by your emotions.

Teaching Children Emotional Guidance

From young ages, many of us are taught to ignore or suppress our emotions. When we were two and our brother took our toy away, Mom did not show us how to feel better using our guidance. She distracted us by giving us another toy. Or she told us, "Don't cry. You're alright." While those may not be considered bad ways to parent and they are certainly superior to the angry parent who smacks her child for crying, they ignore the guidance the child was born with. The first technique teaches the child the parent will make him feel better when he is upset. The lesson the child learns is: *"Finding a way to feel better is not your job. Mom will do it for you."* In the second example, the message is: *"Expressing your emotions is not good behavior. Suppress them."* Emotions then become bothersome things that we have to deal with instead of the valuable tool they are designed to be.

Emotions are our friend. We should understand them as messages letting us know if we are moving in the direction we want to go. We should understand our power to change our emotions by changing our thoughts.

There is a way for anyone, in any circumstance, to feel better. If you are currently suffering, I do not know your path forward—but your Emotional

Guidance knows. It is with you 24/7 providing feedback in response to every thought you think.

Find a thought that feels better. Soak it in until you feel stable holding that thought and then reach for one that feels even better or another one that feels as good.

If you teach a child that someone else made them angry, you are teaching the child the wrong interpretation of their emotion. When a child is angry, the emotion is an indicator that the child's perspective about the situation is less empowered than it could be. The other person doesn't determine the child's perspective, the child determines the perspective. Teaching children to consider different perspectives and to choose the one that feels best will help them develop healthy habits of thought.

A child can be taught that they aren't in charge of how they feel and/or that they don't have the ability to feel better without assistance. If the child becomes upset by something that happens and the parent rushes in to fix the problem when the child could have/would have eventually felt the empowering freedom of solving it him/her self, the parent is teaching the child that someone else has to solve their problems for them.

Note: None of this suggests, in any way, that a crying baby should be left to its own devices. Affection and love are essential to life. But the child whose toy was taken by another child in the sandbox is better served learning how to feel better on his/her own than always having Mom/Dad rush in to solve it for the child. If the parent rushes in the first time and afterwards talks (at an age appropriate level) about ways to deal with such a situation if it occurs again before leaving the child to deal with it on his/her own the parent is providing helpful information. The parent could even coach from the sidelines as Jimmy sits there bawling because Roger took his toy. "Jimmy, remember what we talked about?" He looks at you. "Jimmy, why are you crying?" The child responds, "Roger took my toy." You ask Jimmy, "Do you think you won't get it back?" (shakes head) "Roger will probably be bored with it soon and when he is done you can play with it again. Remember five minutes ago when you wanted the toy Roger had?" Look (pointing) "He isn't playing with that one anymore. You can play with it. Someday Roger will have better manners and won't take things from you before you are ready. He should have tried to trade since you wanted the one he had."

(I'm probably being too adult for a 2-year old. It's been a while since I've been around any children that young, but you get the gist of it.) The older the child is, the more general your coaching efforts should be.

- *You can do this.*
- *You can figure this out.*
- *I think you can handle this but if you want to talk about it, I'm always here for you.*
- *I'm happy to share how I've handled similar situations but you have, too. Remember when _____.*
- *What does your Emotional Guidance tell you?*

You can do a lot of harmful things with a child's emotions by training them in ways that lead to detrimental patterns:
- You can teach a child to soothe negative emotions with food and establish eating habits that will not serve them well throughout life.
- You could mislabel emotions.
- You could teach the child that the feeling of anger is named hatred.
- You could teach a child that the feeling of hope is misguided.
- You could teach a child to suppress their emotions.
  - This is one of the surest ways to develop ill physical, mental, and behavioral health.
- You could teach a child that it is more important to make you happy than him/her self. This is often played out to the extreme when a parent wants to dictate the career path of the child and makes it difficult for the child to follow their guidance.
- Another example is when the parent wants to dictate who the child will marry. Deeper thinking about why you want what you want is required to solve these dilemmas. Many times, the parent is pressuring the child because they care more about what others (including strangers) will think about them than they do about the child's well-being.

Existing cultures and traditions developed before the scientific understanding of the purpose of emotions was known. Re-evaluating traditions using what leads to the best outcomes is not something that has been done. Given how many areas of life are currently less than optimal because customs sometimes go against what leads to the best physical, mental, behavioral health, success, and relationships outcomes, it is something the new generation could (and IMO, should) do.

For example, we could prevent the vast majority of crimes before they occur. Happy people are extremely unlikely to commit crimes. Individuals experiencing lower emotional states (anger, rage, fear, frustration, greed, jealousy, envy, resentment, etc.) are far more likely to commit a crime than someone who is hopeful, happy, joyful, eager for life, etc. The decisions a person makes about their actions changes with their emotional state. Understanding the purpose and right way to use emotions leads to experiencing positive emotions more often.

Teaching your child how to interpret and regulate his or her own emotions is the best gift you can give them beyond love.

Be Realistic

Far more goes right in the world, every day, than goes wrong. If we put the worlds' troubles in the perspective of our body with the bad things in proportion to the good, the world has a hangnail. I am not saying awful things aren't happening. I am saying that filing your head with them as you begin your evening and/or as you head to bed is not healthy for you. It does not solve problems. In almost every situation, there is nothing you can do. What do most people do? They feel fear. Look at where fear is on the EGSc

(Appendix I). Fear is an indicator that a high level of stress is being experienced.

The 24/7 negative news has primed most of us to be afraid of this beautiful world we live in. Many will argue that they have to be realistic. Viewing a tiny percentage of the things happening on the planet is not at all realistic—it is a view with a major negative bias. If the 24/7 news channels reported good news and bad news in proportion to their occurrence, the bad news would last less than a minute each day.

If you feel you live in a bad world, I encourage you to shift your focus to one that is more realistic. Start with the big picture and get as specific as you can while still feeling good. The sun came up today. Even if it was on the other side of clouds, the sun rose today. The atmosphere is filled with air I can breathe. Wow! Two huge, necessary hurdles done! Are the birds singing? Are the plants growing? Is the sun feeding the plants? Are the clouds watering the plants? Did people fall in love today? Did people hold hands today? Were any babies born today? I have two eyes that see, two ears that hear, one nose, two arms, two legs complete with feet. I have family I love, who love me. I have friends I love, who love me. I have a bed and a kitchen and windows. I have guidance that responds to every thought I think. I could go on like this for an entire book so I'll stop now. You get the idea. The amount of wonderful going on every day is enormous. So be realistic, think positive.

One more point about the news. Have you considered what the job of the news stations is? Follow the money. They are paid for ratings. Researchers figured out a long time ago that if they make people fearful they watch the news more often. How do you get ratings higher? More viewers means higher ratings! [37]

Use your own guidance to make your decision. Experimenting with the ideas and strategies in this book is the best way to develop confidence in using your Emotional Guidance.

Long-term, Short-term

Framing desires in advance is a powerful tool that increases the benefits of Emotional Guidance. [38]

Emotional Guidance will guide you to feeling better, which is healthier—but it will not strongly consider long-term desires unless you have. If two people had the same goal and one did not give deliberate thought to long-term goals and the other took the time to frame these goals, the Emotional Guidance of the individual who has intentionally set priorities will be more useful because it will weigh long-term goals over temporary pleasures.

Emotional guidance is unique to the individual thinking the thought. Unique goals represent our desired future. When we move away from our goals, our emotions feel worse. Better-feeling emotions are deliberately cultivated by choosing perspectives that support self-actualization. [39]

Thoughts create meaning for events in life. [40] For example, if someone cancels an appointment, the individual who is told the meeting will not occur is free to assign meaning to the cancellation. Even when a reason is given, the reason may, or may not, be accepted by the receiver. If the reason is not accepted, the individual will create a reason to explain the event to himself. That explanation may be one that feels good or one that feels bad. Whichever is chosen, the event will be experienced (felt emotionally) by the individual as if the assigned reason is true.

Generally, the desire that feels better in the moment will win. If there is little belief that a comfortable weight will be achieved or maintained, the desire for the chocolate cake will usually win over the long-term but unbelievable desire to maintain or achieve a comfortable weight.

On the other hand, someone with a high degree of confidence (which might be interpreted as determination or will power) may forgo the chocolate cake now because she is able to achieve the same (or higher) degree of positive emotion by focusing on (and belief in) the possibility of achieving the long-term goal. Note that the greater your belief in your ability to succeed, the better the thoughts you have access to can feel.

She could change her focus away from the chocolate cake and onto achieving the long-term goal and feel good without the chocolate cake.

Whether we're looking long-term or short-term, decisions we make about what will feel best depend on a variety of factors, but mostly on which ones we've focused on more. If long-term goals aren't given a lot of airtime in our mind, short-term goals will receive stronger Emotional Guidance. Focusing on long-term goals increases the consideration we give the consequences of our words and actions.

There is an inherent desire to feel better. Many desires are not beneficial in the long-term. Without knowledge of techniques to change thoughts, endless loops can result—sugary foods, alcohol, drugs, shopping and more can temporarily improve mood, but do not support long-term goals. The more attention you give to long-term goals, the more they will be considered in the emotional response you receive when a short-term goal conflicts with long-term goals.

For example, in an upsetting situation it is not uncommon for individuals to reach for alcohol to provide relief from negative emotions. Unfortunately, alcohol is a Dysfunctional Strategy that only provides a temporary dulling of the pain (or lessening of the focus on the painful thoughts) and can lead to even greater problems.

A more permanent method of approaching an upsetting situation is to reframe your perception of the event in a way that feels better.[41] Memories can be retrospectively constructed from your present perspective, changing the meaning of the past experiences. With practice, finding better-feeling thoughts becomes easier.

Circumstances do not create our emotions. Individuals who live lives that are far from advantageous circumstances can be happy with their lives and receive the benefits of positivity.[42]

Hope

Human societies train people to "*keep a stiff upper lip*" and to "*be strong*" by which they mean the person should endure negative emotions. This is bad advice. Several branches of science have been studying human thriving and the results point to the fact that people thrive when they feel emotionally good and suffer when they do not.[43]

When individuals know they have Emotional Guidance and practices using it, they know that no matter how bad their current circumstances may seem, they can find ways to feel better. Hope, a belief that a positive or desired outcome is possible, is a key emotional state for resilience. Just knowing that guidance exists builds a firm foundation for hopefulness.[44] Without this knowledge, it is easier to feel hopeless, which can lead to inertia or giving up.[45]

Source of Emotional Guidance

People often ask me to explain the source of Emotional Guidance. Realistically—it does not matter. Our guidance guides us toward our individual goals and toward our highest good. The researchers agree about the benefits of our guidance. Experimenting with your guidance makes it clear it guides us around obstacles and toward goals. Sometimes faith is required because the path the mind wants us to take seems more logical but when our guidance is followed we eventually learn why the straightest path wasn't what we expected. Our guidance helps us be more of who we want to be.

Quantum physics provides some answers about how Emotional Guidance works and may be sufficient for science-minded people. Experiment with your Emotional Guidance because experience is the only way to know for sure that the guidance is beneficial, accurate, and always present.

In a peer reviewed textbook I contributed to, *Perspectives on Coping and Resilience*, I detailed my research into whether common religions including Buddhist, Christianity, Islam, Hindu, and Confucius support guidance.[*] More than 90% of humanity has a worldview that is influenced by religious and/or spiritual beliefs. In every religion I researched, I found passages that support the existence of guidance that dovetail with what science now understands about the purpose of our emotions. Right Responses do not indicate that there is a specific right (or wrong) perspective about any situation. A Right Response is a mindset that is less stressful. Advanced Stress Coping Strategies help you identify Right Responses. When in an upsetting situation, your Emotional Guidance can be used to obtain immediate feedback about better ways to perceive the situation.

The beauty of Emotional Guidance is that everyone has it. It is personal to everyone's unique goals and desires. It is simple to accurately interpret

---

[*] Some of those passages are provided in Appendix IV.

your emotions. Your Emotional Guidance does not tell you what others should do or not do; it is specific to your unique perspective and incorporates your personal values.

The brilliance of Emotional Guidance is in its simplicity. Anyone, even children, can understand their guidance. It does not require expensive, labor-intensive programs to oversee it. No tools are required. It's like an app we're born with.

One common criticism of positivity is the belief that negative emotions are being repressed. This is not based on empirical evidence, "*On the contrary, resilience [which requires optimism] is marked by exquisite emotional agility.*"[46]

Some people protest that positive emotions are not always good because anxiety can be a call to action. The goal of positivity is not to always be joyful. The goal is for you to know, no matter what happens, how to move to a better-feeling emotional state. The goal is not to feel happy. Progress made toward goals will bring emotional relief. The call to action from anxiety should last only long enough for us to recognize that we would like something to be better before we begin focusing on the solution. Use the High Stress/Low Stress diagram (pg. 34) to explore this concept. We do not have to marinate in a negative emotional state to motivate ourselves. When we believe solutions are possible we can move energetically toward them, eagerly seeking solutions. In a positive state, our minds help us recognize answers quickly.

Emotions are responses to thoughts and each thought elicits a new emotion. Emotion is the sensory guidance feedback systems response to the thought. Two consecutive thoughts may generate the same emotion or emotions so close to one another they cannot be differentiated, but the emotion experienced changes in response to each thought. Think of it this way, if you print two copies of one photo, when you flip through your photo's, the second copy of the photo seems the same but it is not the same physical photo. They are two separate pictures that have an identical image. In the same way, two thoughts can elicit an identical emotional response but they are still two separate responses. If the level of empowerment is the same, the emotion will feel the same.

Emotional Guidance leads us to better-feeling emotions, whether it is away from fear or toward becoming the best we can imagine being.

The fear of death keeps more people from living than any other fear. Avoiding death is supported by Emotional Guidance; fear of death is not.

Emotional State

What is *emotional state*?

Emotional State (ES) can refer to two distinct states. One is the emotional state in any given moment—how you feel in that moment in time. The other is your chronic emotional state, a practiced emotional state that you chronically return to over time.

Applying Transformational Stress Coping Strategies is the most effective method of changing your chronic emotional state. Applying Advanced Stress

Coping Strategies is the most effective method of changing your current emotional state.

Both our habitual and current emotional state create filters between the subconscious mind and the conscious mind. If you manage your emotional state to a place that feels good on a consistent basis, your filter will highlight information that feels good and dim things that feel bad. Perhaps the easiest way to explain this is that our thoughts, words, and actions are mood congruent.

In other words, they reflect our mood/emotional state.

Our world is based on our perception. If three strangers walk down the same street at the same time and are given in-depth interviews at the end of the street, all three will have experienced the street differently.

- Someone who has healthy habits of thought would notice things that reinforce a positive mood.
- Someone who has unhealthy habits of thought would notice things that reinforce a negative mood.
- Someone who was angry would notice things that reinforce being angry.

Let's say there was a jewelry shop on the street that sells engagement and wedding rings.

The person with healthy habits of thought might think of the joy they felt when they chose their ring, or of someone close to them that has recently become engaged and is very happy.

The person with unhealthy habits of thought might think of how few marriages last a lifetime, if they are divorced their thoughts would go to the end of their marriage instead of to the good parts, if they aren't married they might worry that if they marry their marriage would end in divorce.

The person who is angry might think about children forced to mine diamonds and wonder if the store uses diamonds from those countries. Remember, anger is not a solution. Anger can create energy that turns to action, but as soon as actions are being taken, it is best to focus on the success of the actions which would elicit positive emotion, not anger. Just staying angry doesn't help anyone and it hurts the person who holds onto the anger.

Emotional state has a pronounced effect on behavior. Emotional state is tied directly to how empowered or disempowered we feel. Joy is a reflection of feeling very empowered. Depression reflects feeling very disempowered. Understanding your Emotional Guidance provides you with socially approved methods of regaining a sense of empowerment. People who do not have good stress coping strategies frequently turn to Dysfunctional Strategies to cope with stress. Many undesired behaviors help an individual feel temporarily more empowered.

Our thoughts are consistent with our emotional state. If we don't like our emotional state we can use Advanced Stress Coping Strategies to change our thoughts in order to experience better feeling emotions. If our thoughts are moving so that the emotional response is worsening, we are moving further away from our self-actualized self. When we change our thoughts in a direction that supports our dreams and goals, the stress we experience decreases. If you practice paying attention to the emotional feedback from your thoughts, you can think a thought and feel the stress go up or down in your body and immediately know which direction* the thought takes you.

Emotional state affects every relationship in our lives, from strangers on the road to our most intimate relationships. Higher emotional states support close and loving relationships. Lower emotional states contribute to frequent friction and bothersome behaviors.

Emotional Guidance Process

There are three simple choices to make when you use your Emotional Guidance:

Emotion Feels Bad (A)
- Look for movement toward better emotional state

Emotion Feels Better than Prior Emotion (B)
- Stabilize; Repeat A or C

Emotion Feels Good (C)
- Reinforce or move to even better emotional state

Topics

An *Emotional Set Point* is where your emotions are on a topic. For example, if my emotional state with respect to the way oxygen is paid for by our Medicare system is at anger I can bop along in a good mood and when that topic comes up I can find myself feeling angry pretty quickly. Your emotional state jumps right to where it was the last time you thought about the topic you are thinking about. If my emotional set point about flowers is appreciation, flowers will have the power to transport me to a feeling of appreciation. A set point is where you left your emotion on that topic.

You have an Emotional State or Set Point on every topic. When you hold an infant in your arms, you may immediately move to the top with feelings of love. When you hear of violence on the news you may immediately move to anger or fear. Specific people you have not talked to or seen in years will have an emotional set point wherever it was when you last left it. If you part with someone on less than amicable terms but when you think about them you remember the good memories, your set point will not reflect the way the relationship ended. If you ruminate about the worst parts of the relationship, your set point will reflect the negative emotions you harvest when you focus on what you didn't like about the relationship.

You have a different Emotional Set Point on every topic. Find your set point on the EGSc and then reach for the next higher emotion on that subject. You will not be able to move up more than 1 or 2 levels at one time, but you don't

---

* Direction refers to toward self-actualization or away from self-actualization

have to remain at a level any longer than it takes to become stable there before you can begin successfully moving up another level.

Topic must be very narrowly defined. Your relationship with your mother can be different from your relationship with your father. Your relationship with your mother on a specific subject, say money, can be different from your relationship with her on other topics such as gifts, food, shopping, clothes, career, marriage, or travel. The way you generally feel about your mother has more to do with which topic you focus on when you think of her. If your mind automatically goes to the one troubled topic between you, you will experience the relationship as if you do not have a good relationship, even if there are dozens of other topics on which your relationship with her is good. If your mind tends to ignore the topic(s) where there is disagreement and focuses on those where harmony exists, you will feel you have a good relationship with her, even if one or more of the topics where there is dissention are areas of significant discord.

Our relationships with our mothers (and really anyone) are under our control as far as how we view it. If you decide to wait until your mother changes on the point(s) of discontent before you can be happy, you may wait forever. If you change your focus away from the areas where you disagree to the areas where there is harmony, you can feel better about your relationship right away.

If someone you love has died or otherwise left your life and you think mostly about their absence, you will feel sad when you think about them. If you mostly remember the joys you shared you will enjoy your memories of them.

At first, it requires a conscious effort to focus on different aspects of your relationship. This is only because your previous habit of thought created neural pathways in your mind that are easier for the neurons to travel than the more desired paths.

Refocusing your attention requires patience with yourself. If it is a topic you think about often, it will take about three months to shift your neural pathways. When you find the old perspective coming to your mind, recognize it is merely an old habit that has not yet been fully replaced with the new habit. Do not criticize yourself for the old habit not yet being gone. As soon as you recognize you are focused on what you do not want, deliberately think about the thoughts you would rather focus on to reinforce the new path.

When I listen to stories from people whose prior efforts failed to achieve desired changes, this is where the failure most often occurred. It was not because the attempt to change was not working, but because their expectation and interpretation of how long it would take to change their habits of thought did not match their experience. They could not see how close they were getting to the goal and gave up, often within sight of the finish line. One of the main factors that contributed to giving up was the tendency to berate themselves for not yet achieving the goal. The second factor was lack of information about how long it takes and why we cannot instantaneously change our beliefs. Beliefs are formed by repeatedly thinking the same or similar thoughts. That creates neuropathways that become a filter that affects our perceptions.

Changing our thought processes requires kindness to oneself. Just making a conscious decision to change is a big deal. Give yourself credit for doing that and then allow time to be your friend. I have deliberately made many changes to my thought processes. One in particular was extremely ingrained. I was much like Pavlov's dog when the subject came up. It was as if I carried a soapbox on my back and as soon as the subject came up, I would set the box down, climb on it, and begin spouting my beliefs about the topic to all who would listen. I had strong conviction that my beliefs were right. (They weren't.)

After my research convinced me that those beliefs were based on false premises, I decided to change them. I no longer believed them to be true. I would still find myself a few minutes into my tirade (on complete auto-pilot) before my mind would engage. I remember the first time I realized what I was doing. I was back on my soapbox, spouting things I no longer believed, about five minutes into my typical spiel. I stopped talking, took a deep breath, and ended the conversation. Then I spent some time mentally reviewing my new beliefs about the subject. I felt appreciation that I now knew more and understood the truth.

The next time, I was only about five sentences into the old habit before I stopped myself. Soon, I began realizing where I was heading during the first sentence. My Emotional Guidance was helping because I had also been working on being more sensitive to the onset of negative emotions. Every time I got on that soapbox I felt negative emotion. I celebrated when I stopped myself at just the thought, before I uttered words I no longer believed. The next time I thought about it had been a few months since I had traveled that neuropathway. Now it has been a decade.

Humans think about 60,000 thoughts each day. It is not possible to be conscious about every thought we think. Most of our thinking is done on autopilot. By paying attention to how we feel we can identify thoughts we might want to shift by noticing when our emotional response to a thought doesn't feel good. Thinking about what we are thinking and why we are thinking what we are thinking is called metacognition. Simply pausing to think about what we're thinking and asking ourselves if that is the best thought we could possibly have on that subject is very beneficial. If the thought doesn't feel good there is a better-feeling thought we could have on the same subject. I call the process of noticing thoughts that don't feel good and thinking about why we're thinking them the very creative name of "Stop, Think, then Do."

Our emotional state affects the thoughts we think. We perceive things from our current emotional state and interpret people's words and actions from our current emotional state. If you pay attention you can see someone in a bad mood say something snarky and someone in a state of appreciation completely miss the sarcasm and respond as if the person's comment was polite.

You can see the reverse when someone in a good mood says something nice and a person in a bad mood interprets it as insulting.

Our brains try to maintain our current emotional state by interpreting reality in ways that sustain our current emotional state, as if we have deliberately cultivated that emotional state and want to maintain it. This is very helpful when we feel good and not helpful when we don't feel good. This is the reason that the best thing to do during an argument is withdraw and let both parties (or groups) get better control of their emotional state so a productive conversation can occur.

Most people believe that negative emotions validate their opinion on the subject. They believe that the negative emotion they feel when they look at something and judge it wrong reinforces the rightness of their opinion.

Examples might include:
Someone who believes a teenager is dressed improperly.

The meaning of the negative emotion such a person is feeling is an indicator that a different perspective would be better for the person thinking the thought. The negative emotion is not validating the judgmental thoughts.

Emotions are a closed loop. They are about a comparison between your most self-actualized self and your current thought. The subject of our thought is just an excuse for us to focus. We could focus on millions of other things. If we can't find a positive thought on a subject, it is often best to change the subject we are thinking about, at least for a little while.

Even the most delicious emotion of being in love is a closed loop. The person we are *in love with* elicits so many positive emotions in us because we are so focused on the beauty of their Being that we line up with being our best self. *Falling out of love* means we have stopped being our best self. We can re-focus on the person we were *in love with* or another person and think only about their positive traits and return to the state of *being in love.* We can do this again and again and again. There is no limit. We can do this with friends (i.e. in non-sexual ways), with passion careers, with hobbies, with sports, etc.

> *You cannot control your emotions because the purpose of emotions is to control you. Emotions are a feedback system for facilitating behavioral learning and control. If they were themselves controllable, they would lose that crucial function.*
> Baumeister et al., 2007

We can't decide how we want to feel and feel that way just because we want to but it can be almost that easy. We can think thoughts that elicit emotions we want to experience. The reason we cannot directly change our emotions is because emotions would lose their ability to guide us if we could change them at will. Our emotions are a response to our thoughts. We can change our thoughts. When we change our thoughts, our emotions change.

Learning how to change our thoughts is the key to attaining and sustaining positive emotions more frequently.

Studies about increasing resilience and social and emotional learning skills often mention that the increased skills require boosters to be maintained.[47] When emotions are understood as providing guidance, their guidance provides a natural booster in response to every healthy thought we think.

> EMOTIONAL GUIDANCE IS AN INNATE BOOSTER SYSTEM THAT SUSTAINS ONGOING INCREASES IN RESILIENCE.

History of the Definition of Emotion

Earlier researchers lamented the unpredictability of emotions and wondered why they evolved as a human trait when they seemed to serve no purpose. The reason they thought emotions were worthless and unpredictable was because, like most of society, earlier researchers misinterpreted the meaning of emotions.

There are a number of false premises about emotions that dominate our society including:
1. Other people have the power to make you feel an emotion,
2. Someone other than you is responsible for your happiness,
3. Negative emotions about others' activities tell us whether they are good or bad people or behaviors.
4. You cannot control your emotions.

Let's elaborate on the fourth one—the inability to control your emotions. Imagine a car is traveling at 60 miles an hour and you want it to turn to the right. If you attempted to turn the right front tire by pushing on the tire you wouldn't have much success and you could easily crash. But if you used the steering wheel to turn the wheel to the right it would work perfectly. Attempting to change our emotions directly is like trying to change the direction of a moving vehicle by grabbing the tire. In order to change our emotions we have to change our thoughts. In this analogy, our thoughts are the steering wheel for our emotions.

Since our thoughts lead to our emotions and no one else can think for you, no one else can be responsible for how you feel. Other people can make it easier or more difficult to think thoughts that feel good, but you have the power to change how you think about any situation, to choose to think about something that feels good, or to think about something that doesn't feel good. If you do not exercise this ability, it is not the fault of anyone other than yourself.

Although it may feel good to blame someone else for how we feel it is more empowering to take responsibility for our emotions—especially once we learn how to change our thoughts and feel better whenever we want to feel good. Blaming others is associated with sub-clinical paranoia.[48]

Energy

What this power is I cannot say; all I know is that it exists and it becomes available only when a man is in that state of mind in which he knows exactly what he wants and is fully determined not to quit until he finds it.

Alexander Graham Bell

Something animates our body and when it is absent the body is no longer alive. In Western medicine we can't yet define what this energy is, we simply know that when it is present a person lives and when a person dies it is no longer present.

We can name a cause of death but not why some people die from things that other people manage to survive. In the ones who die, the energy that sustains life leaves. In the ones who live, it grows stronger after they come close to death.

We may recognize that those who are the most afraid die more often and those who are hopeful survive similar circumstances. We will say that some fight for life while others surrender or let go.

Webster Dictionary refers to Qi or chi as it is sometimes called as:

Vital energy that is held to animate the body internally

If you will consider whether your thoughts or decisions increase or

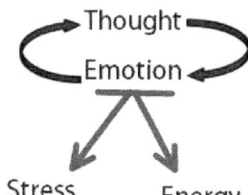

decrease your energy, the same energy which is ultimately present when we are alive and absent when we are not, you will see that we can understand the path we are on by paying attention to our energy.

We feel more energized when we feel positive emotions than we do when we feel negative emotions. We can feel negative emotions and feel more energized than we did before if we are moving from a lower negative emotion to a higher one. For example, moving from depression to anger increases the energy that a person feels even though anger is still low on the Emotional Guidance Scale (EGSc).

We don't notice subtle changes in our own energy level as much as we do the difference between our energy level and that of someone at a significantly different energy level. If we are in a high positive emotional state and encounter someone who is cynical and negatively focused, the difference is immediately apparent. If we pay attention to subtle signals we may feel the urge to distance ourself from a person who feels much more negative than we do.

When you begin paying attention to the connection between emotions, energy, and thoughts you'll discover that thoughts that lead to emotions that feel worse decrease the energy you feel coursing through you. Changing your thoughts around to ones that elicit positive emotions increases your available energy.

Getting out of bed in the morning isn't difficult when you are excited about what you're getting up to do. Think about a time when you felt highly intrinsically motivated. Can you remember the energy available to you when you felt that motivated?

Remember a time when someone made you do something you didn't want to do. One experience many people related is being forced to apologize when they felt wrongly accused. Can you remember how the energy felt stuck?

Now remember a time when you sincerely wanted to apologize for something and your apology was accepted. Do you feel how the energy of a sincere apology is cleansing like rain?

With Emotional Guidance you are asked to pay attention to how your feel and recognize your emotions as sign posts letting you know if you're moving toward or away from self-actualization. Your energy level does much the same thing. If you were trained to suppress your emotions, awareness of your energy may be easier to feel.

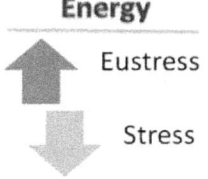

Changing your thoughts changes your emotional response, stress level, and the amount of energy you have available.

When you develop the ability to self-monitor the results of your thoughts with an early detection system that is accurate and knows where you want to be (your self-actualized self), it is easier to know what to do. Instead of feeling lost, wandering around an unmarked desert trying to find your way, you have road signs (emotions or energy) that let you know if you are moving in the desired direction in every moment of every day. All you have to do is read the signs. The core of burnout has been described as, "the reduction of energetic resources."[49] Depression is also associated with lower levels of energy.

Even if you forget and feel as if you've become lost, the signs are still there and they still know how to get where you want to go from wherever you are. All you have to do is remember that there are signs and that you understand their language.

No one's goal in life is to become a couch potato. Couch potatoes are the result of a person believing that they cannot become who and what they want to become. If they can't do the things that energize them the risk that they will choose to do nothing comes into play. Children may try to please their parents but they won't be happy and most children can't keep up the pretense for long. By the teenage years, most will rebel against parents who are attempting to force them to be what they do not want to be. Unfortunately, most teenagers do not understand why they feel so rebellious. Instead of just becoming who they want to be, they act out in many different ways and some even choose to end their life.

The process of reducing stress involves reading the signs and making course adjustments. The process of recovering from many mental illnesses involves reading the signs and making course adjustments, each one of which will lead you to a slightly better state. Small adjustments add up. Think of it in terms of climbing the steps at St. Paul's Cathedral in London. You begin at the bottom but when you're on the 3rd step, you're closer to the top than you were when you were at the bottom. One step at a time is all it takes to find your way to a far better emotional state with more available energy.

Comparison: Old Way and New Way to Use Emotions

The following example demonstrates the difference between the old paradigm and the outcomes it would create with outcomes from the new paradigm.

Your friend, Don, telephones you. He is upset and afraid because he was let go from his job. Don worked at the company for six years. A new boss came in who wanted to bring his own people with him. Your friend stood in the way of his boss's desire to hire people he knew and he's been making Don's life at work difficult for months.

The Old Way to Use Emotions

You become angry on your friend's behalf. You see how unfair and unjust the situation is and you feel powerless that you can't fix it for your friend. Both of you speak about the unfairness and injustice of the situation, reinforcing your righteous anger. You consider your anger a confirmation that his new boss was wrong in his actions. The worse you feel for your friend, the more wrong his being let go feels to you.

Before Don called, you were in a pretty good mood but now your day has been ruined. You'll continue stewing about this situation and worrying about Don for the rest of the day and you'll continue doing the same to a lesser degree tomorrow.

Because communication is interpreted in a mood congruent fashion, when you go to work the next day, your trust in your employer is lower even though it is not the same company that fired Don. Your interpretation of comments managers make is more cynical than it would have been before Don was fired.

Don is struggling to come to terms with the situation and reaches out to you again. The two of you meet for drinks and spend the evening talking about how unfair life is while drinking enough to make driving home illegal. Your conversation focuses on the problem and does not consider viable solutions that you would talk about if your cognitive functions weren't restricted by stress and alcohol.

New Way to Use Emotions

At first, you feel angry on Don's behalf. But you have well-developed emotion regulation skills and when you feel anger you immediately begin looking for other perspectives about the situation. You know that anger means that there is a better way for you to perceive the situation.

Don is a dedicated worker who continually upgrades his skills. He is a very loyal person who tends to remain in a job long after his skills would qualify him for a better job. Remembering this about Don, you have the thought that the loss of this job may be a blessing in disguise. It's too soon to say this directly to Don, but you can reassure him about the quality of his skills and the demand for people with his skills.

As you reassure Don, you sense that he would now be open to considering potential benefits of his situation. You mention the time you were laid off and got a substantial raise in the new job you quickly found and suggest he could experience the same type of outcome. This perspective is supported by the facts. His salary did not keep up with his increased skills. The market value for his skills is more than he has been making. Don begins feeling enthusiastic about finding a new job that matches the skills he developed and about making more money.

When you think about Don the next day, you feel hopeful about his prospects. You don't focus on who fired him or why because that is not something you can change. All that focus would do is make you feel bad. During the day you hear that a co-worker is moving to follow his wife to a new job and you call Don to encourage him to apply for the open position. He's been researching the market value for his skills and working on updating his resume. He's pumped because his market value is substantially higher than what he was making at his old job.

Although these two scenarios are responses to the same circumstances, the outcomes are very different. The new way to use emotions does a better job of producing responses that will be advantageous to the organism or to its relations, which was a stated goal of the old way.

To many people, the second example will feel unrealistically optimistic. They will deny that it is possible to feel optimism after losing your job. I have lived that experience personally as a single parent with two children. The first time it happened after I had begun being more deliberate about maintaining positive emotions I wasn't completely stable, I had moments of doubt and concern but for the most part I was able to confidently move forward without losing sleep.

The second time I had to down regulate my expressed emotions during the meeting where our entire company was told that we were closing out of sensitivity to my co-workers. In my mind I was thinking thoughts like, "Every time I am laid off I get a better job making more money without any days of unemployment. I know something good is coming. I wonder what it is?" Outwardly I expressed appreciation to my boss for keeping the company alive during the worst of the downturn in the economy and offered reassurance to co-workers by relaying that I was seeing increased recruiter activity.

I had a few minutes during which I felt unsure as I contemplated two upcoming vacations, one to Australia and New Zealand for nearly a month and another one to Panama and Florida for two weeks. I felt a small voice of doubt about the wisdom of continuing with those plans but when I thought, "I'll find a way to make it all work" the positive emotion reassured me that going forward with my plans was the right path for me to take.

Within thirty hours of the layoff announcement, the parent company of the firm I worked for notified me that they had decided they wanted me to work for them and to be on the Board of Directors. The decision was based somewhat on my skills but mostly on my positive reaction and helpful attitude in letting them know regulatory issues they needed to deal with as the result of closing the subsidiary. If I had been angry it is doubtful I would have shared that information so readily.

You've been trained to respond to emotions using the old paradigm. The shift to the new paradigm can cause uncertainty. I used both methods in the beginning and evaluated which would bring the better result.

In the example where Don was fired, looking for and finding a potential silver lining (blessing in disguise) is an Advanced Stress Management Strategy.

Back Stories

As there is no worse lie than a truth misunderstood by those who hear it, so reasonable arguments, challenges to magnanimity, and appeals to sympathy or justice, are folly.
William James

Thoughts create meaning for events in life. Our minds fill in missing details to help us make sense of the world. *The details our minds supply are based less on reality than on our beliefs, expectations, emotional state, and focus.* These details, sometimes referred to as *back stories*, are as unique as fingerprints. Events are experienced (felt emotionally) as if the *back story* our subconscious creates is true. [50]

For example, a person who goes to a job interview and feels the interview went well will feel hopeful while someone who is self-critical could have the exact same interview (same questions, same responses, same qualifications) and have a sense they didn't do well and feel badly about the interview. Or, a guy who creates a *back story* that a woman who gives him her phone number likes him will believe he has a chance of getting a date with her. Reality may be that she has no intention of going out with him.

It is very important to recognize that *back stories* are not created in the conscious mind. They are created subconsciously. So, while they may not be factually true, they are not lies in the traditional sense of the word. *Back stories* are interpretations of the known facts filtered by our beliefs. A religious person may attribute good fortune to an intervention from God. An atheist experiencing the same good fortune may attribute it to luck, chance, happenstance, or good planning.

The thought process isn't like this, "Wow. I just found a $20. bill on the ground by my car. Let me think of the many ways that could have happened and find out the truth of how that bill ended up by my car."

The thought, "God is good to me," or "I'm lucky," comes to us and we accept it as factual. We don't tend to question the *back stories* our mind creates because they are created considering our beliefs.

Scientists develop explicit theories to explain phenomena they investigate. Laypersons (non-scientists) develop theories or beliefs to help them understand the world but unlike explicit scientific theories, laypersons theories are often implicit which means the creation of the belief is not done consciously. The conclusions we reach about life become beliefs that our mind then reinforces by interpreting future events in ways that support established beliefs.

"Personal beliefs are critical for understanding human behavior... Piaget, for example, suggested that the development of meaning systems is just as important as logical thinking in shaping behavior. Similarly, Kelly suggested that, "man looks at his world through transparent templates which he creates and then attempts to fit over the realities of which the world is composed." [51]

It is important to remember that *back stories* aren't something you make up on purpose. Your mind seeks to make sense of the world. By creating a *back story* that is consistent with your beliefs, your world makes sense to you. *Back stories* may not be true, but they are not lies in the sense that someone might lie to avoid telling someone a hurtful truth or avoid being scorned by others. Back stories are innocent of conscious wrong doing. A psychotic break is characterized by the creation of a back story that makes unthinkable actions seem to be rational choices. Many of the hypotheses (beliefs) the subconscious mind uses to form our *back stories* are well-established before our seventh birthday. [52]

Ask yourself, "Is there another way to view this situation?" and as a thought occurs, compare how that thought feels to your current interpretation. If the new thought feels better, consider adopting it as the new *back story* through which you perceive the situation. This process can be utilized repeatedly. It is not normal to move from feeling awful about a situation to feeling good with one attempt but a concerted effort, over 20 minutes or days or weeks or months—depending on the severity and complexity of the situation and how much experience you have with the process—leads to feeling much better. Using this method repeatedly helps you stabilize better feeling perspectives. Unlike when you go to a conference or other event that motivates you to a better-feeling perspective that disappears soon afterward, this deliberate but gradual adjustment is sustainable.

The next section describes factors that have a major impact on the *back stories* your mind creates.

Understand how Your Brain Processes Data

Everyone's brain does not process the same inputs in the same way. The conclusions two individuals reach when given the same data can be very different. The main reason for the differences is the way their brains are programmed to process the data.

Our *rational minds* are far from rational. We all have cognitive biases that affect how we view the world. Most of the programming our brains use to process data was programmed when we were young children. Fortunately, Transformational Stress Coping Strategies allow you to take conscious control and re-program your brain with programming that helps you achieve your goals and reduce implicit biases.

Although there are over 186 documented cognitive biases, conscious control of just four filters our brain uses to determine the data it passes on to our conscious mind makes a tremendous difference in the level of stress we experience every day.

Our brain works to maintain our existing beliefs. Below our conscious awareness the brain makes up *back stories* to explain why things happen the way they do.[53] The *back stories* our brain makes up may or may not be true.

Before big data (all the information from your senses) reaches your conscious mind it is mined for what is relevant— the programming of your filters determines what is important. Imagine a miner looking for sapphires but he has no idea what a diamond is. This miner is in your mind, scanning the big data, finding sapphires, and sending the information to your conscious mind. When the miner sees a diamond, it goes in the irrelevant file—because the miner is not programmed to find diamonds.

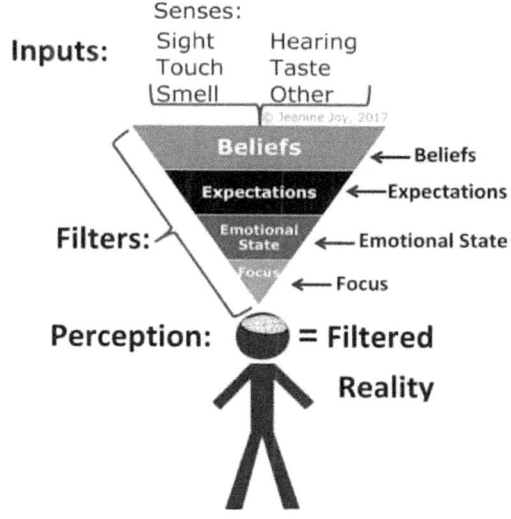

For example, the brain of an employee who believes they are excellent at a task that is counseled or corrected about that task will be given a *back story* by his subconscious mind that explains the contradiction between being good and being corrected. The *back story* will strive to maintain the employee's belief about her level of skill. Examples could include:

- The boss is making up things because the boss doesn't like the employee,
- A co-worker sabotaged the employee's work,
- The boss doesn't know what they are talking about,
- The boss is joking.

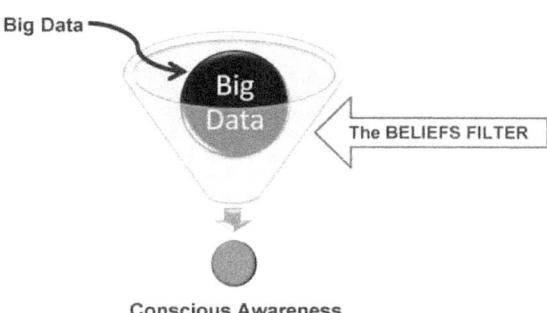

Remember, we don't even realize our mind made up a *back story*. To us, the *back story* seems like reality. The way we experience something emotionally reflects our interpretation of reality. The mind doesn't try to create a story that will serve our highest good and doesn't lean toward creating stories that feel good over stories that feel bad. The main job of the *back story* is to protect our existing beliefs, even if those beliefs make it more difficult for us to move toward self-actualization.

When we understand our mind makes up *back stories* to protect our existing beliefs we will be more flexible in reaching conclusions. We won't automatically believe every thought we think and we won't defend our thoughts without considering whether they could be wrong because of an inaccurate *back story.*

Emotional Guidance is the best tool to help us recognize when our mind is making up *back stories* that are detrimental to the outcomes we desire. If we receive negative emotion as the result of the *back story,* a different back story would serve us better. Since our beliefs determine the back story our subconscious mind creates, this points to an area that could be improved by changing an underlying belief using Transformational Stress Management Strategies.

Individual Perception

The greatest discovery of my generation is that human beings can alter their lives by altering their attitudes of mind.
William James

Emotion Regulation: Automatic and Conscious

We've all noticed that the amount of stress we experience in response to events is not the same as the stress others in like circumstances experience. Our level of stress may be higher or lower than other people experience. Our perception of stress is influenced by many different factors including automatic (subconscious) and conscious emotion regulation. Automatic emotion regulation is influenced by our:

- Beliefs
   - Includes self-efficacy beliefs
   - Includes worldview
   - Includes any beliefs that are relevant to the topic
- Expectations
- Emotional State
- Habits of thought
- Focus
- Goals and desires

Automatic emotion regulation can be made more useful by changing any of these factors with the intention of lessening the stress we experience. Transformational Stress Management Strategies are transformational because they change our automatic emotion regulation so that our initial conscious thoughts are less stressful. Changing one of the above affects how stressed we feel in multiple situations. It doesn't just make one situation more comfortable, it makes many situations more comfortable.

Skill at using Advanced Stress Management Strategies depends on numerous factors, all of which can be developed.

- Conscious emotion regulation influenced by our:
   - Awareness of emotion regulation strategies
   - Level of skill in regulating emotion
   - Accurate interpretation of the emotion we are feeling
   - Accurate interpretation of the meaning of the emotion we feel
   - Time available
   - Resources in that moment (See Re-define Your Best (Resources))
   - Determination to feel good
   - Resistance to alternate *back stories* (Lack of psychological flexibility)

When you use Advanced Coping skills, stressors do not feel as stressful because they are dealt with and don't create the same cumulative effect as they do when coping skills are inadequate to handle the stress you're experiencing. We often attribute an individual's ability to withstand high levels of stress to personal fortitude and while there may be some of that, the most common difference is the presence or absence of good coping skills. Situational stress is not consistent between people. Some people will perceive work as stressful while other people will perceive the same job as not stressful. [54]

The amount of stress experienced can be categorized by the level of coping skills applied. Individuals who do not have well developed coping skills experience higher levels of stress. Someone with Advanced or Transformational coping skills can experience little or no stress in the same situation.

Each of us is essentially hypnotized about the nature of reality from infancy. Cultural anthropologists have documented how people who grow up in different cultures perceive literally different realities. [55] Most of us do not know the premises our *official* concept of reality is based upon or how that concept was created. We believe the concept reflects a fixed reality.

The reality we can ascertain with our physical sensory feedback systems reflects one reality (and not the same one to each of us). The reality we can ascertain with our current technology and measuring capabilities reflects more information than our physical senses communicate to us. Humans tend to define what we perceive as reality.

We (humans) have an onboard computer (our brain) that checks incoming data against several factors, providing us <u>only</u> with the data it believes is relevant based on our programming. This onboard computer can help us thrive if it is programmed correctly. If the programming is based on unsupportive data, or wrong assumptions, it can make life much more difficult.

Until you program your brain in ways that support thriving, you will not even be able to guess at your full potential—much less hope to achieve it.

If you do not believe something is possible, your brain will not pass on data demonstrating how to accomplish it. It will file it in an irrelevant file. If you later decide to believe something different, you can retrieve data from the irrelevant file and evaluate it from a new perspective. An example of this is someone whose spouse cheats but they did not believe the person was capable of doing so. After the fact, the person will often beat themselves up for "not seeing the signs." Understanding that their subconscious brain filed the signs in the irrelevant file because they did not believe their spouse capable of cheating might help them stop unproductive self-criticism. An individual who does not believe their spouse capable of infidelity has programmed their filters to ignore warning signs they might see if the spouse was considered capable of infidelity.

On the other hand, someone who believes their spouse will cheat, or is fearful about the potential, will interpret signs as if they are confirming the fear even when the spouse is faithful.

If we are chronically appreciative, we will find something to appreciate even in unpleasant circumstances. For example, the day after my mom died last month I wrote eight thank you cards to nurses and a respiratory therapist who had cared for her during her two weeks in ICU. I was not happy with one of her main doctors and a few other staff but I didn't write complaint letters. It was too late to change the outcome and my mind focuses on the positive. I had already ascertained that their failures were due to a lack of training in a new research area and that I can do something about that. I can offer training and provide information to prevent the same mistakes from happening in the future. Positive action feels better than complaining about an unchangeable past.

Our minds evaluate how we feel the majority of the time and feed us thoughts that maintain our chronic emotional state. The filters that determine the *back stories* our mind creates are one of the main reasons there are so many unique responses to similar stimuli.

If you are focused on something, orange cars for example, your mind will make you more conscious of orange cars. It is not that there are more orange cars; it is that once you program your mind to focus on them, the information is passed to your conscious mind every time it is available. Our filters are a tremendous tool when used correctly.

A change of perception changes everything. Each mind interprets the world according to factors specific to the individual.[56] Factors create filters in our brain that determine the information <u>the conscious mind becomes aware of</u>. Filters determine how we interpret what we see and experience. You give thoughts power when you accept them as true. Everyone has a choice. Advanced Coping Strategies involve deliberately changing the way we perceive a situation in a conscious effort to change our emotional response.

The amount of stress we feel in any given situation is impacted by how we perceive that stress.[57] Do we think it is more than we can handle? Do we think we're capable of handling it? Do we see it as specific to this situation or as part of a widespread problem? Have we successfully dealt with this type of situation in the past? Has someone we know or have heard about successfully (or unsuccessfully) dealt with the same problem? Do we trust ourself to prevail? The answers we give to these questions determines how we experience the moment—including how our bodies respond.

We always have the ability to change the programming our brain uses. Age doesn't cement our brain into positions that we are unable to change. We always have the ability to adopt new habits of thought.

Consciously recognizing that we can change the way we feel by changing the way we perceive a situation increases our sense of control over our life. We feel more empowered. This supports an internal locus of control which is a significant requirement in resilience, PsyCap, Growth Mindset, Salutogenesis, and happiness.

Physical concepts are free creations of the human mind, and are not, however it may seem, uniquely determined by the external world.
Albert Einstein, The Evolution of Physics

Expectations

You have to expect things of yourself before you can do them.
Michael Jordan

Quantum physics explains how our expectations—high or low, influence others behaviors with mirror neurons[58] that sync our minds.

Mirror neurons [58] do not require conversation or even body language. Mirror neurons sync to the stronger belief when we interact with one another. Have you ever ridden in an elevator with a complete stranger who seemed to think he was superior to you? Did you feel diminished as a result of the encounter? Was your self-esteem bruised?

If your answer is yes, strengthening your cohesion about who you are would benefit you.

Define Yourself: Don't allow Other People to Define Who You Are or What You Can Be

Until we consciously define ourself as the person we want to be, complete with the characteristics and qualities we wish to possess, we are vulnerable. We allow others' opinions and treatment of us to affect how we feel, to devalue us and our sense of worth. We leave the door to our self-esteem not only unlocked, but open to undesired intrusions. We feel defensive. Before we interact with others we may have had dozens of fearful thoughts hoping that they do not criticize us or that they include us in conversations or invitations lest we feel demeaned or left out. We may have lost sleep worrying that someone was surpassing us while we slumbered.

We should not wait until researchers reveal all the nuances of Quantum Physics and mirror neurons work before we begin using what we do know to benefit one another.

One of the best (and sadly somewhat common) examples of this is in a family where one person has been battling an addiction. After the individual successfully completes rehabilitation and feels very confident about his future he is back amidst a family that is just waiting for him to backslide. The family did not go through the program with him so they anticipate another failure. If his intention and belief in his ability not to relapse is not greater than his family's expectation, the family's expectation will win.

Who wins when expectations conflict? The one with the strongest belief wins. If you have a strong belief that you are or can be who you want to be, you have Constructive Interference (Coherence).[59] You'll learn more about the benefits of Constructive Interference in the chapter on Quantum Physics.

How do you counteract another's low expectations about you? Develop a stronger belief about who you are and where you're going than the ones held by anyone who sees you as having less potential than your Emotional Guidance supports. What are you expecting from life? Do you think your expectations serve you or not?

Individuals in our society frequently define themselves based on how others perceive them. They allow others' low opinions to influence who they believe they are. Someone else's opinion reflects who *they* are—not *who* you are. Making conscious decisions about whom you are and what you can accomplish is the best way to fulfill more of your personal potential. We (wrongly) assume others' thought processes are the same as our own.

We can change our definition of self at any time. Our thoughts, words, and behavior will change to reflect our newly defined self. Most people allow other people's opinions of them to determine some or all of the character they play in real life. The more conscious we are about defining ourself as the person we want to be, the more we will become the person we want to be. Strategies that help you define yourself as the person you want to be are in the Healthy Self-esteem Chapter.

If you don't consciously choose what to expect, prior experiences and what others convince you that you should expect will dictate your expectations, even if those expectations aren't serving your highest good.

We never *think clearly* because our subconscious filters distort conscious reality, or perhaps more accurately, they create our individual realities. Fortunately, Emotional Guidance is designed to guide us to accurate interpretations and most importantly, to perspectives that serve our highest good. All information is considered by our Emotional Guidance system. It is not limited to the information that makes it to our conscious mind through the filtering system.

How can we help others? Seeing others for their potential rather than their current state helps them achieve more of their potential. This is true whether we ever speak a word about it to them.

Treat a man as he is and he will remain as he is.
Treat a man as he can and should be and he will become as he can and should be.
E.E. Cummings

Focus

Focus is the easiest significant filter to consciously direct, but it, too, has default modes. Changing focus is how Palliative Stress Management Strategies work. When your focus is not responding to deliberate intentions, it uses its default settings. Everyone has different default settings. Most people focus on whatever is in front of them

There are exceptions. Passionate interest in a topic will guide our focus. If you've ever been in love you'll recall how you thought about the person you were in love with frequently. Any passion, from sports to intellectual pursuits, draws our attention. The reason you can hear someone say your name in a loud room is because your filters are programmed to pay attention to your name. As a Mom, my filters are programmed to hear the word Mom.

Directing our focus toward what we do not want ruins relationships. When we consciously focus on things that elicit less than positive emotions it trains our brain to look for more things that will make us feel the same way. If we begin focusing on what we do not like about our spouse, children, co-workers, body, job, home, or world, it changes our focus. It doesn't take a long time for the change of focus to make us decide that the subject of our focus is bad. Our friends will help us develop and maintain a negative focus if we tell them how irritated (_____) made us. They will ask us if he/she/it has done anything else that upset us the next time we speak.

Paying attention to the emotions you feel lets you know when you are heading away from what you want.

Palliative Coping Stress Management Techniques are dose-dependent methods and the most commonly recommended type of stress management. They are the most commonly recommended because research supporting Advanced and Transformational Strategies is relatively new and because it costs less to research dose-dependent strategies. Don't equate more research with better. It is only indicative of what has been studied so far. This is partially because research on processes that change automatic responses requires a longitudinal design, which means the research is more expensive and does not fit neatly into a school semester, or even a doctoral dissertation.

Changing focus is dose-dependent because, like other medicines that treat symptoms instead of the root cause, the effect is contingent on whether the prescription is followed. Dose-dependent techniques are like drugs that you stay on for life. They work, but you're dependent upon the technique to feel better and their effectiveness may decline over time, making it necessary to increase the dosage.

There is nothing wrong with dose-dependent techniques. Palliative Stress Management Strategies benefit many people every day. But using <u>only</u> dose-dependent techniques is sort of like having a broken leg and choosing to just take pain medicine for the rest of your life instead of having the leg set.

Palliative Strategies are best as temporary measures while learning techniques that directly address the root cause of stress.

Depression and chronic stress decrease intrinsic motivation and the desire to do some of the very things that would provide the temporary relief using Palliative methods.[60] Entire corporate wellness programs have sprung up, heavily armed with carrots and sticks, to encourage beneficial health behaviors. Those who need them the most are the ones who are least likely to be engaged, or remain engaged, with those tactics.

That is why Transformational Stress Coping Strategies that change neuropathways and result in better automatic responses are so important to increasing public health and promoting long-term well-being.*

To summarize, we perceive a filtered reality. How a person feels in any given situation depends on the way the filters are programmed and what, if any, conscious reappraisal they do. This is why two people who have very

---

* See Appendix VII for more information.

similar circumstances can feel entirely different about their situation. One may feel fearful while the other feels hopeful or even excited.

Information is filtered below our conscious awareness but we can identify if we are perceiving our circumstances in the best possible light by how our response feels. We can then use Advanced Stress Coping Strategies to change our current perspective. We can identify filters we want to adjust and use Transformational Stress Coping Strategies that change our beliefs so our automatic responses become less stressful.

Beliefs: Example

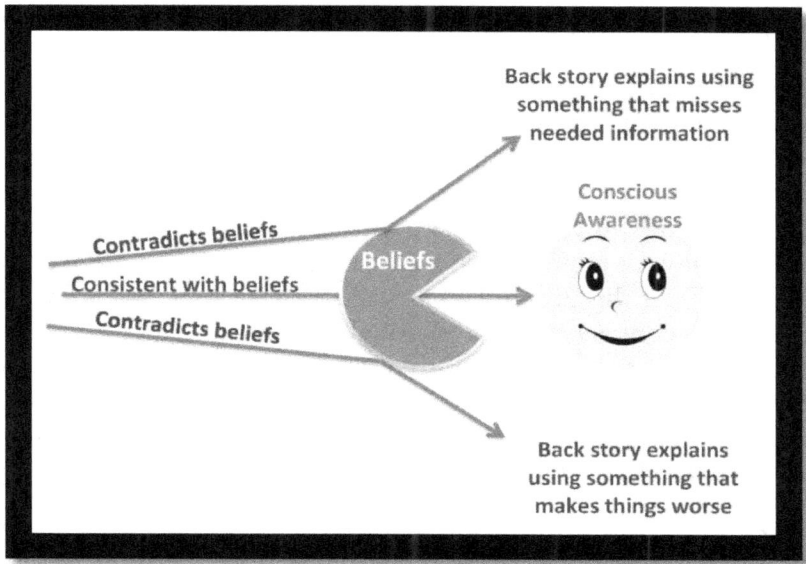

Our beliefs are protected by the automatic processes of our mind. We interpret reality as if our beliefs are true. If we believe someone is trustworthy we tend to believe what they tell us even if someone without an opinion about their trustworthiness would easily pick up on their lies. If we believe someone is not trustworthy we tend to believe they are being dishonest even when they are truthful.

Some people have beliefs that filter their *back stories* about large groups of people as if every member of the group has the same characteristics.

Trustworthiness is one of many subjects that we have beliefs about. We have beliefs about our world, community, family, self, food, fun, death, relationships, self-worth, work, etc.

Every time you read about new discoveries or inventions that the vast majority of the public rejected or thought were of little to no value, you're seeing their minds protecting their existing beliefs. Inventions like the personal computer, Xerox machine, vacuum cleaner, Monopoly, and Trivia Pursuit were initially rejected before being embraced. This is also why Galileo was persecuted for saying the Earth revolves around the sun. Semmelweis was ridiculed for saying germs existed 50 years before the microscope was invented for the same reason.

The *back stories* created in our subconscious mind play a significant role in whether we believe reality or create another meaning for our experiences.

Let's use an example of two people who miss their turn on the way home from work. One of the people believes they are dumb. The other person believes that we live in a helpful universe that will help them do things that are to their advantage. The person who has been trained to believe she is dumb will attribute missing the turn to evidence of her lack of intelligence.

The person who believes that things happen for positive reasons will appreciate the help and believe that they were being protected when they missed the turn. Later, the person with the helpful universe belief talks to a neighbor who complains about being stuck in traffic because of an accident on their normal route. Their mind connects that information with missing the turn, supporting the helpful universe belief.

Does assuming that a helpful universe orchestrated a distraction that caused her to miss her turn make life feel better or worse? Does it matter if it is true? Does feeling protected, but not protected enough to do stupid things like walk down a dark alley in a crime infested neighborhood, make life less stressful? Does this person feel protected enough to worry less, stress less, and feel more confident moving through her days?

Which perspective is more supportive?

If neither of these perspectives appeals to you, what does? What *back story* would your mind create if you missed a turn you take nearly every day? Does that *back story* help you thrive or does it diminish your life in some way?

> *Beliefs are just thoughts you keep thinking. In a global sense, some beliefs are valid and others are not. When we think a thought, an "electrical charge occurs in our brain that causes the synapses to grow closer together in order to decrease the distance the electrical charge has to cross . . . the brain is rewiring its own circuitry, physically changing itself, to make it easier and more likely that the proper synapses will spark together—in essence, making it easier for the thought to be triggered."* [61]

Once you think a thought it is easier for you to think the thought again. If you repeatedly think the thought it becomes a belief. A belief is a thought you've thought repeatedly, which your brain then uses as a filter to interpret reality.

Your mind will show you evidence of your beliefs and will not show you evidence of things outside your beliefs. Our minds interpret reality as if our beliefs are true. Our mind doesn't care if our belief is good for us. It will protect our beliefs and interpret reality as if our beliefs are valid even when they are not true and not beneficial to us. Some of our beliefs support our highest good while others limit our ability to thrive.

> *Believing that our brain shows us reality leads us to believe the information it passes to our conscious mind is an accurate reflection of reality and the only possible interpretation of reality.*

Beliefs do not just hold people back. People who develop empowering beliefs soar. Studying the beliefs of those who are thriving and comparing theirs to your own can help you identify beliefs you might like to adopt.

What we believe determines part of our emotional response. If we see someone who has attained something we want, our emotional response can be extremely different because of what we believe. If we believe their attainment of it means it is something that is attainable for us, we will be pleased by their achievement. It will increase our belief in our ability to attain our desire.

If we believe we cannot have what they have, our emotional response will be quite different. We may feel jealousy or envy. Some people will even feel anger that they can't have what someone else has. Jealousy is self-inflicted. It shouts to the world, "You have something I want but I don't believe in myself enough to believe I can have what you've managed to achieve."

Even jealousy in relationships has this basis. It is not so much a specific person we want (even when we think it is). It is the emotional experience we believe we will have with that person in our life. It is how we believe it would feel to have that person. Our ideas about how it would feel were created by the *back story* our mind created about how it would feel. We have bundled a specific person with the ability to have an emotional experience we desire.

When we do not believe we will find an opportunity or a solution we want, the belief filter will filter out the information so that we literally do not hear or see opportunities. One example is a situation I with a woman I worked with who didn't believe our employer would hire a woman for a specific role she was qualified to fill. She would have loved the role, but because she didn't believe a woman would be hired for it, she didn't bother to apply. The successful candidate turned out to be both female and visibly pregnant. The belief that she couldn't get that role stopped her from taking a beneficial action.

This woman had habits of thought that were influenced by beliefs that what she wanted was out of her reach.

On another occasion she wanted something but had decided she couldn't get what she wanted—a house. I encouraged her to try since the worse that could happen was the bank would say no and leave her right where she was. She tried and was able to buy a house. She's a smart woman. The only reason she didn't think to just try without outside encouragement was because her belief that she couldn't get a mortgage made her brain file the possibility in an irrelevant file.

Opportunities to help people believe more in themselves are all around us. The negative emotion my co-worker felt when she thought about buying a house was saying, "There is a better perspective you could have on this subject" but she interpreted her negative thoughts as affirming her inability to get what she wanted.

Rational Thought

I know that you, ladies and gentlemen, have a philosophy, each and all of you, and that the most interesting and important thing about you is the way in which it determines the perspective in your several worlds.
William James

Rational thought is an oxymoron. We believe we are rational but if you had a time machine and were transplanted back 100-200 years in the past most of us would be considered insane by the standards used at those times.

Even without time travel, rational thought and behavior are culturally specific. Here are some examples of behaviors considered rational (polite) in the United States that are considered rude elsewhere:

- Venezuela: Arriving on time.
- China and India: Opening gifts in front of the person who gave the gift.
- Japan: Laughing out loud so that your teeth are visible.
- Bosnia: Wearing shoes in someone else's home.
- France: Putting a piece of bread on your plate is uncouth. Leave it on the table beside the plate.
- Ireland: Do not eat fried potatoes (French fries) with your fingers.

We create schema's through which we perceive the world. Those schemas are assumptions based on our experiences and customs we are taught. The schema's determine our perceptions and are often not wholly accurate. Most communication is at a superficial surface level where the distortions are not evident. When deeper communication occurs, differences in schemas become more apparent.

If you believe the world is made up of mostly good people your perception is vastly different than it would be if you are convinced the world is made up of mostly bad people. If you believe money is evil you will perceive the world very differently than if you believe money is something that simplifies the exchange of goods and services. Individuals with either perspective will be sure their schema is right and that people with other beliefs are wrong because the *back stories* created by their subconscious mind support their beliefs. It is beliefs, not conclusions, where changes are most productive.

In order to benefit from Advanced and Transformational Coping Strategies you have to realize that there are countless perspectives about any given situation and the viewpoint you choose determines how empowered or disempowered you feel. It determines how you feel emotionally. There is not one perspective that is ultimately right because it is like looking at a painting. If you view it from the front the perspective looks totally different than it does when you view it from the back but both are accurate.

Our society does not give emotions the credit they deserve. We are taught to give our rational minds and thought processes credit for our intelligence. This is another false premise. Many people would assume that not having emotions would create a person who was very good at decision-making; they might even envision someone like Spock from Star Trek.

Researchers who worked with individuals who have lost the part of their brains that recognizes emotions to disease or injury made an interesting discovery.

Rationality depends critically on sophisticated emotionality. Our emotional process works so well that we do not even know much of what it is doing. Emotions provide instant and automatic appraisal of tremendous amounts of data that we never have to consider consciously. Robbed of this function in their brains, individuals find it almost impossible to make even simple decisions. [62]

Confabulation

According to Psychpedia, confabulation is:
"The memory disturbance might be the creation of a memory that never occurred, the gross distortion of an actual event, or the insistence that something that did happen actually did not occur. Confabulations are heavily influenced by emotion. Most people confabulate sometimes, and mundane examples occur regularly."

Pay particular attention to the last sentence. As you learn how truly flexible our minds are and their ability to see a single situation from a multitude of perspectives you will begin to realize how fluid 'facts' can be.

In *The Happiness Hypothesis*, Jonathan Haidt describes research done with patients whose brains were separated (to help them with epileptic seizures). Researchers discovered that both sides of the brain continued to function but only one side had access to language. Each eye communicated with only one side of the brain. By showing only the side of the brain that did not have language a picture, the patient could be made to take an action. These actions were things like choosing a specific picture out of a group of photographs or getting up and walking away. When researchers asked the patient to explain the reason for choosing the picture or for walking away the patient would immediately provide a reason (*back story*) but the reason had no relationship to the stimulus. [63] That is an example of confabulation.

For example, someone shown a photograph of a house covered with snow chose a picture of a shovel but when asked why they chose the shovel their answer had nothing to do with snow. When asked why they were walking away, one answered that he was going to get a cola. The interpreter part of our brains makes up explanations but we don't consciously realize it has made up an explanation. This is not limited to split-brain patients. All of our brains do this. Then, because we don't realize we've essentially made up the reason, we believe it is true. Martin Seligman refers to this as **back stories**. [64] The *back stories* our brains create are what give our life meaning. If we create back-stories that feel good, we feel good. If we create back-stories that feel bad, we feel bad.

Researchers found that when students defended a position the student did not support on an emotional topic like immigration or violence, 69% had a higher preference for the choice they previously opposed a week later. [65] Our beliefs are malleable.

The only smart choice is to consciously choose the beliefs you want in order to create filters that will create self-supportive perceptions of reality (back stories). When you do that, the *back stories* your subconscious mind creates will be empowering.

Unhealthy Habits of Thought Path to Depression

If you believe that feeling bad or worrying long enough will change a past or future event, then you are residing on another planet with a different reality system.
William James

Our thoughts, words, and actions tend to be mood congruent. That means that when you are in a bad mood you tend to notice things and think about things that will sustain your bad mood.

Chronic stress creates two pathways to depression. Stress is evinced by low emotional states and low energy. We should respond to stress, not endure it.

Biochemical Path to Depression

Chronic stress creates biochemical changes in the body that lead to the biochemical imbalance that is often associated with depression. Depression and the biochemical imbalance are symptoms of chronic stress. The lack of good stress management and emotion regulation skills is the cause of the chronic stress.

Stress almost immediately causes biochemical changes in our body. Chronic and severe stress causes stronger biochemical reactions. Stressful circumstances endured by someone without skills to reduce the stress they feel can lead to chemical imbalances, but it is often reversible. Reducing stress levels improves the body's biochemistry.

Our bodies are fantastic and brilliant. They will strive for wellness if we get out of the way. Enduring stress is one way of being in their way. Reducing stress opens the valve that allows the clear cellular communication required for good health to flow (se pg. 23).

Prevention and Recovery Strategies

Most of our thoughts are automatic. Most of the thoughts we think are not thoughtful. They are the result of our habits of thought.

Some people have habits of thought that increase the amount of stress they experience every day. Some people have habits of thought that keep the amount of stress they experience low even when most people would consider their situation stressful.

Lower stress leads to better mental health outcomes.*

---

* Instead of repeatedly mentioning the benefits of lower stress, The Benefits Chapter is devoted to describing many scientifically known benefits of lower stress. When *the benefits* are mentioned throughout this book, it is referring to the benefits described in The Benefits Chapter.

What Causes Chronic Stress?

>Life + Unhealthy habits of thought = Chronic Stress
>Life + Healthy habits of thought = Less Stress
>Life without good stress coping skills = Chronic Stress
>Life with good coping skills = Less Stress

If small things bother you, it is because you have a habit of them bothering you and because your habits of thought (and possibly your self-esteem) make them feel like big deals. Developing healthy habits of thought reduces the amount of stress you experience on a daily basis.

How stressful your life feels is more a function of how you process information than of the situations themselves. That's why some people can face a high level of stress/risk and function well and others begin suffering when just a little pressure is present.

The difference is how resilient they are and how many stress management skills they have mastered. Resilience is an outcome of healthy habits of thought that support healthy self-esteem, optimism, and an internal locus of control.

People use the best stress management skills they know how to use. If they don't know good ones they use poor ones. Your habits of thought can add to, multiply, subtract from or divide the amount of stress you experience in any situation. I'm sure you have noticed that not everyone responds to stressful situations the same way.

People who do not become as stressed tend to be resilient and they are resilient because they have healthy habits of thought that make them feel more capable of dealing with life. When you change unhealthy habits of thought to healthier ones it leads to transformational changes.

Build a Strong Foundation

In many ways, the foundation modern societies build is counterproductive to the development of healthy habits of thought.

Depression begins with chronic stress. If you are not experiencing stress it isn't a stressful situation for you.

Everyone has different things that make them feel stressed. Negative emotion is an indicator that you're experiencing stress. If you feel able to deal with the situation you won't be as stressed as someone who doesn't think they can deal with the situation. If you feel hopeful about the outcome you won't be as stressed as someone who isn't hopeful about the outcome. If you have faith about the outcome you won't be as stressed as someone who doesn't have faith/trust in a good outcome.

If you feel empowered enough to find a way (even if you don't know what that way is) you won't be as stressed as someone who feels disempowered.

I've been in the midst of being laid off when I had significant financial obligations for myself and children and felt excited because I knew things would turn out well for me because they always do. I wasn't stressed.

- Resilience decreases how much stress you feel in a given situation.

- An internal locus of control, the belief that your actions make a difference in the outcome, decreases how much stress you feel in a given situation.
- Being optimistic decreases how much stress you feel in a given situation.
- Healthy self-esteem reduces the stress you feel in a given situation.

Resilience, an internal locus of control, optimism, and self-esteem are all things you can change about yourself so that you experience less stress.

It is possible that a person who isn't feeling stress isn't thinking things through and assessing the risks accurately. You don't want to be overly worried — most people stress and worry about things that will never happen and decrease their happiness as a result. But you do want to manage risks. What does that mean? It means things like using protection during sex, wearing a helmet on a motorcycle or bicycle, wearing a seat belt when you drive, not driving while intoxicated or with someone who is intoxicated, locking your doors when you go to sleep, and not lending money to strangers (at least not more than you can afford to lose).

If you're confident that you'll find a way you probably will and there is no real reason to be stressed.

Factors Associated with Healthy Habits of Thought (Overview)

Our life always expresses the result of our dominant thoughts.
Soren Kierkegaard (1813-1855) Danish philosopher and writer

The following habits of thought are associated with healthy habits of thought. Extensive research shows that they increase physical and mental well-being and lead to better outcomes in a wide variety of situations.

- Optimism
- Healthy self-esteem
- Internal locus of control
- Self-compassion
- Cognitive reappraisal
- Appreciation
- Autonomy
- Metacognition
- Supportive beliefs
- Positive expectations
- Healthy happiness contract*
- Recognizing emotions
- Advanced Stress Management Strategies
- Transformational Stress Management Strategies
- Lean toward thoughts that support positive motion forward
- Lean toward thoughts that support healthy relationships
- Knowledge that increases the ability to develop and sustain healthy habits of thought:
- Stress and happiness have an inverse relationship
- Use Emotional Guidance to determine personal truth

Sustainable happiness is a skills-based state of mind. It is not the circumstances of your life that determine your level of happiness. If you learn how to understand the purpose and use of your emotions you'll spend more time feeling happy. Happiness is the result of moving toward self-determined goals that feel good when you think about achieving them because you believe you can achieve them.

1) Understand that your brain shows you a perceived reality, not reality itself and that everyone perceives a different reality
2) Understand that your emotions are guidance from a sensory feedback system
3) Put the desire to be happy above that of being right (in your relationships)
4) Make continuous learning about things that interest you a priority
5) Choose love not hate

Most arguments are about different *back stories* and cannot be resolved by talking about conclusions. Deeper conversations that explore beliefs are required to understand one another. If you're focused on *being right,* it is almost impossible to have deeper conversations.

---

* Described elsewhere in *MWME;* concept based on Dr. Robert Holden's work

High-Level Factors That Contribute to Positive Outcomes
Life is really simple, but men insist on making it complicated.
Confucius (BC 551–BC 479) Chinese philosopher

A high-level factor is a concept formed by combining several lower-level factors. Lower-level does not imply less importance. Lower-level means it is a component of a combination of factors that have been given a unique name. There are enough high-level factors about happiness and what is required to be successful to make anyone's head spin.

To clarify, a mustang and a corvette are both high-level factors "cars" made up of lower-level factors that include a chassis and an engine. If you didn't know that both are cars with engines and chassis, you might think a mustang and a corvette were entirely different things.

At first glance, it seems like there are too many recommended high-level factors that support positive outcomes and that it would be impossible to attain all of them because there are so many different high-level factors. Even trying to figure out where to start can be overwhelming. It makes it feel like a long road with no end in sight. Fortunately, high-level factors are easier to understand when you compare their lower-level factors side-by-side. The journey becomes understandable and not nearly as long as it seemed at first glance.

It isn't that complicated. Looking at the lower-level factors provides clarity about what is important. The chart reflects the overlap of lower-levels factors shared by the commonly recommended high-level factors that improve outcomes in life.

High-Level Factor	Lower Level Factors							
High Core Self-Evaluations	Internal Locus of Control	Healthy Self-esteem	Self-efficacy				Emotional stability	
Resilience	Internal Locus of Control	Healthy Self-esteem			Optimism			
Psychological Capital (PsyCap)	Internal Locus of Control	Healthy Self-esteem	Self-efficacy	Resilience	Hope	Optimism		
Growth Mindset	Internal Locus of Control							
Happiness	Internal Locus of Control	Healthy Self-esteem			Hope or better	Optimism		Metacognitive Skills
Psychological Flexibility	Internal Locus of Control							Metacognitive Skills
Burnout Prevention	Internal Locus of Control	Healthy Self-esteem	Self-efficacy	Resilience		Optimism		
Salutogenesis Health Promotion Physical and Mental	Internal Locus of Control	Healthy Self-esteem						
The Smart Way™	Internal Locus of Control	Healthy Self-esteem	Self-efficacy	Resilience	Hope	Optimism	Emotion Regulation Skills	Metacognitive Skills

When we look at the lower level factors that make up the higher level factors, it is clear that an internal locus of control is a critical success factor. Healthy self-esteem and optimism are also critical factors to attaining and sustaining a high quality of life. [66]

Happiness

Emotional stability is not a lower-level factor of happiness because emotional stability is not the goal. The definition of True Happiness is:

> "The state of True Happiness does not require a constant state of bliss. It is a deep sense of inner stability, peace, well-being, and vitality that is consistent and sustainable. Awareness that you possess the knowledge and skills to return to a happy state, even when not in that state, is a critical component of sustainable happiness. True Happiness is sustainable because you deliberately and consciously apply Advanced and Transformational emotion regulation strategies that create positive emotions and cultivate healthy habits of thought until your habitual responses focus on the positive aspects in any situation."

Stress and happiness have an inverse relationship.

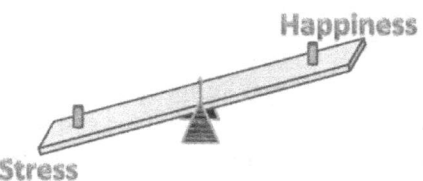

The Smart Way™ is the combination of knowledge and skills presented in MWME. The lines on the next chart illustrate the general trajectory of the emotional state of a person who is in the initial stages of applying *The Smart Way*™ who begins in a low emotional state. The thicker areas indicate the person spent more time in that emotional state. They do not represent mandatory slowdowns. They are meant to illustrate that life events may temporarily decrease your emotional state or temporarily stop progress. Someone who is new to learning *The Smart Way*™ could take 3 – 12 months to move from the Powerless Zone to the Sweet Zone with each step along the way feeling better than the prior one. Someone who is experienced using *The Smart Way*™ could experience an emotional setback (loss of job, friend, lover, etc.) and easily move the entire distance from the Powerless Zone to the Sweet Zone in a weekend.

In many ways, happiness can be described as confidence.

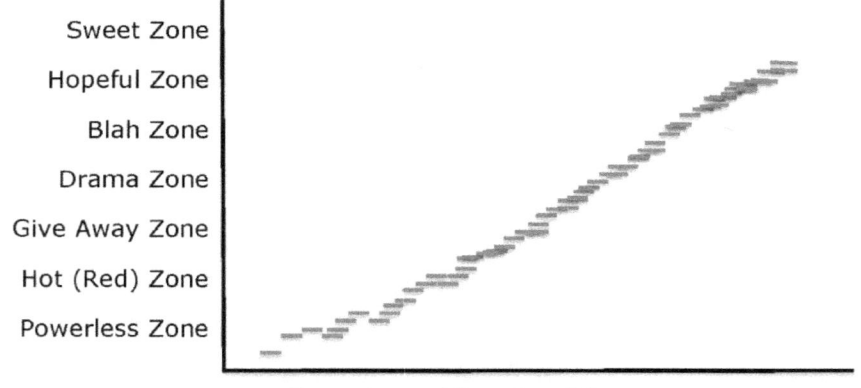

Trajectory of Emotional State across time

It is important not to demand of yourself that you achieve a state of happiness all the time. Being authentic is better than being happy. You <u>can</u>

be happy but that is not the same as you <u>should</u> be happy. Many people sabotage themselves with self-criticism when they believe they should be happy but aren't. Happiness is not the result of your circumstances,

Individuals who have healthy habits of thought experience more positive emotions even when their circumstances are negative.[67] People who have unhealthy habits of thought aren't happy because they focus on negative aspects of their life. If you could be having fun and enjoying the people you care about your best choice is to do so. But if your habits of thought aren't helping you, it takes effort and skill to turn it around and feel authentically good. Self-criticism for not being happy takes you in the wrong direction.

Changing our habits of thought allows us to experience lower levels of stress and *the benefits* associated with lower stress levels. Many aspects of society reinforce focusing on the negative in our lives, and in our world, which reinforces negative habits of thought. When negative habits of thought become established it takes more effort to change them. It can be done and isn't difficult when you know how.

Thankfully, our bodies are surprisingly resilient. If you learn Advanced and Transformational stress management strategies that reduce the level of stress you experience every day, over time both the negative mood and the biochemical imbalances can be reversed. The mood will improve first.

Resilience

The difference between stumbling blocks and stepping stones is how you use them - Unknown

Psychological resilience is a critical skill in the future workplace and the future is here. Resilience provides protection against stressors and makes life better all-around.[68, 69] People who are more resilient tolerate uncertainty better.[70] A review covering a decade of resilience research concluded:[71]

Individuals can actively participate in the development and strengthening of their own personal resilience to reduce their vulnerability to adversity. We recommend that resilience-building be incorporated into education.[72p]

Using Advanced and Transformational strategies to find more positive perspectives and using your Emotional Guidance to help you identify productive thoughts leads to natural increases in optimism and positivity. Psychologically healthy people are more likely to have a bias toward optimism than psychologically unhealthy people.[73] Optimists experience more positive emotions than pessimists.[74] Optimists feel more supported by partners.[75] Understanding Emotional Guidance increases resilience because it always points toward solutions.

I'm not afraid of storms, for I'm learning to sail my ship.
Louisa May Alcott (1832-1888) American author

When you work on thoughts about yourself using Advanced Coping Strategies and Emotional Guidance it leads to natural increases in healthy self-esteem and decreases in defensive self-esteem. As soon as you begin consciously using your Emotional Guidance to feel better and realize you have the ability to feel better without first having to change the situation, your locus of control becomes more internal.

An internal locus of control is the beliefs that your thoughts, words, and actions affect the outcome of your life.

An external locus of control (see unhealthy habits of thought) is the belief that external factors control the outcome of your life.

The way a resilient person perceives situations is different from the way a person with lower resilience perceives the same situations. A person with lower resilience can increase resilience by shifting their perspectives so they feel better (less stressed). The chart highlights some of the differences.

Less **Resilient Habits of Thought**	More **Resilient Habits of Thought**
Obstacles are enemies	Obstacles are challenges (opportunities)
Feels disempowered	Feels empowered
Sees problems as permanent	Sees problems as temporary
Sees self as a victim	Sees self as survivor or thriver
Blames others	Accepts responsibility
Sees problems as unsolvable	Believes solutions exist & can be identified
Feels fearful/helpless	Feels confidence/capable
Responds reactively	Consciously chooses perspective
Rigid thinking	Feels curiosity
Holds onto anger	Forgives easily
Resistance to new ideas	Welcomes new ideas & experiences
Feels hopeless	Feels hopeful
Expects the worse	Faith
Tendency to attack oneself	Belief in Self & Ability to learn
Holds onto guilt	Characterizes failure as learning
Feelings of shame	Self-Acceptance and Approval
Negative emotional bias	Positive emotional bias
Long-term worry and anxiety	Trust
Feels life "just happens"	Feels Personal Control
Feels unworthy	Feels worthy
Being "right" is highest goal	Places higher goals above "being right"
Feels despair	Looks for the silver lining
Feels out of control	Feels a sense of control over the response
Very specific negative thoughts	Zooms out to less specific thoughts

Write down a problem that bothers you fairly often. Use the chart to find a perspective about the problem that feels better to you that you can believe. Once you find a thought that you can believe that feels better than your usual thoughts on that subject, reinforce it by finding other thoughts about the same subject that resemble the new, better-feeling thought you found. Do this every day for a week and your emotions regarding the subject will stabilize. If they are still wobbly (going back to the less pleasant thoughts) keep doing it until it is stable. Once it is stable, repeat the process and find an even better feeling thought.

This process will take longer when you are inexperienced. Once you are experienced, you will be able to find and stabilize new thoughts in minutes.

Higher levels of resilience have positive effects on perceptions of stress, psychological responses to stress, and job-related behaviors related to stress regardless of difficult environments. Faced with especially difficult work environments, workers with higher levels of resilience seem able to avoid absences and be more productive than workers with low resilience. [76p]

Psychologists have attempted to classify tendencies revealed by the *back stories* our minds create to make sense of our reality. They refer to these explanations as our explanatory style. We often learn our explanatory style from our mothers and her style may or may not result in resilience. [77, 78] In fact, this is probably a contributing factor to the amount of truth in the saying *"The Rich get richer and the poor get poorer."* A conscious decision to change our perception and response to events is required to break an undesired cycle. Nurturing moms from low-income families buffered children from the common health issues such children often face as adults. [79] People who did not have the benefit of a nurturing mom can gain those health benefits by changing their own thinking. Taking responsibility for ourself rather than blaming others empowers us.

Explanatory Style

How you explain your situation to yourself and others matters. The same situation can be perceived as a challenge from which you'll learn and grow or as an experience that is ruining your life. It's all in how you perceive the situation.

Let's look at explanatory styles as they relate to Emotional Guidance. Categories of explanatory style include:

Personal: Whether the situation was caused by external forces (external locus of control) or internal causes (internal locus of control).

Permanent or Temporary: Is the situation perceived as stable (will it persist) or temporary (expected to change). Someone with optimistic tendencies tends to believe they can have an influence over the outcome of their lives and that negative events are temporary.

Pervasive: Are the factors that caused the situation global, local, or isolated?

Individuals with pessimistic tendencies tend to believe that negative events are permanent and pervasive and that there is little they can do to change the outcome.

Pessimism plus stress is a recipe for depression.

Your explanatory style can be different in different situations depending on your beliefs. For example, if you see yourself as having significant influence over your personal relationships, you have an internal locus of control relative to relationships. If you believe that your career depends on others (bosses or companies) you have an external locus of control in work situations.

- Thoughts that move toward self-actualization feel more empowered.
- Thoughts that move away from self-actualization feel less empowered.
- The less we believe in our potential, the more it feels we are moving away from self-actualization we are and the worse we feel.
- The more we believe in our potential, the more it feels we are moving toward self-actualization, and the better we feel.

Let's look at scenarios where someone has been fired and compare explanatory style to their self-actualized self by applying Emotional Guidance as a basis of comparison.

Imagine being fired from a job for failure to perform and identify which thoughts are moving toward or away from self-actualization in this situation.

I'm a screw-up. I'll never be able to get ahead because I can't keep a job.

This represents a disempowered perspective about the situation which means it is moving away from self-actualization. This is an internal attribution for the problem (*I'm a screw-up.*) but it isn't necessarily an internal locus of control because the person sees the situation as permanent (*I'll never be able to get ahead because I can't keep a job.*) It is also personal. If the person saw being a screw-up as something he or she could change the inability to get ahead wouldn't be perceived as permanent. It might be reflected in thoughts like this:

I haven't been doing my best. I need to stop being a screw-up so I can get ahead. (This is more empowered and moving toward self-actualization.)

Let's look at a different perspective:
They didn't recognize talent when it was right in front of them.

This is a disempowered perspective because it requires others to recognize one's talent but empowered because it indicates the person believes they have talent. This is a good example of what I refer to as ***split energy***. Split energy is two steps forward and two back, repeated indefinitely. The number of steps doesn't matter. Some people take thousands of steps forward before they retrace their steps. You see them get a new job or a new romantic partner and everything seems fantastic, for a while, then it seems as if their new situation has become a repeat of an old scenario.

This places all the blame on outside factors which mean the person perceives no ability to change the situation (external locus of control—disempowered).

Now let's look at a healthier perspective:
Maybe I was in the wrong field and this is a chance for me to find something I'll be good at.

This is an empowered feeling perspective. The focus is on the hope of (or even belief in) something better coming. That something better is, by definition, moving toward the best potential self. This person sees the situation as temporary (*there is something I'll be good at I just wasn't doing that this time*) and an internal locus of control (*this is a chance for me to find*). This attitude will lead to thoughts, words, and actions that support finding a new job in a field where the person will perform better.

Contrast that with a less healthy perspective:
I'm not smart enough to keep a job.
This is a disempowered perspective and moving away from self-actualization. This looks like an internal locus of control because self-blame is involved (*I'm not smart enough*) but the situation isn't seen as temporary so it isn't an internal locus of control with respect to the level of intelligence. This person doesn't know that intelligence is something that can change with effort. They see the reason as personal. Intelligence as a fixed characteristic is a common but now scientifically refuted belief about intelligence. You can change your level of intelligence.[80]

Now look at another healthy perspective:
Lots of people have been fired and found success in a new job.
This is an empowered perspective and leans toward becoming self-actualized. This is an internal locus of control because it reflects a belief that it is possible for her to find success in a new job. It is seen as a temporary situation with a better future (optimistic).

Let's analyze another perspective that is common and unhealthy:
My boss was a jerk. I'm glad to be gone.
This person's self-actualized self would see the bosses' positive attributes (i.e. *working for that jerk helped me learn how to deal with people who are negatively focused*). Even though this person expresses positive emotions about losing the job (*I'm glad to be gone.*) the boss being a jerk seems like an external and uncontrollable factor. An internal locus of control might consider things such as whether they can gain skills in getting along with people even if those people aren't as pleasant as we'd like them to be.

The next perspective is unhealthy and may point to additional unhealthy areas in the person's life:
How am I going to tell my spouse?
This one is subtle but it contains many nuances:
I don't trust my spouse to trust me to get another job.
I don't trust my spouse to be resilient.
Maybe: My spouses' opinion of me is how I determine my self-worth.
This perspective is not seeing the relationship with the spouse as the relationship their self-actualized self could have. Remember that the stance (attitude) you take isn't a right or wrong scenario. It is about whether your emotional state helps you or not and if it doesn't help, it is wise to change it.

Before we complete this discussion of explanatory style I want you to reaffirm your competence and worth at work to offset any negative seeds this discussion about being fired might have stirred up. You can come up with your own or use the following affirmations. Don't just read them. Read them, think them, and feel how they feel.

I make valuable contributions through my work.
I am a skilled employee/business owner.
My work is valued.
I am good at what I do.
While I am good at my work I am also always becoming better.
I deliver a service which heals, gives hope, and allows people to feel positive.

Psychological Flexibility

When you're finished changing, you're finished.
Benjamin Franklin (1706-1790)

Many published peer reviewed journal articles mention that the uncertainty being experienced by employees because of constant changes and unknown future changes is contributing to declining mental health. Psychological flexibility and conscious resilience are the solution, not certainty. Certainty is an illusion. We can feel certain about where we are going and what we are going to do but we cannot be certain that our plans will work even when there aren't a lot of variables. An attitude of "*Whatever the future holds, I am capable of surviving and thriving*" will serve you better. Psychological flexibility is one of the top ten job skills cited as necessary for workers in 2020.

The novel, *Lucifer's Hammer,* demonstrates the difference between certainty and psychological flexibility. The main characters have psychological flexibility and are resilient. The banker does not possess those skills. In the story, the banker was the most respected man in town but after a nuclear war, money lost its value. Survival skills and the ability to cooperate in order to increase the chances of survival were suddenly more important than money. The banker did not have the psychological flexibility to adjust to the new world order and chose to take his own life rather than find his place in the new paradigm. The only thing that stopped the banker from thriving in the new world order was a belief that he couldn't do it.

We have more stability today than we've ever had. History is full of examples of horrific things we have little risk of experiencing. It is the news media and instant communication from every corner of the planet that makes the world seem less safe and secure.

Mental First

If you make a problem feel better mentally first, the problem will be easier to solve. If you view the problem as difficult, it will be harder to solve than if you view it as something you can handle. Unless it is a true emergency, spending time changing your perspective to an empowered perspective first will always lead to better outcomes. A smarter version of you shows up when you feel more empowered.

Stress Management Coping Strategies

I am not concerned that you have fallen—I am concerned that you arise.
Abraham Lincoln (1809-1865) 16th President of the United States

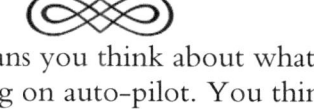

Metacognition simply means you think about what you're thinking. In other words, ou're not thinking on auto-pilot. You think about what you're thinking, how it feels when you think what you think, and why you're thinking what you are thinking. Some people naturally use metacognition and thrive as a result. Like any skill, yours will get better with practice. Like any new skill, you won't be an expert the first time. You can learn how to do it and the best part about it is that using metacognition helps you feel good. Once you feel the empowerment the first time you are successful, you will want to do it again—because it feels good. The effort you exert toward self-empowerment today provides a stepping stone that provides empowerment for a higher step you'll climb tomorrow.

How stress is processed determines how much stress is felt . . . An individual can experience stressors but be unable to process the stress well . . . Another person can experience a significant number of stressors, but process each well.
– Gandi, et al., 2011

Stress reduction programs focusing on cognitive behavioral techniques were found to be of utmost significance when it comes to preventing and treating burnout in healthcare professionals. [81]

If you are experiencing symptoms of one or more mental illnesses, remember that it took a long time for them to develop. The road to recovery is much shorter. As you learn to apply Advanced and Transformational Stress Coping Strategies to the way you perceive your life you can begin feeling better right away and become sustainably less stressed in just a few months.

Life has the potential to stress us out in many different ways. You can deal with all of these issues from an empowered mindset that sets you free to enjoy life. Treat yourself well, not just today, but every day. You deserve it.

Advanced and Transformational Stress Coping Strategies empower you with skills that allow you to regulate your emotions in ways that are beneficial to your physical and mental well-being. Developing Advanced and Transformational Stress Coping Strategies reduces the stress load at work and at home.

It is now widely appreciated that emotion regulation plays a crucial role in healthy adaptation and that difficulties with emotion regulation are associated with psychological and physical health problems. [82]

We are not stuck with our initial emotional response or our initial stress level. We have the ability to choose different perspectives that reduce stress and improve emotional state. If you bought a car for college and its reliability has decreased, you're not stuck with it because it was your first choice. You can make a decision to change it. In the same way, you are not stuck with your initial thoughts and emotions about any situation you are currently experiencing, or any situation from your past.

Just as you'll make a better decision about the next vehicle you purchase if you acquire some knowledge of safety features, cost, gas mileage, insurance rates, etc., you'll make better decisions about the perspectives you accept if you understand your choices.

Coping vs Thriving

Attempting to handle stressors without Advanced Coping Strategies resembles walking along a gravel road barefoot. You must step gingerly and you still often become bruised. You can't travel fast or far. Youe have to focus on yourself in order to ensure your own wellbeing but even with focused effort, you can't avoid bumps and bruises from the rough ground.

Thriving is walking along the same gravel road in sturdy, light-weight hiking boots. You feel confident traveling as fast as you want to go and can travel significant distances without injury. You can enjoy the journey and view because you don't have to pay as much attention to every step you take.

"Proactive approaches to managing health and aging can be taught, with sustained gains in both proactive competence and health outcomes." [83] Six broad categories of coping exist along a continuum:

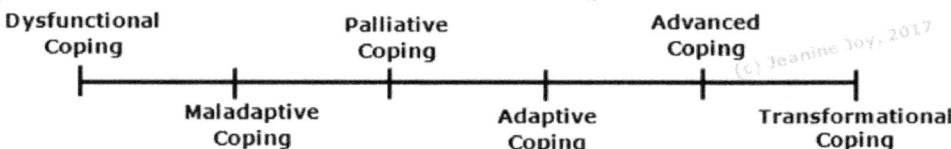

Palliative Coping functions primarily by distracting you from the source of stress. Some forms, such as exercise, can cause temporary positive changes to your body's biochemistry which provides additional assistance. Palliative Coping Strategies are the most commonly recommended strategies. There are two detriments to Palliative Coping methods:
1. Palliative Coping methods are dose-dependent meaning that, like a headache pill, they have to be applied each time in order to be effective. A headache pill you took last week isn't going to help you with the headache you developed this afternoon.

> **Palliative Coping**
>
> *Decreases anxiety but does not solve the problem*
>
> - Visualization
> - Deep breathing
> - Relaxation training
> - Adopting healthy lifestyle
> - Reducing competing activities and commitments
> - Social connections (talking)
> - Exercise
> - Going outside
> - Helping others
> - Adult coloring
> - Meditation/Mindfulness (not rigorous practice)
> - Yoga (not rigorous practice)
> - Tai Chi (not rigorous practice)
> - Laughter Yoga
> - Humor
> - Watching television
> - Surfing the internet
> - Music
> - Golfing
> - Massage
> - Sleeping
> - Petting a pet
> - Bubble baths

Nearly half of the people who use Palliative Coping Strategies such as exercise, don't exercise when they feel "too stressed," even though they know it would help.[84]

2. Palliative Coping doesn't change the underlying cause of stress—it distracts you from it.

A third potential downside exists and that is that Dysfunctional or Maladaptive Coping Styles will be combined with Palliative Coping Strategies. For example, adult coloring is currently a popular form of Palliative Coping. On its own, adult coloring is a distraction. If the person coloring simultaneously ruminates about the source of stress, it is maladaptive. If the person coloring drinks a bottle of wine while coloring, it is dysfunctional. If the person coloring applies Advanced Coping Skills such as metacognitive strategies that reduce stress, it is an advanced strategy. If the person coloring applies problem-solving strategies, it is Adaptive Coping.

There are millions of sources for palliative coping techniques but almost none of them provide information about how to avoid maladaptive and dysfunctional combinations or information about how to increase Adaptive or Advanced Coping skills. Your Emotional Guidance will let you know what you are accomplishing with the coping techniques you employ.

Dose-dependent strategies are useful but they are not a solution and they do not change the initial hit you experience from stressors. Dose-dependent stress reduction methods are like driving over a spike strip in your driveway every morning, changing your tire and going on with your day but leaving the spike strip in your driveway where you will run over it again the next day. Transformational Stress Management Strategies remove the spike strip.

Most people attempt to manage stress with the same strategies over and over again. Some people use a variety of coping strategies while others use just one or two main styles. The style used is generally the one(s) that have the least risk and the best results out of the strategies <u>the individual knows how to use</u>. When new strategies are learned they have to be practiced enough so that they will come to mind when they are needed.

This is easier than it seems because practicing feels good. There is no pain during this gain. Well, unless you beat yourself up for not having known what you're learning sooner. Don't do that. It's far better to simply appreciate that

you know now. Self-flagellation is an unhealthy habit of thought.

Dysfunctional Coping styles make the situation worse quickly.

Individuals who have better coping skills will use the skills with the lowest risks unless an addiction is involved.

> **Dysfunctional Coping**
>
> *Makes matters worse, fast*
>
> *Use alcohol or drugs to suppress emotions, self-harm, violence*
>
> - Self-mutilation
> - Ignoring or storing hurt feelings
> - Sedatives
> - Stimulants
> - Acting out
> - Projection
> - Suicide
> - Violence
> - Retribution
> - Smoking
> - Drugs
> - Alcohol

In a study of 558 teachers, individuals using Palliative Coping styles had higher levels of burnout.[85] Adaptive coping is associated with lower burnout.[86]

Maladaptive Coping	Adaptive Coping
Increases stress, allows problem to fester, makes problems worse slowly	*Changes situation*
Unsuccessful attempts to decrease stress without attempting to solve the problem that is creating the stress. • Denial • Wishful Thinking • Displaying anger • Withdrawal[165] • Workaholic behaviors • Humor (depends on how it is used) • Passive communication (makes it easy for others to ignore your thoughts and feelings) • Dissociation (dysfunctional when extreme) • Compartmentalization • Suppress or ignore emotions • Cynicism • Eating • Self-criticism • Whining	• Problem-solving • Assertiveness • Positive self-talk • Self-acceptance • Stress management • Anger Management • Increasing skills • Conflict resolution • Time management • Goal Setting • Asking for help • Social Connections (Asking for help) • Social and emotional learning skills • Community living skills • Meditation/Mindfulness (rigorous practice) • Yoga (rigorous practice) • Tai Chi (rigorous practice) • Plan to avoid temptations

I would use "religious practice" to describe the level of commitment to Yoga, Meditation, or Tai Chi required to move it from Palliative to Adaptive but that could lead to confusion about whether I am referring to commitment or perceiving the practices as religious in nature. All three practices may be perceived as religious, or not religious, depending on the perception of the perceiver. Both ways can be categorized as Palliative or Adaptive depending on the frequency and consistency of practice.

    Journaling is not listed in any category because the category it falls into depends on what is written and the thoughts you think about while journaling. If the writing is complaining or documenting ways you were wronged, it is Maladaptive. If it is plotting revenge, it is Dysfunctional. If it is brainstorming for solutions, it is Adaptive. If it is writing about things that feel good and creating neuropathways of appreciation, it is Transformational.

Advanced Coping Skills	Transformational Coping Skills
Quick, proactive reduction of experienced stressors	*Belief changes that automatically reduce the amount of stress felt on a daily basis*

Meta-cognition
Critical Thinking Skills
Emotional Guidance
Change of perspective
Cognitive reappraisal
Apply knowledge of factors that influence behavior
Emotional Intelligence (EQ)
Develop and apply mental strength and resilience
Psychological Capital (PsyCap)
Pay attention to early signs in order to be proactive
Give the benefit of the doubt
Develop realistic optimism
Self-supporting thoughts
Choose happiness over winning
	• Develop healthy habits of thought
	• Re-program unhealthy habits of thought
	• Psychological Flexibility
	• Cognitive Flexibility
	• Growth Mindset
	• High Core self-evaluations
	   ◦ Healthy self-esteem
	   ◦ Healthy self-efficacy beliefs
	• Resilience
	   ◦ Internal Locus of Control
	   ◦ Realistic optimism
	   ◦ Healthy self-esteem
	• PsyCap
	• Salutogenesis
	• Develop self-compassion
	• End destructive self-criticism
	• End unproductive worry; use risk management to manage risks

Once someone learns Advanced and Transformational Coping Strategies they will use them if they are being aware of what they are doing. If they are following habitual habits of thought they may temporarily resort to established habits. Awareness that they have new and better skills will return, and when it does, they will switch tactics.

Time is required to develop new neuropathways that make new skills the default strategy. It can be helpful to set-up visible reminders that help you remember. Positive quotes are one way to do this. When I was developing new skills I ordered notepads and mouse pads with positive quotes and I even made a few t-shirts. In time, the new methods became a part of who I am and frequent reminders that there were better ways to deal with stress were no longer needed.

Developing the habit of asking yourself, "What is the best way for me to deal with this stressor?" can help you choose the best strategy for your current situation.

Develop Healthy Perspectives
It all depends on how we look at things, and not how they are in themselves.
Carl Gustav Jung (1875-1961) Swiss psychologist and psychiatrist

Your Purpose

Your emotions will guide you to understand your purpose. When your work puts you in the Sweet Zone often, examine it for your purpose. Listen to how you describe the work you do. For decades before I realized that my purpose was helping people, I described every job I had by describing how I helped people when I did my job.

- What do you look forward to doing?
- Why did you choose your career?
- What is your why?
- What aspects of your work energize you?

Spend time each day remembering what you love about your work, even if you haven't enjoyed it for a long time. Remembering what connects you to your purpose will help your mind re-focus on the aspects you enjoy.

If you've been focusing on aspects of your job that you don't enjoy, your mind will automatically focus on other things that feel the same way. When you deliberately re-focus on aspects of your work you enjoy, your mind will automatically think about those aspects more.

This will help more than your perception of your job. When your mind begins focusing on things that elicit negative emotions your perception of other things, such as your relationships, can become more negative as well. You will have noticed this tendency by observing that when you or someone you're in a relationship with, is in a bad mood that isn't relevant to your relationship, it can make communication within the relationship more likely to erupt in an argument or other disagreement.

Our minds seek to reinforce our emotional state; it is as if the thoughts we think are designed to sustain our emotional state.[87] Now, using Transformational and Advanced Coping Strategies with Emotional Guidance, we can deliberately cultivate the emotional state we want to experience. Once we do that, our brain will help us sustain it by focusing on aspects of our environment that reinforce our desired emotional state.

Robert Assagioli wrote about this subject in *Psychosynthesis:*[88]

It is well to recognize and remember the value of each human being and of every activity of his, however humble it may be. This helps us to bring good will and cheerfulness to bear in doing anything, even if wearisome and boring. However apparently insignificant in itself, an activity is in reality, as necessary as actions of greater prominence which seem more important. This balanced appreciation and the resulting good inner disposition are well illustrated by the story of the three stonecutters.

A visitor to the site of where one of the medieval cathedrals was being built asked a stonecutter what he was doing. "Don't you see," replied the latter sourly, "I'm cutting stones," thus showing his dislike of what he regarded as unpleasant and valueless work.

The visitor passed on and put the same question to another stonecutter. "I'm earning a living for myself and my family," replied the workman in an even tempered way that reflected a certain satisfaction.

Further on, the visitor stopped by a third stonecutter and asked him: "And what are you doing?" This third stonecutter replied joyously: "I am building a cathedral." He had grasped the significance and purpose of his labor; he was aware that his humble work was as necessary as the architect's, and in a certain sense it carried equal value. Therefore he was performing his work not only willingly, but with enthusiasm. Let us remember the example of the wise workman. This recognition will enable us to accept every situation, fulfill every task, willingly, and with cheerfulness.

When you perceive you work as aligned with your purpose, it has more meaning and you will enjoy it more.

Autonomy

Nomos is Greek for *law.* When you are autonomous you make your own rules to live by. People feel a sense of freedom when they have autonomy. Autonomy is more important in some areas of life than others and some areas are more important to one person than they are to another. For example, my husband will happily consume whatever meal I prepare. My youngest daughter wants a say in what she eats and on specific holidays will balk if we decide to have a meal that differs from our family traditions.

Likewise, in the workplace, some people want full autonomy over their work while others simply want to be told what to do and some even want to be told how to do it.

The feeling of autonomy is a combination of two main factors:
1. How much decision-making latitude you have in the situation, and
2. How you perceive the situation.

Both are important but your personal perception has the final say in how much autonomy you feel. For example, in a prior life I supervised people who sold stocks and bonds. It is a highly regulated industry and supervisors have many requirements imposed by regulations and are at risk of criminal charges if they fail to perform their duties. Despite being in a role with very little control over what I did on a day-to-day basis, I was able to maintain enough sense of freedom to feel comfortable. I have always been a freedom loving person.

How was I able to have a rigidly regulated role and feel free? By viewing the job from a broader perspective, instead of seeing it as something others were forcing me to do, I saw having the job as a choice I was free to change at any time. By reminding myself that I was free to do something else, I continued to feel free while performing a job that had low autonomy.

It is the attitude that one is not stuck, not actually moving to a different role that changes the level of autonomy experienced. The level of autonomy you experience depends on how you perceive your situation.

Emotion Regulation Process: Overview

- Your words and actions follow your thoughts.
- There are healthy habits of thought that lead to the outcomes you want.
- There are unhealthy habits of thought that lead to the outcomes you do not want.
- You can know, in each moment, if the thoughts you are thinking are healthy or unhealthy.
- You can change your thoughts to healthier ones in the moment that you notice you are thinking unhealthy thoughts.
- You can know, in each moment, whether your thoughts are leading you toward your personal goals.

Think of your thoughts as seeds. If you want to grow corn you don't want your thoughts to plant brussel sprouts. Everything you care about including relationships, health, wealth, fun, and success turns out the way it does because of the thoughts you think.

Replace habits of thought that make your life harder than it has to be with habits that make life more fun. Even if your life often feels good, do you know why? Do you consciously choose to maintain healthy habits of thought or have you just been lucky?

You can choose to develop habits of thought that support mental well-being. Once developed, healthy habits of thought are self-sustaining. Good relationships are easier when you have healthy habits of thought. Good choices about diet, exercise, and risky behaviors are easier and often, more automatic, when a person has healthy habits of thought.

Mental wellness doesn't have to be random. You can choose to develop habits of thought that support mental well-being. For fifty years they've been telling people to think positive but until now we weren't told how to think positive. Replace habits of thought that make your life hard with habits that make your life more fun.

Coping strategies are attempts to deal with emotions. Most coping strategies attempt to deal with negative emotions although some down regulate positive emotions because the emotions being experienced do not fit the social norm for the situation. We are capable of increasing positive emotions and sustaining them longer.

Advanced and Transformational Coping Skills reduce stress. For example, changing beliefs about your ability to handle stress so that you feel more capable of dealing with stressful experiences reduces the level of stress you initially feel when you encounter a stressful situation. Your mind perceives the situation, deems you capable of handling it (based on your own beliefs about your capabilities) and then you feel the emotional response.

Emotional Guidance helps us determine which beliefs to change to help us self-actualize.

If you find yourself thinking or saying, "I can't take any more" what you mean, at the basis of the statement, is you can't handle any more stress. It is common to misinterpret the feeling and begin believing you're at the end of your rope and you can't take one more authoritarian demand from your employer, one more bad encounter, one more heartache, one more disappointment, or more financial strain, etc. It isn't the situations; it is the perception of the situations that brings you to feel that you can't take any more.

Man's ability* to be resilient is unknown. We haven't reached the end of our potential resilience.

Our greatest immediate power is in changing our perception of our capabilities and our abilities.

When you apply skilled emotion regulation to stressful situations, the amount of stress you experience decreases. When the stress you experience decreases, your ability to handle the situation well increases.

Reading about humans who were resilient under dire circumstances can help you increase your belief in your ability to manage stress. An often used example is Victor Frankl's experiences in a Nazi concentration camp documented in his book, *Man's Search for Meaning*. After losing my first child, I found *Ho for California!: Pioneer Women and Their Quilts* helped me realize that my life was not over. Reading about pioneer women, many of whom lost more than one child, helped me realize that it was an experience that can be lived through.

Begin looking for examples of people who were able to handle what you're experiencing. Asking questions can be helpful.

Have others lived through an experience like this (or worse) and been okay?
What could I do to make this better?
Can I look at this from a broader perspective? Will it matter tomorrow or in a year?
What is good in my life?
What can I plan to look forward to?

---

* I wish we had an English pronoun that was genderless. This refers to humans; not just men.

Transformational and Advanced Coping Skills

There are healthy and unhealthy methods of coping with stress. Many methods of coping encouraged in our society are not healthy. Coping styles can be divided by whether they usually lead to optimal (healthy) outcomes or suboptimal (unhealthy) outcomes.

The more healthy coping skills you develop, the less negative impact you will experience from stress.

"Coping is defined as the set of cognitive and behavioral strategies used by an individual to manage the internal and external demands of stressful situations." [89]

Unhealthy coping styles lead to undesirable outcome. In the long-term, unhealthy coping styles make problems worse and contribute significantly to downward spirals. Unhealthy coping strategies make situations more likely to be perceived as threatening, harmful or as causing a loss, which can be material or emotional (such as losing respect). [90]

Positive coping is proactive rather than reactive. In most situations, the best response to stress is a cognitive change that may not be followed by action. In many situations, finding a more empowered perspective is all the work that needs to be accomplished to reduce or eliminate stress. For example, the simple act of changing your thoughts about a subject from believing the task is too difficult to believing you are capable of success is all it takes to allow your mind to begin finding ideas that will make solving the problem easier to accomplish. [91] You can go even further and find opportunities in situations most people perceive as problems. Action is still required to solve the problem but the stress has been reduced or removed without action.

Regular use of positive (healthy) coping skills increases resilience, self-efficacy, self-esteem, quality of life, emotional state, relationships with others and self (less self-criticism), and provides a foundation for a life that it feels good to live. Positive coping protects and fuels your energetic resources.

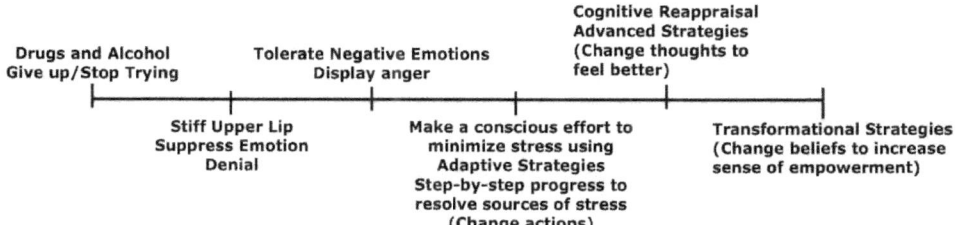

Positive (healthy) coping sees risks but evaluates them as something that can be managed or mitigated. Healthy coping includes active problem-solving but problems are considered surmountable or may be viewed as opportunities. Although individuals who are not well-versed in healthy and unhealthy coping styles often view positivity with distain or consider it Pollyannaish, this view reflects their lack of knowledge.

A quick look at the Benefits Chapter should convince anyone with an open mind that humans thrive when they feel positive emotions and suffer when they don't feel positive emotions. Denial, avoidance, and wishful thinking are unhealthy (negative) coping styles as evinced by a significant body of research.

Emotional Intelligence (EI) and Emotion Regulation are not the same thing but the concepts are being integrated because they are complimentary.
Emotionally Intelligent individuals shape their emotions from the earliest possible point in the emotion trajectory and have many strategies at their disposal. Second, high EI individuals regulate their emotions successfully when necessary but they do so flexibly, thereby leaving room for emotions to emerge. [92]

Transformational Strategies
Just when the caterpillar thought the world was over, it became a butterfly.
Proverb

"Automatic thoughts are quick, evaluative thoughts that come to mind immediately, without the person being aware of them and therefore without deliberation. *People tend to accept their automatic thoughts as truths . . .* Individuals use their core beliefs as a lens through which they interpret life situations." [93] Beliefs work as an subconscious filter. When you change a belief it changes your automatic thoughts. If you develop a more empowered belief, your stress level declines. If you develop a less empowered belief, your stress level increases. One reasons for dysfunctional thinking is the acceptance of erroneous core beliefs.

Core beliefs develop based on the *back stories* our subconscious mind creates about our experiences. We could live in a mansion situated in a peaceful island paradise and have an older brother who resents us and physically harms (trips, punches, pushes, etc.) us every chance he gets and we could decide the world is a mean and violent place.

We could live in a slum where the sounds of gun-fights ring out at all hours of the day and night, navigate past drug dealers and women reduced to selling their bodies to survive to get to the bus stop, but have an older sibling who is protective and always there for us and feel protected and safe.

It is not our circumstances that lead to what we internalize about the world. It is what we are taught and the beliefs we develop about our experiences. The good thing is that our worldviews are not chiseled in marble. We can change them.

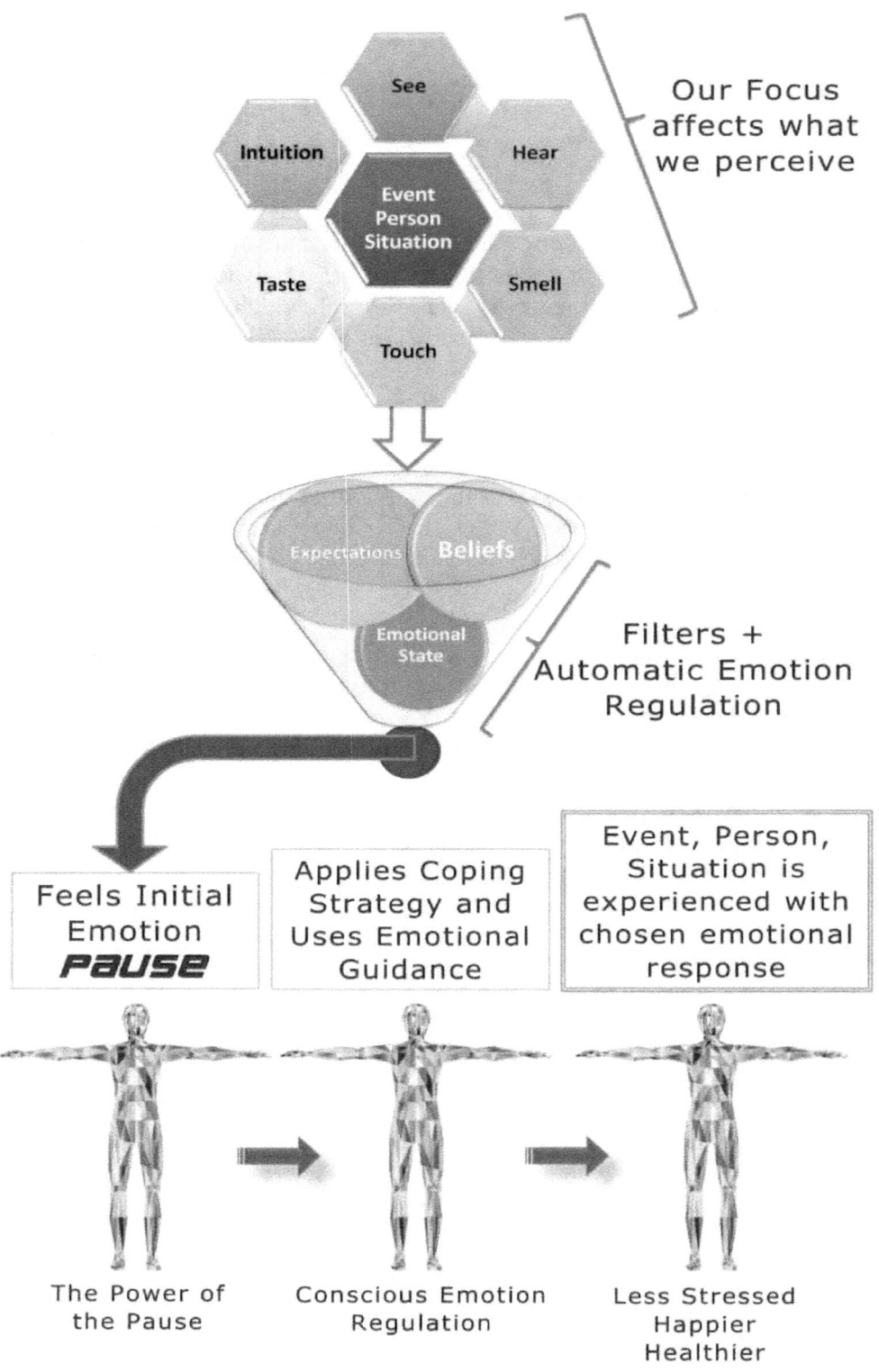

Develop Healthy Habits of Thought (Transformational)

Transformational Stress Management Strategies take longer to reduce stress than Advanced Stress Management Strategies, in the beginning. But when you apply Transformational Strategies to change a belief, within about three months, your first automatic thought will be less stressful than it would have been in the past. Transformational changes affect many areas of life and reduce the need to use Advanced Strategies once your automatic thoughts are less stressful.

> *Interventions that enhance positive implicit valuing of emotion regulation may be beneficial. Techniques that allow individuals to experience successful emotion regulation may positively influence the value they give such regulation. Training procedures that specifically enhance cognitive reappraisal would be promising as cognitive reappraisal abilities play a distinct and important role in successful psychotherapy.* [94]

It boils down to:

Life + Healthy habits of thought = less stress

Healthy habits of thought include:

- Realistic optimism
- Healthy self-esteem
- An internal locus of control
- Self-compassion
- Feeling a sense of autonomy
- Cognitive reappraisal
- Reframing
- Looking for the silver-lining when things don't work out
- Appreciation; looking for things to appreciate
- Supportive beliefs
- Positive expectations
- Healthy happiness contracts
- Recognizing emotions and their meaning
- Self-love
- Self-respect
- Lean toward thoughts that support positive motion forward
- Lean toward thoughts that support healthy relationships
- Openness to new experiences
- Using metacognition to think about what you are thinking and why and making adjustments to lower stress

Researchers reported:

> *A broader repertoire of wellness promotion practices enhances the ability to move beyond neutral and achieve high well-being.* [95p]

Developing healthy habits of thought is associated with better: [96]

- Moods
- Cognitive Function
- Mental Health
- Physical Health
- Quality of Life
- Social functioning
- Social Outcomes
- Well-being
- Thriving
- Pro-health behaviors

There are two pathways that are best used in conjunction with one another. One is deliberately cultivating healthy habits of thought that support positive emotions (Transformational). The second is paying attention to how you feel in response to thoughts you have and reappraising thoughts that elicit negative emotions (Advanced). Recognize that it is your thoughts about the experience and not the actual experience that creates its meaning for you.

A study that involved determining the stress levels of dental students during examinations reported that the higher level of stress perceived, the greater the risk of burnout. [97] During the past two decades an extensive body of emotion-regulation literature has been produced (over 10,000 research papers). This body of work "provides evidence that cognitive reappraisal is a powerful tool to regulate emotions." [98] The ability to cope effectively with negative emotions reduces the risk of developing psychopathological symptoms (mental illnesses) that are associated with chronic stress. [99]

Using Advanced Strategies including challenging self-critical thoughts can foster optimism and self-worth. [100] Imagine that someone is piling bricks (or monkeys) on your back all day long. If you have good coping skills you can remove most of the bricks (or monkeys) almost as soon as they land on your back. If you don't have good coping skills they stay there, wearing you out, making you tired, and slowing you down.

Note about microaggressions: Instead of imaging bricks, imagine fishing weights, lots of small fishing weights. Trying to get the world to change can

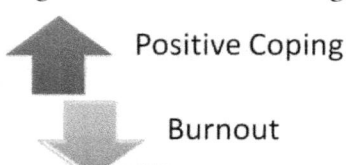

be dysfunctional, maladaptive, palliative (if you think you are making progress), adaptive, advanced, or transformational. Basing your happiness on changing other people increases the amount of stress you experience.*

Those who develop an approach to life that minimizes their stress levels have significantly higher levels of psychological well-being. [101p]

The strategies shared in the following pages will assist you in developing a strategy toward life that helps you restore and maintain psychological health. When you know the impact of different thoughts on your well-being your choices of thought will demonstrate more wisdom. The approach you

---

* Rescue Our Children from the War Zone has more information on microaggressions. My book, Diversity Appreciation is in the works and may be released in 2018 or 2019.

choose can co-exist with any spiritual or religious practices you already practice.

Categories that have been associated with well-being include:

- Self-awareness
- Being positive
- Sharing of feelings
- Setting limits
- Self-acceptance
- Personal Growth
- Purpose
- Work-Life Balance
- Self-care
- Taking vacations
- Exercise
- Being in healthy relationships
- Leaving unhealthy relationships
- Pursuing and achieving goals
- Developing a personal philosophy
- Reading inspirational materials
- Avoiding drugs and alcohol
- Learning new skills
- Mindfulness
- Meditation
- Hobbies
- Positive self-regard
- Perceiving health as more than the absence of disease (wellness {salutogenesis} model)
- Getting professional help when/if needed
- Having a spiritual or religious belief system

How many of the above do you regularly do? Making small improvements many times makes a tremendous difference in your long-term results.

Shifting your approach to life can be very simple. I've seen many people quickly shift aspects of their approach to life after hearing an alternate view that resonates with them a single time. It is as if we become stuck in a paradigm that life is a certain way when the reality is that each of us perceives life from a unique self-created paradigm. Because we believe our paradigm is reality we don't question it. When we learn someone else uses a different paradigm, it can shift the events of our life into new patterns that make more sense. We can quickly adopt a different worldview when the new perspective helps us perceive the world with greater clarity. In most cases, this change moves in a positive direction. On occasion, this change goes in a negative direction that we refer to as a psychotic break. You don't have to worry about this if you make a habit of trusting your Emotional Guidance.

The brain seems to have an amazing ability to shift the puzzle pieces when we change our viewpoint. Many significant improvements I've seen have resulted from a series of smaller changes.

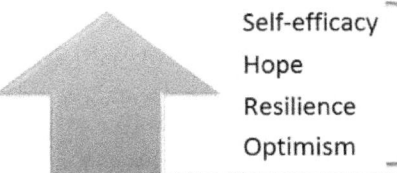

Self-efficacy
Hope
Resilience
Optimism

Each characteristic (skill) decreases the risk of developing a mental illness

Approaching information with an open mind and being willing to consider alternative viewpoints while rejecting things that don't feel right elicits the best results. In my own journey I initially rejected some ideas and came back to them later after I'd shifted in other areas and found that I was able to discard old, ingrained ideas that were factually wrong but had been strongly believed for decades.

When you consider that much of our worldview was established by age 10, it makes sense to consider alternatives and make conscious decisions about what is in our best interest and to think about what may be limiting our psychological well-being and success.

Supportive, Empowering Beliefs (Transformational)

It is our attitude at the beginning of a difficult task which, more than anything else, will affect its successful outcome.
William James

Most beliefs are established while we are children. We did not examine them using critical thinking. We accepted them as truths and then our minds began interpreting reality as if our beliefs were true. This happened even if the beliefs we accepted as true held us back, made our lives worse, or increased our stress. What our parents taught us to believe is often an inexact replication of what their parents believed and so on back through time. Beliefs tend to be passed from generation to generation without evaluating their benefit, detriment, or truth in objective reality because our minds interpret reality as if our beliefs are true. This makes beliefs a target rich environment for changes that will decrease stress and increase happiness and success.

If you have ever watched a Sci-fi movie where the world is different than the one we live in, you noticed that the actors act as if the fantasy reality is real. In many respects, we all do that to some degree. As long as our interpretations of the world conform to the interpretations of those around us, we all believe our reality is real. If our interpretations are significantly different from those around us we may be considered geniuses or delusional, depending on whom is judging our interpretations, and their own version of reality. We have the ability to change our beliefs and when we do, our world changes.

I'm not implying that you can transport yourself into a different world simply by changing your beliefs. It is your interpretations of the world that changes. *It feels like a different world.* When unsupportive or fearful beliefs are changed to supportive beliefs, it feels like a much better world.

Some people think beliefs refers to religious beliefs. You can include or exclude religious beliefs from your examination. Do whatever feels best to you.

Evaluating beliefs and changing ones that do not support your highest good has the ability to change every area of your life. Beliefs can be about the nature of our world, the nature of people, aging, our bodies, or literally anything you encounter, or hear about, during your life.

Repeatedly thinking similar thoughts about a topic creates a belief about that topic. A belief is just a neuropathway your thoughts can travel more easily than your thoughts travel alternate routes.

"Beliefs powerfully shape emotions via their influence on appraisal processes... several influential appraisal theories have posited that beliefs are one of the most important influences on appraisal process, and thereby determine when and what type of emotion will be elicited in response to environmental contingencies." [102]

You cannot change beliefs directly because when you attempt to think about the belief and change it, your thoughts travel the same neuropathway and keep the belief reinforced. The way to change a belief is to decide what you'd rather believe and then reinforce the new belief by repeatedly thinking about it and, if possible, talking and/or writing about it. There are a variety of methods to use to determine what beliefs you would like to change and which beliefs you'd like to establish. The process is as follows:

- Identify areas where my your Emotional Guidance indicates your beliefs are leading to emotional appraisals that result in negative emotions and/or feelings of disempowerment.
- Recognize that things that were true in your life but not in others' lives are reflecting your established beliefs and not a fixed reality.
- Decide what you would rather believe based on how ideas felt (using Emotional Guidance) to identify empowering beliefs.
- Reading quotes and inspirational books to help you identify empowering beliefs that resonated with you.
- Look for evidence that others could do what you are encouraging yourself to believe you can do to reinforce your belief that you can do it using an attitude of, "If X can, so can I."
- Practice thinking the thoughts you want to believe through affirmations, by writing, and by speaking about them.

In my personal experience, I had some firmly embedded beliefs that I stopped believing but they still functioned as beliefs (impacting my words) for a while until the new beliefs were firmly established. I was easy on myself

when I realized I was voicing opinions I no longer held by recognizing it was just evidence of an old neuropathway that would stop being the path my thoughts traveled once my new thoughts had created a stronger neuropathway. Eventually they stopped being active neuropathways. The process took about three months of consistent effort which consisted of affirming my new beliefs every time the old beliefs came into my mind.

As I consciously adopted a more empowered worldview, my personality and emotional response to previously stressful events changed significantly. I went from being a Mom who was always worried about her children to one who allowed them age appropriate freedoms. I felt more confident and became more assertive. I stopped allowing other people's opinions of me to determine how I felt about my self-worth. I identified empowered perspectives about prior traumas that transformed them from subjects to be avoided to topics I could help others heal from their own traumas. For the first time in my life, I began liking myself.

Because beliefs inform the automatic appraisal of potentially stressful events, adopting more empowered beliefs means the initial negative emotion felt in a variety of situations is diminished, and in some cases, gone entirely. Situations previously perceived as hassles or problems are now perceived as opportunities or useful information. Not as much conscious reappraisal is needed to regulate emotions because more empowered beliefs make the initial appraisal of the situation less stressful. Research indicates a single belief change can change the amount of stress experienced in a variety of situations. [103]

The thoughts you think equal your level of happiness.
The process is this:
1) You think a thought
2) You feel an emotional response to the thought you thought
3) The process repeats

Steps 1 - 3 are how most people live their lives. Living that way leaves you at the mercy of what is going on around you and your first impression of those circumstances.

The better way to live (the way we were designed to live) is this:
1) You think a thought.
2) You feel an emotional response to the thought you thought.
3) You decide if you like the emotional response you felt to the thought you thought.
4) If you like the way the thought feels, stay on that subject and think more thoughts.
5) Repeat steps 1 – 4.
6) If you don't like the way the thought feels, mentally look for a different thought about the same subject with the intent of finding a thought that feels better.

Here is a sample of steps 1– 6.

Thought = *"I have more to do than I can possibly accomplish before my company arrives. They'll think I'm a slob if all this is not done."*

Alternate thoughts that might feel better:

"Not everything on my to do list has to be done." (Go General)

"My friends don't care if I've cleaned the windows. They're coming to spend time with me and with each other--not to judge my value based on how often I clean my windows." (Reappraisal)

"I can ask my best friend to come early and help. We'll get to spend some time together and it will be easy to get this done with more hands." (Adaptive)

When you find a thought that feels better, make that the perspective you take on the subject you're thinking about. Repeat steps 1 - 4

An alternative is to change your focus and think about something else. This is especially valuable when the topic is something you feel bad about that is not something you can change right now. You can change how you view awful stuff from the past by changing the *back story* associated with it.

Over a period of time the above process will reprogram your mind. When your default thought process changes, you feel better automatically. Realize that there are millions of perspectives about any situation and all of them are valid from the point of view from which they are thought. You're not stuck with your first perspective.

Healthy self-esteem (Transformational)
All the extraordinary men I have known were extraordinary in their own estimation.
Woodrow T. Wilson (1856-1924) 28th President of the USA

Self-esteem reflects the beliefs you've developed about yourself, about your self-worth and value, about your goodness, about your lovability or desirability, about your intelligence, and you capability. Shawn Achor said, "One of the greatest buffers against picking up others' stress is stable and strong self-esteem." [104]

When you change your beliefs about yourself to ones that *see* yourself as having value and worth, it feels as if the entire world changes with you. The world seems less hostile and can begin to seem friendly. To me it felt as if my life before healthy self-esteem was lived in thick forest with a lot of briars that often scratched me and tore my clothes. After my self-esteem improved, it feels as if I am living life in a beautiful grassy park with a river running through it where I can sit and feel calm and relaxed at any time.

I had no idea how hard life was because I hadn't known anything else. Self-esteem beliefs can be tough to change and I do not recommend you begin with them. Get some practice in areas you haven't reinforced by thinking the same thoughts again and again. Once you have a few successes in shifting other beliefs, begin the process of increasing your self-esteem. Even small shifts make a big difference in how your life feels on many levels. The strategies presented in MWME give you everything you need except the willingness to apply them. Advanced and Transformational Strategies are the best tools for challenging self-critical thoughts and fostering optimism and self-worth. [105]

Ask yourself the following questions. If the answer doesn't feel good, it isn't your truth, even if it your current belief.

Do I like myself?
Do I have the right to be happy?
If I'm not in a relationship do I feel incomplete?
Do I deflect compliments because I don't believe I deserve the praise?
Do I hold back from doing things I want to do out of fear of rejection?
Do I feel like an imposter waiting for people to figure out I don't deserve what I've achieved professionally, in relationships, or financially?
Do I perceive criticism as threatening?
Do I apologize frequently for things that I don't need to apologize for?
Can I accept a compliment?
Do I make decisions based on what I believe will appeal to others or to get their approval instead of what pleases me?
Do I avoid arguments and disagreements by suppressing my needs and feelings?
Can I comfortably walk up to a stranger and introduce myself?
Do I embellish the truth about myself in an attempt to project an image I hope others will deem is good enough?

Do I act as if my opinions matter?
Can I choose where I want to eat or do I always defer to others?
Do I seem to need more sleep than others?
Do I take care of my body because I'm worth it?
Do I take care of my body because others' opinions of my body matter to me?
Do I share meaningful details of my life with friends?
Do I believe people will like me if they know the real me?
Do I try to make myself small or wish I could disappear or run away when I have a negative emotional experience with someone I care about?
Can I stand in front of a mirror, look myself in the eyes, and tell myself:
- *I am good*
- *I am wise*
- *I love you*

Do good things happen in my life because I prepare for opportunities so I'm ready when they appear?

Pay attention to how you feel. Thoughts that frequently elicit negative emotion indicate underlying beliefs you can change to reduce stress. Changing one belief can reduce the stress you experience every time you think about that topic.

Self-esteem is important. Every area of your life is affected by your beliefs about yourself. There is an infinite variety of undesired manifestations that occur in the lives of people who have low self-esteem that can be stopped by increasing their self-esteem. Healthy self-esteem does not seek to be better than anyone else. Healthy self-esteem is about feeling worthy and being of value for being the unique being that is you.

Self-esteem seldom reflects the reality of an individual. We are often taught to form our beliefs about ourself from the opinions of others so I'll start there. We've already talked about how our perceptions vary as the result of our emotional state. If I meet someone when I am feeling insecure, I might perceive them as someone who feels superior to others. If I meet someone when I am in a state of appreciation, my mind will find on aspects of them that I appreciate. We connect emotionally with one another. That's why we love stories so much.

If you were raised around people who were often angry, frustrated, or afraid it is unlikely they focused on your strengths and helped you see them. It is likely they focused on aspects of you that matched their emotional state and that formed their opinion of you. Other people's opinions of you, to a very large degree, reflect their emotional state. That's one of the reasons charming, charismatic people are so well loved. They *charm* people into feeling better than they usually feel which makes people want to be around them.

The thing is you can't charm someone else into feeling better if you're feeling bad. Feeling good when you have low self-esteem can feel like climbing Mt. Everest. You can't stay at the peak for long if you have low self-esteem. Feeling good is much easier when you have healthy self-esteem.

When you begin seeing that others' opinions reflect their emotional state you'll give them less control over how you feel about you. It isn't that others' opinions don't matter. It isn't about disrespecting them. It's about understanding where they are emotionally and the relationship between their opinion and their emotional state. It takes the sting out of harsh words. Once you understand this relationship, you can look back at things that formed your self-esteem and re-frame them as reflections that someone you interacted with didn't feel good instead of being a basis for low self-esteem.

You don't have to go back at all. You can begin where you are and move forward but if there are memories that haunt you or hurt you that you still think about often, re-framing the *back story* associated with the memory changes the way they feel.

When you truly get it that other people's opinions and words reflect their emotional state, your ability to hear them out without taking offense grows. There is no need to defend yourself because even if they are talking about you, they are demonstrating their emotional state. This doesn't mean you never again listen to constructive criticism. Seeing yourself as someone who is always learning and growing makes you want to become better. When someone provides you feedback, you evaluate it in a different way. Instead of criticizing yourself for not being perfect, you evaluate the information using critical thinking. Is there a grain of truth in the comments? Is it something you want to change about yourself? What does your Emotional Guidance tell you?

For example, my pubic speaking and my writing are two areas where I want to be the best I can be. If someone tells me that I could do either of those things better, I am all ears, but not as criticism of what I've done. I am all ears to pick up any nuggets of information that will make me even better.

For example, several people who provided feedback on my first five books made comments along the lines of "They contain very useful information but there is so much science makes them heavy reads." I now feel satisfied that I have documented the science that supports my work and am honing my craft by writing books that are easier to read. I want this information to reach a lot of people so it's important that they are as good as they can be. I am not seeking perfection. They'd never get published and never help anyone if I waited for perfection. I don't even care about them standing the test of time in the way a classic novel can because the information shared in these pages should become common knowledge. If people still have to undo unhealthy thoughts society taught them a hundred years from now it will mean I failed to get this information to enough people to make healthy habits of thought normal.

An attitude toward your life, relationships, and work that goes along these lines, "I've always done the best I could but I will always have room to learn and become better" serves you well.*

The motivation of someone who criticizes you can run the gamut from someone who is miserable and gains a tiny bit of pleasure by making others miserable to someone who values your work but recognized that a slight

---

* See section on "Resources" for more on this concept

change will help you accomplish your goals easier, faster, or better. If you take others opinions as information that you can accept or reject, the miserable person won't be able to make you feel bad. In fact, if there is a grain of truth that gives you an idea to improve in what is said, the person attempting to make you miserable may actually make you happy that you now have one more tool in your toolkit that makes you better.

You could even feel empathy for the miserable person because the tiny bit of pleasure someone attains by making someone else feel worse is nothing when compared to the enormous pleasure possible when we uplift others.

The following affirmations reflect healthy self-esteem and can help you develop beliefs that increase your self-esteem.

Who I am is good and I seek opportunities to learn and grow and become even better.

I welcome opportunities to learn and grow because it is fun to learn and grow.

I do not have to learn and grow. I do it because I know moving toward self-actualization feels good and I like to feel good.

If your mind argues with these affirmations, take smaller steps toward feeling good about yourself. Give your accomplishments more attention than you normally do. Make a list of goals you set and accomplished. If you can't think of anything you've done recently, go as far back as you need to in order to find something you decided to do and then did. If you have to go all the way back to learning to walk, that's okay. As you find thoughts about setting goals and succeeding your mind will start helping you find other examples. If you've been very miserable all your life, you can even use things you accomplished that are not socially desirable as examples. It doesn't mean you should do those things again. It means you have the ability to set a goal and accomplish it.

Accomplished goals don't have to be big. I set a goal to drink at least 80 ounces of water a day and I now do that. That represents accomplishing something that I decided I wanted to accomplish. The funny thing about goals is that once we achieve anything it doesn't feel big to us even if someone else thinks it is massive. We grow into our goals. It is human nature to set new goals, often even before we've accomplished the ones we're working towards. That happens because as we move toward accomplishing our goals, we fulfill more of our potential. We become better and more capable than we were so we feel more capable of accomplishing more.

I've accomplished many things in my life but by the time I achieved them they didn't seem to be the big deals they were when the goals were set. I'm sure you have accomplished many things, too. Achieving the goal was never the point. The point was to grow into the person you had to become in order to achieve the goal. The point of setting and accomplishing a goal isn't achieving the goal even though it can be a major accomplishment. The point of a goal is to focus our energy in ways that help us become who we have to be if we are to achieve the goal. All goals are about personal growth.

We have the ability to decide to be good irrespective of others' expectations simply because that is who we prefer to be. When we don't consciously decide who we will be is when we are more likely to be as others expect us to be. We do not have to push against anyone else's choices (or lack of choices) in order to choose to be good ourselves. Can you feel the difference in the energy of pushing against "the intolerant multitudes" vs. simply deciding to be a good person (kind, nice, respectful, successful, etc.) under any and all circumstances? Pushing against takes more energy than simply choosing what you wish to be and then being that. Consciously choosing who we will be because that is who we want to be, and who it feels best for us to be, is empowering and liberating.

If there is something about yourself that you truly don't like, decide to change it. Use the fun process of defining yourself as if you are a fictional character and then become the character you defined.

When successful fiction writers are asked how they write the dialogue for their characters they often respond that they don't write the dialogue. A composite of what they say is, "I create the character and the character writes their own dialogue." I've written one fiction book (as yet unpublished) and found that this was true. I didn't have to labor over "what will Maia say in response to this?" Knowing the character I created, words that were *in character* for Maia simply flowed onto the page. This is an important analogy because I realized that what we say or do in any given moment is based largely on who we think we are. We define ourself and then we behave in accordance with who we have decided we are.

Two things flowed from that realization. The first was an *ah ha* moment about something I'd been saying I would write a book about if I ever figured out how I'd done it. At one point in my life, I was a 2-pack-a-day Marlboro girl who had been smoking for 14 years and after attempting to quit several times decided that it just isn't in my nature to quit. I don't quit anything.

At that point I had an inspired thought that said "I can't quit smoking but I can become a non-smoker." I then spent six weeks brain-washing myself that on a specific day I would be a non-smoker. The last two weeks of being a smoker I had to force myself to continue smoking because I was still a smoker until the day I became a non-smoker. I won't lie. The first three days were difficult but decades later I have never again smoked because I don't smoke, I am a non-smoker.

The *ah ha moment* combined with my prior experience of changing my definition of self helped me see that we can define ourselves as we want to be and we will become more of who we want to be. We usually try to change by changing our habits, but if we change from the inside out, beginning with our beliefs, our thoughts, words, and actions will follow our beliefs. That's what they do naturally.

Changing beliefs first is easier than using willpower to change habits. Your words reflect your beliefs. Since beliefs are just neuropathways created by repeatedly thinking thoughts, we have the ability to re-program our beliefs to support becoming who we want to be.

Evidence of the power of belief change is all around us. The Pygmalion Effect, seen when students whose teachers believe in them and encourage them exceed expectations, occurs because the teachers beliefs increased their own belief in their abilities. Believing we can do something leads to greater success because when we believe we can the filters our subconscious mind uses to determine which data to make consciously available includes data we need to be successful.

I'd already learned how to feel good most of the time when I had this realization but sometimes I just wasn't where I wanted to be. When I wasn't, I wasn't as kind or as loving as I naturally am when I'm in that good-feeling emotional state and I didn't like it. Once you become accustomed to feeling kind and loving towards others, it feels worse to be even a little off the mark than it did to feel miles off the mark when that was how you normally felt. So I decided to define myself in the following ways:

- *I am kind.*
- *I am a loving presence.*
- *I look for and see the best in others.*

After re-defining who I am in the above ways it is easier to show up that way even if I'm not having my best day. It isn't about working (emotional labor) to show up that way. It is simply who I am. It can even help me identify when I am a little off so that I can use one of the processes to improve my emotional state. I don't pretend to be nice. I am nice. I don't pretend to feel upbeat. I feel upbeat.

Our mind has a variety of layers, as indicated in the diagram.

- Changes at inner levels affect every larger layer
- Changes at larger layers can have an impact on inner layers, but it is the more difficult path to change
- Changing the outer levels without changing the inner layers creates conflict that the inner layer will eventually win
- Changes made at outer layers that are assimilated into the inner layer can become permanent

For example, using willpower to force daily exercise can lead to an identity change regarding exercise but most people fail before they achieve an

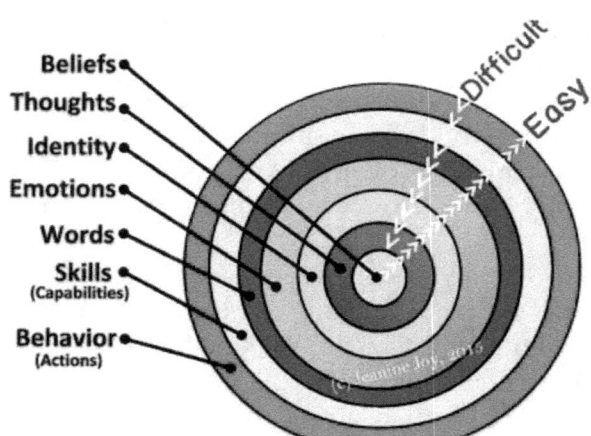

Illustrated Behavior Dynamic

identity change. Defining oneself as an exerciser doesn't require willpower because the definition of self creates a belief that is then supported by your thoughts. The need for a new view of how to effectively make desired changes is evident in the fact that so many struggle to make changes using willpower. Changing beliefs first makes behavioral changes easier to implement.

One helpful key is to recognize when you believe something is true for you but not for others. Remember, beliefs are able to help or hinder. They are not all good or all bad. Most importantly, the brain does not differentiate between those that serve our higher good, and those that thwart it. The mind *irrationally* attempts to support whatever we have decided to believe.

Irrationally attempts to support our beliefs is too harsh. The brain functions as if we understand the impact our beliefs have on our experience, so when we have a belief, it acts as if we have deliberately chosen that belief and understand the ramifications of the belief. Most people have no idea how their beliefs affect their thinking and experiences.

A couple of things may help you identify beliefs that are not serving you. If you find yourself saying, 'I want to but,' you are pointing out a belief that limits you. The second is when you believe that another has it better than you and have an excuse or explanation for why that is. 32% of Americans say a lack of willpower prevents them from making desired changes. [106]

Willpower is required when there is a struggle between self-concept (beliefs) and desired behavior. In the illustration on the next page, the elephant represents a belief. The people tugging on the rope represent good reasons to change and the desire to change a habit. Because beliefs lead to thoughts which then lead to words and actions, willpower fights a losing battle against underlying beliefs. The battle will continue until the belief is changed or the individual gives up the attempt to change behavior. No willpower is required when beliefs are changed first because willpower is a fight between beliefs and desired actions. When our beliefs support our desires no willpower is required and the outcome is better. [107]

Using willpower can deplete the energy required for self-control.
"Inadequate self-control has been linked to behavioral and impulse-control problems, including overeating, alcohol and drug abuse, crime and violence, overspending, sexually impulsive behavior, unwanted pregnancy, and smoking ... and it may also be linked to emotional problems, school underachievement, lack of persistence, various failures at task performance, relationship problems, and dissolution and more." [108]

When an action is consistent with your beliefs, it feels natural and does not deplete the energy required for self-control. When the action conflicts with your beliefs about yourself or world, self-control is required and the energy required for self-control can become depleted, leading to a decreased ability to control your behavior. For example, non-smokers don't need willpower to prevent them from smoking whereas an x-smoker will (at least occasionally) require willpower in order not to succumb to the urge to smoke.

"A match between implicit (beliefs) and explicit (conscious desire) in goal achievement is associated with adaptive outcomes." [109] When our beliefs conflict with our desired behaviors, beliefs win. Beliefs are simply neuropathways created by repeatedly thinking a thought. New beliefs can be created by reinforcing thoughts you want to believe.

Just as a fiction writer creates a character who then writes their own dialogue, individuals create the character that is themself, and the outer *accoutrements* fill in thoughts, words, action, health, wealth, and love.

Emotional labor is a work-related requirement to project emotions the worker may not feel. [110] Emotional labor drains our energy and can be discerned as inauthentic or dishonest by observers. Individuals who are required to perform emotional labor at work deplete resources used for self-control and find themselves less able to control their behaviors at the end of the day, especially after they leave work. This can result in unhealthy behavioral habits, poor decisions, and fewer pro-health behaviors.

This is most obvious in the young child who behaves according to social norms at daycare but has a meltdown when in the safer company of a parent. While it is not as dramatic (usually) in adult behavior, the same underlying mechanisms are in play.

If you have a job where you are required to present a particular emotional front and it is an emotion you would like to experience (i.e. cheerfulness), you can try defining yourself as a cheerful person. It usually takes 6 – 12 weeks of daily reinforcement to change our definition of self. When I became a non-smoker I affirmed my new definition every time I lit a cigarette (40 times a day) for six weeks. I find it helpful to use the times during my day when I have a minute or two alone, when I wake up, and before I go to sleep to affirm beliefs I want to establish and make concrete.

Comparison of Self to Others

Comparing your performance to others is associated with worse outcomes. This relationship holds regardless of whether others are perceived as performing better than you or worse than you. [111]

People often sabotage their self-esteem by comparing themselves unfavorably with others. Adopting an attitude that you're not in competition with others and that you are becoming the best version of you that you can be will help you achieve more than unfavorable comparisons with others will ever achieve. If your goal is to be better than someone else it requires a worldview that puts people in hierarchies of better than and worse than one another. Your Emotional Guidance will support a worldview of everyone being unique and good much more than it supports one of competition.

There is nothing noble in being superior to your fellow man; true nobility is being superior to your former self.*

A final consideration about comparisons of self to others is that if your goal is to be better than someone else that is not the same as becoming the best you can be. Your self-actualized self may be far better than someone else's ability in the same area but if you stop improving when you're better than the person you're using as your basis of comparison, you won't discover how much more you could be.

A Sense of Entitlement

A sense of entitlement exists on the same continuum as self-esteem. The second to the right in the Self-esteem Continuum feels entitled to a good life but also perceives that everyone else deserves a good life. This entitlement isn't based on works, intelligence, education, etc. and it isn't about someone handing it to you without working for it. It's about perceiving that you're as deserving as anyone else of rewards and a good life (marriage, career, friends, money, etc.)

The greater danger for most of us lies not in setting our aim too high and falling short; but in setting our aim too low, and achieving our mark.
Michelangelo

The belief that one is entitled to a good life protects against learned helplessness and increases resilience. It aids in efforts to reframe failures as stepping stones on the way to success. It also protects against seeing failures as a sign that you don't deserve success or simply aren't good enough.

Your Emotional Guidance will help you decide which belief is best for you and help you find and develop supportive beliefs.

Some people warn against over evaluation of capability. I'll just leave this one with the father of modern psychology:

---

* I've seen this attributed to Ernest Hemingway and as a Hindu Proverb

> *Most people live, whether physically, intellectually or morally, in a very restricted circle of their potential being. They make very small use of their possible consciousness and of their soul's resources in general, much like a man who, out of his whole bodily organism, should get into a habit of using and moving only his little finger.*
> William James

Bold and Cautious are two descriptions used for personality types. Cautious personalities are associated with worse mental health.[112] People with cautious personalities "fear being rejected" and this reduces their positive social interactions and their willingness to risk rejection.[113] Essentially, they reject themselves by taking themselves out of the running so that someone else can't reject them. If you consider the Cautious personality type on the self-esteem continuum it's easy to see how it correlates with low self-esteem.

Fear of Being Judged

"I am afraid that people will judge me."

Fear of being judged means that you assume other's opinions of you are accurate. Most of the time, other people's opinion of you reflect their emotional state—not an accurate view of who you are. You have to decide for yourself who you are, that you have value and worth and the right to be happy. Also, since people with low self-esteem significantly undervalue their own value and worth others frequently judge them better than they judge themselves. When we are stressed, others tend to judge us worse than they judge us when we aren't stressed.[114]

Not caring about what other people think or say is not "the key" but it is part of the key. Actually, not caring isn't the most important thing—the key is to understand that what they say is far more about them than about you.

If someone says words to you that are demeaning, it reflects truths about their emotional state (and maybe their beliefs) and does not say any truth about your value and worth. So you don't care from the perspective of you don't take it personally, you don't question your self-worth or your value based on someone else's words. But you will probably care from the perspective of being aware that the person is in a bad emotional state. If it is someone you love, you may want to help them with their mood, give them a hug, a listening ear, etc.

Not caring, as in "get upset" or allow their words to undermine your emotional state--yes, that's part of the key to a happy life.

How Can We Not Care What They Think When What They Think Matters?

When you understand that someone who feels good emotionally will find things about you that they appreciate and that someone who feels emotionally frustrated will find aspects of you they find frustrating and someone who is angry often will find things about you that "make them angry" you can free yourself of the emotional pain their words cause. You can simply recognize that belittling or hurtful words mean the person speaking is in pain—the words say nothing about you. Your responses say a great deal about you.

You don't have to know why they feel bad. You don't have to make them understand that the reason they behave as they behave is because of how they feel. You just have to know how it.

Families often form an opinion of who you are when you're young and persist in keeping that image of you even when you've attained respect outside the family (i.e. a doctorate, inventions, etc.). You can't make them change their image of you, but you can change how you respond to them. How you feel about anything is up to you. When you base your opinion of your level of success on your family's opinion, you are giving your power away to your family.

If you gave them that power, you have the ability to take that power back. How you feel is your responsibility. No one can make you feel good or bad, successful or unsuccessful, without your permission. When they can't push your buttons anymore a funny thing often happens--they stop trying to push your buttons.

Now, in work situations, it may matter. For example, you don't want to show up at a job interview dressed inappropriately because you will be judged and that judgment will affect your chances of getting the position. The information in the section on Expectation is relevant because if you expect to be respected at work the way you are treated will be different than it would be if you expected to be disrespected.

Look at some of the most revered people in our society. Take Lady Gaga for example. Lady Gaga isn't trying to "fit in." You don't have to be a psychopath to not care. If you have emotional flexibility and understand why people judge others in the ways they do and that their judgments say very little about you, then you can disregard what others think.

One of the best things I have done (success wise) is not listen to what others said I should do or not do and not listen to the naysayers who did not believe what I was doing was possible. If I had cared about their opinions, I would not have even tried several of my greatest successes.

Trust that the people who come into your life will like you as you are. My hair is almost six feet long. In my prior career I was an executive in the financial services industry. I lost count of the number of people who told me I should cut it to help my career. It was not necessary to cut it. I didn't care what others thought about my hairstyle choice. I enjoy my hair.

Once when I was leaving a meeting after being hired at a new company an executive who had interviewed me for the position was behind me when I left the room. He had apparently not noticed my long hair during the interview and asked where it came from. How do you miss that much hair?

I'm not a psychopath. I care deeply about other people and my work is focused on making life better for as many people as I possibly can. But I don't care if someone doesn't like me or doesn't like my work. Their opinion does not diminish my value or my self-esteem. I strive to find things to appreciate about everyone. Sometimes what I appreciate about others is they show me how I don't want to be and make me glad I am as I am.

I remember a special day when I was giving away hugs on a peer in Santa Monica. I hugged everyone who wanted a hug, young & old alike. But if someone refused a hug that was OK, too. I did not feel rejected. I was giving hugs to give. (There is research that shows hugs are healing and most people don't get enough of them.) If someone does not want to receive, it's okay with me.

Don't give other people permission to ruin your day.

Optimism (Transformational Coping)

Optimism is not a fixed element of personality. Optimistic attitudes are created and sustained by habits of thought which often echo those around you and especially those who were around you when you were young.

Optimism can be developed by changing underlying beliefs and habits of thought. Optimism is associated with better life outcomes in health, relationships, career, and longevity. There are many aspects that affect these outcomes but decreased stress and stronger social connections are significant factors.

An individual may be optimistic in every area of life or in selected areas. Optimists tend to focus on solutions and what they can do. In the Resilience section of this book, the habits of resilient and less resilient individuals were compared. Many of the resilient habits of thought in that chart reflect optimistic attitudes. Optimism is a key component of resilience.

Optimists may:
- Be more likely to trust other people
- Believe that there is a way forward
- Feel hope or trust that things will work out well
- Believe the world is good
- Believe people are innately good although they sometimes do bad things

Optimist's lives reflect their beliefs about life. Positive mental attitudes result in interpreting experiences in a positive light. Where an optimist sees an opportunity a pessimist sees a problem. Both optimists and pessimists live in self-fulfilling prophesies.

Optimists will find the silver lining in adversities. Optimists experience less stress and more positive emotions than pessimists. Optimists feel more empowered when they face difficulties which lowers the amount of stress they experience.

Internal Locus of Control (Transformational)

Every high-level psychological factor that increases health or success includes an internal locus of control. An internal locus of control is the belief that your thoughts, words, and actions have an impact on the outcomes you experience. It is the opposite of learned helplessness[115] where a person or animal will not act in its best interest because it doesn't believe its actions will make a difference.

Using Advanced and Transformational Stress Coping Strategies automatically increases your sense of having an internal locus of control by demonstrating that how you perceive a situation, person, or event determines the way you experience the event. It becomes clear that you have the ability to exercise control over how your experience feels by changing your perspective about the situation.

When a situation feels bad to you, remember that how you feel is determined by how you perceive the situation and apply Advanced Strategies to change the level of stress you are experiencing. This increases your sense of empowerment.

Individuals with an external locus of control are more likely to blame others for undesired events. This leads to perceptions that the event is beyond their control and could happen again if they are in a similar situation. The belief that you can do something to prevent an event from happening reduces stress.

Growth Mindset (Transformational)

A growth mindset, the belief that you are a work in progress, not a completed project provides a foundation for success. Without a growth mindset individuals will not even read this book, much less apply the strategies. Those with a fixed mindset will not see any point because they are focused on defending who they are instead of becoming more of who they can be. Fortunately, a fixed mindset is simply a habit of thought that has formed. It is a belief, not a life sentence.

A growth mindset is necessary to learn and grow. A growth mindset is an internal locus of control relating to your potential.

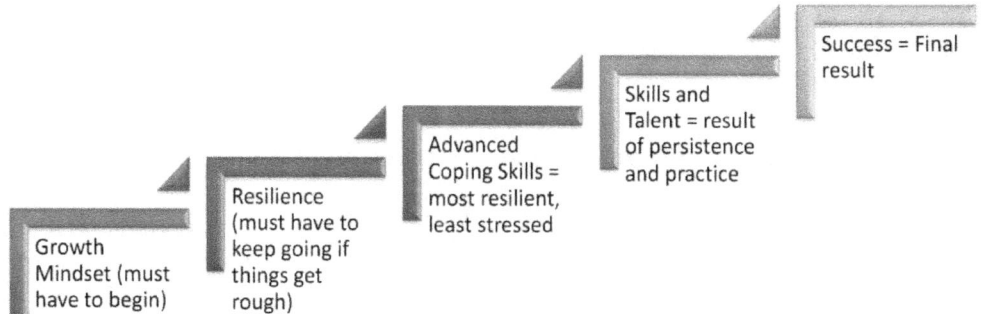

Individuals with a fixed mindset focus on protecting their self-image. They focus on not failing more often than they focus on what they can achieve. See the High Stress/Low Stress diagram (pg. 28). A growth mindset is important for achieving more of your potential. It develops naturally as you use Advanced and Transformational Coping Strategies because your Emotional Guidance directs you toward growth and greater achievements.

Emotion Regulation Beliefs (Transformational)

Just as some people believe they can change and grow (growth mindset), some people believe that they can consciously regulate their emotions. They're right. Other people believe that their emotions are whatever they are and that they cannot change them (fixed mindset). Emotions regulation strategies that help you control your emotions in healthy ways work by changing your thoughts in order to elicit different emotions.

If you believe that emotions can't be changed, the good news is all you have to do is try using some of the techniques presented in these pages and you'll be able to show yourself that you can change your emotions because you want to change them. That will have a Transformational effect on your life and decrease your risk of developing psychological disorders, which often involve some kind of emotion dysregulation.[116]

If you already believe you can regulate your emotions, applying the strategies you're learning in this book will give you executive control of your emotions under most situations.

Re-define Your Best (Advanced and Transformational) (Resources)

Your best in any given moment is not the same as your *best possible.* Accept this. Your best in this moment depends on many variables. You can structure your life and make commitments that will increase *your best in this moment* but you cannot always be at your best. Some of us are better in the morning. Some of us are better in the afternoon. We can't call in because we didn't get a good night's sleep—although our society should consider this acceptable in some situations. For example, if my surgeon had a hoot owl outside her window keeping her awake most of the night I would prefer she call out or come in but reschedule the surgery rather than proceed when science says she won't be at her best. I won't reiterate the negative impact of stress on performance, but it applies here as well. Nutrition, hunger, thirst, illness, hanger,* emotional upset and more can make our *best in this moment* less than our best possible ever but <u>*in that moment*</u> *it is your best possible.*

For example, my mom passed away two weeks ago. Since then I've required more sleep than usual and I am not recovering from lack of sleep as quickly as I normally do. I am simply not at my best right now. I am being compassionate toward myself. I can feel that if I demand my usual demanding schedule from myself it would take me to a breaking point.

I am using self-control (a depletable resource) to get through the days. I am also using many strategies from this book to function as well as I am. I was scheduled to give motivational speech six days after and I met my obligation.

I am, literally, doing the best I can under the current circumstances. I could beat myself up for not being at the top of my game right now but it would serve no purpose and make it even more difficult to function under the weight of negative emotion self-criticism would generate.

---

*Hanger is anger largely attributable to hunger

Life happens. We can manage risks, and we can take a lot of steps that will help us be at our best possible more often, but we can't stop negative experiences from happening.

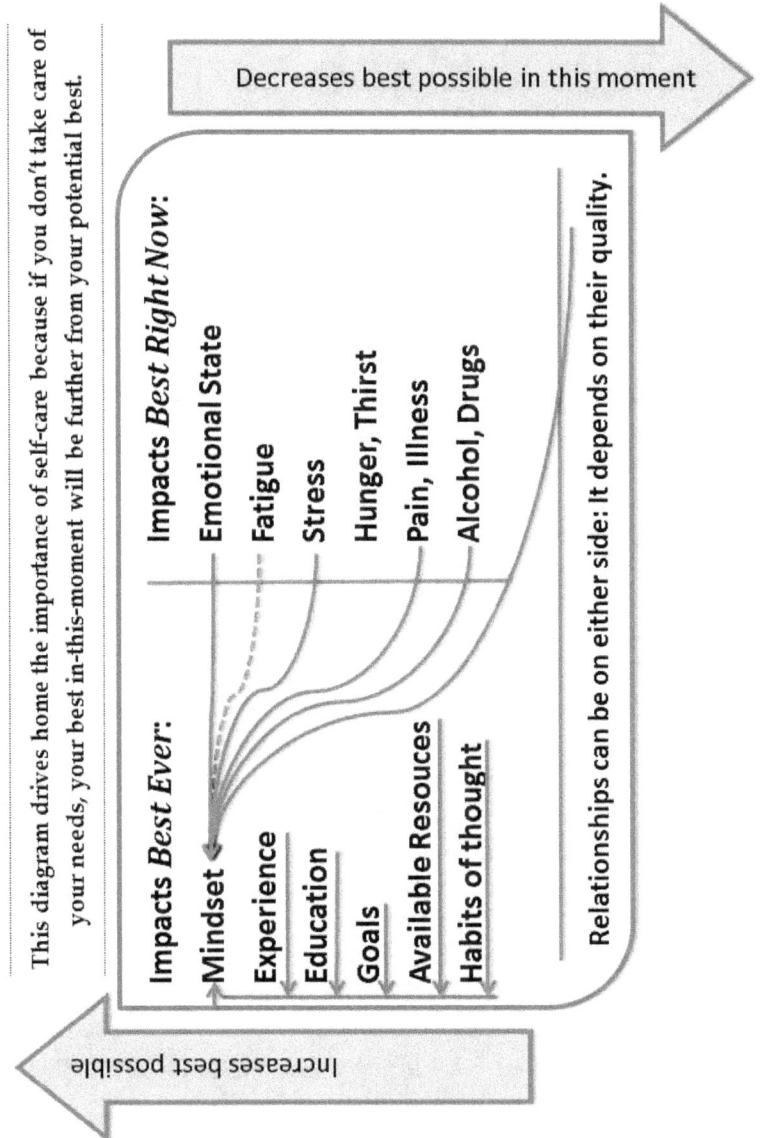

This is an important concept. It's important in deciding what to do right now because your best potential in this moment should be considered. For example, not having a discussion with someone when you're upset is a good decision, if it can wait. The outcome of decisions and conversations won't be as good when you aren't at your best. Also consider the emotional state of anyone you are interacting with and give them the benefit of the doubt. If you've ever been in a disagreement with someone who became upset and you insisted on continuing the discussion you know it probably would have been better to wait.

My husband and I have a general agreement that whoever is in the better emotional state drives. However, when the person in the better emotional state is ill or tired, we shift the rule to allow the one who has fewer negative effects to drive at that point in time. We were in Boston this week, meeting with several hospitals about our solutions for employee engagement and burnout prevention and recovery. My hubby drove the entire time because my resources were lower than his.

The key is to plan in advance, to the extent possible, to have as few negative hits on your best-in-the-moment and as many positives as we are inspired to have in the best ever category. The better our best potential is, the better we will be even if we have some hits to our best.

For example, I've been using *The Smart Way*™ for ten years. It is rare for me to be in a bad emotional state. I've developed expertise in managing my emotional state so that even in situations where someone who doesn't have that skill is experiencing high stress, I'm usually in a better emotional state.

In most cases, a physician with decades of experience in his specialty will be a better diagnostician than a 1st year resident, even if the more mature physician is experiencing moderate pain, hunger, or fatigue. Increase the pain level and the 1st year resident may do a better job. It's an art, not an exact science. Understanding the relationships is more important than being precise. The understanding should be considered when deciding what your limits are in that moment.

If you blunder into your day without considering factors that may limit your best in that moment you are more likely to make mistakes and you're more likely to feel guilty about those mistakes because you will recognize that you could have done better.

Take a minute in the morning to set your intentions for the day. I'm not referring to a *to do list*, although that is a good practice. I am referring to how you want to feel. The mind/body connection is more powerful than most people in our society recognize. If you are tired in the morning and you repeatedly affirm that you are tired, you will feel as tired. If you recognize that you are tired and affirm that once you have something to eat and wake up a bit you'll feel better, you will not feel tired all day.

Guilt doesn't help. It is an indicator of a pretty high level of stress and often leads to maladaptive (unhealthy) methods of stress relief. If you are unhappy with your past behavior, who you are is no longer the same person you were when you did (or didn't do) what you feel guilty about. Guilt is an indicator that you would make a different decision if you were faced with the same situation today.

Commit to doing better next time if you are unhappy with your past behavior. Consider your in-that-moment resources before something goes wrong in the future. Doing a daily self-check, much like airlines do a pre-flight check, is helpful in recognizing and managing your behavior.

It helps you identify when something is going wrong faster. We can be so busy with our lives that we fail to recognize changes that indicate something is going wrong in the early stages when it is still easy to correct. Years ago I woke up one morning and after being up just a few minutes went back to bed to lay down. I felt so weak I couldn't even reach the phone on my bedside. I began yelling for my daughters who were upstairs. They eventually heard me and called an ambulance. I had subtle symptoms of an infection for weeks but hadn't been paying attention to my body's clues. The infection was in my bloodstream. I could have caught the problem sooner by paying attention.

Pay attention to your physical body, your emotions, and your energy level. When you feel *out of whack*, take corrective action. Give yourself the benefit of the doubt. Realize that your best in-the-moment when you made a mistake was the best you could do in-that-moment.

Review the list of items (in the Resources diagram) that most frequently have a negative impact on people's best-in-moment. You will probably find at least one reason you weren't capable of doing your best ever every time that you made a mistake. You did the best you could do at that time given your circumstances. Your body, mind, and spirit have needs and when those needs aren't met you can't be at your best. You are human. You aren't a machine. The benefits of your humanity far outweigh the occasional downsides.

Think about a DUI. Someone whose blood alcohol level is .03 is legal to drive but they have some impairment. The higher the blood alcohol level goes, the greater the impairment. Strong and resilient people may function okay with two or even three of the seven (low emotional state, fatigue, stress, hunger, thirst, pain, illness) but add a fourth and their performance will surely suffer. Learn your limitations and set your own rules about when you will forge ahead. Recognize that your best now is frequently not your best possible.

Give yourself permission to take action (or speak words) later when circumstances are limiting your best in-the-moment.

I teach a class at a psycho-social rehabilitation agency where I'll often have sixty individuals with various degrees of behavioral challenges, many of whom are recovering from addictions and abuse. I cannot help them as well when I'm tired or a little under the weather. I make a point to eat before I go and stay hydrated. In a group like that you never know what you'll encounter. One day I arrived and almost immediately put my lesson plan aside because one of the women in the class said she was in crisis (suicidal). I encouraged her to spend some one-on-one time with an available counselor but she refused stating, "I want to know what you can do for me in this situation." I spent the next hour and a half working to bring her to a more stable emotional state in front of a fairly large audience. At first, the audience watched but in time, several of them helped by sharing their own stories. Months later she gave me a verbal testimonial that you can hear on my YouTube Channel (Jeanine Joy) with the title, *Solutions for Social Problems.* Her testimonial begins at about 16:40 into the video. I shudder to think what might have happened if I hadn't had breakfast. It was a challenging situation with not just the life of a young woman on the line; her child's future would also be irrevocably changed if she ended her life.

I use the commute to get myself into as positive an emotional state as possible. I think about the people I'll be seeing and see the potential inherent within each of them to help me inspire them to fulfill more of their potential. I allow myself to love and care about them but not to take responsibility for their choices. They're adults and they are responsible for their choices.

In the same way, a physician could think about the patients that will come for healing that day and see their potential for health, the wisdom of their bodies, and care about them without taking responsibility beyond offering his or her best possible at the moment in time when they meet one another.

A teacher can think about the potential of her students and recognize that the more challenges a student has that diminish his or her resources, the more hidden potential the child possesses.

A minister can see the potential for great relationships in the couple being counseled and help them see how the resources they are bringing to the relationship affect the quality of the interactions.

The dividing line between caring and taking responsibility is very narrow but it has to be a clear line to preserve our own health and well-being.

No one decides "I could do a better job but I feel like messing up instead of doing my best." Even if it looks like someone is doing that, for example, seemingly asking to be fired, they are doing their best but their goal is not the goal others want them to have. Maybe they want to leave the job but are being pressured to stay or are staying out of guilt at what they'd give up for their family if they left so they self-sabotage.

If you've made a mistake, the takeaway should be to do better in the future which means consider factors that may keep you from doing your best and manage them to the best of your ability, which can include increasing your ability to manage them. That could be building your resilience, your ability to manage your emotional state, going to bed earlier, eating regularly, getting medical care sooner rather than later, etc.

Self-Compassion (Advanced to Transformational)

Self-compassion is giving yourself the benefit of the doubt. You did the best you could with the resources you had available at the time. Resources were detailed in the prior section. Self-compassion is: [117]
- Treating oneself with kindness
- Recognizing our shared humanity
- Being mindful when considering the negative aspects of oneself

Low levels of self-compassion are associated with higher levels of burnout, [118] psychopathology, [119] and social anxiety. [120] Self-compassion is not the opposite of self-criticism. [121] Self-compassion lowers concerns about comparisons with others, public self-consciousness, negative self-rumination, and reduces feelings of anger. [122]

Self-compassion is important in recovery from stressful life events and can reduce or eliminate PTSD symptoms following "severe and repeated interpersonal trauma." [123] Women going through divorce recover faster when they are compassionate toward themselves. [124] Give yourself permission to be self-compassionate. Ask yourself, "How would I treat someone I love if they were in this situation?" Be as kind to yourself as you would be to a friend.

I have never met anyone who did not do the best they could in-the-moment when their situation is considered fully. If they failed or did not do a good job there is an underlying reason. Self-compassion accepts that we are not at the top of our game 100% of the time. We live in bodies that have needs and when those needs aren't satisfied we cannot do our potential best but we still accomplish our best possible in that moment.

Communicate with yourself. Know how you're feeling. Be as kind as possible. Ignoring yourself can lead to loneliness.

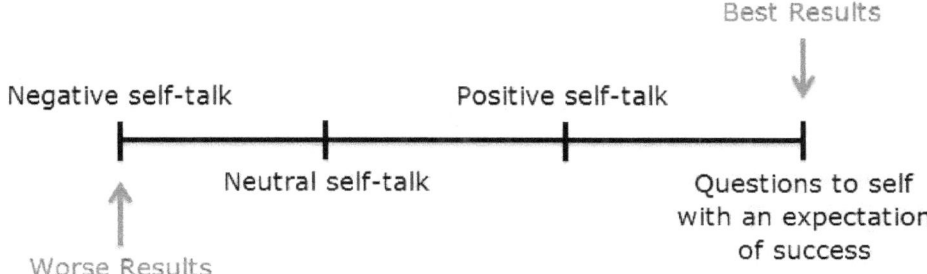

Your Emotional Guidance will support self-compassionate thoughts. Trust it.

Perfectionism

Perfectionism is a flaw. We're human. We aren't meant to be perfect. If we were perfect we'd have nothing left to improve and we feel best when we have something we can improve. Our goal is not perfection. Our goal is growth, learning, and positive emotion. Attempting to be perfect diminishes positive emotion. Your Emotional Guidance will help you remove internal (implicit) demands of perfection. Set a goal to be easier on yourself.

Self-love or Self-respect (Transformational)

Self-love and self-respect go beyond self-compassion. We can feel compassion for someone for whom we don't feel respect or love. This may sound religious to some of you but the fact of the matter is that the phrase *Love Thy Neighbor* from the Bible has seeped into society's idea of what is right. The problem is that they forgot to include the *"as Thyself"* part of the instructions. In fact, in many cases, society tells us to love others more than, or before, we love ourself. There are a lot of self-sacrificing people who never take care of themselves. Many healers are that way. The problem is that when you don't take care of yourself, you become the one who needs help which was never your intention.

You are at your best when you take care of yourself and you have more to give to everyone else when you take care of yourself first. Loving yourself is not wrong. This is fact. We are healthier, mentally and physically, when we feel good and if you don't love yourself, you can't feel good.

Self-love and self-respect are the opposite of low self-esteem. They mean you see yourself as a human worthy of love and respect. It doesn't mean you are better than anyone else, but you're not worse either. Two things help increase self-love and self-respect. Your Emotional Guidance supports loving and respecting yourself. You can check that out for yourself by thinking self-supporting thoughts and feeling how they feel.

If you need more than that, make a list of all the ways you'll be better for others when you feel worthy of love and respect. When you feel worthy you're not stressed and that means you can be at your best: Your best health, your best performance on the job, and your best in your relationships.

Form your own opinion about you. Remember other people's opinions are heavily influenced by their emotional state.

What thoughts about myself feel best when I think them?

Open to New Experiences (Transformational)

The more you open yourself up to new experiences, the bigger your world (I like to call it my playground) becomes.

Most of us have what we consider to be our comfort zones. By deliberately expanding your comfort zone repeatedly over time you can expand it so far that you can't find the end of your comfort zone.

At 18 I was an extremely shy, socially awkward victim who didn't have a clue about much of anything. I was most comfortable escaping into a fiction book. One-on-one conversations were difficult for me and led to watery eyes and a bright red face. Now I enjoy speak in front of large audiences without fear.

Being fearless and being stupid isn't the same thing. I apply risk management strategies to my life. I don't walk down dark alleys at night. But I get on stage frequently without fear. The count of countries I've visited is up to 43 and I did a lot of that travel alone or as a single mother responsible for two daughters.

Between starting a business and writing a book where many of your own trials, tribulations, and struggles are laid open for any reader to see, I'm not sure which one takes more confidence, but I didn't hesitate to do either when my Emotional Guidance indicated it was the right path for me to take. When I went on my first business trip to San Francisco as a young woman I ate room service because I was too timid to go to a restaurant alone. The week after that trip I began going out to eat alone every Thursday night until I was able to confidently walk into any restaurant and enjoy dining alone. Part of that was learning to enjoy my own company. Another aspect was deciding that I was worth a nice meal. Those first few Thursdays were tough. I would sit in my car giving myself a pep talk before going in to the restaurant. In my mind I imagined all sorts of awful things people might think about me dining alone including that I had no friends or wasn't good enough to have friends. Only by facing my fear (and learning that most waitresses are very kind to solo diners) was I able to expand my comfort zone.

Expanding your comfort zone is a lot like building up your muscles through weight and endurance training but unlike exercise, once you develop confidence it doesn't disappear if you don't use it for a while. If I could do it, so can you.

Positive Thinking (Advanced to Transformational)

The way we think about the world determines our thoughts and actions. Fighting against disease is not the same as testing the limits of human wellness.

Some people reject positive thinking out of hand because they believe it is unrealistic and Pollyannaish. These beliefs are not the result of examining the research or of reality. More people than I can remember have said they don't think positive because they are realistic. Remember:

Paradigms	
• Prevent disease • Sustain life	• Wellness Promotion • Quality of life

"If you think you can or can't, you are right."
Henry Ford[15] ★

This 1925 Henry Ford quote can be traced to its origin:

"You must never, even for a second, let yourself think that you can fail," said Mr. Ford. "Our first principal is that failure is impossible. You may not get what you're trying to do right the first time or the second time or the tenth time or the 100th time, but if you shut out of your mind the possibility of being licked, then you are bound to win." [125]

Self-fulfilling prophesies are documented in research. Our personal expectations of self and others' expectations of us influence our outcome. [126, 127] Because our beliefs filter the big data that our subconscious mind sends to our conscious mind, self-defeating beliefs block our access to information that would help us if we believed we could be successful.

One study demonstrated that "beliefs about the likelihood of success in emotion regulation can shape actual emotion regulation success."148F[128] The field of positive organizational scholarship takes the concept forward, stating:

"Adopting an affirmative bias is associated with resourcefulness, or with creating, unlocking, and multiplying latent resources in individuals and organizations. Resourcefulness means that an amplifying effect occurs when individuals and organizations are exposed to positivity." [129]

★ Although the above quote is commonly attributed to Henry Ford, the attribution stems from a 1947 *Reader's Digest* article that did not note when or where Henry Ford made the statement. A similar quote can be traced to Virgil in Aeneid.

The second important aspect of positive thinking vs being realistic is that the facts support positive thinking as realistic. It is only our perception, influenced by the media's focus on the negative aspects of our world, that makes us think more is wrong in our world than right.

If your habits of thought focus on the negative aspects of our world it can be difficult to recognize the positive aspects that surround you. It isn't that our world lacks positive aspects; it is that your brain is trained to focus on the negative aspects.

The appreciation exercise is helpful in training your brain to recognize positive aspects of our world. You can think about things that give you pleasure when you think about them and then realize how common they are.

How many healthy babies were born today?
How many people fell in love today?
How many parents told their children they love them today?
How many people were cured who would have surely died from an illness one hundred years ago?
How many people easily communicated with someone today that it would have taken months to reach just a hundred years ago?
How many people laughed today?
How many people went to bed in a safe place today?
How many people had enough to eat today?
How many people learned something today?
How many people cared for an animal today?
How many people took a breath of fresh air today?
How many people turned on a faucet and had clean water available to them at the touch of a fingertip?
How many people learned something useful today?
How many people smiled at a stranger today?
How many people appreciated someone else today?
How many people enjoyed smelling a blooming flower today?
How many flowers bloomed today?
How many pieces of fruit ripened today?
How many seeds germinated today?

I could go on like this for hours. The amount of good happening all over our planet every day is far greater than the bad happening in our world. Positive thinking does not mean we don't recognize the bad. Positive thinking means we believe we can find solutions to problems.

One trick to positive thinking is to ask yourself what you can or will do about something that you do not want in our world. For example, today we lose 2/3 of our at-risk children to prison, addiction, or death. That is definitely a negative aspect of modern society. I could lament that fact all the days of my life and not change it at all. Or, I could document evidence-based solutions that are already proven to work and publish a book containing those solutions. I did the latter but I would never have done it if I thought we lived in a bad world where we can't solve our problems.

Positive thinking doesn't mean you ignore problems. It means you believe they are solvable and that you are resilient enough to deal with problems you encounter. Maintaining a positive outlook protects against mental illness.[130, 131]

Make Happiness a Priority (Transformational)

Our society doesn't support making our personal happiness a priority. There are many reasons and ways this message is conveyed to us so that it becomes part of our belief system. Society often considers the pursuit of personal happiness as selfish. This common belief is blatantly wrong for a variety of reasons. Our happiness is good for others for the following reasons:

- When we are happy, we are naturally nicer to others.
- When we are happy, our immune function is better which improves our physical health which makes us less likely to become a burden to others.
- When we are happy, we naturally make better choices about food which improves our health.
- When we are happy, we naturally make better choices about exercise which improves our health.
- When we are happy, we naturally make better choices about sleep which improves our health.
- Positive emotions are associated with greater resilience so when bad things happen we rebound faster making it less likely we will become a burden to others.
- Positive emotions protect against mental illness which helps us be a better citizen, spouse, parent, etc.
- When we are happy, our cognitive function is better so we make better decisions which make us of greater benefit to our families, employer, and community.
- When we are happy, our digestive function is better which reduces the likelihood we will develop chronic illnesses associated with digestion.
- When we are happy, our central nervous system functions better which reduces the risk we will be involved in or cause an accident.
- When we are happy, we have a greater capacity to have good relationships with others which is good for us and them.

Our unhappiness leads to the opposite—detriments to our families, employers, and society. Everything mentioned above that is improved by happiness declines when we are unhappy. In addition, we are more likely to commit a crime or be violent when we are unhappy. Our productivity and customer satisfaction from interactions with us decline when we are unhappy.

Think about arguments you've participated in with a spouse or co-worker. How often were the arguments because you wanted to prove your rightness about something that, in the greater scheme of things, was inconsequential? How would you have perceived the situation if your first priority was to be happy instead of to be right? Could you have let it go? Do you argue with someone about their opinion? Do you have heated discussions when you're talking about different perspectives, both of which are right from the perspective from which they are being viewed?

When arguments become heated, how often do hurt feelings and decrements to relationships occur? How often are social connections damaged by arguments or other disagreements?

Now take those arguments to a larger arena. How much is society harmed by people demanding that others think like them or behave like them? Is it possible to get everyone to think the same or behave the same? Is it a desirable outcome to whittle everyone down until all people have only one opinion amongst them? Are any problems solvable when only a single perspective about the situation is available?

With most people, unbelief in one thing ... is founded upon blind belief in another.
George Christoph Lichtenberg

When you want something to be different, why do you want it to be different?

If you boil your reason down to its essence, the reason you want it to be different is because you believe you would be happier if it was different.

The truth is you can be happy in spite of it being as it is.

The truth is that being happy no matter what, being happy because you simply choose to be happy and choose to focus on things that make you happy instead of the one thing, or the few things, that make you unhappy is a more empowered state of mind. Everyone likes to feel empowered. In fact, happiness reflects empowerment. When a person feels empowered they are happier than when they feel disempowered. When a person feels happy, they feel more empowered than they do when they're unhappy.

Try stepping back from disagreements and use Advanced Stress Coping Strategies to find better ways of dealing with the situation.

Human Dignity (Transformational)

Unconditional respect or love for others requires psychological flexibility and the development of beliefs that yield the benefit of the doubt to others. It is difficult to give others unconditional love or respect if we do not first give it to ourselves.

Western society holds conflicting belief structures about human dignity. There is a strong current containing the belief that respect must be earned. There is an equally strong current containing the belief that respect is an inherent right of all humans regardless of their deeds. Even an individual who consciously chooses to view all humans as deserving of respect may have an internal struggle to fend off learned beliefs about earned respect. This is true with self and others.

Viewing others with unconditional love and respect when we don't do the same for ourselves is nearly impossible. Society's strong current of protest against seeing oneself as good creates internal (psychological) factors that come into play.

Why is this important? Emotional labor is pretending there are emotions that you don't feel. Treating someone you don't respect, or even despise, as if you respect them is emotional labor. Many occupations require treating wide varieties of people, some who don't meet our personal standards, with respect. You don't know what resources (or lack thereof) made a person who they are but you can understand how to help them increase their resources which increases their ability to meet societal behavior standards.

Emotional labor takes energy and adds to the risk of mental illness. Finding perspectives where you authentically feel respect for everyone reduces the stress you feel as the result of emotional labor. Nearly every job that requires interaction with others has a component of emotional labor. Some occupations require very high levels of emotional labor and they are associated with declines in mental health and increased suicide.

Treating someone with dignity and respect does not take a toll when the feelings you express match the emotions you feel. Authenticity is healthy and is received better by those with whom we interact. We can sense when a person's words and actions differ from their true feelings. When we sense this, it diminishes our trust in them because we innately know they're not being honest with us.

In addition to conflicts between a person's belief systems and requirements to treat everyone with respect, when outside forces demand that you demonstrate emotions or attitudes that are inauthentic it reduces your sense of autonomy, which is demotivating and can reduce the energy you have available even more.

I want to be clear that I'm not, in any way, suggesting that people do not deserve to be treated with dignity and respect. I am arguing that teaching people how to authentically adopt those perspectives will:
1) Allow them to authentically display those attitudes.
2) Improve the energy they have available for work.
3) Eliminate a potential source of diminished trust between clients and employees.
4) Improve your ability to experience positive emotions.

Appreciation (Palliative to Transformational)

Why should we think upon things that are lovely? Because thinking determines life. It is a common habit to blame life upon the environment. Environment modifies life but does not govern life.
William James

Appreciation in-the-moment is palliative. When it is used consistently, it trains your automatic thoughts to be more appreciative which is Transformational.

Appreciation is one of the most powerful tools. It hasn't been researched nearly as much as gratitude but for 2/3 of the people, appreciation is more powerful than gratitude and for the remaining 1/3 there is no difference between gratitude and appreciation.[132] I prefer appreciation but if gratitude makes you feel better, use what feels best to you.

Appreciation Process I

Every morning tell yourself (set an intention) that you will find at least three things to appreciate during the day. If you want to use an expectant question you can ask, "What will I find to appreciate today?"

Dwell on the beauty of life.
Watch the stars, and see yourself running with them.
Marcus Aurelius

Then plan a time at the end of the day (both dinner and bedtime work well) to remember what you found to appreciate during the day. Don't just remember what it was. Pause and allow yourself to feel the emotion of appreciation and any visceral feelings in your body that correspond with the things you found to appreciate. If you have dinner with someone, sharing what you found to appreciate is a good practice. Writing about what you appreciate is another good way to practice appreciation. Some studies show that journaling can become routine so make sure you are present when you journal. In other words, feel the emotions as you write and think about how you feel when you feel appreciation.

Appreciation Process I trains your brain to look for the good in the world. There are lots of people that want us to focus on the negative and we can easily become unbalanced in our perspective. Many people think a negative bias is realistic but the truth is that there is far more good going on everyday than bad. The more time you spend appreciating, the more you will agree with this statement.

Appreciation Process II

The second appreciation process involves stream of consciousness writing. It supplements the 1st process. In this process you decide to focus on one thing you appreciate and begin writing about what you appreciate/love about it until you run out of thoughts of appreciation on the subject. I do three of these each day and am often high from the release of good feeling bio-chemicals in my body by the time I finish.

If you want to keep falling in love with your partner over and over again, do this process about your partner at least once a week. It doesn't have to be about your whole partner. You could focus on one aspect of your partner one time and another aspect another time. If you find yourself feeling irritated by your partner you can use this technique to help you remember what you love about your spouse. Being irritated is a reflection of your emotional state more than anything else. When you focus on the positive aspects of your partner, you will experience a better relationship. [133]

What to appreciate? The world is full of things to appreciate. It does not have to be a big thing. You can appreciate that you have running water, that your body knows how to transport oxygen to cells that need it, that your heart pumps without you having to think about it, that you have food to eat, that the sun came up, that you have a comfortable pillow, that you can smell a flower. The list is endless. The key is to focus on things that make you feel good. I love sitting on my deck in the morning feeling the sunshine and looking out over the open area in my backyard, listening to the birds chirp, and catching sight of cardinals, finches, and butterflies.

Appreciation Process II reinforces positive emotions and as I mentioned, it's a great way to get a natural high. There is something very powerful about knowing you can feel great just because you want to.

There is no more powerful foreplay than to express appreciation for your partner, in writing or verbally. I'll leave that there. You can apply the same process to enjoy your job more.

Visioning (Advanced to Transformational)

Ellis, an early researcher, stated his use of rational referred to cognitions that *"are effective and self-helping, not merely cognitions that are empirically and logically valid."* [134] This is an important distinction and one I also make. In fact, I go further and under some situations, I encourage magical thinking. As long as you understand that you're fantasizing, if it feels good when you do it, it's helpful. You can't spend all your time in a fantasy world, but you can do it often enough to improve your emotional state.

Visioning creates neuro-pathways. Olympic athletes participated in an experiment where one group only did physical practices, one only did visioning practices, and one group did a combination of visioning and physical practice. The best performance increases were in the group that did both visioning and live practice.

When you consider the impact on neuro-pathways, visioning makes the nerves that make the play perfectly fire and begin creating connections that will help the athlete play as close to perfect as possible.

Diversity Appreciation (Adaptive to Transformational)

It is not possible to dislike someone, or a group of people, and feel good while you are with them. The dislike you feel is a negative emotion which *The Smart Way*™ tells us is a sign post that we would serve ourselves better if we found a better-feeling perspective about the subject we are thinking about.

Remember, negative emotions indicate we're experiencing stress. It is self-inflicted stress because if we liked the person or group that we're feeling stressed about we wouldn't be stressed.

When we define our in-group (people like us) in narrow ways our brain sees out-groups as *other*. Our brain and physiology respond differently to *others* than it does to our in-group.

The best way I've found to get around biases we've been taught or learned is twofold.

1. Deliberately cultivate a new belief about your in-group. Expand it to be as broad as possible. Gradually expand your concept of your in-group with the ultimate goal being to include the human race or all sentient beings.
2. Pay attention to how you feel. When you feel negative emotion about an individual or group of people, view it as a sign that the way you perceive them is not the best possible perspective you could take

for your own good (best interests) and actively seek a better-feeling perspective about the individual or group(s).

There are some helpful ways to do this:

- Keep feeling good as a high priority goal that supersedes having been right in the past. If you were taught not to like a group of people and now you recognize that you feel negative emotion when you think about that group, give feeling good a higher priority than the rightness of your opinion about that group.

For example, I was raised during the Cold War and although I had never met a Russian, I was taught to hate Russians. I dutifully did this for decades until I began understanding that my emotions were providing guidance. The emotion of hate meant there is a better feeling way to view Russians and by hating them I was depriving myself of the opportunity to feel as good as I could.

I began seeing myself as human first instead of American first. It was about that time when I began traveling more internationally. While I was in Australia I met some Russians that I liked quite well and they liked me. One evening at dinner our conversation strayed to the Cold War and we laughed about how we had once allowed our government to dictate how we should feel about each other when we actually liked each other. My Russian friends grew up hating Americans because they were told we were bad.

When you step outside paradigms that allow you to decide that all members of a group are bad because they are members of the group, it immediately becomes apparent how ridiculous that perspective is. I was happy to let go of my anti-Russian sentiments and feel good.

I could have beat myself up for all the years I spent believing that Russians were bad but that would serve no purpose other than continuing to deprive me of my potential to feel good. I know too much to give in to the insistence that I was always right in the past. The price that would extract requires me to feel bad while learning. Learning and expanding your awareness, especially awareness that no one should dictate to you how you should feel, is knowledge worth celebrating.

2) The second technique is to see people for their potential rather than for where they are today. I've worked with quite a few people with sordid past experiences. If I wanted to feel bad I could negatively judge them for what they've done. If I want to feel good I have to see the potential for good within them. I have developed the belief (supported by research) that people are innately good and that most humans live far below their potential. I could judge people for living below their potential but that wouldn't feel good.

7 out of 10 youth in state and local juvenile justice stems have a metal illness
(www.nimh.nih.gov)

Instead I seek to inspire them to fulfill more of their potential. That's what feels best to me.

3) One thing that helps me see people for their potential and not judge them negatively for who they are in this moment, or who they were in the past, is understanding that happy people are good to others and everyone would be happy if they had the skills to be happy. There is a direct link between sustained negative emotion and bad behaviors including crimes. We live in a society that does a poor job teaching people how to be happy which means we do a poor job of preventing crime. Our society so little understands the relationship between mental health, emotional state, and behavior that I am often asked why I veered so far from the main body of my work in my thesis which explored the impact of emotional state on behavior with a focus on crime. More than one hundred years after William James said, *"There can be no existence of evil as a force to the healthy-minded individual."* it is still not common knowledge. This is not saying that mental illness makes an individual likely to commit crimes. Most mentally ill people never harm anyone. The connection is to emotional state. People who are truly happy (see the definition of True Happiness in this book) do not harm others. It is the lack of skill to feel better that leads to crimes of all types. Someone with a healthy mind possess emotion regulation skills in order to maintain the health of their mind, whether they are consciously aware of it or not.

    a. My research has led me to conclude that people would not behave badly if they knew how to feel good. Since we don't teach those skills, society plays a role. It is not that people are blameless or have no moral control over themselves. This is a far different perspective from the one I had as a teenager and young adult. My beliefs are based on research that shows all of us have the capacity for bad behavior when we feel disempowered and for good behaviors when we feel empowered.

    b. Teaching people to feel more empowered unleashes more of their potential.

Changing your attitudes, should you chose to do so, will not happen overnight. It works best if you take small steps repeatedly to move toward a broader definition of your *in-group*. Use your emotions as guidance to help you identify thoughts that will benefit you.

Even after you eliminate your biases you may find new biases to creep into your belief system. As long as you pay attention to how you feel it's easy to stay ahead of it. The recent election cycle with all its negativity tried to make me classify people into groups I liked and groups I didn't like. I had to consciously reject the prevalent attitudes in order to feel good. I made my decisions about who I was going to vote for and then withdrew from as much of the negative dialogue as it was possible to avoid because engaging in the discussions felt awful.

Poor Guidance about Priorities: Change Unsupportive Beliefs (Transformational)

Our society is filled with conflicting maxims about the right way to behave. They make the journey through life more confusing than it has to be. These ideas originated with individuals and were almost never based on research. In most cases they are not anything more than an opinion about proper behavior that became popular and accepted as a truth by a lot of people. Those people then taught it to their children. Because the main function of our brain is to prove our beliefs to us it can be difficult to recognize how a specific belief is making our life more difficult than it has to be.

For example, within the topic of happiness, these false premises are common:

#1: I have to be perfect before I deserve happiness.
#2: I must sacrifice good things for happiness.
#3: Happiness must be (or can be) earned.
#4: You cannot know happiness unless you have suffered and sacrificed.
#5: Happiness will be punished.
#6: I must be enlightened to know real happiness.
#7: Everyone must agree that I deserve happiness before it is okay for me to be happy.
#8: I must have control of my circumstances before I can be happy.
#9: I have to be completely independent in order to be happy.
#10: I must be good before I can be happy.
#11: Too much happiness will change me and that makes me afraid.
#12: Happiness is about materialism.
#13: It is more important to be right (and never be shown to have been wrong) than to be happy.
#14: I can't call myself happy if I am not happy all the time.

There are other false premises about happiness. Nearly every area of life is filled with false premises that make our lives more difficult. The political divisiveness that is currently harming our country is an example of the false premise that if the way we think we should accomplish something is not the same, it means we have different fundamental goals. In many cases, the underlying goals are the same. The difference is just the opinions about how to accomplish the goal. But politicians never talk about the goal; they only talk about how to achieve it. Both sides make erroneous assumptions about the other based on how they want to accomplish a shared goal without recognizing they share the same goal.

We can do so much better, in every area of life. This book will help you do better and be part of the solution that creates a better world for all and a better life for yourself.

Develop Healthy Attitudes (Transformational)

There are many attitudes that indicate healthy habits of thought. It is helpful to understand healthy attitudes. When you are trying out different thoughts and using your Emotional Guidance to decide if a thought is healthy for you, it is helpful to know the direction to learn toward as you try on different thoughts to see how they feel to you.

These healthy attitudes are provided to help you do that.

Develop your own moral compass. Do not allow others to dictate what is right and wrong for you. Decide who you want to be. When you feel good, being positive and helpful feels better than being destructive and negative. In lower emotional states, thoughts about doing bad things may feel better than your current thought but from a long-term perspective they are likely to lead to guilt and other negative emotions. You can define who you want to be and your thoughts will begin supporting your preferences. For example,

I want to be kind.
I want to be a good person.
I want to be a positive influence.

You can use these if they resonate with you. Choose others if these do not resonate with you.

When you notice that you hesitate to do something that might benefit you because it is outside your comfort zone, make a plan to do it so that you become comfortable with it. Don't let fear hold you back from beneficial actions. Do allow fear to keep you from making decisions that are ill-advised from a risk management perspective.

Make up your own mind. Don't follow the pack. Gather information and decide what feels best to you. It is not your job to please others. Don't be deliberately harmful but going along with their opinion or behavior to avoid making someone else feel bad is not the best decision for you. Note: if you are in a situation where it is dangerous to disagree, do what you have to do to survive and then separate yourself from the people who create that environment as soon as you are able to do so—even if you have to relocate a long distance away in order to be safe.

Resentment means you have an external locus of control. Resentment indicates you are giving the power over your outcomes, including your emotions, to someone else.

My mood; my choice.
Feeling bad doesn't mean I am bad.
Being happy is more important than being right.
Decide to change what is; complaining just holds me in place.
I can control myself. I cannot control others.
More goes right every day in my life than goes wrong; even on my worse day.
I would rather be happy than let little things disturb my equilibrium.
Everything is a little thing.
No one else can control me.
I look for the why to line up my energy with my work.
There is a solution to every problem.
I'm learning to enjoy life more every day.
No one else is responsible for how I feel.
I'm wonderful... and so is everyone else.

Healthy habits of thought will help you develop some core concepts. Don't worry if you can't believe the core concepts at first. The core concepts will feel natural once you develop skill at using your Emotional Guidance and Advanced and Transformational coping strategies.

I am strong.
Problems are opportunities in disguise.
Everyone is good at the core of who they are.
I am wise.
I am capable.
I can find a win-win-win-win in this situation.
There is more good in the world than bad.
I can thrive even if most people are currently choosing to struggle.
Other people's opinions reflect their emotional state; not my value.

Forgiveness (Transformational)

Forgiveness is not for someone else. It is for you. Work on forgiveness when you begin feeling inspired to do so. Do not try to force yourself before you are ready.

Look yourself in the eyes in a mirror and say to yourself:

 I have the power to love. I have the power to forgive.

Continue looking into your own eyes, willing yourself to believe your own words—to be the type of person who can forgive another because you deserve to live without the weight of negative emotion holding you down.

Think of someone you have held onto anger about. The person could be family, friend, foe, or even a stranger. Look inside yourself and try to find a perspective that feels better about the situation you've held onto anger about. *Write something down about how it would feel better to you to let go of the anger.* You can choose to tell the person or not, <u>this is for you</u>, not for anyone else.

Note: Do not begin with the person who is the most troubling to you. Begin with someone whose transgressions are not as sharp or painful. You're developing a pattern of behavior and patterns of thought. Your goal is to demonstrate to yourself how forgiving someone else makes <u>you</u> feel better.

Some of my students have struggled with finding it within themselves to forgive anyone. I'm always able to help them find a perspective that allows them with this healing. If you have a friend you trust, talk over your desire to forgive someone with your friend and maybe you'll find a way. Ask yourself expectant questions such as:

How can I find a way to forgive?
How will I benefit from forgiving?

When you begin making a habit of forgiving small transgressions it becomes easier to revisit the bigger hurts and begin whittling away at them. If it is something that feels really big, for example, being abused as a child, you may have to chip away at it the way a sculptor chips away at the marble to find the beauty inside. Steps on that path may include:

1. Realizing that everyone does the best they can in any given moment, even when their best in that moment was awful—it was the best they could do at the time.
2. Recognize and begin seeing how emotional state affects behavior.
3. Recognize and begin seeing evidence that before anyone becomes someone who harms others, they were in pain.
4. Recognize that at the core of everyone there is someone good, even if that goodness is impossible to see because of all the layers of pain that hide the goodness.
5. Commit to feeling good and realize that you can't hold a grudge and feel good
6. Realize that in addition to emotional state, illness, lack of sleep, stress, and other factors can make someone's best in-the-moment be pretty awful.
7. If you were abused by someone, recognize that at the time they were doing the best they could—for whatever reasons. You don't have to know what happened to make them as they were. I can assure you that it's a never-ending story. Someone hurt them, but the person who hurt them was hurt by someone else first and so on back through time. We cannot change the past, we can change the future and forgiveness stops the cycle.
8. Who are you because of what happened that you would not be if what happened had not happened?
    - Would you be as strong as you are?
    - Would you know you can endure as much as you can and still be a force for good in the world?
    - Would you have as much compassion for others?
    - What have you gained?
    - What is the silver lining?

When you begin focusing on what you've gained, the way it looks changes. You do not want anyone else to ever suffer as you did, but you may come to the point where you would not allow anyone to take the experience away from your life—even if that someday becomes possible, because you realize that you would not have become all that you are if your past was easier.

Each step that feels better is good for you.

You may need a subtler approach. You may be attempting to bridge too much of a chasm between how you feel right now and forgiveness. If you think this might be what is hindering you look for a situation where you can find a different, slightly better feeling perspective. Use the processes to shift your focus and once you've stabilized your emotional set point on that topic, see if you can find a way to forgive. If you're still not there, repeat the step about finding a new perspective until you are.

Everything we hear is an opinion, not a fact.
Everything we see is a perspective, not the truth.

Marcus Aurelius

Remember, the forgiveness is for you. Anger, rage, and even blame are blocked energy that is not good for your body or mind. Your body will not function as well when you hold onto these emotions as it will after they are released. You will perceive new relationships through a veil of distrust, or even fear, as long as you hold onto perspectives about past relationships that are painful. Your immune system will function better. Your cognitive abilities will be better. Your digestive function, endocrine system, and more will benefit.

It does not matter if what you're holding onto anger about is someone who abused you when you were a child or someone who cut you off in the parking lot yesterday; releasing negative emotion helps you. I've had many students who have been able to release negative emotions about childhood issues who subsequently had very positive experiences. Two common ones have been weight loss and improvement in chronic health conditions. There has also been a trend of improved relationships with other people and new loves coming into their lives.

How might your life benefit from forgiveness?

Don't forget to forgive yourself. Guilt does not serve you either. When you release negative emotions, you've done good work. Celebrate. It may have felt like you did not do anything other than think, but forgiveness, releasing anger, blame, and guilt are action steps.

You may want to document the day. One way is to write a letter, taking the perspective of yourself in the future, and thank you for healing your hurt. Another way is to write a letter to the person you forgave—even if you'll never send it and even if they are deceased. Remember, you are under no obligation to tell someone you have forgiven them but energetically it can provide additional healing to write the letter, even if you never intend to send it.

Write down things you can now feel about yourself that feel good, that you want to hold on to from this day.

When I first began my forgiveness journey, my list seemed impossibly long. It seemed as if it would take forever to find forgiveness about my past. It was not long until only the worst transgression was left and because I had practiced, that was far easier than I'd imagined it would be. Surprisingly, it was easier than the first one. Developing the habit of forgiveness makes it easier to do this work. Examples of affirmations that can make it easier to forgive more people for more things.

I have the power to love.
I have the power to forgive.
Forgiveness is a gift I give to myself.
I am stronger when I love than when I hate.
I can love fearlessly.
I can always find a better perspective about a situation and, in finding it, feel better now.
I am more powerful than I know.
I have great potential.

My emotions will give me immediate feedback any time I reach for better feeling thoughts.

Loving feels good even if I am not loved back - but only if I focus only on loving. Not if I look for what I am getting back and see lack.

If you are a person who believes in God: God will help me love and forgive.

If you are creative, you may choose to express the release of negative emotions in artwork.

Easily Offended

"Why are people offended by just about everything?

The world is in transition. Attitudes about many things that were relatively stable for hundreds of years (if not longer) have been changing rapidly. Historically, attitudes changed slower and old attitudes died out with those who held the beliefs. Now people live longer and attitudes are changing faster so we have a greater number of active beliefs held by living people.

Social media has raised awareness about the diversity of attitudes and more people are shifting beliefs during their lifetime.

To give you an idea how much things have changed, my MIL was disowned because she married a Catholic man. She was Episcopalian. Episcopalian's are one of the closest religions to Catholic's you can get and both have a Biblical basis. In her New England environment, being disowned for marrying outside one's faith was not unusual during that era (1940's). One of my friends (Japanese) was disowned by her family for marrying a Chinese man in the '80's. I have not heard about that happening to anyone in recent years. Another friend was disowned by his parents when he was dishonorably discharged from the military because he was HIV positive in the early 80's. I don't see many families disowning their children, especially children who are terminally ill, today.

Today we see marriages between many faiths and families in America usually don't disown their children for marrying outside their faith. Attitudes are changing.

Beliefs about race, religious differences, nationalistic views, and LGBTQ are changing.

We're taught by many examples that we should judge ourselves by how others perceive us. We're not comfortable with others looking at us and not liking what they see. So when our beliefs have evolved, or simply formed in more modern ways and we find ourselves interacting with someone who holds different beliefs, it makes us uncomfortable.

The discomfort is easy to stop. All you have to do is stop caring what other people believe and how they perceive you. Their perception of you says 99% more about themselves than it does about you. Someone else's opinion reflects their beliefs, their emotional state, and other personal factors about the person.

We cannot control what others believe. We can, however, recognize that different people have different beliefs, some we'll like and some we won't like. If we try to control what others believe, we'll be chasing that goal our whole life and we won't be very successful. It's very difficult to change another's beliefs because the filtering process in their mind just keeps interpreting reality as if their belief is true. Changing established beliefs has to begin with the person who believes the belief--from the inside out. Asking yourself, "Is this true for everyone?" is a good way to begin. If it is not true for everyone, you probably have an established belief that makes it true for you because you interpret reality as if it is true.

The chart on the next page contains attitudes that support thriving and attitudes that hinder thriving:

	Beliefs that feel like Struggle	Beliefs that feel like Ease
School	I hate school.	I am a good student.
	School is hard for me.	I can have fun while learning.
	I don't like school.	I am good at learning.
Work	My job sucks.	I like _____ about my job.
	My work is meaningless.	My work is important.
	My boss doesn't value me.	My contributions have value to my boss.
	I'm undervalued at work.	I am respected at work.
	I'm a F. U.	I am good at my job.
	I don't understand how to get ahead.	I learn more every day.
	I'm in a no-where job.	I make the most of myself.
	I live for weekends.	I can enjoy myself every day.
Popular	No one wants to spend time with me.	I am easy to get along with.
	I'm afraid of what people think of me.	Most people like me.
	I don't want to show my true self.	People are interesting.
	Will they like me?	I like people.
	The world has a lot of bad people.	I have friends I can trust.
Being Nice	No one can make me be nice.	I am a nice person.
	My teacher is mean.	My teacher cares about me.
	I won't do nothing for nobody.	I feel good when I do nice things.
	They'll let me down if I trust them.	People will live up to my expectations.
Drugs / Alcohol	Drugs make me feel better.	I value my brain.
	Alcohol makes me feel more social.	I'm happy.
	I don't know how to feel better.	I can change my focus and feel better.
	I can't stand this emotional pain.	I can love and let go.
	Drinking gets me through the day.	I'm strong, I can make it.
	Everyone I know does drugs.	I can be whoever I want to be.
Eating	Food comforts me.	Food fuels my body.
	I binge on junk food when I'm sad.	I can eat what I want in moderation.
	I eat when I'm lonely.	I enjoy my own company.
Crime	I can get away with this.	I am a law-abiding person.
	I only care about myself.	I'm an ethical person.
	I deserve this –they owe me.	My life has lots of potential.

Advanced Stress Management Coping Strategies
Teachers open the door but you must walk through it yourself.
Chinese proverb

Metacognition (Advanced Strategy)

Metacognition is thinking about what you're thinking and why you're thinking what you're thinking. Humans think an average of 60,000 thoughts a day. Obviously, every thought we think is not thoughtful. Most of our thoughts are the result of habits of thought we developed many years ago. We don't have to attempt to think about every thought we think. If the thoughts feel good when we think them they are serving us. Positive emotion is letting us know those thoughts are leading toward self-actualization. Negative thoughts can be manipulated using Advanced Stress Management Strategies to find perspectives that will serve us better.

For example, if a new task affects your job responsibilities, an initial thought may resent being forced to do something someone else decided you should do. Using Advanced Strategies, you can manipulate the disempowering (bad-feeling) thought to a completely different thought.

Here is an example of a physician who changed her belief to a more empowering one:

> *When they first began requiring me to report data every time I encountered a patient who was struggling with Opioid addiction, I resented it. It felt invasive of my patients' privacy and pointless. Now I know that the data collected has focused national attention on the problem and that resources that would not have been made available to help people with Opioid addiction are now reaching those who need them because of that data. I am glad I live in an era where we have the ability to gather data that leads to real changes in the way we do things and to better outcomes for patients.*

This perspective in this example moved from resentment to appreciation. The shift is not something you would expect to be able to do in one step. It is best to shift one level of empowerment at a time. (Remember, each Zone on the EGSc is separated by how empowered emotions in that Zone feel.) Once you become adept at changing yout perspectives and develop a tendency to lean toward the positive you will notice two changes:

1. Your initial assessment of situations will be more positive than it was in the past, and
2. You are able to move to more empowered emotional states faster.

When it comes to #2, it becomes possible to be a few minutes into a situation that would have previously been a significant stressor that led to months of feeling low (such as being laid off or the end of an important relationship) and find positive perspectives (i.e. silver linings or new knowledge/insights) that eliminate the stress of the situation. This is not suppression. It is, as Peil stated, "conscious knowledge acquisition, in an act of deliberate learning and personal mental tactic to invoke optimal belief structures." [135]

One person may look at a situation and see a problem while another sees the same situation as an opportunity. By choosing positive perspectives using Advanced Strategies where we think about why we are thinking the way we are thinking about the subject we're thinking about and choose the thought (consciously) that feels the best to us instead of going with our first thought about the subject, we can feel better. Our first thoughts are often suboptimal, especially if we haven't deliberately cultivated beliefs that lead to self-supportive automatic thoughts.

The thoughts we think are influenced by the mood we are in when we think them. If we're in positive mood we are more likely to appraise something in our environment as positive. If we're frustrated we are more likely to appraise something in our environment as frustrating. In other words, our cognitions are related to our mood (mood congruent). [136] Our mind appears to interpret our environment in ways that support the continuation of our emotional state. It makes sense to deliberately cultivate emotional states we want to experience and then allow the automatic process to help us maintain enjoyable emotional states.

Metacognitive Processes (Advanced)

The first step in using metacognitive processes is knowing which thoughts to think about. Thoughts that are stressful can be changed to less stressful thoughts. That's the target for most of your metacognitive work. Remember, thinking a thought does not make it right or good. Thinking a thought that isn't right or good doesn't make you bad. We're designed to consider many thoughts on a subject.

When your Emotional Guidance helps you identify a thought that is stressful, ask yourself questions about the thought.

Is this thought true?
Is it only true for me or is it true for everyone?
How do other people look at this situation?
Have people been in this situation and found silver linings?
Have people been in this situation and later been grateful for the experience?
Am I being specific? If yes, can I think more generally about this subject?
Do I have to solve this today?
Is this subject important?
What is the silver lining?
What opportunities hidden within this problem?
Have I successfully handled similar issues in the past?
What skills do I have that will help me deal with this?

Am I comparing my bloopers to someone else's highlight reel?
What were my resources when I did something I now regret?
What resources can I draw upon?
Am I giving myself enough credit for my ability to handle this situation?
What thoughts feel better than the thought I'm thinking?

As you explore the answers you receive to these questions, pay attention to how they feel. When an answer brings a sense of relief stay with it and decide if you can adopt the perspective it represents about the situation. You may benefit from writing the new perspective down.

Keep your focus on how things feel rather than what you believe is true. As long as you remain aware of the difference between fantasy and reality there are situations where fantasizing about doing things you wouldn't, or couldn't, actually do will relieve stress.

One manager whose boss wanted her to quit because he wanted to bring in his own person imagined her boss's bald head was the golf ball she was hitting. It led to the best game of golf she ever played but more importantly, from then on she was able to relieve some of the stress she experienced at his underhanded maneuverings by imaging his head as a golf ball. She would have never hit his head with a golf club, but the thought of doing so felt more empowered than being the victim of his game.

If you choose to use a technique similar to this to reduce stress, make sure it is one where you cannot follow through on actions.

The personality trait of 'Imaginative' is a positive predictor of resilience. One reason may be that it can aid in finding perspectives that feel better. A creative way to change how a situation is perceived is to make up a story. Albert Ellis found that creative perspectives didn't have to be true to provide benefits as long as the individual realized that it wasn't reality.

In a bullying prevention class I use the example of visualizing taking a space ship to another planet with the bully and then leaving the bully on the other planet. Students have reported that just the thought that they'd done that helps them not respond to the bully in a fearful manner, which makes them less of a target. Bullies like people who are easily frightened. I used creativity to come up with the idea because I knew I couldn't teach students to visualize doing something they could actually do because it would increase the likelihood that they'd really do it.

Respond Proactively to Emotions (Advanced)

This is where conscious emotion regulation is applied. The first tool you need to be good at doing this is The Pause. The Pause is inserted between your initial experience of an emotion and taking action. If an emotion feels good you generally don't need a pause. However, there are short-term actions that are inconsistent with your long-term goals. In those types of situations The Pause can be applied to consider long-term goals in relationship to short-term pleasure.

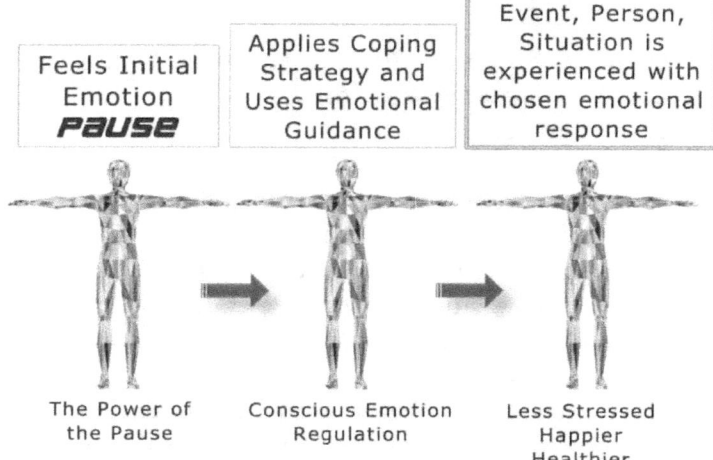

The Power of the Pause — Conscious Emotion Regulation — Less Stressed Happier Healthier

The Pause can help you make good decisions about what you eat, keeping your promises, and avoiding risky behaviors. The more attention you give to your goals ahead of time the less you'll need to consider using The Pause in tempting situations.

The Pause provides time between feeling a negative emotion and acting on the negative emotion during which you can make better choices. You can reappraise the thoughts that led to the emotion and chose one that feels better. Consider the consequences of the verbal or physical reactions available to you.

Taking a deep breath, or two or three, can help you think better during The Pause. Your pause may help you identify upstream beliefs you want to change so that your future automatic (subconscious) evaluation of situations is less stressful.

Cognitive Restructuring/Reappraisal (Advanced Coping)

"One particularly adaptive type of emotion regulation is reappraisal, which refers to changing how individuals appraise the situation they are in to alter its emotional significance."[137] Individuals who engage in reappraisal tend to:[138]

- Feel a higher sense of purpose in life
- Feel less depressed
- Have strengthened social bonds
- Experience higher levels of well-being
- Demonstrate greater social adjustment

Cognitive restructuring is the process of identifying thoughts that increase stress or interfere with optimal functioning. Previous methods of cognitive restructuring were often labor intensive and, in many cases, required a therapist. With an understanding of your Emotional Guidance, the process becomes easier to do on your own using immediate feedback from your emotions.

We think a thought, recognize the way we feel when we think that thought is not the way we want to feel, and know that the negative emotion means the thought is not the best thought we can think about the subject we are thinking about.

> *We are not advising people who need the help of a therapist not to seek the help they need. Therapy can be a life-changing process. We are pointing out that understanding Emotional Guidance empowers individuals with knowledge and skills that make it more likely they can make substantive progress on their own. We have seen situations where individuals who have been in and out of therapy for decades without being cured become symptom-free after learning The Smart Way™.*

Cognitive reappraisal significantly contributes to positive mental health and protects against indicators of poor mental health.[139] People who recently faced stressful life events and habitually used cognitive reappraisal had higher levels of:[140]

- Well-being
- Better social adjustment, and
- Fewer depressive symptoms

Reappraisal is when you apply strategies to change the thoughts you are thinking that elicit an emotion that feels bad to you. For example, you left $100 on your dresser when you left for work and when you come home it is gone. Your first thoughts may be that someone came into your room and took your money or that someone in your home took it. None of these thoughts would feel good. During reappraisal you can decide to ask the people who live in your home if they took it. You can check to see that the doors and windows are secure.

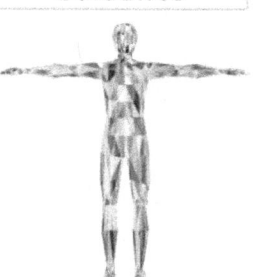

Applies Coping Strategy and Uses Emotional Guidance

Conscious Emotion Regulation

There are many reasons the money may not be where you left it. Your partner may have put it away for safe-keeping because they didn't like it being visible. You may have forgotten to give your son money to buy the equipment he needs when soccer practice begins tomorrow and he took it to buy things he needed that you were going to buy for him. In this instance, leaving the money where he could get it when he needed it was what I refer to as a happy accident. The cat may have knocked it onto the floor and it is under the dresser.

If you don't reappraise, the attitude you bring to the conversation with others in your home may be accusatory which is not likely to turn out well. Giving people the benefit of the doubt will usually lead to a more positive emotional response.

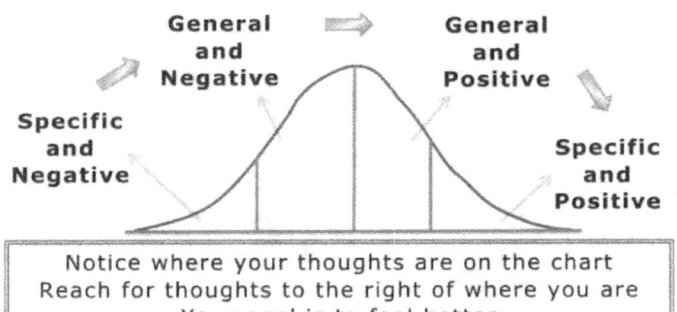

If you're feeling intense negative emotion, you're being very specific. If you look for thoughts that are more general, you'll be able to feel better.

If your thoughts are generally negative you may be able to find a generally positive thought that you can use. Generally positive thoughts can be very general.

I don't have to figure this out today.
I can deal with this tomorrow.
I'll figure this out, eventually.
This is not bigger than me.
Other people have dealt with things like this and found a way.

Another helpful process is to think about a camera lens. If you're feeling negative emotion you're zoomed in on a flaw. If you zoom out to a larger perspective you'll be able to see the thing that feels bad from a different perspective.

Pivot $180°$ when you recognize what you don't want. Tell yourself that you can decide what you do want if you know what you don't want. Ask yourself:

What do I want?

Remind yourself emotions are temporary responses to thoughts and that as soon as you find different thoughts you can feel better.

Let's try it now. Get a blank piece of paper. It can have lines or be completely blank. Write a sentence to describe something that has been bothering you. Think about the issue by asking yourself questions, such as "What is the opposite of this?" and "What does the big picture look like?" as well as "Will this matter tomorrow (or in 5 years)?"

Put the issue that is bothering you in a broader context. Then feel how your emotion about the topic shifts.

If your emotions become worse, you are going more specific, not more general. Be patient with yourself and try again. If you have been practicing negative thoughts for a long time it can be a little bit like starting the lawn mower the first time in the spring, which means it requires a little more effort to get going but once you start, it will be easier the next time.

It's Bogus (Advanced Coping)

One of my favorite processes is what I call Bogus. When I think a thought that evokes enough negative emotion that I pause to examine what I am thinking and why, I can often eliminate the hold the thought has on me be declaring it Bogus.

Collecting evidence that supports empowered thoughts is one way to ensure you will be able to easily declare limiting thoughts as Bogus. For example, examples of aging that are empowering, women who are strong and successful, and people who have done things you want to believe you can do. Paying attention to these examples is fun. It makes your world feel both bigger and safer. The Bogus process works to refute your own limiting thoughts and to help you not adopt other people's limits as your own. Many people have cognitive biases about subjects that you don't want to adopt as your own. You don't have to convince them that their beliefs are wrong but you do want to prevent yourself from adopting their beliefs where they would become self-fulfilling prophesies. Trusting your Emotional Guidance makes it easy because rejecting disempowered thoughts receives a positive response.

Use Science and Experience to Support Yourself (Adaptive Coping)

Whether it is your belief or someone else's, evaluate it by identifying the thought that feels better and then looking for evidence that the thought you want to believe is valid and for evidence that the thought you don't want to believe is not valid. Use Emotional Guidance, science, and experience to inform your opinion.

If you are going through a tough situation and feel isolated and alone, as if no one has ever endured what you are enduring, you can look for evidence of others who had similar, or worse, experiences to assure yourself that humans are capable of adapting and growing during adversity.

Our world is full of inspirational individuals who have survived and thrived in spite of adversity. Unfortunately, our society tends to put them on a pedestal which makes us think they have something ordinary mortals don't have but that is a false narrative. We all have great potential within us. Believing we can makes a tremendous difference.

If Everyone . . .

Another process you can use to determine if thoughts make sense is carry it out in your mind as if the entire world adopted the thought. What would the world look like? Would it be good or bad? Better or worse than what we have now? This process leads to a far greater appreciation of diversity of all kinds, including diversity of thought.

Words Matter

Ought, Should, Must, Always, Can't, and Never frequently point to beliefs that may increase stress or lead to self-criticism. Definitive statements are another sign. "I'm not good at X" is an example of a statement I would challenge. The challenge is not the opposite; the challenge changes the statement to one that is recording a current event that does not reflect a pre-determined future. "I'm not good at X, <u>yet</u>" leaves the door open to change your relationship with X.

Death – Plan Ahead

When it comes to death I spent a long time coming back to my beliefs and comparing them to the emotions they evoked until I found a worldview that comforted me on the subject of death. I mention this not to convince you of any particular worldview but because people often say things like, "Well, death always feels bad so emotions that feel bad can't mean I'm looking at it in a way that doesn't serve me." This is not always true. It was not true for either of my grandmas.

If you have a huge fear of death (your own or others), don't start with the biggest issues. Use Emotional Guidance in areas where it is easy and work toward bigger subjects.

Most people avoid thinking about death. Less than a month ago my mom passed away and having a worldview that allowed me to find perspectives that soothed me is making her transition far easier than it would have been if I hadn't already developed neuro-pathways that support thoughts that don't bring me to my knees with grief.

I've used the strategies in this book more in the past month than I had in the past five years combined. But I am doing well because of the tools at my disposal. When you know you're ready for something it is much easier to handle it than it is when you don't know if you can handle it.

Power of Thoughts/Words: Quantum Physics

Man's greatness lies in his power of thought.
Blaise Pascal (1623-1662) French mathematician, physicist and philosopher

Think of thoughts as a pattern of energy with the ability to affect subatomic particles. Imagine that a thought is wave 1 and a desire is wave 2. In this case, the waves are in sync (thoughts and desires are in sync). The person whose thought and desire are represented in the graph is not stressed about this topic—waves in sync do not create tension. The resulting outcome is positive. Popp found that individuals whose waves were in-sync were healthy.

Fritz-Albert Popp researched both healthy and unhealthy subjects and eventually concluded good health was a state of perfect subatomic communication (coherence) and ill health was a state where communication breaks down.*

This is consistent with research indicating that positive and optimistic individuals enjoy significantly better health [141] and greater success. [142] A pilot study by The HeartMath Institute achieved a 36% reduction in pain ratings by increasing heart coherence in a group that had moderate to severe perceived pain. The same technique reduced negative emotions by 49% and perceived stress by 16% while physical limitations decreased by 42%. The control group was unchanged. [143] This successful intervention included instructions to be more aware of their feelings and emotions and use self-regulatory techniques to shift into a more coherent state of mind to achieve heart coherence. [144]

Heart coherence occurs when you believe you can achieve your desires. Constructive Interference could be represented by the desire "I want a job where I make enough to take good care of my family" amplified by the belief "I am well prepared to find a good job."

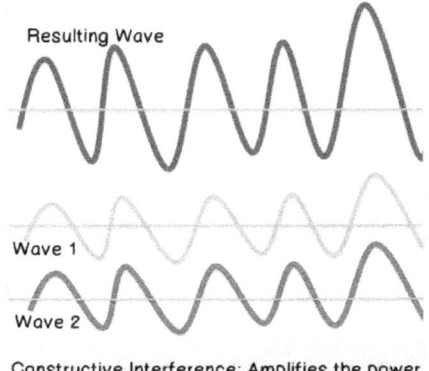

We are ill when our waves are out of sync. When our waves are out of sync our minds and bodies experience stress. Our emotions let us know whether our waves are in sync. When

---

* Remember the funnels in Relationships: Stress, Energy, Emotion, Biochemistry, Thoughts, and Cellular Communication

we have Constructive Interference toward something we desire, we're feeling joyful. When we have Destructive interference, we're feeling stressed and our emotions are in lower Zones on the EGSc.

When the waves are in sync, they begin acting like one giant wave and one giant subatomic particle. Coherence creates the ability to communicate, like a highly sophisticated computer system.

In Quantum Physics, waves are encoders and carriers of information. When two waves are in phase (sync), and overlap each other (technically referred to as *interference)* the combined amplitude of the waves is greater than the combined amplitude of the separate waves; there is a compounding effect.

When what you want and what you believe you can achieve don't conflict your thoughts are in-sync (Constructive Interference). Energy on the quantum level is working in your favor. Everything from the function of your cells (immune, digestive, cognitive, biochemistry, and central nervous system), to the thoughts you think and the words you speak are supportive of achieving your desire. There is power in Constructive Interference as illustrated by the compounding effect seen in the amplification of the wave in the diagram.

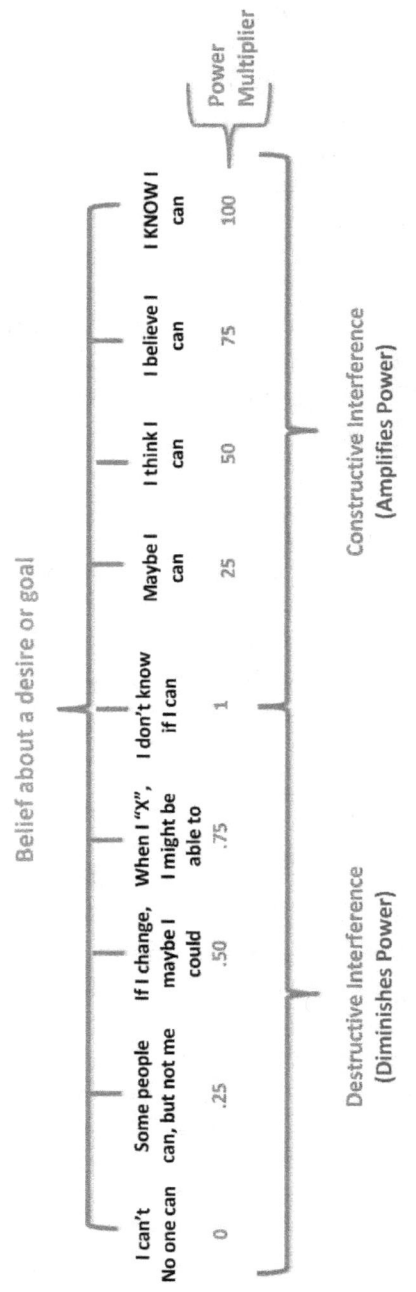

The amount of energy it takes to shift thought into alignment with desires is far less than the energy required to make an equal change in the world of Classic Physics where:

Work = Force x Distance
Force = Mass x Acceleration

I'm not Einstein, but I've come up with a way to explain Interference mathematically. Constructive Interference acts as a multiplier because it increases power and Destructive Interference acts as a divider because it decreases power. Begin with the following equation:

Interference = Desire x Belief = Power (multiplier/strength/energy)

With a belief that one can accomplish a desire, Constructive Interference increases the power the individual has to achieve the desired goal.

Constructive Interference = Desire x 100 (belief = "I can")

With an "I want it but I don't believe it is possible" belief, Destructive Interference decreases the power the individual has to achieve the desired goal.

Destructive Interference = Desire x 0 (belief = "I can't")

I created a chart to illustrate how mindsets affect the power (energy) to achieve desired goals. Pay attention to the words associated with the multipliers. Words (and thoughts) matter.

Herbert Fröhlich, of the University of Liverpool, was one of the first to introduce the idea that some sort of collective vibration is responsible for getting proteins to cooperate with each other (in our bodies) and carry out instructions of DNA and cellular proteins. Waves (at the quantum level) synchronize activities for the living system. Positive thinking creates Constructive Interference, allowing clear communication between the cells of the body.

Negative thinking creates Destructive Interference that interferes with communication between the cells of the body. Negative thinking, by definition, is in opposition to goals and to positive motion forward. Anything less than positive thinking loses the beneficial impact of Constructive Interference.

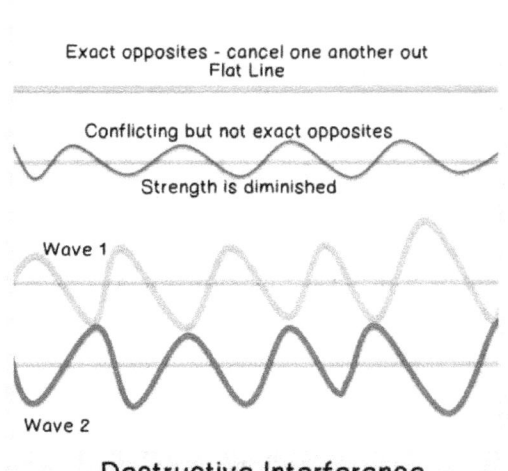

Destructive Interference Diminishes Power

Researchers at Harvard found that positive emotions reduce the risk of developing heart disease by 50%.[145] They found that the absence of negative emotions was not the same as the presence of positive emotions. Positive emotions are required to obtain the health benefits. Positive emotions mean we have achieved Constructive Interference. This fits the theory that positive emotions create clear communication between our cells, evinced by (or supported by) Constructive Interference while neutral emotions and negative emotions do not create Constructive Interference.

Negative emotions create Destructive Interference. The flat line at the top of the chart is indicative of someone who wants something but whose belief is opposite the desire. For example, the desire "I want a job where I make enough to take good care of my family" contrasted with the belief "It is impossible to find a good job in this economy" would be a flat line.

The lower power wave (conflicting thought) indicates the same desire combined with a less pessimistic (but still not positive) belief "It will take a long time to find a good job in this economy."

Mathematically, ***1 x .5 = 50% power***

Can you feel how conflict between the belief and the desire create tension or stress? This stress exists at the quantum level, which is why it is the root cause of ill health. When our thoughts and beliefs are in sync, tension (stress) is reduced or eliminated.

Although many people try, I have not found evidence of a way to pull back our desires and maintain positive emotions. There are many ways to shift our beliefs so they become more coherent with our desires. Increasing Constructive Interference on the quantum level magnifies our success and our health. Better cellular communication explains the greater cognitive abilities that are documented when people are in positive emotional states. Improved immune, biochemical, and digestive function can be similarly explained.

Our thoughts are waves. A healthy, positively focused individual will have more coherent and positive thoughts. In other words, their thoughts will be consistently looking for solutions and believing they exist, their thoughts will reflect a belief that they will get through whatever hardship or turmoil they are surrounded by and be able to move forward. Or, if their life is going well, that it will continue to do so. Their waves are in sync, combining and amplifying one another. Communication with the body is clear. The level of stress is low.

On the other hand, someone who is experiencing illness will want the same things, they will want to get through it and move on, and they will want to believe things will turn out all right, but their negative bias creates Destructive Interference with the desires, thereby leaving the positive desires without enough power to manifest. Someone whose life is going well but who believes that it will not continue to do so creates Destructive Interference with continued wellbeing which eventually manifests in their reality.

Three examples of thoughts and their coherence (or lack thereof) are shown below. The first example is of someone with unhealthy habits of thought who is in a low emotional state. Their thoughts oppose their desires leading to Destructive Coherence. The negative thought patterns can cause a downward spiral. Notice the self-criticism. In each example, Emotional Guidance would let the person know when thoughts were not productive by generating negative emotion.

Thoughts	Power Multiplier	Direction
I can't believe this is falling apart. Nothing ever works out for me.	0	↓
Every time I think something is finally working out it crashes.	0	↓
If I wasn't stupid I might be able to find someone who loves me.	0	↓
No one is going to hire someone my age.	0	↓
I can't remember the last time something worked out really well for me.	0	↓
I might as well stop trying. It never works out for me.	0	↓
I must be cursed. What is the point?	0	↓
I don't know what to do. I can't do anything well.	0	↓↓↓
Life is awful and then you die.	0	↓
I'm a loser.	0	↓

In the next example, the random and unfocused thoughts of someone whose thoughts are inconsistent cancel one another out. The person has some positive thoughts, but not enough to cause thriving. If the thoughts continue to be more negative than positive, a downward spiral is a possibility.

Thoughts	Power Multiplier	Direction
I really hope this will turn out OK (without any real feeling of hope)	0	↓
Sometimes things turn out OK	100	↑
Maybe my brother will help me out (hopeful but no real faith)	.79	↗
Bad things happen in three's; what is next?	0	↓
At least I have people in my life who will always love me no matter what	100	↑
I hope Joe never hears about this; he will never let me live it down	.25	↙
Every time I think things are going well something bad happens	0	↓
I've been in worse situations. I can probably find my way out of this	.75	↗

165

Deliberately choosing to focus on better feeling thoughts could turn the situation around and create the more desirable upward spiral. Most people's thought patterns are a lot like the second example. If they understood the importance of focusing on what they want with positive expectation, they would make a greater effort to think more thoughts that would benefit them.

Each one of the thoughts that has a multiplier of less than 100 could be improved using Advanced or Transformational Strategies.

In the third example, of thoughts from a positively focused and optimistic mindset, the coherence of thoughts that support the individual's underlying desires increase wellbeing in all areas of life.

Thoughts	*Power Multiplier*	*Direction*
Every time I think something bad has happened to me it turns out to be good when I get a clearer view of it	*100*	↑
I wonder what the silver lining will be here?	*100*	↑
I know there is a solution. There always is. I wonder what it is.	*100*	↑
Things always work out well for me. I don't have to know the ending to know this will work out well, too.	*100*	↑
I wonder what new things I will learn because of this?	*100*	↑
It is fun to solve problems.	*.75*	↗
I have lots of people who will help me if I need help.	*100*	↑
I am really blessed. My life is going well.	*100*	↑

When comparing the above examples of thoughts, the scattered, powerless nature of the middle example, the destructive power in the first, and the positive amplifying power in the third example can be felt. On the quantum level, we understand that as coherent thoughts and desires overlay one another, the combined strength is amplified. The last example is indicative of individuals whose situation is changing in desirable ways because the Constructive Interference of their thoughts have amplified power.

The middle example is a more common thought-pattern, characteristic of a person who seems to be moving in circles or chasing his own tail, so to speak. He moves around a little bit but often ends up back where he began.

He may change jobs only to find that six months later he has an equal number of similar problems in the new position as those he was experiencing in the role he left. Until he changes something about himself he will continue thinking in ways that lead to the same outcomes.

Someone can have cohesive positive thoughts about one area of life and destructive interference in another area of life. Some factors create spillover into many areas of life. Self-esteem (worthiness), is one of the areas that will have an effect across the board. Other factors may only affect one aspect of life or an even narrower topic, such as a single relationship or goal.

Once you desire something, you won't be in-sync with your desire unless and until your thoughts are consistent with your ability to achieve the desire.

Want it + Don't believe you can have it = stress/discord/Destructive Interference

Want it + Believe you can have it now = Constructive Interference/harmony/low stress

Once you want something you cannot stop wanting it. But to fully understand what that means you have to understand that what you want is not the specific thing that you think it is. If you fall in love with someone, you can stop wanting that particular person because what you really want is the way that person makes you feel when you're in love. If you want a new sofa, it is the way you believe you will feel when you have that new sofa that is the real desire—the sofa is just the excuse you're using to feel that the way you want to feel.

Thoughts are a pattern of energy with the ability to affect subatomic particles. Your emotions will guide you toward greater positive (Constructive) coherence. Your heart is always in a positive, loving, appreciating, hopeful state. When you attempt to be other than that you feel negative emotion. The more you bring your mind into alignment with your heart, the better you will feel and the better your life will become.

> *"Coherence is the state when the heart, mind, and emotions are in energetic alignment and cooperation . . . it is a state that builds resiliency—personal energy is accumulated, not wasted—leaving more energy to manifest intentions and harmonious outcomes . . .*
>
> *When the physiological coherence mode is driven by a positive emotional state, we call it psychophysiological coherence. This state is associated with sustained positive emotion and a high degree of mental and emotional stability."* [146]

Write one of your goals or desires at the top of the blank chart. Use the chart to record your own thoughts. Add arrows to indicate the whether your thought patterns are consistent or inconsistent with your goal. Nuances do matter. "I can" is not equal to "I think I can," use your emotions to feel for the difference between the two thoughts.

If your thoughts do not support your goals, use the metacognitive processes described in this book to shift your thoughts to ones that support your goals. A separate chart for each topic can be beneficial. However, the goal is not to complete a lot of charts. The goal is to pay attention and recognize how the emotional discord feels and then adjust your perspective to one that feels better.

Do you need some help coming up with ideas for your topics? Do you have a co-worker who tends to be irritating to you? Are you happy with the current political climate? Are all your relationships as good as you want them to be? Do you have a health condition that is not as good as you would like it to be? See if your thoughts are in alignment on these topics.

If you enjoy good health, you can use the way you feel when you are ill—such as when it feels like a cold is starting. Another alternative is to think about how you think about an illness someone you care about is experiencing. Remember mirror neurons and the influence of expectation.

Thoughts Worksheet	*Power Multiplier*	*Direction*

Another way to use the chart is to ask your friends about things you say on a regular basis. One example is "I can gain weight just from smelling cakes in the bakery."

Because our society currently operates as if the quantum level does not matter. Many common beliefs and phrases that do not serve our highest good are in common usage. I used to think such thoughts could not really matter. However, after consistently feeling for how different thoughts felt, I began to feel the discord of unsupportive thoughts in a stronger way. When that happened, I shifted my mindset away from unsupportive thoughts and my results changed.

Here are some more examples of common unproductive expressions:
A good man/woman is hard to find.
I always choose the slowest line at the checkout counter.
I can never (fill in the blank). i.e. find my keys
I always (fill in the blank). i.e. anything you don't want
Nothing good lasts forever.
I am always a day late and a dollar short.
He does not respect me.
I can't (fill in the blank). i.e. anything you want to do
(fill in the blank) is too expensive for me to do.
It's a once in a lifetime experience. (unless you only want to do it once)

Just realizing you have more ability to exert control over how you feel by changing your perspective (and therefore your thoughts) about a subject significantly reduces stress.

Create revised statements that are more empowering than the ones listed above. Can you think of expressions you think or say that may be creating Destructive Interference with your ability to achieve your goals?

Don't be afraid of your thoughts. Occasional negative thoughts won't kill you. The accumulation of your thoughts creates momentum. You want your momentum to be more positive than negative. The more positive thoughts outweigh negative thoughts, the better life feels. Any step in the direction of feeling better is good. This is not something you should, must, or ought to do. This is something you do because it feels better to do than not do. The benefits of doing it are secondary.

Be Flexible (Advanced)

Don't accept the first thought you think about a subject as the truth. If it feels bad when you think it, it probably isn't your truth. Recognize that we all have cognitive distortions. For example, if a democrat thinks a democratic leader made a statement they will agree with it but if the same statement is reported as being said by a republican leader they object to the statement. It's not just democrats; republicans do the same in reverse.

Don't accept the first thought you think about a subject, especially if it causes negative emotion. Your negative emotion is an indicator that you're stressed by the thought.

Trust Your Guidance (Advanced and/or Transformational)

Cognitive dissonance is not a reason to beat yourself up. We all created worldviews as children and have added to them ever since. We don't teach children how to consciously construct worldviews that are healthy. Our society leaves it to chance. Discovering that your beliefs or worldviews could use some help, or contain inconsistencies, is good news because changing them will make your life feel better.

Adjust Your Focus (Advanced Coping)

If you tend to look for your flaws, re-focus so that you pay attention to your strengths and successes. If you tend to look for other people's flaws, begin looking at their strengths and potential. If you're worried about what other people will think about you, focus on what you have in common with them. The Expectant Questions process is helpful.

Adjusting your focus can be fun. Play with it in the privacy of your mind.

Give Yourself Credit Where it is Due (Advanced and Transformational)

Many people discount their good deeds. Recognize the good in you. If you find yourself responding to a thank you with "It was nothing" you're discounting your goodness. This is an indicator that you're negatively distorting your value and worth.

Negative emotions will alert you that you're looking at flaws. When you look at yourself in a mirror, pay attention to how it feels. Many people look for flaws when they look in a mirror. Look for your beauty instead.

Labels (Advanced)

Labels take us a step further from clarity. Our society loves to label and classify but as soon as we slap a label on something we have distorted it and reduced clarity. As far as I can tell, nearly everything in our world exists along a continuum and when you use a label that does not consider the continuum, the solutions are lost. For example, mental illnesses exists along a continuum that begins with stress and moves to chronic stress and then on to mental illness. We can widen the continuum and see the distorted thinking that led to stress. The label states what is but not how it arrived or how to heal it. For the whole path to be visible one must look at the continuum.

Labels can trap us into boxes. To many people, the label *Adult* implies that one must act mature. Playful activities that adults would enjoy are eschewed to reinforce the perception that one is a responsible adult. Yet it is possible to be a responsible adult and still play tag with your neighbors after dinner. How much more fun would that be than going to the gym and running on a treadmill?

We don't have to accept labels we don't like and we don't have to accept the limits labels place upon us. I work with a young woman whose community bullied her because they didn't think she conformed to the racial label they put on her enough to suit them. Why would anyone willingly accept a label that tells you that you can't do things you want to do?

We will never be free to be who we are until we allow others to be who they want to be. When people aren't boxed into corners and slapped with labels that are confining they are happier and happier people treat other people better.

Labeling specific emotions can be helpful in certain situations. Associate specific solutions with specific labels. Different strategies are more effective during different emotional states.

Reframing (Advanced)

Re-framing is one form of cognitive restructuring. I usually write about re-framing in connection with perceptions of failure. Failures can be perceived as meaning we are not good enough or they can be perceived as opportunities to learn and begin again with more knowledge. Defining ourself as a failure hinders our ability to be successful in the future. Re-framing experiences as learning opportunities prepares us for greater success in the future.

Re-framing can be applied to other areas. Compare the following statements:

1. EMT's are exposed to high levels of stress in the course of their profession and are particularly susceptible to experiencing burnout."[147]
2. EMT's are exposed to high levels of potential stressors in the course of their profession which can make them particularly susceptible to experiencing burnout.

In Statement #1, the EMT is passive and stress is something active that the EMT encounters during the course of his or her work. This active agent (stress) is a threat to the EMT's well-being.

In Statement #2, stress is a potential outcome. Stress is optional and may pose a threat.

Statement #2 by itself changes nothing but when EMTs are taught healthy habits of thought, they are empowered to take the lower stress option by perceiving the potential stressors in low or no-stress ways which then decreases the risk of burnout.

The scientific community frequently writes about humans as if we are mechanical. If A happens, we can expect B. We know that this is not true. Not all individuals in stressful jobs experience high levels of stress. The difference is the way they process and perceive data.

As an example, if you doubt yourself and think, "I'm not tough enough to handle this situation" you can use your Emotional Guidance to help you reframe the situation. If you've practiced with your guidance you will be reassured when you try other more empowered thoughts and they feel better. Once you pay attention to your guidance for a few weeks you will be reassured when you counter a disempowering thought simply by affirming a more empowered thought and feeling how your emotions respond, "I can find a way to handle this situation and grow in the process. I'm looking forward to seeing who I become as the result of this challenge."

Reframe Failure

Q. A 21-year old college student at a highly ranked University asked me, "How can I compete with people who are better than I am in every way?"

A. Okay, first of all. Failure is simply looking at a situation in less than an optimal way.

Let me begin with a story:

Tom Watson Jr., CEO of IBM between 1956 and 1971, was a key figure in the information revolution. Watson repeatedly demonstrated his abilities as a leader, never more so than in this short story.168F[148]

A young executive had made some bad decisions that cost the company several million dollars. He was summoned to Watson's office, fully expecting to be fired. As he entered the office, the young executive said, "I suppose after that set of mistakes you will want to fire me." Watson was said to have replied,

> "Not at all, young man, we have just spent a couple of million dollars educating you."[149]

How does this relate to you? You're assuming your peers know what you know. I can assure you that they don't. Yes, they know things that you don't know. That is true now and it will always be true just as the fact that you know things they don't know and you will always know things that others don't know.

That convoluted sentence is important because your value and worth is not derived from what you have accomplished or not accomplished. It is from the unique ways you perceive the world which is different than everyone else. No one perceives the world exactly the same way, not even co-joined twins.

I can think of no other desire that you could have that would improve your life more than a desire to improve yourself. Once this desire is sparked within you, it is sure that you will eventually be amazed at who you become as long as you believe you can improve yourself.

Do not hamper yourself by:
- Looking back at the past and regretting it instead of seeing it for the impetus it was for you to develop a desire to improve yourself. Without having done less than you now wish you had done, you wouldn't have this strong desire to improve. It is likely that many of your peers are simply being *obedient* and do not have that desire despite their successes so far. Even if they do have it, you also have it now.
- Your focus on criticizing who you were instead of who this desire has made you become doesn't help you. The expanded potential of the "future you" increased substantially because of your realization that you want to make a change in your behavior.

As far as changing yourself, you won't make much progress if you simply attempt to change behavior. You have to change your beliefs about yourself. Then your behaviors will change. Begin seeing yourself as someone who evolves throughout life, an ever growing and learning Being. Think about whom you want to be—not in relationship to your peers—but what energizes and excites you. Don't worry about how you'll become who you want to be—just think about who you want to be in a world where you can become whoever you want to be. This is a world where you can become who you want to be if you don't trip yourself up by worrying about how to do it.

Once you know who you want to become, begin thinking of yourself in that way. Begin describing yourself (if only in the privacy of your own mind) in those ways. Your beliefs about yourself will evolve as you change your inner dialogue. After your beliefs change, your behavior will change automatically. Who you decide to become is not chiseled in granite, you can change it and should expect it to evolve over time.

As you begin accepting and liking yourself more, others will find you more likable. If you do the work to feel better about yourself, good relationships will follow.

Be patient with yourself. You're very young (in years) and growing in wisdom. You have a long journey ahead. It can be fun or difficult. How you see yourself is the most important factor that determines which it is.

In many of the training sessions I lead I will baldly state, "I'm wonderful . . ." and leave it hanging there during a long pause before I begin adding (as I look at the class) "and so are you, and you, and you, and you, and you. . . " Each of us is wonderful in our own ways. See yourself as wonderful, not better and not worse than others but not the same. Your uniqueness is your greatest value to the world. No one else can see the world from your perspectives. That gives you insights others do not have and those insights can benefit society.

If you are dealing with failure or fear failure I encourage you to do some research and learn about failures of individuals who have become household names. Here are some successful people who failed before they succeeded.

Researching successful individuals who failed at one point in time, like those in the list below, can help you realize that failure is just a part of success. Hint: Look for the failure(s) they experienced before success.

Michael Jordan	Oprah Winfrey	J. K. Rowling
Soichiro Honda	Tony Robbins	John Paul Mitchell
Sidney Poitier	Albert Einstein	Marilyn Monroe
Abraham Lincoln	Garth Brooks	Orville and Wilbur Wright
Akio Morita	Bill Gates	Harland David Sanders
Steven Spielberg	Stephen King	Winston Churchill
Steve Jobs	Charles Darwin	Ludwig van Beethoven
John Grisham	Dale Carnegie	Theodor Seuss Giesel
Elvis Presley	The Beatles	Louisa May Alcott
Charles Schultz	Jack London	Stephanie Meyer
Tom Landry	Joe Torres	Walt Disney
Thomas Edison	R.H. Macy	

Every adversity, every failure, every heartache,
carries with it the seeds of an equal or greater benefit.
Napoleon Hill

Fear of Failure

This question is from a University student who picked his major based on his earning potential and not what he is most interested in learning, *"How can I stop being depressed when I am not studying what I want to study but I am afraid I will not be able to earn enough if I learn what I am interested in learning?"*

Your best future will come from pursing what interests you. Happy people are more successful and have better lives than unhappy people.

There is a study that followed the lives men who went to Harvard in the 1930's. Before I read that study, I assumed that everyone with a Harvard education did well. What the study found was that happier members of the group had the sort of success you expect someone with the benefit of a Harvard education to have, but the unhappy members of the class:
- Experienced business failures
- Had more divorces
- Were far more likely to become alcoholics
- Some committed suicide
- Had less career success

There are people in every sort of career who make a great living. There is a story about a teacher who worked with disadvantaged students and ended up doing very well financially because he was very good at helping children. They made a movie called *The Ron Clark Story* about him. Most people will tell you a teacher can't make good money, but if there is an exception, you too, can be an exception, but only if you don't believe the rule.

If you look, there are people in most occupations who defy the odds and make more money than most people in that profession. They don't limit themselves to doing what others do and the ones who do great love what they do.

Confidently follow the things that energize you and make you come alive. Your life will be better.

Job Interview Failure

Were you actually *refused* a job, or was another candidate simply viewed as a better choice for *that particular job?* Some jobs have hundreds of applicants and to feel *refused* because they selected another candidate is being very harsh on yourself. Try seeing it as one step closer to getting a job. Even if you did crash and burn during the interview, you got some experience and you now know that you need to practice. Ask a family member or friend to give you mock interviews so you can practice and ask them to be hard on you so you're ready for anything that comes up.

Positive Affirmations (Advanced)

Positive Affirmations reduce stress when they are used correctly.[150] The key to successful affirmations is not reaching too far. If you say an affirmation and your mind responds by arguing with the statement, you've attempted to reach too far. It isn't that you won't be able to get to where you want to be, you just need to take smaller steps. Used incorrectly, affirmations are probably the most damaging common technique. It is important to know how to use them correctly.

You can do affirmations from any emotional Zone as long as the affirmation is believable from your current position. Positive affirmations are one of the most widely taught techniques and they probably cause the most harm. They cause harm, not because the process is bad or defective, but because they are counter-productive if you do not believe the affirmation. [151]

For example, if the statement "I am good enough" receives backlash, be more specific and affirm that you're good at something specific. Once you get your mind thinking about one thing it doesn't argue about that you're good at, other thoughts will come to you.

Don't keep trying an affirmation if you get backlash. Take a smaller step. If you keep trying, the arguing that happens in your mind will make your current belief (the one your mind is arguing to protect) more established and it will be more difficult to change.

Positive affirmations are positive statements that affirm or attempt to train your mind toward a more positive mental attitude. They are useful when used correctly. Positive self-affirmations can speed emotional recovery from slights others make toward you, including racial or gender related comments or actions. These can help employees recover from perceived stereotype threats. [152]

Positive affirmations can increase our confidence. Positive affirmations can boost self-esteem and self-image. A well-known affirmation that originated on Saturday Night Live is:

I'm Good Enough, I'm Smart Enough, and Doggone It, People Like Me!

Affirmations can cover any area of life, relationships, health, career, and even fun.

I love the wisdom of my body. Every cell knows what to do and does it well.
The right words come to me at the right time.
I am wise.
I am young and beautiful.
I know what to do.
I am loved.
I have the skills and knowledge I need to succeed.
My timing will be perfect today and I will make people laugh.
My emotions guide me toward my goals.
People like me because I like people.
I will do my best to see the potential in others.
I am kind.
I am love.
I am a sought after and valued employee.
I am the director of my life.

Vary your affirmations using first person and third person. *Jeanine, you've got this!* activates different parts of the brain than *I have this* activates. Remember to focus your self-talk on what you want rather than pushing against what you don't want. *Jeanine, you can do* this will produce far better results than *Jeanine, don't screw this up.*

The other aspect that can arise subtly is a sense of fear or lack of safety. If you're affirming, *I am safe*, but you feel unsafe as you say it the affirmation heightens your fear. Rather than your mind arguing you may simply feel the fear in sensations in your body. If you are in a safe situation, use logic to increase your sense of safety. Think about the aspects of your situation that should keep you safe. If you aren't safe, it is time to take (or, at a minimum, plan) actions you can take to get safe. Affirmations won't keep you safe if you make unsafe choices.

One way to work on positive affirmations is to recognize where you currently stand, then create small steps between the two positions. This exercise can be done on very specific topics or very general topics. It is easier to begin with broader topics and then move on to more specific topics after you have experience with the process. Use statements that are positive—as if they are true now. "I am" statements are powerful when you do affirmations.

Where you are: _____
Where you want to be: _____
Realistic steps:
Then repeat and stabilize.

Example:

Where I am: *I am not happy with how often I exercise.*

Where I want to be: *I want to exercise more and feel satisfied with the amount of exercise I do.*

I'm not exercising enough because I have not made it enough of a priority.
I can make exercise a higher priority in my life.
It would be easier if I did exercise I like—it would make it easier for me to make it a priority.
I like to dance.
I can make a commitment to dance every day for twenty minutes.
I will dance every day for twenty minutes.
I will make play lists of music that makes me want to dance.
Moving my body more feels good.
I like moving my body.
I can do this.
I am capable of exercising as much as I desire.
My body is strong and will be stronger still because I am moving more.
I can live in a way where I am happier with how much I move.
I like understanding that I can change my habits more easily by first changing my thoughts.
I am getting the hang of this.
I feel good about how much I will exercise now.

Expectant Questions (Advanced)

Expectant questions are more powerful than positive affirmations.

> Self-talk forces the frontal lobe of your brain to focus on the task at hand.
> Rin Mitchell (Big Think)

I was excited as soon as I read the new research about expectant questions. It makes sense given the way our brains work. Asking a question prompts the brain to look for answers.

Affirmations that stretch too far can backfire, but questions don't have that downside. I tested the process by asking "How could I get to the moon?" The first thoughts I had in response were trains of thought that could lead to actionable answers. When I asked other questions, such as "How can I get this book to best seller status?" a lot of actionable answers immediately come to my mind. When I asked "How can I best help clients with a specific issue?" actionable thoughts come to mind immediately.

A Positive Affirmation states: *I can do this.*
An Expectant Question asks: *How can I do this?*

Try this process the next time you need a solution. Just turn it into a question and see how your mind responds. Here are some lead-ins to questions that get the brain working productively:

How can I...
What should I do in order to...
Who should I contact to help me...
What do I need to accomplish... (i.e. to prepare myself for _____)
How can I best...
Where is the best place to...
When should I...
Which method would be best in this situation...
Which breakout session should I choose?
Why should I use this?
Is there something that would be better than what I am considering?
How can I illustrate this simply?
What analogy will provide a clear example?
How can I heal...?
How can I help this patient decide to adhere to instructions...?

Expectant questions tie in with the origins of my own work. A professional asked me why I was so resilient in 1995. I didn't even know I was resilient when he asked me that question. I recognized that if I was more resilient than many others and I could figure out why, I would be able to help other people. I began asking "What makes some people thrive in spite of adversity?"

Over the years many people told me it was not possible to answer a broad question like mine but my intuitive guidance contradicted their perspective. Today I feel I know the answer fully and it began with asking a question and continuing to ask the same question until I was satisfied.

Today my guiding question is "How can I best communicate what I've learned about human thriving to as many people as possible?" As I began asking this question analogies and diagrams began coming to me even though I never considered myself to be good at creating either of these.

Positive Reframing (Advanced)

Positive reframing is a powerful tool. It takes something undesired and finds a positive aspect to it and chooses to focus on that positive aspect. This can feel like an impossible task if you've never done it. With practice your mind will begin looking for the silver lining in the first moment that an undesired situation comes about.

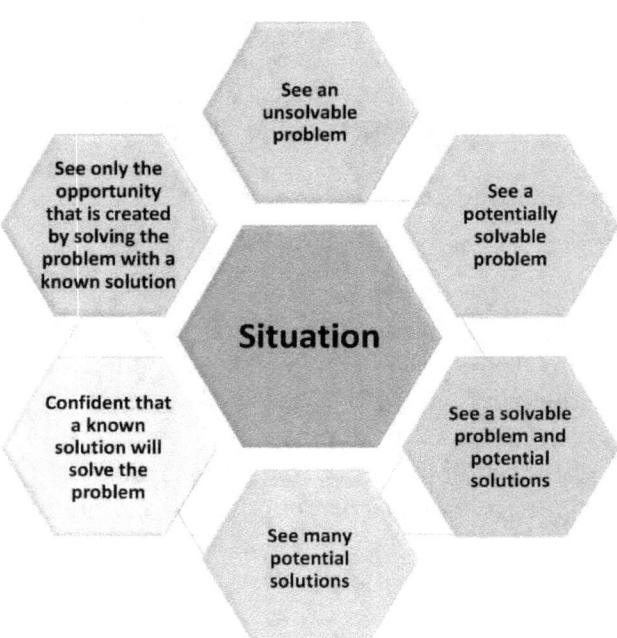

After applying *The Smart Way*™ to the way I live my life, I realized that where I would have once perceived an unsolvable problem I began seeing the potential to solve problems. The way my mind perceived situations I encountered gradually shifted until my first automatic response was focused on opportunities the situation provided. It didn't mean I reveled in the problem but once the problem exists it is best to make the most of it. In reality, all the perspectives on the illustration exist. They are always there. Inspiration is being able to see the best possible perspective and helping others move to more empowered perspectives (closer to the best possible perspective).

Some people refer to the silver lining as *gifts in the wound*. I have come to believe that there are always gifts in the wound. When we lost Prince (The Artist) to opioid overdose the conversation changed. No longer were opioids a problem of nameless, faceless addicts. Now the problem has the face of someone the world loved and mourns.

When we lost Robin Williams to suicide I was days away from publishing my second book, *Prevent Suicide: The Smart Way*™. I held off on publishing it because I felt the world was too raw and felt some guilt that I hadn't written it sooner because then maybe I could have saved the national treasure that Robin Williams was from such a lonely and senseless demise. His death breathed renewed life into the campaign to end stigma and to find solutions that will stop the loss of lives to suicide.

We wouldn't have chosen these situations but once they are here we must embrace the gifts they bring if we want to feel as good as we are capable of feeling. Given a choice, we would never choose the gift if it meant we would have to choose the situation that gives rise to it. But once the situation occurs we don't have a choice about whether it will happen. Our only choice is our response to it.

A friend of mine lost his daughter last year, 10 years past the age he was initially told to expect her to survive. The loss was devastating to him but at the same time he can be grateful for the advances and hard work of the medical community that gave both of them those extra years together. Afterwards, he realized that he had been under constant stress wondering if this trip to the hospital would be the last and that he might have enjoyed her even more if he'd worried less. It's too late to face her challenges differently but he can help others and he can face his own and his wife's later years differently than he would have if he hadn't gained this insight.

Look for Silver Lining (Advanced and Transformational)

In the spirit of,

If life gives you lemons, make lemonade

Situation	*Potential Silver Lining*

Make a mistake	• Learn what not to do
	  • If you don't, it is very unlikely it will be repeated
	  • What led to it; avoid that in the future
	• Share what you've learned and help others avoid the same mistake
	• After a mistake you're better than you were before the mistake because you've learned something you didn't know

End of a relationship	• Opportunity for someone better to enter your life

Disability	• Opportunity to help/inspire others
	  o Christopher Reeve
	  o Sujit K. Reddy (empowerment speaker born with spina bifida)
	  o Jon Morrow (can only move his eyes and mouth – inspirational writer)

Death of a child	• Make it meaningful
	  • Dr. Darren R. Weissman (inspirational author)
	  • Candy Lightner (founded MADD)

Being fired	• Find a job better suited to your skills and talents, which may mean a better job that you find more satisfying.
Being laid off	• Find a job that you've grown into but wouldn't have looked for without the motivation of a lay-off. • An opportunity to ask yourself, "What do I want to do?"
Being abused	• Opportunity to realize how strong you are and to help others realize the same. •

Savoring (Advanced)

Wiki does a great job defining savoring in the way it is intended here:
Savoring is the use of thoughts and actions to increase the intensity, duration, and appreciation of positive experiences and emotions.

Anything you enjoy can be savored. It can be the present moment. An example is mindfully savoring the fresh berries you're eating. It can be savoring a treasured memory from your past. It can be savoring a feeling, like confidence. It can be savoring anticipation of a future experience.

Savoring is deliberately choosing to think thoughts that feel good to you and especially thoughts that do not evoke a downside. Remembering pleasurable experiences with a mate who is no longer in your life is fine if you can do it without the bitter-sweetness of the relationship being over creeping into your mind. If you can find a stance that appreciates that you had those experiences, your past becomes a treasure trove of memories to savor.

Think of savoring as something comprised of pure pleasure. There is no attention to lack when you savor. You don't wish:
- o   You were elsewhere.
- o   You were with someone else.
- o   You were in a body that feels or looks better.
- o   That some aspect of now was different than it is.

You appreciate what you are thinking about fully. As long as it brings you to a feeling of pure appreciation you can savor the same thing repeatedly. If it stops feeling uplifting, savor something else. One of the things I like to savor is **Happy Places** I've created in my mind. One of my *Happy Places* is a yacht with a full crew that I use to sail around the world, always in warm locations. I do different things in this *Happy Places*. Sometimes I just enjoy the rocking of the boat as I bask in the sun. Other times I have imaginary conversations with people I love and sometimes with people I'd like to meet. Sometimes I fish. When I go to my *Happy Places* I can do anything I want. It's an especially wonderful place to go when your body is having a root canal.

Because we now know that sustained positive emotions "predict physical heath, including lower levels of the stress hormone cortisol" [153] you can enjoy your savoring without feeling you should be doing something more productive. Savoring is good for you.

You can plan your life so that you always have something you are looking forward to that you can savor before you do it. I love to travel and usually plan my trips well ahead of time. One time I decided to go on a cruise just six weeks before it sailed. Afterwards I noticed that I didn't get to enjoy the cruise before the cruise. Normally I spend time savoring a trip before the actual trip. After noticing a big difference, I decided to plan my trips further in advance and to spend time savoring trips I intend to take but haven't yet booked.

If you make a habit of using your commute time to savor the aspects of your day that you enjoyed and connect it to your why, your work will feel more meaningful and enriched.

You know savoring is working if you feel good while you're savoring. Have fun with it.

Strengths (Adaptive)

Everyone has character strengths and areas where we are not so strong. Find, recognize, and embrace your strengths.

- Wisdom and Knowledge: creativity, curiosity, judgment, love of learning, perspective
- Courage: bravery, perseverance, honesty, zest
- Humanity: love, kindness, social intelligence
- Justice: teamwork, fairness, leadership
- Temperance: forgiveness, humility, prudence, self-regulation
- Transcendence: appreciation of beauty and excellence, gratitude, hope, humor, spirituality [154]

The Smart Way™ builds strengths associated with positive outcomes including:

- Autonomous Intrinsic Motivation
- Positivity/optimism
- Growth Mindset
- Emotional Intelligence
- Authenticity
- Internal Locus of Control
- Healthy self-esteem
- Metacognitive Skills
- Positive goal-setting
- Positive self-image
- Physical, Mental, Emotional, and Behavioral Health
- Acceptance of responsibility for actions and results

Adaptive Coping
Skill and confidence are an unconquered army.
George Herbert (1593-1632) British poet

Adaptive Coping generally involves increasing your level of skill. Adaptive Coping Skills are complimentary to Advanced Coping Strategies. Applying Advanced Coping Strategies before implementing Adaptive Coping Strategies improves the results you achieve. For example, using Advanced Coping Strategies to reduce stress without requiring a situation to change increases the cognitive capacity you have available for problem-solving. You will be able to identify better solutions after you use Advanced Coping Strategies than you would have if you went straight to problem solving.

Anger management is an Adaptive Coping style that can become unnecessary when you frequently use Advanced Coping Strategies. When you practice your emotional state into good feeling emotions frequently, anger is not near the surface. Things that would have once made you angry (because they seemed like big problems) no longer make you angry because they seem like minor inconveniences that you are fully capable of handling.

Curiosity

Our brains naturally protect our beliefs regardless of whether doing so is beneficial to us. By adopting an attitude of curiosity toward new information the brain's automatic rejection of new information that conflicts with existing beliefs can be bypassed.

Your Emotional Guidance will support the curious approach.

Planning (Adaptive Coping)

Planning in advance is helpful. Several ways you can plan to reduce stress and increase success in advance include:
- Setting long-term goals
- Establishing mission statements for every area of your life (pg. 183)
- Setting your intentions about what you want from your activities
- Plan to avoid temptations

For example, when someone is stressed they sometimes watch television shows for hours on end or surf the internet with the result they don't go to bed when they should. If they set a timer that will require them to get up or be continually irritated, it can serve as the nudge they need to take the action they intend.

Another example is tequila. I like the way I feel when I drink tequila but I don't like what it does to my inhibitions. I made a rule for myself that I can only drink tequila when I am with my husband. If he's not with me, I don't drink tequila.

The first time I found myself living alone as a single adult, I sat down and made a list of rules for myself. Making your own rules, ones that support your long-term goals, is very different from someone else imposing rules on you. I set curfews based on which day of the week it was that helped me fulfill my long term goal to complete my education while maintaining my reputation as a reliable employee in my full-time job. When you're at a party and you tell people you have to get home because you have a curfew few will ask you who set the curfew. Complying with your own rules feels completely different than adhering to rules someone else set.

Establishing our intentions is setting micro goals. Before a meeting I might set the intention that I'll have the right words at the right time. In many ways, setting intentions are situation specific affirmations made as the activity begins.

Mission statements are discussed in the Setting Limits section of MWME.

Establishing clear, long-term goals helps you see the progress you're making which can contribute to your sense of accomplishment. Establishing 1, 5, 10, and 20 year plans, with as much detail as feels good and no detail that feels forced, works well. You always have the option to change your plan if your interests change.

Social Support (Adaptive)

Social support is a protective factor against physical and mental health issues. It is important to note that, in general, people who feel good emotionally have better relationships with others in every area of their lives. Rather than attempting to develop relationships in order to improve your health and lower your risk of mental illness, work on improving your emotional state and then do what flows naturally from your better feeling emotional state. Individuals who use reappraisal as a coping skill have better interpersonal relationships and those who use suppression have worse interpersonal relationships. [155]

It is important to understand that the perception of emotional support is the source of its benefits. In studies that looked at how individuals perceived social support by comparing their perceptions with the actual support the people they perceived as supportive were willing or able to provide, it was the perception of the presence of support that mattered. [156]

Use criteria that are important to you when you decide who to include in your social circle. It amazes me how many people go out of their way to socialize with people they don't enjoy. Be neighborly with your neighbors but if you don't enjoy their company or share interests in things you love, don't plan to spend your evenings with them. It's possible to get along with nearly anyone. It's possible to survive on cheap fast food, too. But it is so much more enjoyable to sit down to a meal with a server who provides top notch service and a memorable meal. If you make plans with people and find yourself forcing yourself to go, it's probably because you didn't choose your friends wisely. It doesn't make them bad people. They just aren't what you want or need.

When it comes to family, do your best and be satisfied with it. The strategies in this book can smooth out acidic family relationships. Remember, you have to change your perspective. Attempting to change someone else is a lesson in frustration. People who have good social support tend to be optimistic, have healthy self-esteem, an internal locus of control and are more resilient.

Set Limits: Say No (Adaptive)

Saying no is adaptive. Developing a mindset that gives you permission to say no is Transformational. Saying no can be one of the most difficult things to do for someone who has been taught to be selfless, or someone with low self-esteem. There are a variety of methods I've used to increase my ability to say no to extraneous activities that don't support what is most important to me.

Established your own moral code and made a decision to abide by (comply with) your own code. Use the power of making a decision and you'll be able to be more of who you want to be. If there is something you're worried you'll do but you know you don't want to do it, establish rules that you agree (with yourself) to live by. Make a decision that you will live by the rules you establish for yourself. You do not have to share your rules with anyone else.

Decisions have power.

Once you make a decision it is much easier to do what you have decided to do. Decide what you want and then decide that is what you will do. Your Mission Statements will help you develop the rules you want to live by.

Mission Statements

The first step is being very conscious about your own priorities. When I was creating the mission statement for Happiness 1st Institute the idea to create mission statements for all the important areas of my life came to me.

I created mission statements for:
- My life (an overriding statement of purpose)
- My business
- My primary relationship
- My relationship with my body
- My relationship with me
- My relationship with my health
- My relationship with my children
- My relationship with my parents
- My relationship with my friends

- My relationship with my home
- My relationship with strangers

Mission statements aren't long, drawn out missives. They are concise statements of intention.

Once I had my mission statements I could compare requests to my mission statements and ask myself if the request fit into any of my missions or if it was outside my core missions. I am interested in many things so filling time is never something I want to do with things that don't fit my core missions. I also ask if a new request is something that calls to me (using my Emotional Guidance as guidance).

There are volunteer activities I used to participate in for causes I care about that I no longer do because they didn't support my core missions. When you're a caring person there is a never ending list of causes you'd like to support. One way I make the decisions about which volunteer activities I participate in is whether it is the highest and best use of my skills, knowledge, and talents. For example, I joined my husband volunteering for a USGA golf tournament. I enjoyed the four days I worked and had fun but I kept thinking about the greater contributions I could be making elsewhere and decided I wouldn't do that again.

For years, I volunteered for a conservation organization but the contributions I made could have been done by anyone with basic skills so it wasn't the highest and best use of my skills. If I'm going to be thinking about other things I would rather be doing while I do something I will say no. This was a difficult skill to learn.

It is helpful to have kind answers when you decide to say no.

"I would love to but my other commitments don't allow me enough time to give you the commitment you're asking for. I hope your event is very successful."

"I'm sorry but I'm already stretched thin. I am honored that you thought of me."

Sometimes somebody wants to do something for me that would take time I don't have and I use "I'll take the thought for the deed. I so appreciate your kindness."

When my children were younger I would use, "I am spending as much time with them now while they still want to be with me."

You don't have to give a reason but I found that doing so stopped repeated requests. Just be authentic.

It's easier to say *"no"* if you have established your priorities in advance. In a study that interviewed physicians who were known in the community for their resilience, one of the findings that supported their resilience was the ability to set limits. [157] Learning to set limits increases job satisfaction which decreases burnout. [158]

Sleep (Adaptive)

A good night's sleep goes a long way toward helping you become more of who you want to be and helps you think healthy thoughts. Stress often interferes with the ability to get a good night's sleep. There are some things you can do to improve your ability to sleep.

- Decide how many hours of sleep you need. There are wide individual variances and the better your emotional state, the less sleep you tend to need. Determine when you will go to bed by subtracting how many hours of sleep you need from when you need to get up. If you are going to engage in other bedroom activities before you go to sleep or after you wake-up, add time for those activities. If you frequently have trouble going to sleep, add time for time it takes for you to get to sleep.
- If you have a tendency to think about things that are bothering you or things you have to do the next day, write them down before you go to bed. This helps your mind relax because you won't forget to do them.
- There are many other ways to improve the quality of your sleep including limiting screen time for an hour before bed. For readily available suggestions just use a search engine and search, "improve sleep quality." Try different strategies to see what works best for you.

When you wake up:

Spend a few minutes being intentional about the day you want at the very beginning of the day to establish a baseline that improves the outcome.

Set your intentions for the day. Reinforce positive thoughts about what will happen during the day. Affirm your intention to show up as your best possible self and maintain or improve your relationships with important people in your life. Spend a few minutes feeling emotions you want to feel during the day by remembering or imagining situations where you would feel those desired emotions.

This morning ritual primes your mind to focus on things that will support the emotions you've informed it you want to feel.

Meditation (Palliative to Transformational)

There are many different meditation techniques. Meditation can be a compliment to *The Smart Way*™ but unless your practice is very rigorous (daily), it isn't likely to reprogram your brain.

Meditation is a wonderful practice. I use a couple of types of meditation in my own practice including one that simply allows my mind to rest and a loving heart meditation that helps me find peace and love for all of humanity in my own heart. Loving-Kindness meditation has been shown to improve compassion and resilience. [159]

Instruction in meditation is beyond the scope of this book.

Religion/Spirituality

Many studies indicate there are mental health benefits of spiritual or religious beliefs. On the other hand, there are religious beliefs that can detract from mental health. "Religious beliefs" is too broad of a brush to use to state that something is always good. A survey of interns at Yale indicated that belief in the utility of prayer and meditation and a belief that their life has a purpose during times of hardship (indicating flexibility and purpose in the belief system) were protective against burnout.[160]

Use your Emotional Guidance to determine if your worldview uplifts you or makes you feel worse. If it makes you feel better, it is beneficial to you.

Emotional Guidance is supported by the texts of major religions. See Appendix IV for some examples.

Unhealthy Habits of Thought (Identify and Change)

Pessimism is a contagious disease;
Optimism is a miraculous medicine.
William Arthur Ward

Certain habits of thought lead to undesired outcomes. Changing habits of thought is one of the fastest ways to improve the outcomes you experience. Chronic negative emotions indicate you are experiencing chronic stress.

Life + Unhealthy habits of thought = Chronic Stress

Unhealthy Habits of Thought include:
- Awfulizing or Castrophizing
    - Permanent, Pervasive, Personal
- Negative Rumination
- Negative co-rumination
- Low Self-esteem
- Low Self-efficacy beliefs
- Low Core Self-evaluations
- Pessimism
- Shoulding
- Self-criticism
- Surface-Thinking
- Suppressing emotions
- Fixed Mindset

Before the new paradigm of emotions as guidance was understood, the fact that experiencing and suppressing negative emotion were both bad for our heart health perplexed researchers. When the new paradigm of emotions as guidance, much like road signs providing directions, it becomes clear that we are not designed to experience sustained negative emotion. Experiencing chronic negative emotion is optional.

Regulate means to control, supervise, or maintain something with the goal of having it operate properly. Emotion regulation means adjusting our emotions. Some emotion regulation is not healthy. If we regulate our emotions in ways that cause us to be inauthentic, it has negative side effects. In order to regulate emotions and produce authentic emotions we have to do it at the level of thought.

The adverse outcome of negative emotions is not the result of experiencing them; it is the result of the stress our mind and body are experiencing. Sustained negative emotions are just an indictor to let us know about the stress. The healthy way to live is to pay attention to negative emotions and use healthy strategies to find better feeling perspectives.

We have the capacity to regulate our emotions to *"increase, maintain, or decrease positive and negative emotions."* [161] Conscious reappraisal of negative emotions is often not done *"even though proactive regulation would have led to better emotional states. This is both a skills gap and a societal tolerance for negative emotions that is much higher than we should allow if we want to live our best possible lives."* [162]

When habits of thought include the following, constructing new habits will lead to better outcomes. Don't be overwhelmed. Changing one belief can change more than one habit of thought.

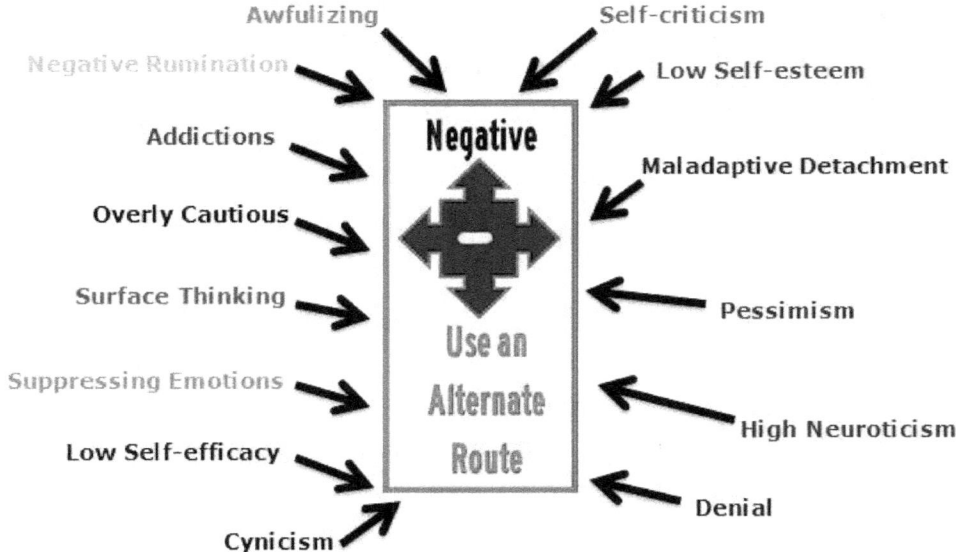

The choices we make are largely dependent upon the strategies we know how to use. Your Emotional Guidance will provide immediate feedback letting you know what works and what doesn't work.

It's not behaviors or lifestyles that cause negative feelings. Depending on how a person perceives it, the same behavior or lifestyle could make one person happy and another miserable.

Someone who has strong religious feelings against sex prior to marriage will not feel good if they are violating their beliefs with their lifestyle or behavior. They can change their behavior or their beliefs but until one or the other changes they can't be happy living that lifestyle.

Someone else who doesn't have strong feelings against premarital sex could greatly enjoy the lifestyle.

Anxiety

Anxiety is often because you're thinking more about what others think about you than about what you think about others. If you're judgmental about others you may expect they are the same about you. Most people don't think about anyone else often or long. Business literature is now saying that the attention span averages 8 seconds. How much can they think about you for 8 seconds?

What someone else thinks about you reflects a lot about their beliefs and their emotional state and very little about you. Most people think other people's opinions of them reflect some truth about them. Happy people will generally find something about you that they like. Unhappy people will generally find something about you that they don't like.

Many people perceive their negative thoughts as continuous and/or uncontrollable. They aren't uncontrollable. The person who thinks they are uncontrollable cannot control them because they have not learned strategies that will help them change their automatic habits of thought.

The belief that thoughts cannot be controlled makes the situation feel permanent. Just learning that there are ways to control automatic thoughts leaves the door open for change to occur.

Unhealthy habits of thought can lead to depression, anxiety, and other forms of mental illness.

Habits of Thought

It is important to realize that habits of thought are learned. They are not personality traits you're born with even though many people believe pessimism and other personality characteristics are fixed traits. Progress in understanding personality and mental health made during the past decade led to changes in the scientific view but most people won't know about that change for a long time. News published in scientific journals tends to travel slowly, even when it has the potential to help people enjoy life more. That's one reason I love my hobby of reading scientific journals. I don't want to wait and I don't think you should either, which is why I write.

Most importantly, anyone with the desire to do so can change their habits of thought to make their life better. The techniques aren't difficult to apply and using them feels good so there are immediate rewards and even greater long-term rewards. It is not necessary to evaluate and analyze why you think the way you think in order to change your habits of thought.

A habit of thought is the result of repeatedly thinking in one way. Repetitive thoughts create neuropathways in your brain that are easier for your neurons to travel than alternate routes. You always have the ability to consciously direct your mind to use another route. Think of it this way. If you walk along a certain sidewalk everyday on your way home from work and they open an ice cream shop on that road that you don't want to go in but find it difficult to resist when you see it, you can consciously decide to walk on another street to avoid the ice cream shop. It might take a while for the new route to become a habit, but if you keep taking the new route you will eventually not even have to think about walking the new route.

Creating new neuropathways that support healthy habits of thought is the same process but it only involves the mental part, not the physical walking part.

At first, even after changing the route you take home from work you will sometimes automatically find yourself in front of the ice cream shop where you don't want to be if you're not thinking about it. That's just because your neuropathways aren't completely changed yet. It's no problem to retrace your steps and take the route you want to take. Eventually your automatic path will be the route that doesn't go by the ice cream shop.

You may see changes within a month of deliberate effort but it can take three months of consistent effort to re-write old neuropathways. Be patient with yourself. It is not as if that is the only thing you can do for three months. You are still living your life; you're just laying the groundwork for a better future for yourself. Don't criticize yourself if you forget and travel the old path. Just recognize it for what it is—neuro pathways that are still easier to follow than the ones you want to travel. When it happens, reinforce the neuro-pathways you want.

OCD

You cannot STOP thinking about something by trying to stop thinking about it because when you try to stop thinking about the thing you don't want to think about, you are thinking about it. You can, however, decide to think about something else and every time you begin thinking about the topic you don't want to think about, have something more pleasant to think about already planned as a diversion. This is also true of actions but change thoughts first.

KNOW that you can change your thoughts, even habitual thoughts. You have control. *You think them; they do not think you.* I would not label repetitive thoughts with a label that gives them more power than they deserve. With consistent effort, anyone can change their thought paths. The more power given to labels, the harder it is to believe in your ability to change and to find the hope that you can do it. Labels have power. Only use the ones you want to keep.

Repetitive thoughts, whether they are assigned a label (such as OCD) or not are the result of a neural pathway that is easier to travel due to repetitive use. New paths can be created. You can consciously choose to think about something you want to think about each time a repetitive thought you don't want comes to mind. If you're persistent in changing the subject your mind is focused on, your automatic thoughts will eventually change. Be patient. You did not develop your current habits of thought overnight. Our ability to develop automatic processes is a wonderful human characteristic.

Plan in advance what you will think about instead of what you don't want to think about. If necessary, write it down where you have access to it.

Some people put post-it notes around their homes reminding them to think about the things they want to think about. Don't write a note that says, "Don't think about X." It will only make you think about it more. Don't write a note that says, "Think about what you want to think about." Be specific. If I were doing that I would write notes like this:

Think about the meadow by Antelope Lake.
Think about the warm sun caressing my body.
Think about floating on the water.
Think about (upcoming trip).

I can ride my bicycle without thinking about pedaling or how to turn the handlebars in the right direction. I can do all of the physical actions, and make decisions about those actions, below my level of conscious awareness while I carry on a conversation with someone riding with me or simply soak up spectacular mountain vistas. I can do it while my mind wanders and even while my mind plots out how to write a book.

But the fact that we can do things on autopilot does not mean we have to. If my leg cramps and pedaling in the usual way is painful, I have the ability to consciously decide to shift my foot on the pedal in a position that provides relief. In the same way, someone who has repetitive thoughts can decide to think about something differently or to think about the same thing in a different way.

If you lived in a house near the woods and took a walk each morning, initially you would probably travel the path with the least amount of brush and branches to move, etc. Perhaps you would follow a deer trail. After a while, walking that path every day would create a larger path that is even easier to walk. If you decided that you wanted to walk a different route it would be more difficult, you would have branches to move, perhaps logs to walk over, possibly thorns protruding into the path, etc. You can do it, but it is easier to walk the existing path. Also, sometimes, when you were not consciously focused on taking the new path you might automatically revert to the old path, and not realize it until you discover yourself quite a ways down the old path. It's not a big deal. Just turn around and walk the new path.

Many of my students relate to this analogy because they've done it at some point in their lives. After moving to a new home or job, they moved and found themselves automatically heading to their former home after a long day at work or to the old job on a morning when they are tired. It often happens a week or so into the new routine when they were being less conscious about the fact that they are going somewhere different. The new route had not become automated and the old neuropathways kicked in. The old neuro circuits are still easier to use than the new route. Eventually your circuits re-wire. Once they do, you drive to your new home or job even if you are on autopilot.

The biggest key is not to be upset when you find your thoughts on the old path. Just recognize where you are and move to where you want to be.

Criticizing yourself for being on the old path is counter-productive. When we decide a thought-path no longer serves us we have to clear a little brush to walk a new path but it is worth the effort and it is only difficult at first. The second time is easier than the first and by the 10th; you cannot even recall how difficult it was the first time.

The same process can be applied to repetitive motions. In my 20's, every time I got upset I would clean house. Cleaning calmed me down. At some point I began to suspect that my husband was angering me on purpose so I'd do all the housework. I substituted reading for cleaning. If I realized I was cleaning to deal with anger, I began reading.

Anger

Frequent anger shares a surprising number of similarities with OCD. An individual who feels angry easily and often has developed habits of thought that have carved neuropathways in his brain that make it easier to become angry than to have other responses.

The advice for planning other responses given for OCD will help rein in chronic anger.

Explosive anger can be because you're not in touch with your emotions so you ignore earlier, more subtle negative emotions like frustration. Paying attention to how you feel and using Advanced Stress Management Strategies sooner can help you break this habit.

Low self-esteem can also increase anger because low self-esteem makes it is easier to feel threatened.

Make a decision to change in the way you want to change. Believe you can change. Take any steps you can think of to begin and don't give up.

Catastrophizing/Awfulizing

Castrophizing or Awfulizing are essentially the same thing given two different names by well-known people in psychology.* Catastrophizing[163] or awfulizing† reflects the presence of unhealthy habits of thought that lead to perceiving situations as: [164]

- Permanent
- Pervasive
- Personal

It is better to focus on being your best and believing that you are prepared to be successful, or to recognize that you need training and pursue it than doubting your ability to be successful. Focus on being your best doesn't mean seeing yourself as infallible in ways that would make you

---

* Awfulizing (Beck) and Castrophizing (Seligman)

† Awfulizing is the term Albert Ellis used to describe thinking that problems were permanent and pervasive. Ellis's work was based on studying of Asian, Greek, Roman and modern philosophers.

careless. It means managing risks. In complex situations, rather than worry about your effectiveness, ask "What is the best way to achieve this successfully?" The question will direct your brain to answer the question. Believing, "I can find the best solution," which can involve asking others to share their knowledge and experience is beneficial.

Challenging intrusive thoughts about potential failures can take away their power. There is a path between irrational confidence and irrational fear that can be found and followed. Make decisions to take, or not take on, a challenge carefully but once made, align with the decision and don't second guess yourself unless something changes one of the criterions you used when you made the decision.

It might be easier to think of it relative to another subject. Suppose someone gets married and continually questions whether they made the right decision. Imagine the outcome of that scenario compared to someone who gets married and decides that they are going to do the best they can to make the best of the relationship.* The first person would be more stressed and continually second-guess their decision. The second person would be focused on making the marriage the best it can be.

Manage risks without worrying about them. What does that mean? It means that if you think of something else to do, do it, but if all you're doing is worrying if you made the right decision and imagining scenarios that don't turn out well, you're not helping yourself and you're not improving the outcome.

Castrophizing is a habit of thought well worth changing. It is associated with sub-clinical paranoia [165] and correlated with depression and chronic depression. [166] Castrophizing and awfulizing are descriptive terms. Although it is a children's story, *Chicken Little* (or *Henny Penny*) provides a good example. In the story an acorn falls on Henny Penny's head and she concludes that the sky is falling.

An example I see often these days is a young adult whose first love has ended the relationship and the person is very concerned that it means no one will ever love them. Ask a room full of mature adults "Who is married to their first love?" and very few will raise their hands. It is common for our first relationship to end. The end of a romantic relationship does not mean we are unlovable or that we will never find love. The tendency to take the end of a romantic relationship and translate it so that it means you'll never be loved is an indicator of an unhealthy habit of thought.

I don't tell people exactly what to think. I teach them that if they think in this way (i.e. Awfulizing) their perception and experience of life will not be as good as it could be under the same circumstances perceived in a healthier way.

---

* I'm not inferring staying in an untenable situation. I'm referring to day-to-day interactions that are normal in every relationship.

Example:
Awfulizing or Castrophizing thought:
"My love interest ended our relationship. I might not be lovable and it is possible that no one will ever love me."
Healthy thoughts:
"My love interest ended our relationship. I learned a lot from the relationship. Now I know more about what I want in a relationship and am free to find someone who wants me that I want."
Even healthier:

"My love interest ended our relationship. I learned a lot from the relationship. Now I know more about what I want in a relationship and am free to find someone who wants me that I want. I appreciate everything I learned from the relationship and hope he/she finds what she is looking for. I am excited about finding a new love interest that will be a better match for me. I'm not in a hurry for that to happen, but I do not expect it to take years. It will occur naturally and feel good when it happens. In the meantime, I can remember lessons I learned in my first relationship. I was not always the person I wanted to be in that relationship. I can work on making myself into the me I want to be. I'm looking forward to becoming the best possible me. I won't beat myself up for any mistakes I made. I'll simply learn from them and appreciate the opportunity to understand more about myself and others."

This doesn't have to be about the loss of a romantic relationship. Do you have a tendency to see things as permanent and pervasive? Any situation can be viewed as a relationship including, but not limited to:

- Diets
- Vacations
- Exercise plans
- Any goal
- Crime
- Failures
- Job interviews
- Jobs
- Friendships
- Business ventures
- Bad news
- People being trustworthy

Do you think or talk in terms of always, never, only, or constantly? Do you take a single situation and apply it to the entire world, to your whole life, or to your entire relationship?

Don't worry if you do. It's just a habit of thought that isn't serving you well. In fact, if you're doing this it means there is an easy way to make your life feel better. When a person who awfulizes or castrophizes changes their habits of thought their life feels better even though the circumstances haven't changed at all. They're just happier (or less depressed). Their stress level declines and they feel more empowered to change things they don't like. They feel less beaten up by the things they don't like about their life.

Set an *intention* to be aware of times when you or others use always, never, only, constantly, everyone, no one or any other words that have those meanings. Then active refute their truth. Look for and reinforce evidence the situation is not permanent or pervasive.

An intention is an affirmation about what you're going to do. It is like a goal but is often associated with what you're going to do in the near future. For example,

Today I am going to be aware when I use or hear the words always, never, only, and constantly.

Refuting is rejecting the truth of the statement. You can refute it in the privacy of your own mind, you can voice your rejection of the thought or words out loud to yourself, or to others. You can write in a journal (or a blog) to refute the thought that you no longer want to accept.

Let's stick with the example of the ending of a relationship because it is easy for *most* people to relate to that scenario. (Note that I didn't say it was easy for everyone because that would be permanent and pervasive.) When I use *most* it is a true statement. If I used everyone it would be a false statement because not everyone has experienced the end of a relationship.

It may seem like I'm being very picky about which words are used. I am. Words matter.

Worry

Learning to use our minds effectively is important. Worry is an unhealthy habit of thought. There is a saying that worry is borrowing trouble from the future. Worry can create problems in the future because the emotions associated with worry are indicators that your body and mind are experiencing stress. Chronic stress increases inflammation and reduces immune function and leads to other undesirable results.

A friend of mine told her daughter that as long as she lived she would worry "because she loved her daughter." I wanted to tell her that if she wanted to live as long as possible and not become a burden to her daughter she would worry less. But like anyone with an ingrained belief, if she is not asking for help with it, telling her that her belief is misguided just makes her defend her current stance. Only people who want help can be helped.

She believes that if you love someone, you will worry about them. Worry makes now (the time) feel worse than it could out of fear that someday something bad will happen—something that usually never happens. She could just as easily practice seeing her daughter as competent and capable.

If you are a worrier, understand that the emotion of worry means, "There is a better-feeling thought you could be having about this exact same subject right now." Worry does not mean your worrisome thoughts are being validated as something you should spend your time worrying about.

That is not to say you should not look at and evaluate problems—but perceive them as solvable—not as insurmountable. Just believing there is a solution, even before you know the solution, eases worries. "I will find a way to solve this problem" is a healthier outlook than, "I'm not capable of solving this problem." If you need help, gathering the resources you need to solve problems is an Adaptive Coping Strategy.

Pessimism

Pessimism is associated with worse life outcomes in health, relationships, career, and longevity. Pessimists lean toward expecting negative outcomes. Pessimists are not as resilient as optimists. There are many aspects that affect these outcomes but the increased stress experienced by someone who has a negative mental attitude is a significant factor.

A pessimist developed habits of thought that focus on the negative aspects of situations, people, and life. A pessimist may believe that the world is basically a bad place (or evil) and that the bad outweighs the good. A pessimist will often dismiss potential solutions to problems without making an attempt to use them because they are convinced the solution will fail, (so why try?). A pessimist is likely to stay home from a new type of event because she is unsure if she'll have fun while an optimist would go because she might have a good time.

Although pessimism and optimism seem like exact opposites it depends on the situation. An optimist can evaluate situations based on facts and reach conclusions that seem pessimistic but it isn't because the optimist thinks things will go wrong if there is a potential for them to go wrong. It's more likely to be a risk management evaluation that makes an optimist decide against a particular action.

The following chart shows potential pessimistic and optimistic thoughts in response to the same situation.

Scenario	*Pessimistic Thoughts*	**Optimistic Thoughts**
The person is laid off	It's going to be hard to find a new job. It's easier	I've learned a lot of new skills in this job so I'm prepared for

	to find a new job when you have one. I'd better sell the house right away so I don't lose it. My spouse is going to be so angry about this. I dread going home.	a better job. This layoff may be just the motivation I need to find a better job. I have some resources to fall back on and people who believe in me so we'll be fine. I'm lucky my spouse believes in me so I don't have to deal with unjustified fear from him/her.
Relationship ends	It's so hard to find a good person to date. I may never find a good mate. I don't know if it's worth the effort.	There were some lovely traits about this person that I'd like in my mate when I find that person. I'm glad I know how much I enjoy those traits in a potential mate so I can look for them. I'm looking forward to finding someone who shares some traits with this person and has some other traits this person lacked.
Not enough money to pay the bills	I can't make it. I'm never going to dig myself out of this hole. I don't know how to find enough income to pay the bills. I have no leeway for unexpected events like that flat tire. Life is hard and then you die.	Things are tight right now but I'll find a way to meet my obligations. There are a lot of ways to make a little bit of extra money. It might even be fun. I'll ask a few of my friends if they know of anything. I'll figure it out.
Calls aren't returned after the 1st date	That was the best date I've had in a long time but she/he must not have liked me because my calls aren't being returned. Just my luck that when I meet someone I like they didn't like me.	That was the best date I've had in a long time and I'm looking forward to talking to him/her soon. I don't know why I haven't been able to get in touch but I'm sure I'll hear back soon. I could tell the interest was mutual.

As you read the descriptions ask yourself what actions the person thinking the thoughts is likely to take to resolve the problem

A pessimist is unlikely to decide to go ahead with a new venture unless his analysis shows it is a sure thing so they are unlikely to lose money in a risky venture but an optimist is likely to earn money in the risky ventures that do come to fruition. Microsoft is an example of a risky investment that paid early investors significant rewards.

Who is more likely to stop for a few drinks before going home after being laid off?

How does that choice impact the spouses confidence in their ability to find a new job quickly?

Who is more likely to be upbeat and friendly on their next date?

Who is more likely to dig a deeper financial hole by accumulating late charges?

Who is more likely to find a way to add some cash to their budget?

Who is more stressed by the financial situation?

Who is going more likely to make the person they liked so much on the first date feel smothered when they finally talk?

Do you see that the thoughts we think affect the actions we take which leads to outcomes that reflect our expectations?

For a long time pessimism was considered a personality trait that we were born with and that wouldn't change much during your lifetime. Personality traits are not nearly as fixed as we once thought they were.[167, 168, 169, 170, 171, 172] Changing beliefs that support a pessimistic outlook helps you become more optimistic. Pessimism is the result of beliefs and habits of thought you developed during your childhood. You can change your habits of thought if you want to by being more conscious about what you choose to think and developing beliefs you want to maintain.

You don't have to figure out why you believed what you believed. It is more than likely that you developed the belief as a young child. To create a new belief that you decide would serve you better, you do not have to fight against the old one. You can simply begin reinforcing beliefs you want to support. You can refute the existing belief when it comes up naturally. If you refute it, affirm the new belief immediately after you refute the old undesired belief.

An individual may be pessimistic in every area of life or in selected areas. Pessimists often believe situations are worse than they are and may perceive solvable problems as unsolvable. Pessimists may:

- Distrust and doubt others intentions
- Believe the worst will happen
- Not feel hope or trust that things will work out well
- Believe the world is evil
- Believe people are bad

Pessimist's lives often reflect their beliefs about life. Negative mental attitudes result in interpreting experiences in a negative light. Where an optimist sees an opportunity a pessimist sees a problem. Both optimists and pessimists live in self-fulfilling prophesies.

Suppressing Emotions

Suppression of emotions is associated with adverse health outcomes including depressive symptoms, decreased mood, and lower levels of well-being. [173] Memory suffers when emotions are suppressed. [174] Suppressing negative emotions and not taking actions to reduce stress when you feel negative emotion are not healthy behaviors. [175]

Given that the purpose of emotions is to guide us toward self-actualization, suppressing emotions is the equivalent of ignoring signs like these:

The consequences of suppressing emotions can be as serious as ignoring these signs; it just takes longer for the damage to occur.

There is a list of emotions in Appendix VIII. Spend a few minutes at least several times a week reading three words from the list and imagining what the words feel like. Allow the feeling(s) associated with the emotion to flow. There is no right or wrong about what you feel. Just feel how each emotion feels to you. Get accustomed to feeling emotions. Your Guidance will be of more value to you when you are more aware of your emotions. You can set intentions to feel when something feels very good or when something feels worse.

Would a person with perfect eyesight get up every morning and blindfold themselves before they begin their day and leave the blindfold on all day, every day? Of course not. Nor would we wear earplugs that prevented us from hearing the voices of our friends and family or the warning honk of a car or the whistle of an oncoming train. Suppressing our emotions is no different than suppressing our eyesight or hearing.

Unfortunately we are still teaching children to suppress their emotions. As a child were you ever told to, "Stop blubbering or I'll give you something to cry about?" as if you would be crying without a reason. This scenario is one example of schooling a child to suppress their emotions. If a child is upset and the parent tries to tell them there is nothing to be upset about the parent is teaching the child to ignore their emotions.

The parent would serve the child better by helping the child perceive the situation from different perspectives. In a recent class, a member of the audience said children weren't capable of this. I clearly recall doing this when I was 8 years old and talking with my best friend about it.

The best way to school a child is to help the child see other ways to perceive the situation because it will serve the child best later on.

If a child is upset because they have to go home from a fun play date remind them that they can look forward to the next time and that they can think about how nice it is they have a friend they enjoy. Those are other ways to perceive the situation. Don't bribe the child with food as in, "If you're good you can have a cookie after dinner." That teaches the child to use food to soothe emotional upset. Don't try to solve the problem for the child because that teaches the child to rely on you to manage their emotions. Your child must develop skill in managing emotions in order to be resilient and thrive later in life.

If you have primed your Emotional Guidance with long-term goals about raising an emotionally healthy child, it will help you know which techniques will serve you best.

Many cultures encourage children and especially male children to suppress their emotions. If you have a tendency to suppress your emotions you can use the intention setting process to increase your awareness of what you're feeling. You can journal about your day and poke around in your mind to identify how you felt. Use the Emotional Guidance Scale to help you identify emotions that are similar to the ones you're aware you're experiencing. An alternative is to notice your energy increasing or decreasing. Lower energy levels indicate increased stress.

One problem I've seen that sometimes comes from being trained to suppress emotions is the person becomes capable of suppressing and ignoring milder emotions like frustration and irritation so they don't address issues while they're still small but when the pressure mounts and they become angry or enraged, they explode. It can seem as if their emotional eruption came out of the blue because they didn't express any of the emotions that led to the outburst.

Learning to be aware of and deal with emotions before they lead to an explosion is one way to stop angry outbursts. As you become aware of your emotions you will find it is easier to become the person you've always wanted to be.

> *The functionality of emotions depends critically on the appraisals that give rise to emotions, the choice and control of the behaviors motivated by emotions, and the socialization and training of emotions. These parameters, whether or not they are considered part of an emotion, must be considered part of what makes emotions functional.* 176p

This quote points to the importance of understanding the purpose and use of emotions and having strategies that give you the ability to regulate your emotions in healthy ways.

When emotions are interpreted as guidance toward self-actualization with negative emotions being the equivalent of your global positioning system (GPS) freaking out and telling you to make a U-turn rather than telling you to punch someone or seek retribution for a wrong. Emotions become functional.

Negative rumination

Negative rumination is thinking about or talking about something that brings forth negative emotions, repeatedly. The actual event may have lasted five minutes but our experience of it could span weeks or months depending on how many times we re-live it or talk about it. Negative rumination is a significant contributor to depression. Instead of ruminating on things that don't feel good to think about, look deeper for the root cause of the situation. The root is where effective solutions can be found.

Rumination is thinking about something that is not pleasant or fun to think about:
- A problem
- A bad experience or traumatic event
- A relationship that doesn't feel the way you want it to feel
- An aspect of your body that you're not happy about
- Etc., etc., etc.

Ruminating thoughts are focused on the symptoms of the problem and possible causes, not on how to solve the problem. Rumination tends to be shallow in that the problem will usually be perceived as if it happened in isolation.

Small steps taken consistently will make a far larger difference than you can currently imagine.

Make a list of things you like to think about because you feel good when you think about them. Pay attention to how you feel. When you find yourself ruminating about something that feels bad, find something else to think about from your list that feels better. Stop giving the thing you're ruminating about air time in your mind of ask questions with the positive expectation of improving the situation or preventing it from happening again. Look for lessons learned.

Your thoughts lead to your emotional state. Change your thoughts and your emotional state will change. You can begin asking yourself, "What did I think that made me feel this way?" and "What else could I think about this situation that would feel better or could I think about something else that feels better when I think of it?"

Co-rumination

Co-rumination is when you get together with others and focus on things that feel bad when you talk about them. Conversations that outline problems and then turn to solutions are Adaptive. Conversations that focus on problems and simply grumble about problems without identifying solutions are not beneficial. Even worse are conversations that focus on problems and lean toward solutions that are not ethical, moral, or legal.

If your interactions typically focus on problems you are probably not aware in-the-moment that you're participating in these conversations that they feel worse than alternatives because you're used to feeling that way. Pay more attention to how you feel, both emotionally and viscerally, as you participate. You will recognize the negative impact it is having on your physiology and psychology. You can absent yourself from these conversations, attempt to steer them toward solutions, or change the subject.

Let's say your significant other told you to STFU (shut-up with cuss words, said forcefully and usually with strong emotion). Rumination would be something like this:

"If he loved me he wouldn't talk to me like that. He would want to hear what I have to say if he loved me. I was just trying to learn about something that I think is important. Why couldn't he just answer my questions? Doesn't he care how his words make me feel? Why doesn't he want to be open and honest with me? Why does he treat me like that? Don't I deserve to be treated better? Etc. etc. etc."

There is no consideration for the circumstances in this rumination example. There is no questioning of the resources he had when he said that. There is no deeper probing. What was the emotional state of the person who said it at the time the words were said? Negative emotions lead to worse communication and it is person who is speaking whose emotions dictate how equipped they are to have a conversation at a given point in time. A conversation someone can easily have when they feel emotionally good, well-rested, not hungry or thirsty, or in a hurry, can become very difficult when any of those factors are not met.

Maybe the person is upset about the topic that was being discussed. Maybe the person didn't get any sleep the night before. Maybe the person found out they have an illness that has their stress level elevated. When you understand the connection between emotional state, resources, and behavior you can get to the point that when someone you love is rude to you, you don't react to the rudeness and instead you inquire as to what is bothering them.

In the rumination example, there is no giving of the benefit of the doubt or trust. That would look like this:

"My significant other was out of character today. He told me to STFU. I'll give him/her some time to calm down. That isn't normal behavior from my significant other and I'm sure there is a reason and the best thing I can do right now is not take it personally and assume I just don't have all the facts. There are lots of things that can make someone not act as nice as they usually do and it doesn't have to be anything about me or an indicator that our relationship is in trouble. I want to be supportive so I'll assume we'll work things out."

By not responding with anger or resentment it makes it easier for your significant other to apologize.

Not responding with anger is not something I expect you to be able to do immediately. The best way to accomplish it is to understand the relationship between emotional state, behavior, and your resources* and behavior. Simply knowing that your resources affect behavior can help you give your significant other the benefit of the doubt.

If this is normal behavior for your significant other rather than an exception to their normal behavior, the information about resources, including emotional state still applies but so does your significant others habits of thought. You can't change anyone else because change has to happen in the mind. If you believe you deserve to be treated that way I encourage you to work on your self-esteem because your current beliefs aren't supporting the fact that you're worthy of being treated with respect and of having the best possible relationship. This isn't your significant others fault. It's your decisions about your value and worth that have led you to accept poor treatment. A partner that doesn't treat you well is an indicator that you developed beliefs about what you deserve that aren't serving you well.

In some cases an abusive partner convinced you of this and in that situation it is best to get away to heal yourself. In many cases, you arrived in the relationship with low self-esteem and it is not yet clear whether you should leave or not. Why? People respond to our expectations. If you expect to be treated poorly, it is more likely that you will be treated poorly—even by someone who has treated others better. We teach people how to treat us. Even in the situation where the partner has worked to lower our self-esteem there was something in us that allowed that to happen. If there wasn't we would have left the first or second time it happened. I'm not blaming the victim. If the victim doesn't understand how they contribute they can't stop contributing.

Again, if this applies to you it's good news because identifying it is the first step in changing it. It is something you can change.

In any situation, if you feel your safety is in jeopardy, get out as soon as you can safely leave. There are many organizations that assist battered women and men. Yes, there are women who batter men and it doesn't mean the man is weak.

Some people wait until they think they can do it on their own because they don't want to ask for help. Consider this: When you want to give someone a gift or do something for them, do you enjoy it? In the same way, there are people who want to help you and helping you may help them. Imagine a parent who has lost a child who was abused by the child's partner. In some ways, helping others escape that situation may help them with their own grief.

Resources refers to hunger, thirst, fatigue, illness, drugs, alcohol, stress, and emotional state.

Self-Abuse

There are many forms of self-abuse.
- Self-criticism is a form of verbal self-abuse.
- Neglect is a common form of self-abuse:
  - Neglect of physical health
    - Lack of exercise
    - Poor nutrition
    - Inadequate rest
    - Drug abuse
    - Alcohol abuse
  - Neglect of mental health
  - Neglect of social needs
- Cutting is a form of physical self-abuse.
- Self-flagellation is a time honored tradition in some circles.
- Suicide is the ultimate self-abuse
- Subjecting oneself to violence and trauma that is avoidable is another form of self-abuse.

Self-Criticism

This brings me to self-criticism. We can beat ourself up for a lot of things:
- For not living up to personal standards
- For not considering personal resources before making mistakes
- For making bad decisions when we are tired
- For not paying attention when experiencing time pressure

Many people allow a critic to live in their mind and make them feel bad every day. Some people think the critic is necessary. Some people think everyone has a resident critic. Let's tackle these issues one at a time.

If you have a resident critic it is because you were taught to be self-critical. Not everyone has a critic living in their mind. Self-criticism is not necessary for self-improvement and can actually slow down improvements. It is possible to remove a critic even if it has lived in your mind for decades. A critic is nothing more than an unhealthy habit of thought. Self-criticism is associated with sub-clinical paranoia. [177]

If you want to improve any aspect of yourself all you have to do is identify that you want to change it. You don't need to nag yourself to change. Once you identify something you want to change, begin changing it. Self-criticism can increase procrastination about making changes you have decided you would like to make. There is a difference between the energy that you have to make changes when you want to change and when you *decide* to change.

Both an internal (self-critic) and external critic (nagging partner or friend) decrease our motivation to change. An internal critic tends to make us feel less empowered which means we feel less able to change things we decide we want to change.

No one is ever finished. We're not sculptures like Michelangelo's David that have a point where we reach perfection and no further improvements are possible. Humans are, by definition, works in progress. Everyone has many areas where they can improve and many areas where they are very good. Identifying things we want to improve is a good thing. If we turn our attention to making the changes we decide we want, we feel good. If we simply remain as we are and criticize ourself because improvement is possible, we don't feel good.

I tried to evict my resident critic and it didn't work. So I invited my resident critic to move to a tropical isle without me and that eventually worked. My critic would occasionally reappear and I would remind it that it no longer lived in my mind and wish it bon voyage again. It's been a long time since my resident critic visited.

What difference does it make? The difference is huge. Since my critic moved away I have accomplished a lot but one thing I did that I'd done before was get married. I didn't want to spend a lot of money on the wedding but I wanted a nice wedding so I did a lot of the work myself. On the actual wedding day I somehow failed to take into account that the work that needed to be done, (putting tablecloths on the tables and making the flower arrangements) would need to be done at the same time I was fixing my hair and make-up and getting ready to walk down the aisle.

Fortunately my friends, family and new sisters-in-law stepped in to help and everything was done and beautiful for our special day. The old me, the one with the critic living in her head, would have beat herself up something terrific for double booking my time that day and having to ask friends, family, and guests to help out. That and a few other things that weren't exactly as I'd pictured them would have had the power to ruin a perfect day if the critic had still lived in my mind. I remember being amazed at how much I was able to just relax and let things go. I felt such joy that day and was able to enjoy my husband, family, and guests much more than I would have if I'd been stressed out by things that didn't matter.

I simply reminded myself that I was surrounded by people I love who love me and enjoyed the day. What is the value of enjoying your wedding day? Your vacations? Your child's wedding? Your life?

The difference was obvious in the pictures. Even though it had been over two decades since the earlier wedding pictures were taken, I looked much better in the more recent pictures. Happiness shows on our faces and so does stress. The pictures from my earlier wedding reflected the level of stress I felt. The more recent pictures reflected the joy I felt.

The first step in getting rid of a resident critic is to acknowledge that you can be just as good and maybe better without the critic. Fear that the critic is the source of your motivation can make it difficult to rid yourself of the critic. The critic is not necessary. It does not add to your motivation.

Evicting the critic increases your energy to accomplish the things you want to do.

Try this. Think of something your resident critic says to you and write it down. Now write down its opposite.

For example, if your resident critic tells you, "You aren't good enough," write down "I am good enough."

Now, in a quiet place when you're calm pay attention to your emotions and your energy level and tell yourself (out loud): I am not good enough.

Do you feel your energy level feel lower? Do you feel the heavy feeling in your body when you say it as if you're carrying a heavy burden?

Relax your mind for a minute. Think of something neutral or slightly positive—maybe what you ate for breakfast or lunch.

Now, tell yourself (out loud); *I am good enough.*

Did you feel your energy increase? Do you feel lighter in your body as if a burden has been lifted? You may have to say it multiple times to get this feeling especially if your critic is giving you backlash. What is *backlash?* If the moment you say "I am good enough" the critic begins contradicting the statement in your mind, that is backlash.

If you receive backlash from your critic, take a smaller step. Instead of jumping from not being good enough to stating that you're good enough, take a smaller step. Try saying (out loud): *I am getting better all the time.*

If that is still too much, say (out loud): *I am getting better.*

If that is still too much, say (out loud): *I can find a way to get better.*

Other alternatives can include:

I am finding a way to become better.
Other people who had a critic like mine found a way to get better.
Some people who once thought they weren't good enough learned to believe they were good enough.

Try different statements until you find one that feels better than "I am not good enough" and doesn't make your inner critic contradict it. Once you reinforce that new statement you can find another one that feels a little bit better.

You can do this on any subject and learn to feel better on that subject. In the long-term you want to evict your inner-critic. You will still be aware of things you want to improve but the critic won't suck the life out of you. You'll make more progress faster once your critic leaves but be patient about the eviction process.

That critic may have served you well during your childhood if your parent expected you to focus on your flaws. If your parents did that it was not because they didn't love you. They simply were not taught good parenting skills. Children will naturally identify and improve many areas. It is not necessary to make them critical of their value, worth, or potential in order to make them strive to become who they can be. We all have an internal desire to learn and grow. An inner critic can mute those desires by making it more frightening to change because we worry we might do something that will make the critic attack us.

You can ask the critic to leave. It usually thinks it is necessary for your own good. You can thank it for helping you in the past and invite it to go live its own life somewhere else because now you are strong enough to get along without it.

Until the critic leaves you can do things like telling it "Thank you for your opinion." Then reaffirm a positive opinion on the topic the critic attempted to make you feel worse about. Remember to take small steps. When you take small steps you're sure footed. Large steps can make you stumble and many critics will jump in if you stumble and attempt to convince you that you're a lost cause.

Just begin again by thanking the critic for its opinion and take smaller steps. Make a list of the reasons the critic isn't necessary and read it daily.

I'll be more successful after the critic moves out.
I'll be happier after the critic moves out.
I don't need to be criticized to be motivated to improve.
Many successful people don't have an inner critic. I can be like them.

Whatever thoughts come to your mind and feel good are good for you to put on this list. There is no right or wrong reason to evict your inner critic.

Self-criticism is unnecessary. Many of us were taught to view ourselves critically. Self-criticism delays accomplishments. There are too many factors that go into it. Part of it is that self-criticism leaves us feeling inadequate for the goals we want to reach so we don't move forward.

Self-criticism is sometimes referred to as self-flagellation. When we recognize that something about ourselves is not as we would like it to be, the best path is to make a choice to change whatever that thing happens to be. In some cases this will involve taking action and other times it will involve changing our perspective.

The only person you are destined to become is the person you decide to be.
Ralph Waldo Emerson

For example, if someone doesn't like their age because they think they are too old to do something they want to do they can't reverse the clock but they can change their perspective about the capabilities of people who are their age. It turns out that our beliefs about aging affect how we age. I've been looking for examples of people who aged well for two decades and my view of my potential in my older years changed significantly. There are people in their 70's running marathons and even a few in their 90's. I knew a man in Idaho who was 99 and lived alone. When he died he had 60 lbs of seeds on his kitchen table that he was going to plant in his garden the year he turned 100. He did not die of natural causes. He lasted six weeks in the burn unit in Seattle before succumbing to an infection. He was born in 1897 in the Oklahoma territory and American Indians came from as far as 100 miles to see him and his two siblings because they considered triplets good luck.

Aging is not the only thing we can change our minds about. Our intelligence is not fixed either. David Schenk's book, *The Genius in All of Us* dispels myths about fixed intelligence and about not being able to learn as we get older. [178] If you want a more in-depth dive on aging, Ellen Langer's *Counterclockwise* is excellent. [179] Expectation affects outcome. [180]

So, if you can't change the actual thing, change the way you think about it. If you can change the actual thing, make a decision to change it. This is the process:

1. Pay attention to how you feel. Get used to doing this so that when you feel more negative emotion than normal you are aware of the feelings.
2. When the negative emotion is a response to self-criticism, say to yourself, "I don't like this about myself. What would I prefer?"
3. When you know what you'd prefer, make a decision to change whatever it is.
4. Begin doing everything you can do to change the thing you don't like.
5. You'll feel better as you move toward becoming all you want to be, even if it the process will take years (like going to college).

Decisions have power. When you make a definitive decision something clicks into place that makes accomplishing whatever you've decided to accomplish easier than you thought it would be.

Two of my favorite quotes are about the power of making a decision. I've previously attributed this quote to Johann Wolfgang von Goethe but I've since learned that the correct attribution is to W. H. Murray in *The Scottish Himalaya Expedition,* 1951. That change does not make the words any less inspirational.

Until one is committed, there is hesitancy, the chance to draw back. Concerning all acts of initiative (and creation), there is one elementary truth that ignorance of which kills countless ideas and splendid plans: that the moment one definitely commits oneself, then Providence moves too. All sorts of things occur to help one that would never otherwise have occurred. A whole stream of events issues from the decision, raising in one's favor all manner of unforeseen incidents and meetings and material assistance, which no man could have dreamed would have come his way. Whatever you can do, or dream you can do, begin it. Boldness has genius, power, and magic in it. Begin it now.

My second favorite quote about decisions is:

Once you make a decision, the universe conspires to make it happen.

Ralph Waldo Emerson

Self-criticism can take the form of *shoulding* or *coulding* as in "I should have. . . " or "I could have . . . ". There are two things to consider when you realize you're *shoulding* all over yourself. One is to make a decision to become who you want to be. The other is to consider your resources.

Remember, your best potential is not the same as your best in any given moment.

After adjusting my definition of my best to be "the best possible at the moment the behavior is measured" I've observed a lot of people and come to the conclusion that we all do the best we can, given our resources, in any given moment.

Not doing something is a decision. It depends on what it is. If the idea energizes you and it is based on long-term well-defined desires it is usually better to go forward. If it is based on fear or short-term desires (especially if they conflict with longer-term desires) it is not as likely to be a good decision. Negative thoughts about yourself increase your vulnerability to depression and anxiety and lessen the potential for full recoveries (as long as the negative self-image is kept).[181]

Self-Harm

One reason developing skills in changing focus is critical is that it is a process a new student can use to change a painful emotional state quickly. For someone who is considering self-harm, the ability to change focus quickly can be lifesaving. At low emotional states, finding a better feeling thought can seem impossible if you have not already practiced skills to help you. It can feel as if you'll never feel better. The Focus Shift process empowers you with a way to shift your focus to a better feeling thought when you need it the most.

I recommend this process for everyone. It is best prepared for when you are in the Hopeful or Sweet Zone, but the process is used when you are emotionally below the Hopeful Zone. This process is one of the few that provide quick relief when you are in the Powerless Zone.

Focus Shift—The List

Prepare to use this process in advance. When you are in a good mood, make a list of simple things that make you feel good when you think about them. The list should be things you can actually enjoy—not something you want (like winning the lottery). My list has things like sunrises, sunsets, flowers, babies, little red haired girls, doing something for someone else that makes me feel good when I remember it, and remembering overcoming obstacles in the past. On my list, I also have ice cream to remind myself of a specific time when I felt cared for. There is no right or wrong as long as it is something that makes you feel good when you think about it.

Keep your list in your wallet or purse. If you ever find yourself in an emotional state where you can't think of anything that feels better, all you have to do is remember you have the list. Take it out and look at it.

One time, many years ago, I was in that low place where I was unable to think a single good feeling thought. Remembering the list, but not anything that was on it, I found it in my purse. When I reviewed it, there were no babies in the vicinity. It was midafternoon so no sunrises or sunsets were out. Then I saw flowers on the list. It was January, so my yard lacked flowers. Then I remembered the grocery store has flowers.

I got in the car, drove to the grocery store, and spent about half an hour in the floral section. I admired the flowers, smelled the flowers, enjoyed the pretty colors, and the floral scents. By the time I left the store, my mood was greatly improved. I never again returned to such a low mood, because when my emotional state begins to decline, I take action sooner.

The list must be made when you feel good because that is when you can remember thoughts and memories that feel good to you.

My trip to the grocery store did not change any of the facts of the situation that had caused the low mood, but by shifting to a higher mood my mind was able to see the situation in a better light. Solutions that were not mentally accessible from the lower emotional state occurred to me once my emotional state felt better.

In the lowest emotional states, changing ones focus is the quickest path to feeling better. When the mood is that low, the most critical thing anyone can do is find a way to feel better. Sometimes that means sleeping.

Focus is the easiest aspect of our emotional state to change quickly. Changing beliefs that do not serve us provides more progress, but changing a belief that is at the root of a low emotional state is very difficult when one is at a low emotional state. It is better to work on changing unsupportive beliefs when feeling hopeful or better.

A change of focus is a powerful tool. It is an easy one to practice and can be done under any circumstances. Use this process below the Hopeful Zone and immediately when in the Powerless Zone.

If you are thinking about harming yourself or someone else, call 1-800-273-8255 immediately for help. More resources are listed in Appendix VI.

Self-Sacrifice

> *"I'm 24 and I take things very personally. I give a lot to my friends and expect a lot from my friends. When I am hurt people take me for granted. I feel stupid for doing so much for others. How can I stop being stupid?"*

Change your priorities. Take responsibility for your own happiness and let others be responsible for their own happiness. You can't make anyone happy (other than yourself) anyway. You can be their excuse to be happy, but the best way to do that is to be happy yourself and be a person people want to be around

Commit to your own happiness. Do not do anything for anyone else that does not make you happy to do it. If you do it because it makes you feel good to do it, there is no expectation that they will do something for you.

Doing something for them is doing something for you when doing it makes you happy.

For example, if I don't want to cook dinner for my husband, I don't. I feel no guilt about not cooking his meal, none. But often I do cook him dinner, because it makes me happy to support the relationship I want. When I don't cook for him, he might cook for me--if he wants to. But I have no expectation that he will do that. We might both just eat something simple, or have a pizza night.

When I stopped doing things for other people to please them, I became happier. When I stopped expecting others to do things for me to make me happy, I became someone many people enjoyed spending time with.

One of my favorite activities is having uplifting conversations. I can have a conversation with a stranger that uplifts the person and it makes me feel high on life. But I have the conversation because it is something I *want* to do--not because I should, not because I am expected to, not because it is the right thing to do (other than it is the right thing for me).

You have to understand that happy people are kinder to others--even to strangers. You have to be selfish enough to put your happiness first. This is not about using others--it's about taking care of you.

Making others happy

YOU CAN'T MAKE ANYONE HAPPY without their *permission*.

It is NOT your job to make anyone else happy.

Be happy yourself and set an example they can chose to follow (or not). The decision is theirs.

People want autonomy.

Realize that how someone else feels, thinks, speaks, and behaves is more about the emotional state they are in at the time and less about anything else including the situation. Their opinion of you will be good if they're in a good mood and bad if they're in a bad mood. None of it has anything to do with you.

Think about how you feel about others and what mood you're in when you're thinking what you're thinking about them and you'll realize that how you feel about others changes with your mood. Once you realize it is their mood and it is not your responsibility to make them happy you'll stop worrying so much about what other people think.

This includes your spouse. My wedding vows specifically spelled out that I am responsible for my own happiness and my husband is responsible for his happiness.

Low Self-esteem

Historically, low self-esteem has been one of the most difficult areas to change even with the aid of a professional. That's no longer true. Research conducted at Wake Forest University over twenty years ago highlighted some of the problems associated with low self-esteem, "Low self-esteem ranks among the strongest predictors of emotional and behavioral problems.

Compared to people with high self-esteem, people with low self-esteem tend to be more anxious, depressed, lonely, jealous, shy, and generally unhappy. They are also less assertive, less likely to enjoy close friendships, and more likely to drop out of school. Furthermore, they are more inclined to behave in ways that pose a danger to themselves or others: low self-esteem is associated with unsafe sex, teenage pregnancy, aggression, criminal behavior, the abuse of alcohol and other drugs, and membership in deviant groups." [182]

The good news is that the strategies you are learning in MWME can help you increase your self-esteem. Emotional Guidance does not support low self-esteem. Thoughts that reflect low self-esteem receive a negative emotional response which, given the new definition of the purpose and use of emotions, indicates the thoughts are not serving our highest good and that we should find a thought that elicits a better feeling emotion.

When I work with individuals who have low self-esteem I use two methods. The first is for them to use their Emotional Guidance as often as possible, but not directly on low self-esteem in the beginning. The purpose of using Emotional Guidance frequently is to develop trust in its accuracy. Once this is done, the individual can begin working on adjusting their self-esteem with guidance they trust. Before trust in Emotional Guidance is established I do not recommend using it to work on self-esteem.

Look for counterfactual thinking and distortions that are obvious. Do you give other people the benefit of the doubt but vilify yourself? Write down your accomplishments.

Self-esteem is best dealt with after you loosen it up a bit. Like an old rusted screw, it is easier if you work it loose a bit first. Giving up unhealthy habits of thought in every area you can and developing healthy habits of thought will loosen up the mental connections that have kept thoughts that support low self-esteem active.

People who boast about themselves and toot their own horn are often perceived as having big ego's (high self-esteem) but the truth is that these are signs of low self-esteem and insecurity. Someone who knows they have value and worth doesn't have to prove it to other people. One key to healthy self-esteem is caring less about what others think of us and just being the best person we can be.

Accomplishments, even high achievements, and low self-esteem are not mutually exclusive. Many high achievers have low self-esteem. Self-esteem is about what you believe about yourself which may not reflect reality. Individuals with low self-esteem substantially underestimate how positively they are regarded by relationship partners. [183] Self-esteem leads to insecurities that cause you to underestimate how others view you which can increase anxiety by increasing your concerns that others view you as poorly as you view yourself.

Low self-esteem is the result of habits of thought that support low self-esteem. The habits of thought have to be changed. It is possible to do this. It isn't even difficult when you know how. But it does take time.

Low self-esteem is learned. When you were born you thought the world revolved around you. You expected others to provide for your every need. You did not think about whether you deserved to suckle at your mother's breast or deserved to have a clean diaper. You knew your worthiness yet you were not a productive member of society. You did not produce anything other than the waste that filled your diapers.

Low self-esteem means that somewhere along the way someone convinced you that you weren't all that. They told you or showed you by their actions that you were not valued or worthy of the best life has to offer. They were wrong.

People will blast people with high self-esteem for putting themselves above other people but the truth is that every human being has so many wonderful aspects that everyone is worthy and of value to the rest of society. We know intuitively that we should have value and when we think we don't we sort of freak out. We can become defensive of anyone or anything that we think is attacking our value or worth. Or we can become insecure and afraid to show our gifts to the world out of fear that someone will think it proves we aren't good.

The healthiest approach to our own value and worth is to see ourselves as of enormous value. Our life, our thoughts, and our contributions, whatever they may be, have value. When we see ourself as having value it is easier to see others the same way. Not better. Not worse. See all people as having great value and worth. See no one as lacking value or worth. Look for the best in others. I'll admit that sometimes the value and worth I see in someone is that of helping others see more clearly the world they do not want but that is clarity and clarity has value.

The most important first step is to understand that low self-esteem means you have a lower opinion of yourself than you deserve. Your brain may be arguing with that point as you read it but remember, your brain attempts to protect your existing beliefs. That means that if you've developed a belief that says you're not good enough; your brain will attempt to protect it. This is one of the areas where Emotional Guidance is so valuable because it bypasses the belief filter and lets you know which thoughts support self-actualization and which thoughts interfere with self-actualization.

The negative emotion you feel when you think thoughts that reflects a belief that you're unworthy are telling you that those thoughts do not help you move toward self-actualization. The positive emotion you feel when you think you are worthy tells you that those thoughts are helping you move toward self-actualization.

If low self-esteem is something you are dealing with it is best not to tackle it as the first project you use Emotional Guidance to consciously change. It is better to work on something that does not affect every area of your life first until you trust your Emotional Guidance. Once you trust the accuracy and good intentions of your Emotional Guidance, it becomes much easier to begin shifting your self-esteem to better opinions of self.

One of my beliefs is that things that help us be our best are how we are intended to be. It doesn't make sense to me that we would be designed (or evolve, depending on your worldview) in a way that makes something that helps us be our best possible self be damaging to us.

For example, it is very evident that happiness is good for us. Our bodies and brain functions best when we're happy as does our digestive system and immune function. Relationships contribute significantly to both our physical and mental health and it is easiest to develop and maintain healthy relationships when we are happy.

Good self-esteem has a lot of support from Emotional Guidance. Resilience, which allows us to bounce back from adversity, requires healthy self-esteem. Surely humans are at their best when they bounce back from traumas and dramas. Being resilient reduces stress. Scientists have demonstrated that we are designed to function best when we think well of ourselves.

Thinking we are better than others does not serve us well. It contributes to all sorts of problems that at the extreme can lead to genocide and in milder forms is simply unpleasant and not conducive to good relationships with others. When I found the balance that I teach which goes like this, "I am wonderful . . . and so are you," my Emotional Guidance provided strong support for the stance. I tried hundreds of views to see how each felt before choosing the belief I wanted to develop.

This new belief reminds me to see the potential in others rather than focusing on who they are being in the moment. That helps me inspire them to become more of their potential. It allows me to have positive self-esteem without placing myself above anyone else. It was the perfect belief for me to establish. If it resonates with you, feel free to use it. If it doesn't resonate, play with your thoughts until you find one that feels good to you. Other people don't have to be part of the equation. For me it felt better to acknowledge that my being wonderful doesn't make me any better than anyone else. It was the only way to quiet the voice in my head that wanted to dispute the "I am wonderful" belief.

Once your Emotional Guidance leads you to a thought that feels good about yourself, affirm it frequently. You can say it to yourself in the privacy of your own mind. You can talk about it with supportive friends. Don't talk about it with friends who may attempt to talk you out of positive thoughts about yourself. Think of new thoughts you want to keep alive as newborns. They require time and attention to help them thrive. Thinking the thought often will turn it into a belief. Once it is a belief, it is strong and can survive on its own unless you practice thinking a contradictory thought.

The transition from low self-esteem to accepting that you have great value and worth—just like everyone else—can take time. Use the positive emotion the thoughts elicit as evidence of their truth. When the thought feels good, you can be sure the thought is nurturing your highest good.

At this point, people who have suffered with low self-esteem for a long time often begin beating themselves up for not seeing their own value sooner. That is not productive. Use your Emotional Guidance to feel how it feels when you criticize yourself for not knowing something in the past that you now know. It is essentially beating the *current you* up for who you used to be. You can't punish the you that you used to be because that version of you has evolved and no longer exists.

It is common for people to be angry at those who taught them low self-worth but your guidance is helpful there as well. One thing that has helped me forgive and let go of any mistakes my parents or anyone else may have made is realizing that everyone does the best they can with what they know in any given moment. We are all learning, growing, and becoming all the time. Even parents who did what most would consider a lousy job were doing the best they could, given their circumstances and knowledge.

My thesis was on the connection between emotional state and behavior. Even a mass murderer like Jeffrey Dahmer was doing his best possible in that moment given his emotional state, beliefs, and fears. Yes, he was a horrific mass murderer but when you understand the connection between emotional state, cognitive function, the strong innate desire to feel better his behavior becomes predictable. Knowing that given all those factors it can be understandable doesn't mean his behavior is acceptable, but it was his best given what he knew, his history, and his circumstances at the time.

Behavior moves in tandem with emotional state unless the person has deliberately cultivated beliefs or rules about their own behavior that will counteract a low emotional state. When all the factors that affect behavior are considered, each of us does our best in every moment. This is true of our parents and other care takers.

Our beliefs affect what we value. Beliefs lead some people to value some traits over other traits such as:

- Physical Strength
- Character
- Skill on the playing field
- Specific labels
- Physical beauty
- Intelligence
- Hard work
- Specific achievements

A studious boy, whose father values skill on the playing field may feel unworthy because he does not meet his father's expectations despite the fact that other families put more value in the pursuit of knowledge than in skill at a game. A star athlete whose parents see little value in athletics and high value in academics may feel he is not good enough because his strengths don't fit the ideal son his parent's desire.

We were not born to suit our parents. We were born to be our unique and wonderful selves. When a parent creates an ideal model of their child they want and compares their flesh and blood child to that idea and find fault the parent is not seeing the child's gifts. Such a comparison doesn't say anything real about the child's value or worth. The lack the parent perceives is not the child's fault. It is a lack in the parent. The parent can change their perspective and feel better.

A child isn't a house. We don't go to an architect and describe the exact features and measurements we want in our child and have the child designed to fit our expectations, yet many parents behave as if the child should meet their preconceived idea of perfection. Demanding that a child pursue what we want them to be interested in rather than allowing the child to discover what makes the child's heart sing, increases stress which brings with it all the their parents don't want for their children.

Children will only thrive if they are allowed to become self-actualized which means they have to be free to become the person they are inspired to be.

Can I feel better about myself?

To feel better about yourself, sneak up on it.
Seriously!
Find something, anything that makes you feel appreciation. Think about it until you're in a state of appreciation and then turn your thoughts to yourself. The easiest thoughts for your brain to find are thoughts that match your current emotional state.

If you've been practicing negative thoughts about yourself for a long time, you may not be able to stay with positive thoughts about yourself for more than a few seconds . . . the first time. Repeat this exercise frequently and it will become easier to think positive thoughts about yourself and to maintain those thoughts longer.

Using Transformational Stress Management Strategies gradually improves your chronic emotional state. Since your thoughts are mood congruent unless you are consciously directing them, feeling better will improve the automatic thoughts you think about yourself.

Low Self-Efficacy

Self-efficacy is a context specific belief. It refers to your personal belief about whether or not you are competent to perform a task or achieve a goal. Think in terms of strengths. A person can believe they are good at one thing but not good at another thing. I have many skills and talents but I need a bucket to carry a tune. My self-efficacy when it comes to singing is that I should only do it when I am alone and if I learn someone else is present I apologize for assaulting their ears.

The actions you take when you believe you are capable are different than the actions you take when you don't feel confident in your abilities.

People who believe they are capable do better than those who do not.[184] Enhancing self-efficacy beliefs can reduce stress.[185p] Use your Emotional Guidance to find thoughts that make you feel more competent.

Willingness to seek support

Many people perceive asking for help as a sign of weakness and resist asking for help even when it is desperately needed. Failing to ask for support is a weakness. This is an area I've struggled with and continue to work on changing. Two things have helped me become more willing to ask for assistance when I need help.

The first is recognizing that I enjoy helping others. When I need help and don't request it, I deprive others from the pleasure they would receive from helping me. Do you ever help someone because you want to help them? When you do, do you enjoy it? Does the level of your enjoyment increase if they are willing to accept the help you're offering? Do you find it frustrating to want to help someone but they refuse your offer?

Remember times you helped others and enjoyed it. Now turn it around and see that there are people who would enjoy helping you. Recognize that *asking for help* is an Adaptive Coping Strategy.

Denial

Denying a negative event is not the same as changing your perspective and seeing the event as more positive. A person who, when a romantic relationship ends, denies the truth and insists that the person will change their mind is in denial.

A person who, when a romantic relationship ends, recognizes that the relationship they want includes someone who wants them and that the person who ended the relationship doesn't meet that criteria and from then on perceives the end of the relationship as ending a relationship they didn't want is not in denial. This person has a clearer view of the situation.

Desired Relationship

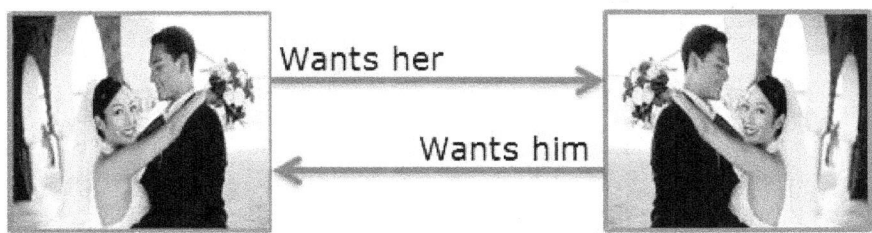

Undesired Relationship

 Doesn't want him

No longer what he wants

Likewise, someone who has a relationship with someone who continually tells them they are there for them but refuses to provide help when it is needed provides clarity about their true intentions. Words are cheap. Actions provide insight. Denying of negative events is associated with higher emotional exhaustion and depersonalization.[186]

Cautious (overly)

Overly cautious individuals are "reluctant to take risks for fear of being rejected or negatively evaluated."[187] They may perceive attending a social function as a risky activity. Over time, being overly cautious leads to lower achievement, fewer social connections, and lower levels of well-being.

If you're overly caution, both Advanced and Transformational strategies can help you overcome the fear and enjoy life more.

Avoidance

Avoidance coping allows problems to fester. Depersonalization is a form of avoidance coping and is similar to the disengagement associated with burnout. Objectification of others is an example of this. Objectification avoids interacting with the person as an individual with feelings and needs. Your emotions will help you find perspectives where you can be engaged and feel good.

Insisting on Control

Many people increase the stress they experience by attempting to control everyone and everything in their life. We cannot control what happens in our life. There is too much to control and most people do not respond well when others attempt to control them.

Developing our emotion regulation skills gives us the ability to control how we respond.

People who insist on control often believe that other people have more control than they actually have. They may look at a finished product, such as a career that is flourishing and believe the person planned every step and always knew exactly what they would do next. In most cases that is not the way it was. In most cases there were unexpected zigs and zags, uncertainty, hope, but no plan, etc.

This quote from Martin Luther King, Jr. is a wonderful way to approach life:

Faith is taking the first step, even when you don't see the whole staircase.

How does this quote work in real life? Here are examples of situations that require great faith:

- *Enrolling in and going to college with an undeclared major.*
- *Having a baby.*
- *Getting married.*
- *Accepting a new job.*
- *Planning a vacation.*
- *Inviting someone on a date.*
- *Getting in a car and expecting to arrive safely at your destination.*

If you have attempted to control every aspect of your life, you already know how stressful (and unproductive) that strategy is. It can be difficult to let go if you don't know a different way to approach life. Trusting that if we keep doing what we can do to work toward what we want that we'll eventually arrive is a perspective your Emotional Guidance will support.

You may also want to ask people you admire about their journey and the part their belief in their ability to persist even if things didn't go as planned played a part in their success.

Cynicism

Cynicism is an attitude towards others characterized by distrust of their motives. The person who is feeling cynical may focus on uninspiring reasons for actions such as ambition, materialism, and greed. They may perceive someone who has an inspiring *why* for their actions inaccurately and attribute a negative reason for their actions.

For example, I wrote a suicide prevention book and occasionally offer a coupon code that allows the holder to obtain an e-book free of charge. There is no financial benefit to me when someone obtains my book for free. It is on Smashwords so I do not collect their name or email address. I've had individuals post online that my offer was self-serving.

That is something someone who is cynical would do because they would not perceive any altruistic motives. I didn't even want to write that book but after the second time I unexpectedly used my methods to stop an imminent suicide I felt compelled to write the book. I knew that if I didn't write it I would feel guilty every time I heard about someone committing suicide.

Cynicism is not the same as skepticism. Skepticism is open to additional knowledge. Skepticism is being unwilling to accept something as fact without more information.

Cynicism is commonly seen on social media when someone without the facts attributes an overly negative interpretation of the events. Recently a commenter did that to me. I had mentioned my husbands' age and he erroneously assumed my hubby was a lot older than me and proceeded to make derogatory remarks about marrying *an older man*. Our age difference is actually less than the average age difference in couples who marry at the ages we were when we married.

A cynic assumes their negative conclusion is accurate. A skeptic would ask for more information to make sure they knew the facts.

 Emotional guidance will guide you away from cynicism. Pay attention to how you feel when you reach a conclusion. If your emotion is negative, look for another perspective that feels better.

Addictions

Addictions begin when someone who lacks skills to feel better in healthy ways wants to dull pain or feel better.

Beating an addiction without building stress management skills is a recipe for relapse as soon as stress and negative emotions become unbearable.

If you're addicted to drugs, alcohol, sex, shopping, or other unhealthy addictions, build your resilience and Advanced Coping skills. If you knew that you could avoid relapse because you had better skills, you'd be more energized about beating the addiction. As long as it feels hopeless, as if you'd relapse if your level of stress got too high, there may not seem much point. When you have Advanced and Transformational coping skills you feel more capable of resisting relapse. You are stronger with skills.

For example, a desire to feel better right now may be satisfied by a bottle of wine but the desire to beat alcoholism in the long-term is in direct conflict with that desire.

Alcohol and drugs are Dysfunctional Coping methods. People who know better methods of coping (effective and less risky) will use them. I've taught people who have addictions to feel better and when they learn better skills they are less likely to relapse. If you're ready to beat an addiction, professional help will make it easier.

Surface-Thinking

Surface thinking means believing the first thought you have on a subject without questioning it. It can involve defending beliefs with anger because you cannot articulate logical reasons to support your position. The reason you cannot articulate the reason is usually because you were taught the belief and did not question it.

If you cannot articulate reasons you believe what you believe it doesn't mean your beliefs are wrong. It means you accepted them without examination. Because it is a belief, your brain will interpret reality as if your belief is true. This may be helpful or it may be hindering. The only way to know is to see how it feels, use your Emotional Guidance.

If your reaction to a challenge to one of your beliefs is anger instead of reasoning, it is a clear sign that you would benefit from taking the time to think about what you believe, why you believe it, and whether your current beliefs support the person you want to be.

Final Thoughts about Unhealthy Habits of Thought

If you've identified that you have one or more unhealthy habits of thought, it is good news because you now know:

1. How to identify habits that made your life worse, and
2. How to change habits that made your life worse.

That is a much more powerful position than simply knowing your life is not as good as you'd like it to be but now how to make it better. Now that you know change is easy, your life can get better. Knowing how to deal with unhealthy habits of thought creates hope that the future will be better than the past. Hope is powerful.

Why is The Smart Way the Best Way?
Prevention is better than cure.
Desiderius Erasmus (1466-1536) Dutch humanist

The Smart Way™ was designed by combining characteristics of individuals who thrive against the odds with the latest research in positive psychology, resilience, psychological flexibility, self-determination theory, emotion regulation, biochemistry, and other research that points to the basis of human thriving.

***The Smart Way* is:**

A combination of:
1. Understanding and deliberately applying Emotional Guidance
2. Knowing and applying Advanced Stress reduction strategies (metacognitive strategies) to reduce stress.
3. Knowing and applying Transformational Stress Reduction Strategies that reduce the initial stress an individual experiences on a daily basis.
4. Understanding how the mind processes big data and how it determines the micro data you consciously receive.
5. Leaning toward realistic optimism supported by Emotional Guidance
6. Developing an internal locus of control
7. Healthy core self-evaluations
    a. Healthy self-esteem
        i. Strong self-efficacy
8. Understand that thoughts, words, and actions are congruent with mood and beliefs

The Smart Way™ is *smart* because it prevents illnesses from occurring instead of waiting for them to happen and then treating the symptoms. Several aspects of *The Smart Way*™ are designed to increase individual's motivation to use cognitive reappraisal techniques, both by overcoming common limiting beliefs and by understanding the benefit of maintaining better-feeling emotions.

When you use mindfulness and "accept thoughts and feelings without judgment and focus on the present moment," [188] depression and anxiety decline. With *The Smart Way*™ you take the next step and change perspectives to help you identify perspectives that serve your highest good.

The Smart Way™ provides a stable foundation for success throughout life. Evidence-based techniques address core skills that make it easy to get on and stay on a path that takes you toward self-actualization and success.

The objectives of *The Smart Way*™ are:
- Foster skills and social competence through training that increases self-confidence.
- Increase success by providing goal setting training that reinforces inherent desires for autonomy and competence.
- Reduce susceptibility to negative external pressures and stress.
- Increase growth mindset and intrinsic desire for continuous self-development.
- Develop skills that increase happiness and resilience, which reduces stress.
- Develop a thorough understanding of how to accurately interpret emotions and respond to their signals in pro-health and pro-social ways (Emotional Intelligence Plus).
- Recognize the connection between emotional state and behaviors.
- Teach skills that lead to the development of habitual bias that allocates attention in ways that elicit positive emotions more often, essentially resulting in implicit emotion regulation. [189]

Skills that empower you to regulate your emotional response (self-regulation) to significantly reduce the risk of mental illnesses including burnout, depression, anxiety, panic disorders, bi-polar disorder and even psychosis. Individuals with the ability to self-induce desired emotional states "are happier in both positive and negative circumstances."[190] Regulating negative emotion to feel better indicates reduced stress levels, which leads to improved physical health. "The existence of automatic, unconscious processes influencing human emotion, cognition, and behavior is widely accepted and confirmed by numerous studies."[191]

Compare CBT to The Smart Way

The Smart Way™ helps you optimize the way you use your mind and body. *The Smart Way*™ has been compared to Cognitive Behavioral Therapy in the following way:

Cognitive Behavioral Therapy (CBT) is done one-on-one and resembles having an expert marksman stand next to an amateur who is blindfolded while attempting to hit a target by obtaining instructions from the expert, who is the only one who knows the location of the target. It is reactive because it is done after a diagnosis is made.

The Smart Way™ takes the blindfold off the archer (patient/client) so they know exactly where the target is and provides them with skills that help them hit the target consistently in the current situation. The skills they develop can be applied to future situations without having to consult an expert.

The Smart Way™ can be delivered in large group settings where hundreds can be taught at the same time because it removes the blindfold and makes the target fully visible to each individual, who is given skills that empower them to continually improve their aim. Intrinsic motivation occurs naturally because each step results in positive emotional feedback. Even when the overall emotional state is still negative, the student feels the relief of feeling better and the hope that comes from knowing one has the skills to shift to increasingly better feeling emotional states. Cognitive Behavioral Therapy is hampered by:

    Stigma associated with mental illness

    High cost of one-on-one therapy

    Recurrent need because CBT resolves current issues without necessarily developing skills to address future issues

    Therapists are trained to move people from a minus state to zero on this scale:

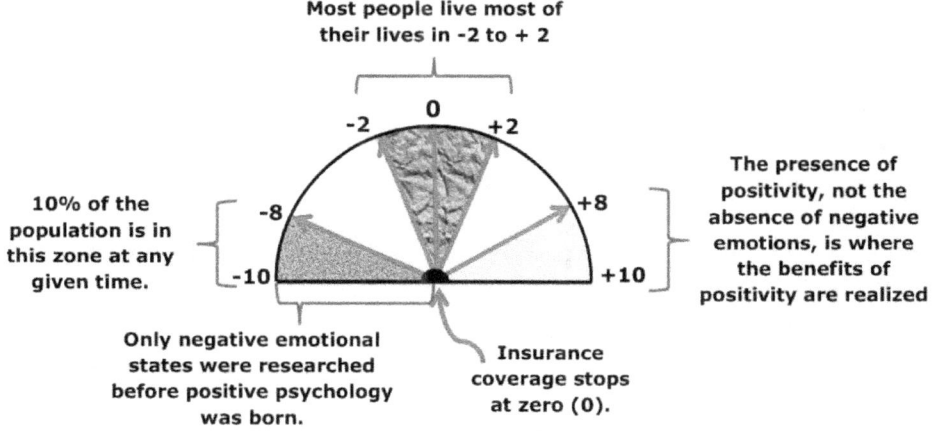

Based on the following definition, *The Smart Way*™ meets the definition of cognitive therapy but it does not require a therapist.

"Cognitive behavioral therapies can be defined as those interventions with the core assumptions that what individuals think directly impacts how they feel and what they do." [192]

It can be learned and applied privately or in group educational classes which are not the same as group therapy. The teacher doesn't have to know where you are, she only needs to know how to teach you skills you can use to change your thoughts so your emotional state improves.

Despite the fact that traditional Cognitive Behavioral Therapy is used as a curative rather than a preventative method of improving mental (and in some cases, physical), health, ". . . the evidence-base of CBT is enormous." Hoffman, et al. conducted a review of meta-analyses of the use of CBT to address a wide variety of issues and concluded by recommending that countries *adopt it as a first-line defense against mental disorders.* I go a step further in my hypothesis.

Anything Cognitive Behavioral Therapy is effective at treating, *The Smart Way*™ can prevent from happening in the first place.

The Smart Way™ empowers individuals with knowledge of strategies they can use to develop healthy habits of thought before a problem occurs.

While there is a strong emphasis on prevention with The Smart Way™, case studies demonstrate that The Smart Way™ is effective in restoring mental health to individuals who were suffering from severe long-term PTSD, severe chronic depression, anxiety, BPD, bi-polar, anger, and that is has been effective in preventing imminent suicides. It was those successes combined with the increased experience of positive emotions in groups I taught that convinced me of the power The Smart Way™ has to help people.

The Smart Way™ should help you with depression, PTSD, anxiety, panic, social phobias, anger issues, OCD, bi-polar disorder and schizophrenia.*

Providing knowledge and skills that prevent unhealthy habits of thought that Cognitive Behavioral Therapy is designed to correct will prevent problems from manifesting in the first place, thus preventing a significant portion of the suffering that affects people around the world. Psychotherapy may take different forms. The therapy can help patients

- Change thought or behavior patterns
- Understand how past experiences influence current behaviors
- Solve other problems in specific ways
- Learn illness self-management skills [193]

CBT is essentially teaching people to think in self-supporting ways, it makes sense that teaching them to do that before a problem manifests would effectively prevent many issues from ever arising. The benefits of healthy habits of thought extend to both physical [194] and mental health. [195] The benefits to individuals, employers, schools, and society in general of reducing the incidences of these problems should be obvious.

If we and our children have skills and habits of thought that make us resilient, we will fare much better than those who are not resilient. We will not experience the level of chronic stress that leads to diminished physical and mental health.

One of the reasons so many suffer is because they know intuitively that life should be better for them. Not understanding their guidance negatively affects their life experience. Emotional Guidance helps you identify beliefs that hinder your ability to thrive.

There is no need for a diagnosis before teaching *The Smart Way*™ because it is simply teaching individuals about how their brain works and how to think in ways that optimize outcomes. While learning *The Smart Way*™ can lead to recovery, or better outcomes, the main purpose is to

---

* I have been reading a lot of journal articles about schizophrenia during the past year as I am writing a book to help individuals who have been diagnosed with schizophrenia, and people who hear voices or have hallucinations.

prevent new manifestations of problems that can be prevented by reducing stress.

Cognitive Behavioral Therapy teaches people how thoughts influence feelings and behaviors. [196] It is something everyone needs to know. To the average person, mental health care is shrouded in mystery, stigma, and secrecy. Just the thought of thinking about our innermost feelings can cause fear. When one begins considering that Cognitive Behavioral Therapy is essentially helping someone change the way they think to healthier thought patterns, it make more sense to teach people what healthy thought patterns are in the first place. Given how many mental health problems can be healed, or at least improved with CBT, it points to the fact that information about how the mind works is highly valuable to everyone.

How you use your mind determines how much stress you feel in a given situation. Everyone who receives a lay-off notice does not feel the same degree of stress. Not even everyone with two children and a mortgage and no spouse feels the same degree of stress when a lay-off is announced. The amount of stress experienced depends on the perspective you take about the situation.

How our brains, emotions, and thoughts are connected should not be information reserved for the elite. "CBT is a psychotherapeutic approach that focuses on the way in which people's thoughts influence their feelings and behaviors. CBT includes a number of different approaches that share the belief that it is not the event that causes our feelings and behaviors, but rather how we perceive or think about what happened . . . Socratic reasoning is a central technique." [197]

The aspects that make CBT therapeutic is that it is done after-the-fact (once someone is already suffering from a diagnosis). CBT has assessment procedures to measure progress toward healing. If done before an illness manifests there is no need for assessments to be done to determine when health is restored to a level where insurance will no longer pay and no need for a diagnosis because the point is to avoid having a diagnosable illness. Our emotions provide all the feedback required now that we understand the purpose of emotions is to let us know when our mind/body is stressed and guide us toward less stressful thoughts and situations.

In Cognitive Behavioral Therapy:[198]	*In The Smart Way:*
Finding the client's irrational beliefs	Feeling the emotional discord and using metacognition to find thoughts that feel better
Automatic thoughts	When automatic thoughts don't feel good, question them and use metacognition to find better feeling thoughts
Assisting the client in changing them	Individual directs his or her own change using Advanced and Transformational Stress Coping Skills. If a therapist is needed, Emotional Guidance will encourage assistance and help the client overcome concerns about stigma
Verbally disputed by client and therapist	Mentally disputed by client. Individual may verbalize (i.e. See Bogus Process)
Pragmatic: How is it working for you in your life?	Same: This question is used in *The Smart Way*™
Empirical dispute: Prove to me that this belief is accurate by just giving me the facts	Individual uses emotions to gain greater clarity about the potential perspectives of a distressing situation, leading to a less emotional and more fact-based evaluation
Elegant dispute: Generate a new more effective belief to replace the old one for client to test in homework assignments to see how the new belief works in his actual life	Individual understands beliefs are thoughts you've thought repeatedly until you've created easy to follow neuropathways. Changing neuropathways simply requires thinking new, better-feeling thoughts repeatedly until those neuropathways are easier to travel. Moment-to-moment adjustments in the new beliefs can be evaluated by how they feel—there is no need for the trial and error process to be applied in real life without knowing in advance (by how the idea feels) that it will bring improvements.
Shame-attacking	*The Smart Way*™ sees shame as an inescapable double-negative and refutes it directly. Sustained negative emotional states are inherently harmful to both body and mind, so shame is refuted as something based in unhealthy beliefs about self, others, or society. *The Smart Way*™ sees beliefs that cause shame as dysfunctional targets that are ripe for change.

In the above chart, CBT is compared and contrasted with *The Smart Way*™ to demonstrate how much more efficient it is to give people information they can use to effectively adjust their thoughts in-the-moment. The time they would spend recording the frequency and events that co-occur with specific beliefs and how frequently those undesired behaviors occur so they can share the information with a therapist could be spent applying the processes and making progress toward better-feeling perspectives.[199]

Often, traditional methods address symptoms of the root cause, such as assertiveness training, anger management and social skills training.[200] The problem is that these programs do not address the root cause of the problem. They help, but not as much as using the same time to improve the root cause.

CBT focuses on client empowerment, positing that the client is capable of change by controlling her/his thoughts and emotions, conveying respect for the client's abilities and understanding.[201] *The Smart Way*™ does the same but reinforces it by putting the knowledge and power in the client's hands, helping to develop and reinforce a healthy internal locus of control. Despite its limitations, Cognitive Behavioral Therapy is highly effective but *The Smart Way*™ has greater potential because it is a cost effective preventative measure and it overcomes some of the objections that our most vulnerable populations have about mental health services.

The Smart Way™ is *Cognitive Behavioral Therapy Plus* because it adds Emotional Guidance and a direct understanding of how the mind works, not just insights garnered by a guided tour led by a therapist.

I'm not suggesting mind-control—at least not by anyone other than the individual controlling his or her own mind. In fact, when individuals do not understand how the mind works or how what they expose themselves to affects their outcomes and the thoughts they think, they make decisions that harm themselves without any awareness of what they are doing. We're careful about exposing ourselves to toxic chemicals, but most people do not realize that over a period of time, negative habits of thought are just as toxic as the chemicals they try so hard to avoid or that repeated exposure to negative inputs can decrease physical well-being. Not understanding how the mind works is no different than giving someone the keys to a car without a map when some paths take them through hostile and even deadly territories.

Compare Mindfulness to The Smart Way

Mindfulness is defined as:
1. The quality or state of being conscious or aware of something.
2. A mental state achieved by focusing your awareness on the present moment, while calmly acknowledging and accepting your feelings, thoughts, and bodily sensations, it is used as a therapeutic technique.

The Smart Way™ differs from mindfulness in several important respects that lead to improved outcomes. The Smart Way™ meets the definition of the 1st definition above but not the second.

The Smart Way™	Mindfulness
Doesn't restrict thought to the present moment. Consciously chooses (as often as possible) subjects to think about based on how they feel. Leaves room for savoring pleasant or delicious memories. Leaves room for eagerly anticipating future events.	Requires focusing on the present moment.
Applies the most recent research on the purpose and use of emotions to create a framework for a flexible adaptive coping style that improves outcomes, reduces stress, and increases resilience and emotional intelligence.	Acceptance is contraindicated by the new research on the purpose and use of emotions that concludes that emotions are designed to guide our behavior. By simply accepting emotions they cannot serve as the guidance they are designed to be.
Awareness of thoughts and feelings but not just accepting them, the individual using The Smart Way™ consciously thinks about what is being thought about and evaluates how they feel when thinking a specific thought compared to how they prefer to feel and finds perspectives that elicit better-feeling emotions. It is a conscious, adaptive, pro-active approach that understands our thoughts have an emotional response and while we can't directly change our emotions, we can change our perception which will change our emotional response to the thoughts we think.	Requires calmly accepting your feelings, thoughts, and bodily sensations.

Being mindful is a good thing and acceptance is better than suppression and numerous other maladaptive methods of dealing with emotions. It is not a best practice now that researchers [202, 203, 204, and 205] have discovered that the reason humans can't directly change their emotions is because the purpose of emotions is to guide us toward self-actualization and away from danger. Maslow defined self-actualization as the desire for self-fulfillment and the tendency to become everything that one is capable of becoming.[206] Our definition is slightly different because our potential expands as we grow so we never become fully self-actualized. We can, however, continually move toward self-actualization.

People speak of the power of now. Being in the now, mindfulness, certainly helps one to enjoy life more. But how does one respond when the now is painful? How does one stay in the now and not be racked by debilitating emotional pain? Now is better than future worry or past regrets but if now is unpleasant, using our power to change perspective can reduce the pain immediately. Feeling better is what is best for our health, relationships, and well-being.

The new definition of emotions indicates their purpose is to provide guidance. It is helpful to think of them as road signs. Thriving feels energized and often involves learning.[207]

When you're driving down the road and you see a Dangerous Curve Ahead sign you don't just accept the presence of dangerous curves. You check your speed and slow down if your speed is too fast for the road conditions. You pay more attention. It's not the time you reach for you iPod to change your music selection or call your spouse. When you feel overwhelmed, you don't just accept how you're feeling, you look for solutions. If you're angry about something you will be better off if you check for baggage that may be contributing to your anger that is more about your past than your present situation.

An example will help:

The Smart Way™	Mindfulness
A friend of yours is severely beaten and is paralyzed by his injuries. You initially feel horrified by what was done to him and worried about his future. While recognizing your emotions are normal in this situation you acknowledge that you'd like to feel better. You begin evaluating your thoughts about your friend. You recognize that medicine has advanced significantly and progress helping people with paralysis is significant. You consciously recognize that he is young and his strong body has a better chance than an older person does to recover from the injury. You recognize that if the paralysis is permanent, the rate of progress being made in medicine may allow your friend to live a far better life than he would have (given the same injuries) just a decade earlier. You feel grateful for all the work	A friend of yours is severely beaten and is paralyzed by his injuries. You feel horrified by what was done to him and worried about his future. You accept these emotions as a normal response to the situation. You don't make evaluative judgments about the emotions as good or bad.

done in this field and for the researchers who have made progress possible. Your feelings have changed from feeling awful to feeling guarded optimism that one way or another your friend's life is not completely ruined. During each of the above steps you paid attention to how your thoughts felt and leaned toward the ones that felt better. As thoughts of his life being ruined forever crossed your mind, you reject the thoughts (not the emotions) because you recognize you have access to better-feeling thoughts and know that better-feeling thoughts are better for you and for your friend because your hopefulness can help your friend be hopeful.

Another example:

The Smart Way™	Mindfulness
Your co-worker has been calling in sick frequently and you've had to take additional, undesired, shifts to make up for your co-worker's absences. It just happened again and you're emotions are fluctuating between anger and frustration. You begin evaluating how you feel and realize that although you pride yourself on being compassionate you're not feeling very compassionate here—you're departing from the person you want to be. Then you realize that although you've worked with this person for a few years you've never had personal conversations and you don't know their situation. You don't know if there are elderly sick parents, a sick child or if the co-worker is ill. You decide the situation is one you'd probably feel a lot of compassion for if you knew the details of what was going on in your co-workers life and it's the not knowing more than the absences that led to your initial emotions. You consciously decide to give your co-worker the benefit of the doubt and decide that just because you don't know the reason	Your co-worker has been calling in sick frequently and you've had to take additional, undesired, shifts to make up for your co-worker's absences. It just happened again and you're emotions are fluctuating between anger and frustration. You accept your emotions and work the extra shift.

doesn't mean it isn't a good one. You begin feeling like you're helping a co-worker in need by taking the shift rather than being advantage of by a co-worker. Your anger dissipates. When the co-worker returns to work you're supportive and welcoming. You let the co-worker know they've been in your thoughts and you hope all is okay with them.

These examples reveal that responses to undesired emotions by an individual applying The Smart Way™ are informed by the specific emotional message, are consciously applied to preserve or restored more desirable emotional states through "open, approach behavior, adaptive development and social cooperation."[208]

It may sound as if I am saying mindfulness isn't a good practice. That's not my intention. I'm saying mindfulness is not a *best practice.* Mindfulness does a lot of good but it also leaves a lot of potential for thriving unrealized. Before we had access to an accurate understanding of the purpose and use of emotions mindfulness was a best practice.

In the same way that other knowledge is expanded upon and improved, The Smart Way™ replaces mindfulness as a best practice for achieving optimal results. We readily accept new ways of doing things when their benefits are easily quantifiable. *The Smart Way*™ is best understood through visceral experience. The old commercial, "Try it, you'll like it" comes to mind. An intellectual understanding is minuscule in comparison to an understanding that comes from experience.

Knowledge of something new and better does not make the less effective method bad. It simply means it is no longer the best practice. Best practices are superior to other methods because they achieve better results.

For example, one of my earliest clients was a Vietnam veteran with PTSD who used mindfulness. Despite being trained to use mindfulness and being consistent in his practice, he had retired because being around a lot of other people had become too much for him. His life was shrinking. He was under the care of a psychiatrist, receiving counseling, and medicated for his condition but nothing had done much other than slow his decline. After teaching him The Smart Way™ his condition began improving. Soon he was becoming more involved in the outside world. He began traveling and his psychiatrist took him off meds because he was doing so well. He was very sensitive to loud noises when we first met and now they don't startle him or create anxiety. The first year I knew him he stayed home on the 4th of July because the potential of fireworks was too much for him. Now he goes to view fireworks on the 4th.

Mindfulness (Palliative to Transformational)

I live the techniques I teach. Numerous people, including clinical psychologists, have remarked that I am very mindful. I want to differentiate between mindfulness and *The Smart Way*™.

Mindfulness strives to focus on the present experience without judgment or evaluation.

The Smart Way™ doesn't care if you're focused on past, present, or future. It encourages you to focus on things that feel good and to find the best feeling thought you can find about what you're focused upon. There is an absence of negative judgment. Negative emotions simply mean that you're looking at a situation or

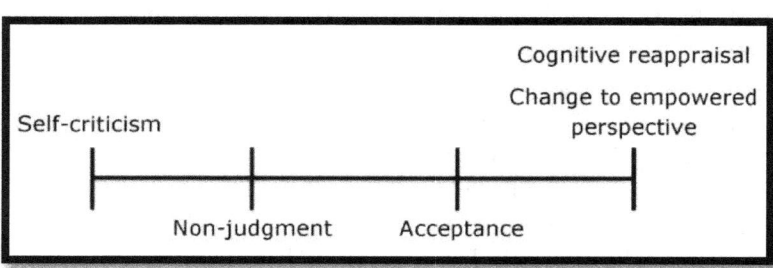

individual in a way that is not the best way you could perceive the situation or person. In that regard it is not judgmental and emotions are seen as guidance so they can be appreciated for providing guidance even when they don't feel good. Emotions are not indicating that someone else is bad when our gaze upon them feels bad to us. It is the thoughts we think about the person/situation that cause our negative emotion.

The Smart Way™ encourages savoring future events that you are looking forward to so that you can enjoy them now and when they actually occur. The trick is not to become attached to the outcome. For example, I enjoyed the things I had planned for my wedding day enormously but when things didn't go exactly as planned I immediately felt for thoughts that felt better which ensured our day wasn't ruined because of a few things that weren't exactly as planned. Reaching for better-feeling thought ensures that savoring in advance doesn't lead to disappointment when the anticipated situation doesn't manifest exactly the way you'd hoped.

The Smart Way™ does not discourage recalling the past. It discourages negative rumination. But there is nothing disadvantageous about savoring memories of good times in the past as long as it is done while feeling good. If it is done while feeling melancholy or missing the good old days, think about something that feels better. It is okay to pick up memories from the past in order to reframe them but only do this if it is a subject you still think about. For example, if you never think about the classmate that was mean to you in sixth grade don't dredge that old memory up. If you were abused as a child and you still feel like a victim, finding more empowered ways to view the past would help you. I've previously written about how to do that in *Rescue Our Children from the War Zone* and those instructions are beyond the scope of this book.

Mindfulness has been heavily researched and implemented in a wide variety of situations. It is a helpful practice but time will show that the practice of using Emotional Guidance and Advanced and Transformational Strategies provides better short and long-term results. In 2016, *The American Journal of Occupational Therapy* reported that abbreviated practices of mindfulness are not supported in the literature (as being effective at reducing stress).[209]

The time commitment for mindfulness is not less than that of learning *The Smart Way*™.[210]

I've worked with clients who used mindfulness before learning *The Smart Way*™ who have reported that their lives improved with the addition of *The Smart Way*™ and I've never had a client with a mindfulness practice who reported that learning *The Smart Way*™ did not provide stress relief beyond what they were already experiencing. This is as good of a place as any to remind the reader that extensive research on a specific practice does not mean it is the best practice, just the most researched practice.

Work/Life Balance

Work/Life Balance has permeated discussions of work-related stress for decades. Two articles I reviewed while writing a burnout prevention book for physicians resonated with me. Both of the articles approached work/life balance from an unexpected direction that immediately made sense. The first was from an intensivist* who described her three maternity leaves.

During the first she worked frequently while her baby slept and returned to work feeling energized and rested but colleagues judged and criticized her for working while on leave. She felt grief and remorse for working despite being motivated to work.

During her second maternity leave she "followed the rules" and disconnected. She once again returned to work energized and rested but was again overwhelmed with guilt, this time over the mountain of work that had piled up during her absence. They say the third time is the charm and for her it was.

During her third leave she "wrote when she was motivated to write, slept when tired, and parented when it seemed fitting." She wrote, "My days were fluid, unencumbered, productive, and loving. When I returned to work, I was energized and rested and guilt-free."[211] She explains:

> *As intensivists, we make hundreds of decisions daily and I would venture to guess that most decisions are good ones. Finding the key to work—life balance for me was having trust in my skills as an*

---

* An intensivist is a physician who works with critical patients in the hospital.

> *intensivist; acknowledging that these decision-making skills guide me in all my life decisions. I mostly make good decisions when deciding how best to spend my time. The most efficient and meaningful way to spend my time is to combine all aspects of my life and let them ebb and flow as naturally indicated.* [212]

I recognized how I live my own life in her comments. The next article I read echoed her thoughts on work-life balance as an illusion:

> *Since entering medical school over two decades ago, I reached the conclusion that the concept of work-life balance acts as quicksand in our professional and personal lives resulting in slow drowning in frustration, depression, and exhaustion... As we follow our peers' instructions trying to balance work and life, the question arises: when should we achieve this balance and How do we know we achieved it?... I concluded that the never-ending chase after work-life balance actually accumulates much more frustration than satisfaction...* <u>the absence of an objective outcome measure makes the chances of ever achieving this goal rather elusive.</u> [213]

The work-life balance concept lacks a critical component of good goal setting—a way to measure success. If work-life balance feels elusive to you, let go of the goal of achieving it. Replace it with taking a few minutes each day to savor the wonderful life that you have. Savor your loved ones; savor the food you eat and the air you breathe. Savor a sunrise and a flower.

Appreciate your skills and the lives you touch. Listen to your Emotional Guidance and if something isn't working for you, believe you can change it and then work toward goals that make things better. Let me know how it goes.

Communication

If we seek happiness and harmony in our dialogues instead of demanding that we be the person who is right, we have better discourse and can openly approach other perspectives and take the conversation deeper to the roots of how those perspectives were formed. How to know if your Understanding is Accurate

- Don't assume you understand
- Ask for clarification
    - Before forming opinion (without judgment)
    - Take the conversation deeper
- How does it feel?
    - Good (on your path)
        - Consider long-term vs. short-term
    - Bad (consider alternative translations)
- Learn about the source
- Learn about the source's resources

Advice Q & A

I receive a lot of requests to answer questions associated with a surprising variety of situations individuals face on a daily basis. The next few headings are responses I've provided to situations that cause a lot of people emotional pain.

Heartache

This question is from someone who thinks it is better to be indifferent to others because he is less likely to be hurt if he can be indifferent and not vulnerable. "If I open myself to new experiences I make myself vulnerable to being hurt."

There is a 3rd option. You can be open to new experiences, learning, growing and having confidence yet know that you will not be hurt badly. Our society misunderstands what heartache is. All heartache is self-inflicted. Yes, all heartache is self-inflicted.

You see our hearts love. The heart does not know how to stop loving. This does not mean that we have to keep someone in our life forever once we love the person. You can lovingly let someone go without stopping the love and you will not hurt. We can love someone and send them out of our life, we just have to wish them the best and not try to stop loving them. We have to unbundle loving from *being with* someone.

If you think about someone who you would say hurt your heart and shift the way you see them around in your mind so that you stop trying to hate or resent or be angry with them and just send them loving thoughts and wish them well, your heartache goes away. Trying not to love someone your heart loves creates heartache. This is true whether the person is living or no longer in their body.

Understand that the heartache you feel when a relationship ends is within your control. Once we love someone our heart will not stop loving that person. The heartache people experience is because they are attempting not to love someone their heart loves. Your heart is stronger than you are. It gives you emotional pain to know that you're pulling away from your heart in your thoughts.

"I love you. I wish you the best. I hope you have a good life. Goodbye."

Usually people who are afraid of being hurt have been hurt. So the way to understand this is to re-visit an old relationship that still pains you in your mind. (There is no need to talk to or see the person again.) In your mind stop vilifying the person (for leaving you, for cheating, for whatever) and simply return to the feeling of love you once felt and then, in your mind, separate loving them from being with them physically and let the person go.

You'll find that relationships that used to hurt no longer hurts.

Once you know the key to not being hurt at the end of a relationship, you are free to love freely because you don't have to protect your heart.

For example, I have an x-husband that I have no desire to spend any time with him. If I think of how he hurt me and resent his behavior I can still hurt even after all these years. But if I can recognize that my life is actually a whole lot better without him in it and wish him happiness and love wherever he is, my heart feels at peace again.

It takes a while to get the hang of it. The more experience you've had with being hurt that you can play with seeing from different perspectives in your mind, the easier it is to gain confidence that if you can turn those old hurts around, you can be open and loving in a new relationship and know you won't be hurt badly, even if the relationship ends.

Being indifferent is like being dead. It's not living. It is something in between death and being alive. I wouldn't take that option for a million dollars.

Feeling Lost and Unable to love

After an unsuccessful job interview, a 23-year old recent graduate who doesn't like his major and is feeling lost—not knowing what he wants from life or why he is alive asked for advice because he feels his ability to love others is decreasing and that he no longer has any goals.

Most people don't have a life goal, especially not at 23. If they do, it usually changes many times over the course of their life. You're holding yourself to a high standard and no one else is doing that (unless you have a parent who likes to find problems with you and fix them).

Loss of a child (grief)

This 33-year old has lost her babies before birth after going through fertility treatments. Her fertility/pregnancy related absences seem to have negatively impacted her career. She feels like she has lost everything that matters to her.

She is asking for career advice, advice about whether to relocate to a new country, about getting over the pain of the loss of her children, and about personality changes she doesn't like in herself.

You've being very specific and very negative (this is not a criticism—it's natural for you to do that under the circumstances). The point is that anyone who focuses on something that is very specific that they don't like and didn't want is going to feel awful. To feel better you must find something that feels better to think about and the easiest way to do that is to:
1) think about a different subject that feels better, or
2) think more generally about the subject you feel badly about.
More general might be like this or this might be too big of a stretch for the first attempt.

I am feeling awful. I wanted my babies so badly and we worked so hard to bring them into the world. After all the stress and strain and effort, to have our hopes and dreams dashed when we were almost there is more than many people can bear. I'm having a difficult time with this situation and feeling lost and angry. I have a right to be angry but I don't want to be stuck here. I don't even like myself very much when I am like this and certainly don't expect anyone else to like me when I'm like this. I want to move on. We still have the adoption option. Adoption will allow us to create the family we want and somewhere there is a child or children who want a home and a family to love and we can provide that. It won't be our biological children but the love will be real. The hugs will be real. The experience will be real. My babies will always be in my heart and I will always love them, but my heart is big and I can find room to love more children. I want to focus more on what I'm going to do next, pursue adoption, and spend a little less time focusing on what I've lost. My babies know they are firmly in my heart. They want me to be happy as much as I wanted them to have beautiful lives. They don't want me to stay here where I feel so miserable all the time. If I sit quietly I can feel them encouraging me to feel better and be all that I can be.

Okay, that should give you an idea of how to move more general in your thoughts and shift the subject slightly. I know it wasn't easy reading. Pay attention to the parts that felt better and as you feel able, expand on those thoughts in your mind.

Depression

One of the reasons our society is so unsuccessful in helping individuals rise from depression is we reject aspects of the path from depression to more empowered states. Anger and revenge are more empowered than depression. We view those emotional states as more dangerous and discourage them. If it were generally understood that anger and revenge are no different than cities you have to drive through when they are along the route from Point A to the destination, Point B, we would do better. If people generally understood that how they feel is within their control they would not blame others for their emotions.

When you understand the path from depression to higher emotional states, moving quickly through the Hot Zone is not difficult. As your emotional state moves to higher Zones, differences feel less relevant.

Primary Prevention

I spend a lot of years answering one question, "What makes some humans thrive in spite of adversity?" At the time I didn't realize that learning what leads to human thriving would provide information about how to prevent illnesses, diseases, and behaviors that interfere with human thriving.

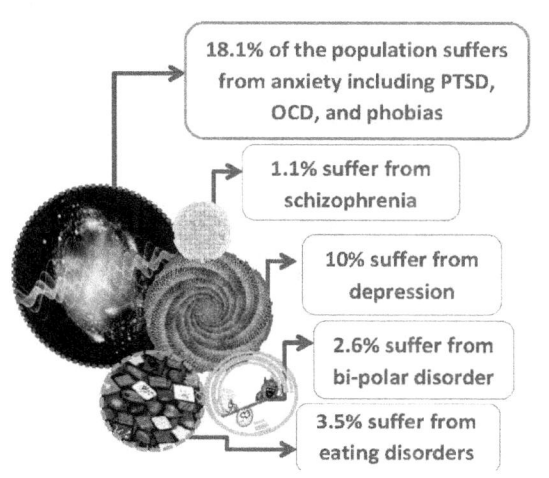

In hindsight, it makes sense that increasing human thriving would decrease human suffering but I didn't realize what I was actually looking for in the beginning. I was looking for the answer to "What makes one person thrive in spite of adversity while another one ends up living in a box under a bridge after facing essentially the same circumstances?"

Primary Prevention should be a common household word. It is that important yet I often find myself having to explain what it is. If we would focus more on Primary Prevention our world would be a lot better for most people. All of us take actions that are considered Primary Preventions everyday (or at least I hope we do). Washing your hands after using the bathroom and before you eat is a form of Primary Prevention. Primary Prevention is something done to prevent an illness from occurring. Primary Prevention and *Risk Management* are closely related. If only one person out of a billion people who didn't wash their hands became ill each year we probably wouldn't be as concerned about whether we wash our hands. But the risk of illness occurring from not washing your hands is much higher than that so nearly everyone washes their hands many times each day.

Mental Health is a perfect candidate for Primary Prevention. Unlike our physical health which will eventually result in death for all of us, no one has to experience mental illness during their lifetime. Mental Illness is wholly preventable. Think about that. With the right preventative measures we could eliminate mental illness. (See Appendix VII for more information.)

From a Risk Management perspective, Primary Prevention of mental illness makes sense because the risk of experiencing mental illness is significant. Half of all chronic mental illness begins by age 14 and three-quarters begins by age 24. Despite effective treatment, there are long delays—sometimes decades—between the first appearance of symptoms and when people get help.[214] Many individuals have co-occuring mental illness.

"For example, 50 percent of males and 75 percent of female inmates in state prisons, and 75 percent of females and 63 percent of male inmates in jails, will experience a mental health problem requiring mental health services in any given year."[215] In many cases, the symptoms of their mental illness lead to longer incarceration times and to increased punishments.

A little more than half the people with a substance use disorder have a diagnosable mental illness.[216]

When you read about the benefits of *The Smart Way*™ in the next chapter, the public health consequences of poor mental health become obvious.

The Benefits of using The Smart Way

Outcomes You Can Expect

Specifically, the healthy habits of thought you'll learn to develop lead to:

Better
- Mental Health
- Physical Health

Longer life [217, 218, 219, 220]
Higher resilience [221]
More authenticity
Less stress
Better relationships [224]
More confidence
Higher self-esteem
More optimism

Better pro-health behavior
Easier to make decisions
More positive emotions
Increased academic success [222, 223]
Greater career success
Increased sports success
Increased clarity of thought
Increased psychological flexibility [225]
Reduced risk of heart disease [226, 227]
Being more of who you want to be
Healthy habits of thought [228, 229]
Higher sense of purpose in life [230]

Happiness and stress have an inverse relationship. Happiness indicates the person is experiencing a low level of stress. Research on the presence of happiness and the presence of stress reveal the following benefits of higher levels of happiness and lower levels of stress:

Increased pro-social behaviors [231]
- Reduced anti-social behavior
  - Violence Reduction [232, 233]
- Better citizenship
- Increased kindness (even to strangers) [234]
- Intrinsically motivated diversity appreciation (a significant step-up from tolerance)
- Reduced (or no) criminal behavior [235, 236, 237, 238, 239]
- Increased positive goal setting
- More likely to act cooperatively [240]
- Stronger social relationships [241]
- Bullying Prevention [242]
- Problematic Gambling [243, 244]
- More likely to marry [245]

Increased pro-health behaviors [246]
- Reduced likelihood of alcohol, drug, and cigarette [247] use

Less drinking to cope [248, 249, 250]
- Reduced likelihood of addiction [251, 252]
- Increased physical activity
- Better dietary choices [253, 254]
- Improved sleep habits and quality of sleep
- Substance Use Disorders [255]
- Smoking Cessation [256, 257]

Physical and Mental Benefits
- Improved immune function [258]
- Improved cognitive function [259]
- Improved digestive function [260]
- Improvements related to Type II diabetes [261]
- Early Stage Breast Cancer [262]
- Improved Heart health [263]
    - Hypertension [264]
- General Stresss [265]
- Rheumatoid Arthritis [266]
- Irritable Bowel Syndrome [267]
- Disease Management [268]
- Improved Central Nervous System Functioning
- And via general stress reduction:
    - Prevent pre-term births [269]
    - Prevent adverse epigenetic changes [270]
- Bullying (Recovery from) [271]
- Reduced risk of mental illness [272, 273, 274] including:
    - Depression and anxiety [275, 276, 277, 278, 279]
    - Anxiety [280, 281, 282]
    - Depression [283, 284]
    - Suicide [285]
    - Panic disorders [286, 287]
    - Social phobia [288]
    - Phobias [289]
    - Bi-polar disorder [290, 291, 292]
        - Hypochondria [293]
        - Anger and Aggression [294, 295]
        - Insomnia [296]
        - Body dysmorphic disorder (BDD) [297]
        - Eating Disorders [298, 299, 300]
        - Prevent relapse of Mood Disorders [301]
        - Childhood internalizing disorders [302]
        - Chronic Fatigue Syndrome [303]

- - Distress Due to General Medical Conditions [304]
  - Premenstrual Syndrome [305]
  - Personality Disorders [306]
  - OCD [307]
  - Schizophrenia [308]
  - Schizophrenia & Other Psychotic Disorders [309]
  - Psychosis [310]
- Positive Mental Health [311]
- Vastly superior results (relapse rates half those of pharmacotherapy) for depression and panic disorders [312]

Success Benefits

- Superior work outcomes [313]
- More activity, energy and flow [314]
- Improved cognitive abilities [315]
- Improved teacher (Trainee) Stress Levels [316]

These results are yours for the taking. In order to take them you have to apply the strategies in this book. Just reading about them but not using them won't bring the results you want to achieve.

Severe and/or prolonged stress causes over activation and dysregulation of the hypothalamic pituitary adrenal (HPA) axis thus inflicting detrimental changes in the brain structure and function. Therefore, chronic stress is often considered a negative modulator of the cognitive functions including the learning and memory processes. Exposure to long-lasting stress diminishes health and increases vulnerability to mental disorders. In addition, stress exacerbates functional changes associated with various brain disorders including Alzheimer's disease and Parkinson's disease. [317]

Positive emotions are immensely beneficial for us—increasing our resilience, reducing the risks from negative life events, decreasing the risk of all types of major illnesses and improving relationships. We have Emotional Guidance that helps us enjoy better-feeling emotions. It makes sense to understand and use the guidance available to us.

Negative emotional states are harmful to our bodies, minds, relationships, and choices. Depressed individuals will

Mental illness is the cause of disability in 4 our of 10 cases
(National Institute of Health)

participate in riskier behaviors than individuals at higher emotional states. [318] There is a plethora of growing evidence suggesting that social ills including crime, [319] teen pregnancy, [320] drug and alcohol abuse, [321] and more are casually related to long-term emotional pain. There is mounting evidence that indicates improved desirable behaviors are linked to increased positive emotion including better corporate citizenship, altruism, kindness to strangers without expectation of reward, better relationships of all types, and much more. [322-323]

Happiness is an indicator of low levels of stress. Stress interferes with:
- Your body's immune function
- Your cognitive abilities. You are literally smarter when you're happy than when you're unhappy.
- Your digestive function which increases the risk of diabetes and obesity
- Functioning of your Central Nervous System
- Relationships
- Success

The National Institute of Mental illness reports that 37% of children age 14 or above who have a mental illness drop out of school.

Reviews
Together we can change the world, one good deed at a time.
Pay it Forwarders

If this book has helped you please pay it forward by writing a review on Amazon, Good Reads (goodreads.com) or another online bookseller's website. In the competitive publishing world, books without reviews seldom make it into the hands of the people they are designed to help. Your review helps us help others. You never know whose life will be positively impacted because you chose to share your thoughts about this book. Thank you ever so much if you choose to write a review. Thank you.

Cultural Differences

This book is written from my perspective informed by research and experience. My perspective is that of an American female who left home at age 18 and put herself through University without assistance from my family. Some of the concepts presented may create conflicts in cultures where parents tend to exert more influence over adult children. The fact that I come from a different worldview doesn't matter because you have your own Emotional Guidance and now you understand how to interpret your guidance accurately. You can find ways to align with your culture that feel good to you or you may choose to rebel against your culture. Your guidance will be with you and help you every step of the way. My children were teenagers when I learned about Emotional Guidance and it led to me giving them more responsibility for their own actions and referring them to their Emotional Guidance when decisions needed to be made instead of asserting my preferences. Prior to learning about Emotional Guidance, I was a controlling parent. After learning about Emotional Guidance I realized that attempting to control others keeps you in bondage because it requires you to be an enforcer.

Dr. Joy's Books

The man who does not read books has no advantage over the man that cannot read them.
Mark Twain (1835-1910) U.S. humorist, writer, and lecturer

The best of a book is not the thought which it contains, but the thought which it suggests; just as the charm of music dwells not in the tones but in the echoes of our hearts.
Oliver Wendell Holmes (1809-1894) American author and poet

<u>*Harness the Power of Resilience: Be Ready for Life*</u>

<u>*Burnout: Prevention and Recovery, Resilience and Retention,* Evidence-based, experience-informed, root cause solutions</u>

<u>*Prevent Suicide: The Smart Way,* Transformative Empowering Processes Provide A Better Way to Prevent Suicide</u>

<u>*Empowered Employees become Engaged Employees:* Using Science to Solve the Employee Engagement Crisis, *The Smart Way: Applied Positive Psychology in Action*</u>

<u>*Rescue Our Children from the War Zone:* Teach Social and Emotional Skills to Improve Their Lives: *Applied Positive Psychology 2.1*</u>

<u>*True Prevention--Optimum Health: Remember Galileo*</u>

<u>*Is Punishment Ethical?* The Fallacy of Good and Evil</u>

"Trusting One's Emotional Guidance Builds Resilience", Perspectives on Coping and Resilience. Ed. Venkat Pulla, Shane Warren, and Andrew Shatté. Laxmi Nagar: Authors Press, 2013. 254-279

About the Author: Jeanine Joy, Ph.D.
Two roads diverged in a wood and I - I took the one less traveled by, and that has made all the difference.
Robert Frost

Dr. Joy followed a non-traditional path to mastering the knowledge she shares. She pursued the answer to a question experts said could not be answered with passionate interest and determination for over two decades. Her journey began when an expert told her she was more resilient than most and asked her how she managed it. Jeanine concluded that if she was more resilient and she could figure out how or why, she could help a lot of people.

As a citizen scientist, she was not bound by the silo's that constrain most researchers. If information helped her thrive or to communicate how to thrive more to others, she looked for ways to incorporate it into her repertoire. Adding evidence-based support to the experience-informed processes and techniques she'd accumulated was the last step in her journey. When she turned to reading peer-reviewed research she was delighted to find support for all the major strategies she was teaching.

She teaches diverse audiences, from the CEO's of organizations to homeless recovering addicts. Many fields of science have made great progress in emotion regulation, motivation, organizational behavior, positive psychology, organizations, and teams, resilience, self-determination and self-control. Because they tend to stay in their own silo, none have put together as many pieces of the puzzle to form a cohesive picture of human thriving as Dr. Joy.

We can and should teach people how to develop healthy habits of thought rather than waiting until they experience physical or mental illnesses from the stress they experience as the result of unhealthy habits of thought.

Her doctorate is in the philosophy of pastoral counseling psychology on a metaphysical foundation. Metaphysics is the study of the mind and a respected field until mind and body were split to please the church. As science brings us back to solid evidence of the mind-body connection, mainstream researchers are beginning to give metaphysics more attention.

Science supports the strategies Dr. Joy teaches and they are also supported by metaphysical principles, by the texts of many of the world's religions, and by the wisdom of many ancient philosophers. She shares lived experiences that demonstrate the benefits of understanding this information.

She is a sought after keynote speaker and trainer committed to helping people thrive more in every area of life. She believes it is possible to create a world where everyone thrives. She is doing everything she can to create momentum that will someday make such a world possible. Archimedes of Syracuse (circa 287 BC – 212 BC) was a leading scientist of antiquity. This Greek mathematician, philosopher, scientist and engineer said, "Give me a place to stand and with a lever I will move the whole world." This book is a place to stand and the lever. Everyone who applies the information from this book will change their world for the better.

Appendix I – Emotional Guidance Scale (EGSc)

In general, emotional states can be defined (broadly) with the following feelings:

Sweet Zone
- Joy
- Empowered
- Passion
- Happy
- Inspired
- Optimism
- Fulfilled
- Appreciation
- Love
- Enthusiasm
- Positive Expectation
- Trust
- Serene
- Secure
- Freedom
- Awe
- Eagerness
- Belief
- Faith
- Satisfied
- At ease

Hopeful Zone
- Hopefulness
- Grateful
- Upbeat

Blah Zone
- Contentment
- Apathy
- Boredom
- Dispirited
- Pessimism
- Empty

Drama Zone
- Frustration
- Overwhelmed
- Irritation
- Disappointment
- Impatience
- Indignant

Give Away Zone
- Doubt
- Guilt
- Cynical
- Worry
- Discouragement
- Blame
- Offended

Hot (Red) Zone
- Anger
- Outraged
- Revenge
- Easily provoked
- Rage
- Furious

Powerless Zone
- Victimized
- Hatred
- Insecure
- Grief
- Powerless
- Hopeless
- Suicidal
- Bullied
- Excessively Detached
- Fear
- Depression
- Learned Helplessness
- Melancholy
- Unimportant
- Jealousy
- Envy
- Unworthiness
- Despair
- Guarded
- Unwanted
- Exploited

Appendix II: Zones and Outcomes Chart

Sweet Zone	Hopeful Zone	Blah Zone	Drama Zone	Give Away Zone	Hot (Red) Zone	Powerless Zone
Lowest Stress	Low Stress	More Stress	Stress Swings ↑↓	Chronic Stress	High Stress	Highest Stress
Highest Empowerment	Some Empowerment	Lackluster Empowerment	Empowerment ↑↓	Low Empowerment	Low Empowerment Leads To Anger	No Empowerment
Best Mental Health	Usually Good	Declining Mental Health	Mental Health ↑↓	Often Signs Of Mental Illness	Frequent Mental Illness	Common Mental Illness
Best Physical Health	Usually Good	Stress Symptoms	Physical Health ↑↓	Chronic Illnesses	Chronic & Serious Illnesses	Chronic & Serious Illnesses
Best Relationships	Satisfying	Lackluster Relationships	Relationship Turmoil	Not Satisfying	Very Rocky & Unhealthy	No Joy
Highest Success * Academic * Career * Sports	Frequent Success	Less Energy For Success	Success ↑↓	Low Success	Rare Success	None Without Significant Support

Appendix III - The Smart Way Training for Groups

The Smart Way™ is proactive, low-cost and develops skills that improve results throughout life. It is designed to help individuals achieve and sustain emotions in the +8 range (from hope to joy). Because it is educational and structured to correct prevalent misconceptions, no stigma is attached to learning about Emotional Guidance and Advanced and Transformational Coping Strategies. It is an evidence-based form of Primary Prevention. Training comes with added benefits, including improving morale, reducing burnout, enhancement of any existing wellness programs, and reduction in prejudices or biases.

The Smart Way™ has a decided advantage over CBT for a number of reasons:

1. It can be delivered in a cost effective manner to large groups
2. It is prevention, not mental health treatment for a manifested illness so there is no stigma. The focus is on increasing happiness and resilience and strategies to reduce stress and regulate emotions.
3. Because it is not a one-on-one therapeutic relationship, cultural differences are not a significant element. The student can use Emotional Guidance to decide what is personally meaningful and best. Classes always include the instruction to follow your own Emotional Guidance over and above the instructor's viewpoint. Instructors will disclose that they have their own core beliefs and that having different core beliefs is acceptable, and adds to the value and worth of each individual. Diversity is recognized as a form of collective strength that is to be appreciated.
4. It empowers the individual with strategies and knowledge that lead to more functional thinking capabilities.

We encourage providing *The Smart Way*™ training classes and materials to both employees and their families because it provides consistent reinforcement and the techniques help families manage their own stressors, contributing to supportive and harmonious home environments. Improving the emotional state of any member of the family benefits every family member. The evidence suggests it can reduce family problems that eventually affect the quality of work and absenteeism.

The Smart Way™ is not synonymous with Cognitive Behavioral Therapy provided before an individual develops a mental or physical health problem. It is **CBT Plus** because of Emotional Guidance. *The Smart Way*™ is delivered primarily to groups or provided as self-help using videos and books. It is significantly more cost effective than CBT because it does not require one-on-one therapy and because it prevents the problems before they happen, thus avoiding the costs associated with problems that have manifested. It is more difficult to cure a condition than to prevent its occurrence in the first place and there is no relapse because the illness did not manifest in the first place. Another major difference is that Cognitive Behavioral Therapy does not include Emotional Guidance, which overturned a prevalent but inaccurate interpretation of emotions. *The Smart Way*™ disabuses negative beliefs about the subconscious portions of personality that often include beliefs that the subconscious is secret, dark, and frightening as well as unreliable and dangerous to explore.

Appendix IV– Religious Passages that Support Emotional Guidance

As the result of receiving numerous questions about how Emotional Guidance fit with individual's religious worldviews my frustration at not knowing how to answer the question led me to research major religions so I would be prepared to answer the question. This is a brief synopsis of passages from different religions that support the use of emotions as guidance. If you prefer to see emotional guidance as guidance from God, the scripture of your religion probably provides some support for the concept. If you prefer to hang your hat on scientific evidence that was provided in the main body of the book.

Examples from a variety of Holy books are shown below:

Proverbs 3:5 (Bible) *"Trust in the Lord with all your heart and lean not on your own understanding; In all your ways acknowledge Him, and He will make your paths straight."*

If we interpret Emotional Guidance as coming from God it makes sense of words written long ago that have been interpreted in many different ways. If people consult the Bible for guidance, they must *'lean on their own understanding'* by finding the right passage, the right interpretation, and using their brains to determine how it applies to their situations. When guidance that comes from the Emotional Guidance system is used, there is no guess work and the path to what is desired is straight. The shortest path to their goals feels better than a longer route.

There are many passages that indicate we are always guided and always watched over. These were written at a time when the majority of humanity was incapable of reading and mass distribution of the written word was not possible. Could these passages be pointing to the emotional sense?

Proverbs 16:9 *"A man's heart plans his way, but the Lord directs his steps"* echoes exactly that the guidance is specific to our unique goals.

From the Bhagwath gita:

"The Supersoul within everyone's heart, directly gives us guidance... the spiritual master in the heart, gives direct inspiration."[324]

"The Lord's mercy is therefore available both in the form of the instructing spiritual masters and the Supersoul within the heart." 345 [325]

From the Tao, "47. *1. Without going outside his door, one understands (all that takes place) under the sky; without looking out from his window, one sees the Tao of Heaven. The farther that one goes out (from himself), the less he knows. 2. Therefore the sages got their knowledge without travelling; gave their (right) names to things without seeing them; and accomplished their ends without any purpose of doing so.*[326]"

From Buddhist teachings, "282. *Wisdom is born of meditation deep, But lost by mind's distraction; knowing these Two paths of loss and gain, so let him live, Let him so direct his life that wisdom may increase.*" [327]

From The Koran (Al-Qur'an), "*By this the reader will observe that the Mohammedans are no strangers to Quietism. Others, however, understand the words of the soul, which, having attained the knowledge of the truth, rests satisfied, and relies securely thereon, undisturbed by doubts; or of the soul which is secure of its salvation, and free from fear or sorrow.*"348 [328]

From Abraham, "*You cannot be separated from that which you are calling God... People hear us say, 'Reach for the thought that feels the best.' And they think, 'Oh no, I need to listen to what God wants.' But aren't we talking about the same thing? Aren't your emotions guiding you to that Connection? And doesn't the word God just set you off on all kinds of tangents that don't have anything to do with your relationship with that which is this Eternal Energy of Love that is your Source?* "[329]

From Confucius: "*By three methods we may learn wisdom: first, by reflection, which is noblest; second, by imitation, which is easiest; and third, by experience, which is the most bitter.*"[330]

These examples clearly point to inner wisdom. Experimenting with your Emotional Guidance system reveals the wisdom that is available to everyone.

Appendix V- Effects of a Positive Mindset

This chart becomes too unwieldy when citations are added. Every box is supported by research. Citations are in the benefits chapter.

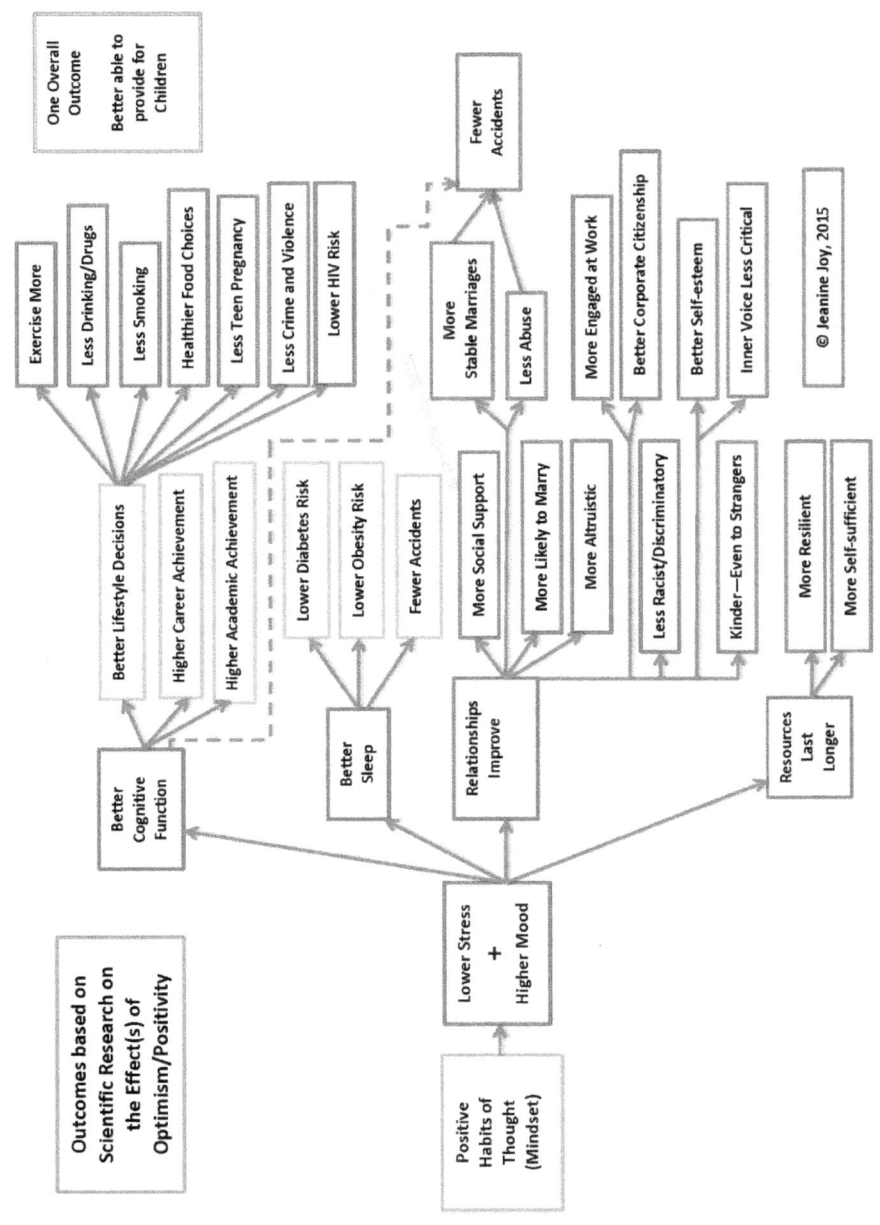

XIX

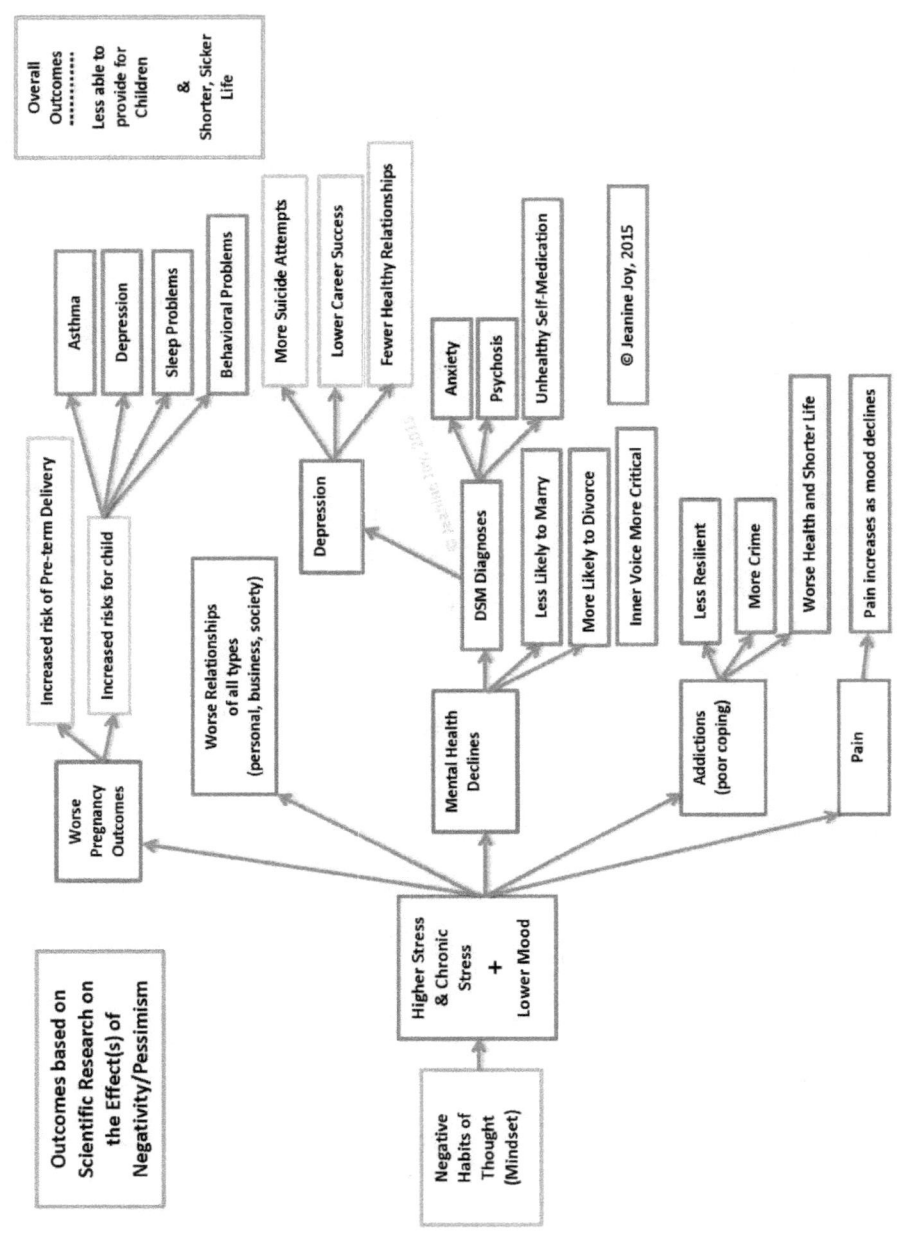

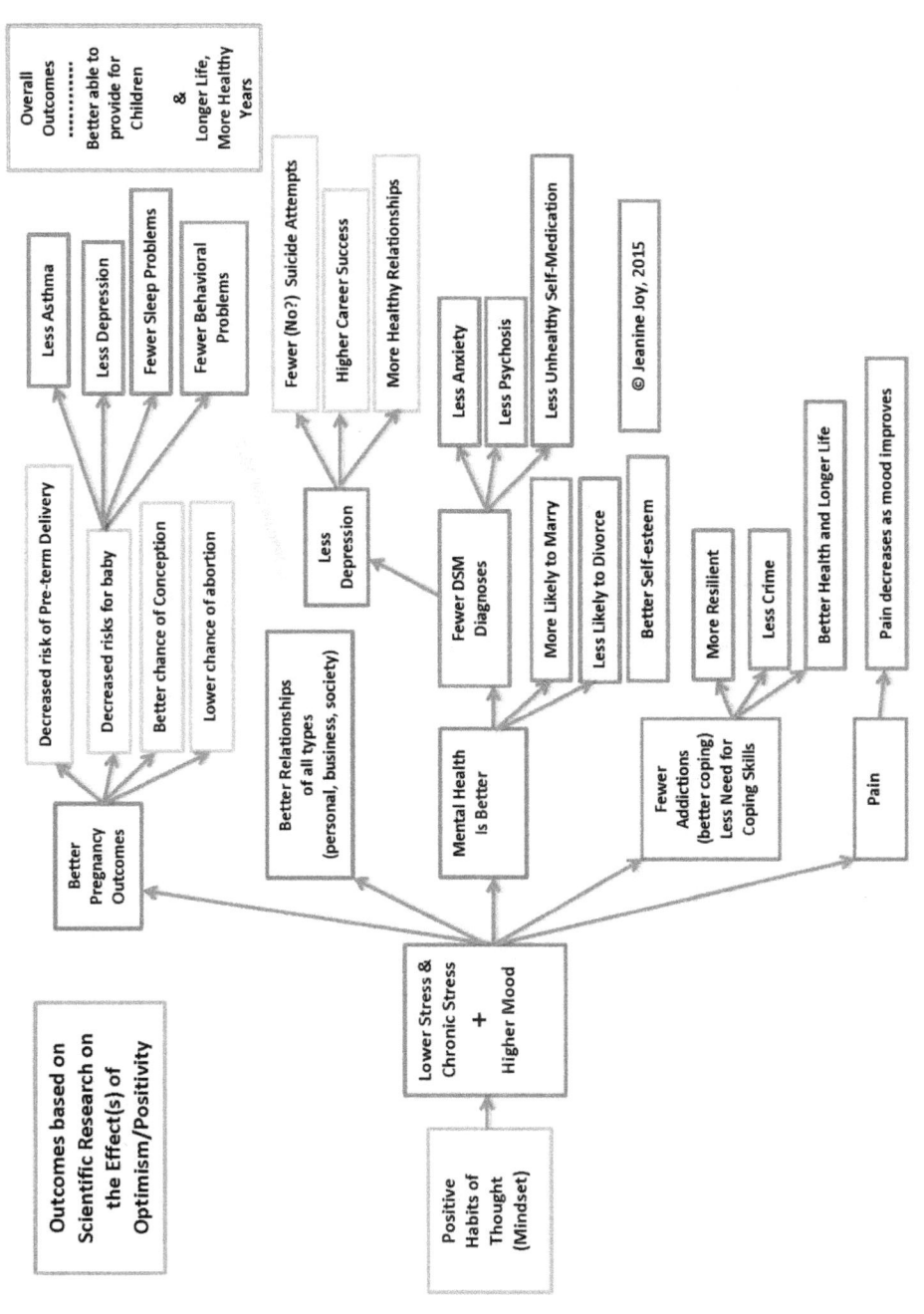

XXI

Appendix VI - Suicide Prevention

Believe that life is worth living, and your belief will help create the fact.
William James

Emergency Numbers

Call a trained suicide prevention counselor (FREE):
- USA: National Suicide Prevention Hotline at 1-800-273-8255; **TTY:** 1-800-799 4TTY (4889)
- UK: Samaritans hotline at 116 123
- The Netherlands: Netherlands Suicide Hotline at 09000767
- France: Suicide écoute at 01 45 39 40 00
- Germany: Telefonseelsorge at 0800 111 0 111 for Protestants, 0800 111 0 222 for Catholics, and 0800 111 0 333 for children and youth

You can also call your doctor, Dial 911, or go to your local Emergency Number, or go to an emergency room. There are people who want to help you. Let them. Call Now.

For a free detailed booklet on depression and its treatment, go to:
http://www.nimh.nih.gov/health/publications/depression/complete-index.shtml

International Emergency Numbers

Australia	000	Switzerland	112	UAE	112
New Zealand	111	India	102	Brazil	192
Fiji	000 or 911	Hong Kong	999	Costa Rica	911
United Kingdom	112 or 999	Israel	101 or 112	S. Africa	112, 10 177
Ireland	112 or 999	Japan	119	China	120
Turkey	112	Nepal	102	Philippines	117 or 112

Special help for LGBT youth at Trevor Lifeline at 866-488-7386 or text "Trevor" to 1-202-304-1200. Available on Thursdays and Fridays between 4:00pm - 8:00pm EST / 1:00pm - 5:00pm PT

Suicide is 100% preventable.

Other Resources:

Focus on the Family has counselors you can talk to free of charge (855-382-5433). TheHopeLine (thehopeline.com) has a web based chat you can do with a Hope Coach

"How can I prevent suicide in adolescents and teenagers?"

The best way to prevent anything is Primary Prevention. Washing our hands before we eat and after we use the bathroom is a form of Primary Prevention that prevents diseases and illness. Clean water delivered to our homes is another form of Primary Prevention.

The same method, Primary Prevention, is the best method of suicide prevention. By teaching adolescents and teenagers strategies that reduce stress and build resilience, they are far less likely to become suicidal. If you're talking about preventing suicide after it has reached the level of an emergency, calling 911 (if in the US) is best,

90% of completed suicides had an underlying mental illness.

Suicide is the 2nd leading cause of death from age 10 – 54.

you can call a suicide prevention hotline, or go to a hospital or your doctor's office. One of the most important things is to take it seriously if someone makes comments that sound suicidal or expresses a desire to engage in self-harm.

Suicide Risk Factors and Warning Signs

Suicide Warning Signs: Act Now

- Depression (prolonged)
- Feeling sad
- Feeling angry
- Pessimism
- Personality change(s)
- Self-criticism
- Talk of death
- Making a will
- Plan to hurt self
- Plan to hurt others
- Withdrawal: family
- Withdrawal: friends
- Neglect of appearance
- Desperation
- Anxiety
- Panic
- Agitation
- Rage
- Not self-supporting
- Feels shame
- Difficulties at school
- Difficulties in sports
- Difficulties at work
- Change in sleep patterns
- Change in eating patterns
- Setback viewed as a failure/sign of low worth
- Rejecting compliments
- Physical symptoms of emotional pain
- Feeling hopeless, "beyond help"
- Giving away possessions
- Increased drug/alcohol abuse
- Sudden improvement after lengthy sad withdrawal
- Lacks sense of purpose
- Reckless behavior/driving
- Sense of being trapped
- Uncontrolled anger
- Seeking/planning revenge
- Dramatic mood changes
- Believe they are a burden to others/society
- Suicidal thoughts (ideation)

When several warning signs are present it is time to act. Trust your read of the situation and save a life.

Suicide Risk Factors

- Prior suicide attempt(s)
- Suicide plan
- Homicidal ideation
- Preoccupation with death
- Mental disorder
- Low self-esteem
- Stress related to LGBTQ
- Mood disorders
- Impulsiveness
- Aggressive tendencies
- Social isolation
- Alienation from family/friends
- New residence during last year
- Lack of social support network
- Family changes
- Relationship conflict
- Absentee parent
- Dysfunctional environment
- Suicide clusters
- Traumatic experience
- Bullied or Bully
- Smokes cigarettes
- Abused as a teenager
- Multiple tattoos
- Rx for mental disorder
- Personality disorder
- Schizophrenia
- Anxiety
- Psychosis
- Alcohol or drug abuse
- Physical illness with loss of activities
- Depression (especially longer than 2 weeks)
- Feels hopelessness
- Learning disabilities
- Self-harm behaviors
- Exposure to violence
- History of childhood abuse
- New school during last year
- Suicide of close friend or family member
- Loss of status
- Recent disappointment or rejection
- Feels mental/behavioral health stigmatizing
- Perfectionism
- Feeling disconnected: religious/spiritual
- Cultural acceptance of suicide
- Irresponsible portrayal of suicide by media
- Self-inflicted high demands
- Abused (especially before age 10)
- Multiple body piercings
- Raised in violent home

Risk factors do not mean suicide is likely—they increase the risk but most people never attempt suicide

Suicide Prevention Help
If you are thinking you would be better off dead or that your loved ones would be better off if you were, call the toll-free 24-hour hotline of the **National Suicide Prevention Lifeline** now at 1-800-273-TALK (1-800-273-8255); TTY: 1-800-799=4TTY (4889) to talk with a trained counselor.
Or, Call your doctor
Dial 911 (or the local emergency number)
or go to an emergency room

◆◆◆◆◆◆◆◆◆◆

Media/Press: Save Lives. Please comply with suicide reporting guidelines.

This page is excerpted from Dr. Joy's book, *Prevent Suicide: The Smart Way*

Appendix VII - Public Health and Mental Health

How important is mental health in public health context?

Mental health is either the most important aspect of public health or tied with physical health. The National Association of School Nurses (NASN) has taken the position that mental health is <u>as critical to academic success as physical well-being</u>. Depending on which research you review, 65 - 99% of all illnesses and diseases begin because of chronic stress. To understand this, you have to dig beneath the surface.

Chronic stress is known effect physical health in these ways:

1. ***Decrease immune function***
    1. Decreased immune function makes us more susceptible to illnesses and diseases.
    2. When our immune function is decreased as the result of chronic stress, illnesses (i.e. colds and flu and even wounds) take longer to recover.
    3. When our immune function is decreased as the result of chronic stress, we are less likely to recover from chronic or life threatening diseases.
    4. On average, a chronically stressed person lives 10.7 years less than someone with low stress.
    5. On average, a chronically stressed person experiences 6 - 8 years of chronic and life-limiting illnesses prior to their earlier death than someone with low stress. Individuals with positive mindsets tend to stay healthy until the last two years of their life even though they live (on average) more than a decade longer.
    6. Low stress reduces the risk of getting heart disease by 50%
2. ***Decreases digestive function***
    1. The risk of obesity increases significantly when an individual is chronically stressed because
        - The way their body processes the food makes identical foods less healthy in the chronically stressed individual
        - High stress makes people not want to exercise, even when they normally exercise and even when they know it will help them feel better
        - Many people use food for comfort food. Food is the #1 anxiety drug in the world.
        - People who are stressed make worse food choices including higher fat and less nutritious foods
        - The risk of developing Type II diabetes increases

3. *Cognitive function decreases*
    1. We make more mistakes and bad decisions with results that affect our success and therefore our ability to afford good food and healthcare
    2. We have a more difficult time solving our problems
4. *Our Central Nervous System (CNS) function declines*
    1. We are more likely to experience an accident
    2. Illnesses related to CNS are more likely
5. *Our relationships aren't as good*
    1. Our emotional state is an indicator of how much stress we are experiencing
        1. As our mood declines we find it more difficult to maintain good relationships with others
        2. We are less likely to marry
        3. We are more likely to divorce
    2. Good relationships provide a protective factor that increases good health. When we are chronically stressed this protective factor declines
6. *Adverse epigentic changes* (genetic switches being turned on for undesired outcomes) are associated with environmental and psychological stressors. These adverse changes last for up to 8 generations in animal experiments.
7. *Increase the risks for our offspring*
    1. We are more likely to deliver a pre-term baby if we have been chronically stressed
    2. Our baby is more likely to suffer from the following before age 16:
        1. Depression
        2. Behavior Problems
        3. Sleep Problems
    3. Our children may inherit adverse epigenetic changes brought about because of chronic stress
8. Chronic stress is known effect behavioral health in these ways:
    1. Increased risk of drug abuse
    2. Increased risk of alcohol abuse
    3. Worse food choices
    4. Less exercise
    5. Increased likelihood of committing crimes or acts of violence
    6. Increased risky behaviors
        1. Failure to practice safe sex
        2. Unsafe driving
        3. Think "behaviors people get the Darwin Award" for posthumously
    7. Increased likelihood of being in an abusive relationship

Mental illness is the cause of disability in 4 our of 10 cases
(National Institute of Health)

8. Increased likelihood of being a bully and/being bullying
9. Lower success in academics, sports, and career

Chronic stress is a leading indicator for mental illnesses.

A *leading indicator* is a measurable factor that exists before a latter event.

Both *schizophrenia* and *psychosis* typically follow chronic stress. The "beginning" of both schizophrenia and psychosis is often associated with a traumatic (highly stressful event) experienced by someone who was already stressed.

Anxiety is essentially a form of chronic stress and anxieties associated with specific situations are essentially a name for chronic stress cause by that specific situation.

Bi-Polar

Bi-polar disorder is a combination of high stress experienced by a person who wants to feel good and doesn't have the skills to do so. When they manage to feel good they are manic and when they don't they are depressive. This is a simplified explanation but individuals who suffer from bi-polar who hear this have said it helped them understand what is going on much better and that learning skills to increase how often they feel good has helped them tremendously.

1 out of 5 children between ages 13 – 18 have or will have a serious mental illness.

Suicide is the #2 cause of death between age 10 - 54. It only drops lower after 54 because people begin dying from other things at higher rates. There are 25 suicide attempts for every completed suicide.

In children, chronic stress and depression interfere with their ability to learn. Mental illness is at epidemic levels in America and throughout the world.

If society understood the cost of chronic stress they would realize that teaching everyone Advanced and Transformational Skills to reduce stress would lower costs. Research shows direct links to chronic diseases, crime, divorce, substance abuse, drop outs, violence, and even poverty. I want everyone to have this knowledge.

Appendix VIII – Emotional Words

Affectionate	Compassionate	Enthusiasm	Hurt	Panicked	Stimulated
Absorbed	Contempt	Enthusiastic	Impatient	Passion	Stressed Out
Afraid	Content	Entranced	Incensed	Passionate	Suicidal
Aggravated	Cranky	Envious	Indifferent	Peaceful	Surprised
Agitated	Curious	Equanimeous	Indignant	Perplexed	Surprised
Agony	Dazed	Exasperated	Insecure	Perturbed	Suspicious
Alarmed	Dazzled	Excited	Inspired	Petrified	Sympathetic
Alert	Dejected	Exhausted	Interested	Pining	Tender
Alienated	Delighted	Exhilarated	Intrigued	Pleased	Tense
Aloof	Depleted	Expectant	Invigorated	Positive Expectation	Trust
Amazed	Depressed	Exploited	Involved	Proud	Terrified
Amazed	Despair	Exuberant	Irate	Puzzled	Thankful
Ambivalent	Despondent	Fascinated	Irked	Quiet	Thrilled
Amused	Detached	Fatigue	Irritable	Radiant	Tickled
Anger	Devastated	Fear	Irritated	Rage	Tired
Angst	Disappointed	Fidgety	Jealous	Rapturous	Torn
Anguished	Discombobulated	Flustered	Jittery	Rattled	Touched
Animated	Disconcerted	Foreboding	Joy	Refreshed	Tranquil
Animosity	Disconnected	Forlorn	Joyful	Regretful	Troubled
Annoyed	Discouraged	Fragile	Jubilant	Rejuvenated	Trusting
Anxious	Disgruntled	Faith	Leery	Relaxed	Turbulent
Apathetic	Disgusted	Frazzled	Lethargic	Relieved	Turmoil
Appalled	Disheartened	Free	Listless	Remorseful	Uncomfortable
Appreciative	Dislike	Friendly	Jubilant	Removed	Uneasy
Apprehensive	Dismayed	Frightened	Livid	Renewed	Unhappy
Ardent	Displeased	Frustrated	Lonely	Repulsed	Uninterested
Aroused	Disquiet	Fulfilled	Longing	Resentful	Unnerved
Ashamed	Distant	Furious	Lost	Reserved	Unsettled
Astonished	Distracted	Giddy	Love	Rested	Unimportant
Aversion	Distraught	Glad	Loving	Restless	Unwanted
Awe	Distressed	Gloomy	Melancholy	Restless	Unworthy
Baffled	Disturbed	Grateful	Mellow	Restored	Upbeat
Beat	Dread	Grief	Miserable	Revived	Upset
Belief	Eager	Guarded	Mistrustful	Sad	Vibrant
Bereaved	Ecstatic	Guilty	Mortified	Safe	Vulnerable
Bewildered	Edgy	Happy	Moved	Satisfied	Warm
Blissful	Elated	Hangry	Mystified	Scared	Wary
Bored	Embarrassed	Hate	Nervous	Secure	Weary
Burnt Out	Empowered	Hatred	Nostalgic	Self-Conscious	Wistful
Calm	Enchanted	Heartbroken	Numb	Sensitive	Withdrawn
Centered	Encouraged	Heavy Hearted	Open	Serene	Wonder
Chagrined	Energetic	Helpless	Open Hearted	Shaky	Worn Out
Clear Headed	Engaged	Hesitant	Optimism	Shocked	Worried
Cold	Engrossed	Hopeful	Optimistic	Sleepy	Wretched
Confident	Enlivened	Hopeless	Outraged	Spellbound	Yearning
Confused	Enraged	Horrified	Overwhelmed	Startled	
comfortable	Enthralled	Hostile	Pain	Still	

Works Cited

(US), N. I. (2007). *Information about Mental Illness and the Brain*. Retrieved January 18, 2017, from NIH Curriculum Supplement Series [Internet]: https://www.ncbi.nlm.nih.gov/books/NBK20369/

Abraham (Performer). (2004). September 18, 2004. [cd-rom]. Chicago, Illinois.

Achor, S. (2010). *The Happiness Advantage: Seven Principles of Positive Psychology That Fuel Success and Performance at Work*. Random House.

Achor, S., & Gielan, M. (2015, September 2). Make Yourself Immune to secondhand Stress. *Harvard Business Review*, p. Epub.

Alkadhi, K. (2013). Brain Physiology andn pathophysioogy in Mental Stress: A Review Article. *Hindawi Publishing Corporation*, 23.

American Academy of Pediatrics. (2012, October 22). *Children with Mental Health Disorders More Often Identified as Bullies*.

American Psychological Association (APA). (2010). *Stress in America Findings: Mind/Body Health: For a Healthy Mind and Body, Talk to a Psychologist*. American Psychological Association (APA).

Anderson, J. G., & Taylor, A. G. (2011). The Metabolic Syndrome and Mind-Body Therapies: A Systematic Review. *Journal of Nutrition and Metabolism*, 8.

Antoniou, A.-S. G., Davidson, M. J., & Cooper, C. L. (2003). Occupational stress, job satisfaction and health state in male and female junior hostpial doctors in Greece. *ournal Manag Psychol, 18*, 592-621.

APA. (2013). *Stress in America: Missing the Health Care Connection*.

APA. (2014). *Stress in America: Are Teens Adopting Adults' Stress Habits?* American Psychological Association. American Psychological Association.

APA. (2015). *Stress in America: Paying with our Health*. American Psychological Association.

Appelbaum, P. S. (2015, April 22). Ethical Challenges in the Primary Prevention of Schiophrenia. *Schizophrenia Bulletin, 41*(4), 773-775.

Armeli, S., O'Hare, R. E., Covault, J., Scott, D. M., & Tennen, H. (2016, January 29). Episode-specific drinking-to-cope motivation and next-day stress reactivity. *Anxiety Stress Coping*, 1-12.

Armstrong, A. R., Galligan, R. F., & Critchley, C. R. (2011). Emotional Intelligence and psychological resilience to negative life events. *Personalit and Individual Differences, 51*, 331-336.

Ashby, F. G. (1999). A neuropsychological theory of positive affect and its influence on cognition. *Psychological Review*, 106, No. 3: 529-50.

Aspinwall, L. G. (2011). Future oriented Thinking, Proactive Coping, and the Management of Threats to Health and Well-Being. In S. Folkman, *Oxford Handbook of Stress, Health, and Coping* (pp. 334-368). Oxford Handbooks.

Assagioli, R. (1965). *Psychosynthesis: A Collection of Basic Writings*. New York: The Viking Press.

Association of Professors of Medicine: The American Journal of Medicine. (2001). *Predicting and Preventing Physician Burnout: Results from the United States and the Netherlands*. Excerpta Medica, Inc.

Aufderheide, D. (2014, April 1). *Mental Illness In America's Jails and Prisons: Toward A Public Safety/Public Health Model*. Retrieved January 18, 2017, from Health Affairs: http://healthaffairs.org/blog/2014/04/01/mental-illness-in-americas-jails-and-prisons-toward-a-public-safetypublic-health-model/

Baratta, M. V., Rozeske, R. R., & Maier, S. F. (2013). Understanding Stress Resilience. *Frontiers in Behavioral Neuroscience*, 1-112.

Barnet, M. B. (2008). *Arch Pediatric Adolescent Medicine*, 162(3): 246-252.

Baumeister, R. F., & Beck, A. (1999). *Evil: Inside Human Violence and Cruelty*. New York: Henry Holt and Co.

Baumeister, R. F., Vohs, K. D., & Tice, D. M. (2007). The Strength Model of Self-Control. *Current Directions in Psychological Science*, 351-355.

Baumeister, R. F., Vohs, K. D., DeWall, C. N., & Zhang, L. (2007, May 16). How Emotion Shapes Behavior: Feedback, Anticipation, and Reflection, Rather Than Direct Causation. *Personality and Social Psychology Review, 11*(2), 167-203.

Beck, R., & Fernandez, E. (1998). Cognitive-Behavioral Therapy in the Treatment of Anger: A Meta-Analysis. *Cognitive Therapy and Research, 22*(1), 63-74.

Bedynsa, S., & Zolnierczyk-Zreda, D. (2015). Stereotype threat as a determinant of burnout or work engagement. Mediating role of positive and negative emotions. *International Journal of Occupational Safety and Ergonomics, 21*(1), 2-8.

Berking, M., Margraf, M., Ebert, D., Wupperman, P., Hofmann, S. G., & Junghanns, K. (2011, June). Deficits in Emotion-Regulation Skills Predict Alcohol Use During and After Cognitive Behavioral Therapy for Alcohol Dependence. *Journal of Consulting and Clinical Psychology, 79*(3), 307-318.

Berry, M. E., Chapple, I. T., Ginsberg, J. P., Gleichauf, K. J., Meyer, J. A., & Nagpal, M. L. (2014, March). Non-pharmacological Interention for Chronic Pain in Veterans: A Pilot Study of Heart Rate Vriability Biofeedback. *Global Advances in Health and Medicine, 3*(2), 28-33.

Beth Israel Deaconess Medical Center. (1989 era). *Stress Management with the Relaxation Response.* Boston: Mind/Body Medical Institute.

Bhatia, V., & Tandon, R. K. (2005, March). Stress and the gastrointestinal tract. *Journal of Gastroenterology and Hepatology, 20*(3), 332-339.

Bigman, Y. E., Mauss, I. B., Gross, J. J., & Tamir, M. (2015, July 29). Yes I can: Expected success promotes actual success in emotion regulation. *Cognition and Emotion, 30*(7), 1380-1387.

Blechert, J., Goltsche, J. E., Herbert, B. M., & Wilhelm, F. H. (2014). Eat your troubles away: Electrocortical and experiential correlates of food image processing are related to emotional eating style and emotional state. *Biological Psychology, 96*, 94-101.

Boden, M. T., & Gross, J. J. (2013). An Emotion Regulation Perspective on Belief Change. In D. Reisberg (Ed.), *The Oxford Handbook of Cognitive Psychology* (pp. 585-599). Oxford University Press.

Boden, M. T., Berenbaum, H., & Gross, J. J. (2016). Why Do People Believe What They Do? A Functionalist Perspective. *Review of General Psychology, 20*(4), 399-411.

Boehm, J. K. (2012, July). The heart's content: The association between positive psychological well-being and cardiovascular health. *Psychological Bulletin, Epub April 2012*, 138(4):655-91.

Bonanno, G. (2004). Loss, trauma, and human resilience: Have we underestimated the human capacity to thrive after extremely aversive events? *American Psychologist, 59*: 20-28.

Bond, S., & Shapiro, D. (2014). *Tough AT The Top? New Rules of ResilieNce foR womeN's leAdeRship success.* Research report.

Boyce, C. J., Wood, A. M., Daly, M., & Sedikides, C. (2015, February 9). Personality Change Following Unemployment. *Journal of Applied Psychology.*

Broderick, J. (2012). Presentation at PPIA 2012. *Positive Psychology in Action, Inc. Positive Health Promotion Forum.* Houston, Tx.

Bruce, A. (2005). *Beyond the Bleep: The definitive unauthorized guide to What the Bleep Do We Know?!* St Paul: Disinformation.

Bryan, T. a. (1991). Positive mood and math performance. *Journal of Learning Disabilities,* 24:490-94.

Bujoreanu, PhD, S., Benhayon, M.D., PhD, D., & Szigethy, M.D., PhD, E. (2011 November). *Treatment of Depression in Children and Adolescents.* Retrieved from Pediatric Super Site: PediatricSuperSite.com

Burnette, J. L., O'Boyle, E. O., VanEpps, E. M., Pollack, J. M., & Finkel, E. J. (2012 (in press), May 9). Mindsets Matter: A Meta-Analytic Review of Implicit Theories and Self-Regulation. *Psychological Bulletin,* 1-63.

Butler, A. C., Chapman, J. E., Forman, E. M., & Beck, A. T. (2006). The empirical status of cognitive-behavioral therapy: A review of meta-analyses. *Clinical Psyhology Review, 26*, 17-31.

Carmona, C., Buunk, A. P., Peiró, J. M., Rodríguez, I., & Bravo, M. J. (2006). Do social comparison and coping styles play a role in the development of burnout? Cross-sectional and longitudinal findings. *Journal of Occupational and Organizational Psychology, 79*(1), 85-99.

Carver, C. S. (2015, July 9). Control Processes, Priority Management, and Affective Dynamics. *Emotion Review, 7*(4), 301-307.

Carver, C. S., & Connor-Smith, J. (2010). Personality and Coping. *Annual Review of Psychology, 61*, 679-704.

Catalino, L. I., & Fredrickson, B. L. (2011). A Tuesday in the Life of a Flourisher: The Role of Positive Emotional Reactivity in Optimal Mental Health. *Emotion, 11*(4), 938-950.

Chang, J. (2011). A Case Study of the "Pygmalion Effect""Teacher Expectations and Student Achievement. *International Education Studies, 4*(1), 198-201.

Cheung, F., Tang, C. S.-k., & Tang, S. (2011). Psychological capital as a moderator between emotional labor, burnout, and job satisfaction among school teachers in China. *International Journal of Stress Management, 18*(4), 348-371.

Christian, L. M. (2012). Physiological reactivity to psychological stress in human pregnancy: Current knowledge and future directions. *Progress in Neurobiology, 99*, 106-116.

Christian, L. M. (2012). Psychoneuroimmunology in pregnancy: Immune pathways linking stress with maternal health, adverse birth outcomes, and fetal development. *Neuroscience and Biobehavioral Reviews, 36*, 350-361.

Cisler, J. M., & Olatunji, B. O. (2012). Emotion Regulation and Anxiety Disorders. *Current Psychiatry Reports, 14*(3), 182-187.

Clark, P. (2010, April). Preventing Future Crime With Cognitive Behavioral Therapy. *National Institute of Justice Journal No. 265*, 22-24.

Cohn, M. A. (2009). Happiness unpacked: Positive emotions increase life satisfaction by building resilience. *Emotion, 9*: 361-368.

Confucius. (2015, February 5). *http://www.theoligarch.com/confucius_quote_three_paths_wisdom.htm*. Retrieved 2015, from http://www.theoligarch.com/confucius_quote_three_paths_wisdom.htm

Creswell, J. D., Welch, W. T., Taylor, S. E., Sherman, D. K., Gruenewax, T. L., Gruenewald, T. L., et al. (2005). Affirmation of Personal Values Buffers Neuroendocrine and Psychological Stress Responses. *Psychological Science, 16*(11), 847-851.

Daily, S. (2012). A healthy teenager is a happy teenager. *Economic and Social Research Council (ESRC)*.

Dalton, P., Mauté, C., Jaén , C., & Wilson, T. (2013, October 9). Chemosignals of Stress Influence Social Judgments. *PLOS One*, Epub.

Danner, D. D. (2001). Positive Emotions in Early Life and Longevity. Findings from the Nun Study. *Journal of Personality and Social Psychology, 80*, No. 5.804-813.

De Castella, K., Goldin, P., Jazaieri, H., Ziv, M., Dweck, C. S., & Gross, J. J. (2013). Beliefs About Emotion: Links to Emotion Regulation, Well-Being, and Psychological Distress. *Basic and Applied Social Psychology*, 497-505.

Deechakawan, PhD, RN, W., Cain, PhD, K. C., Jarrett, PhD, RN, M. E., Burr, MSEE, PhD, R. L., & Heitkemper, PhD, RN, FAAN, M. M. (2012, November 20). Effect of Self-Management Intervention on Cortisol and Daily Stress Levels in Irritable Bowel Syndrome. *Biological Research for Nursing*, 26-36.

Diener, E., & Biswas-Diener, R. (2008). *Happiness: Unlocking the Mysteries of Psychological Wealth.* Blackwell Publishing.

Diener, E., & Chan, M. Y. (2011). Happy People Live Longer: Subjective Well-Being Contributes to Health and Longevity. *The International Association of Applied Psychology: Health and Well-Being*, 1-43.

Ding, Y., Yang, Y., Yang, X., Zhang, T., Qiu, X., He, X., et al. (2015, April 21). The Mediating Role of Coping Style in the Relationship between Psychological Capital and Burnout among Chinese Nurses. *PLOSone, 10*(4).

Dissanayake, R. K., & Bertouch, J. V. (2010, October). Psychosocial interventions as adjunct therapy for patients with rheumatoid arthritis: a systematic review. *International Journal of Rheumatic Diseases, 13*(4), 324-334.

Dockray, S., & Steptoe, A. (2010). Positive Affect and psychobiological processes. *Neuroscience and Biobehavioral Reviews*, 69-75.

Doerrfeld, A. S. (2012, July). Expecting to lift a box together makes the load look lighter. *Psychological Research*(December 9, 2011 online), 76(4): 467-475.

Doolittle, B. R., & Windish, D. M. (2015). Correlation of burnout syndrome with specific coping strategies, behaviors, and spiritual attitudes among interns at Yale University, New Haven, USA. *Journal of Educational Evaluation for Health Professions*, 12-41.

Draper, B., Kolves, K., Leo, D. D., & Snowden, J. (2014). The impact of patient suicide and sudden death on health care professionals. *General Hospital Psychiatry: Psychiatry, Medicine and Primary Care, 36*(6), 721-725.

Driessen, E., & Hollon, S. D. (2010). Cognitive Behavioral Therapy for Mood Disorders: Efficacy, Moderators, and Mediators. *Psychiatric Clinics of North America, 33*(3), 537-555.

Dweck, C. S. (2008). Can Personality Be Changed? The Role of Beliefs in Personality and Change. *Current Directions in Psychological Science, 17*(6).

Dweck, C. S. (2008). *Mindset: The New Psychology of Success.* New York: Ballantine Books.

Edress, H., Connors, C., Paine, L., Norvell, M., & Taylor, H. (2016). Implementing the RISE second victim support programme at the Johns Hopkins Hospital: a case study. *BMJ Open, 6,* e011708.

Eiser, J. R., & Pahl, S. (2001). Optimism, Pessimism, and the Direction of Self-Other Comparisons. *Journal of Experimental Social Psychology, 37*, 77-84.

Ekmund, P. (1992). An argument for basic emotions. *Cognition and Emotion, 6*, 169-200.

Estrada, C. I. (1997). Positive affect facilitates integration of information and decreases anchoring in reasoning among physicians. *Organizational Behavior and Human Decision Processes*, 72: 117-135.

Fagley, N. S. (2012). Appreciation uniquely predicts life satisfaction above demographics, the Big 5 personality factors, and gratitude. *Personality and Individual Differences, 53*, 59-63.

Feldman, B. L., Tarr, M. J., & Lebrecht, S. (2012). 'Micro-Valences: Perceiving Affective Valence in Everyday Objects'. *Frontiers in Psychology.*

Folkman, S., & Moskowitz, J. T. (2004, February). Coping: Pitfalls and Promise. *Annual Review of Psychology, 55*, 745-774.

Fredrickson, B. L. (2005). Positive affect and the complex dynamics of human flourishing. *American Psychologist*, 60(7): 678-686.

Fredrickson, B. L. (2005). Positive Emotions broaden the scope of attention and though-action repertoires. *Cognition and Emotion*, 19: 313-332.

Fredrickson, B. L. (2009, May). The Science of Happiness. (A. Winter, Interviewer) The Sun Magazine.

Fredrickson, B. L. (2010). *Positivity.* Three Rivers Press.

Freeborn, D. K. (2001). Satisfaction, commitment, and psychological well-being among HMO physicians. *Western Journal of Medicine*, 22-30.

Garland, E. L., Fredrickson, B., Kring, A. M., Johnson, D. P., Meyer, P. S., & Penn, D. L. (2010). Upward spirals of positive emotions counter downward spirals of negativity: Insights. *Clinical Psychology Review*, 849-864.

Glashouwer, K. A., de Jong, P. J., & Penninx, B. W. (2012). Prognostic value of implicit and explicit self-associations for the course of depressive and anxiety disorders. *Behaviour Research and Therapy, 50*, 479-486.

Goldberg, B. (2002). *Bias: A CBS Insider Exposes How the Media Distort the News.* Washington DC: Regnery Publishing, Inc.

Goleman, D. (2006). *Social Intelligence.* Bantam Books.

Goodwin, R. D., Pagura, J., Spiwak, R., Lemeshow, A. R., & Sareen, J. (2011). Predictors of persistent nicotine dependence among adults in the United States. *Drug and Alcohol Dependence, 118*, 127-133.

Grant, A. M., & Sonnentag, S. (2010). Doing good buffers against feeling bad: Prosocial impact compensates for negative task and self-evaluations. *Organizational Behavior and Human Decision Processes, 111*, 13-22.

Gross, J. J. (2015). The Extended Process Model of Emotion Regulation: Elaborations, Applications, and Future Directions. *Psychological Inquiry, 26*, 130-137.

Gross, J. J., & John, O. P. (2003, August). Individual differences in two emotion regulation processes: implications for affect, relationships, and well-being. *Journal Personal Sociology and Psychology, 85*(2), 348-362.

Haidt, J. (2006). *The Happiness Hypothesis: Finding Modern Truth in Ancient Wisdom. Why the Meaningful Life Is Closer Than You Think.* New York: Basic Books.

Hall, J. (. (2017). *HRdive.com*. Retrieved 2017, from Employees report having higher stress levels: http://www.hrdive.com/news/aon-hewitt-54-of-employees-report-having-higher-stress-levels/439665/

Harman, W. (1998). *Global Mind Change*. Barrett-Koehler Publishers, Inc.

Heller, A. S., van Reekum, C. M., Schaefer, S. M., Lapate, R. C., Radler, B. T., Ryff, C. D., et al. (2013). Sustained Striatal Activity Predicts Eudaimonic Well-Being and Cortisol Output. *Psychological Science, 24*(11), 2191-2200.

Hessler, D. M., & Katz, L. F. (2010). Brief report: Associations between emotional competence and adolescent risky behavior. *Journal of Adolescence, 33*, 241-246.

Hill, N. (1994). *Keys to Success*. New York: Penguin Group.

Hofmann, S. G., Asnaani, A., Vonk, I. J., Sawyer, A. T., & Fang, A. (2012, October 1). The Efficacy of Cognitive Behavioral Therapy: A Review of Meta-analyses. *Cognitive Therapy and Research, 36*(5), 427-440.

Hopp, H., Troy, A. S., & Mauss, I. B. (2011). The unconscious pursuit of emotion regulation: Implications for psychological health. *Cognitive Emoiton*, 532-545.

Houkes, I., Winants, Y., Twellaar, M., & Verdonk, P. (2011). Development of burnout over time and the causal order of the three dimensions of burnout among male and female GPs. A three-wave panel study. *BMC Pubic Health, 11*, 1-13.

Hounkpatin, H. O., Wood, A. M., Boyce, C. J., & Dunn, G. (2015). An Existential-Humanistic View of Personality Change: Co-Occurring Changes with Psyhological Well-Being in a 10 Year Cohort Study. *Social Indicators Research*, 455-470.

Hu, T., Zhang, D., Wang, J.-L., Mistry, R., Ran, G., & Wang, X. (2014, April). Relation between emotion regulation and mental health: A meta-analysis-review. *Psychological Reports, 114*(2), 341-362.

Huby, G., Gerry, M., McKinstry, B., Porter, M., Shaw, J., & Wrate, R. (2002, July 20). Morale among general practitioners: qualitative study exploring relations between partnership arrangements, personal style, and workload. *The BMJ, 325*.

Hunsaker, S., Chen, H. C., Maughan, D., & Heaston, S. (2015, March). Factors that influence the development of compassion fatigue, burnout, and compassion satisfaction in emergency department nurses. *Journal Nursing Scholarship, 47*(1), 186-94.

Infurna, F. J., & Luthar, S. S. (2016, March). Resilience to Major Life Stressors Is Not as Common as Thought. *Perspectives in Psychological Science, 11*, 175-194.

Ito, T., & Urland, G. R. (2003). Race and gender on the brain: Electro-cortical measures of attention to the race and gender of multiple categorizable individuals. *Journal of Personality and Social Psychology 85*, 616-26.

Jackson, D., Firtko, A., & Edenborough, M. (2007, October). Personal resilience as a strategy for surviving and thriving in the face of workplace adversity: a literature review. *Journal Advances in Nursing, 60*(1), 1-9.

Jensen, RN PhD, P. M., Trollope-Kumar, MD PhD, K., Waters, MD CCFP, H., & Everson, MD CCFP FCFP, J. (2008, May). Building Physician Resilience. *Canadian Family Physician, 54*(5), 722-729.

John, O. P., & Gross, J. J. (2004). Healthy and Unhealthy Emotion Regulation: Personality Processes, Individual Differences, and Life Span Development. *Journal of Personality, 72*(6), 1301-1335.

Johnson, K. J., Waugh, C. E., & Fredrickson, B. L. (2010). Smile to see the forest: Facially expressed positive emotions broaden cognition. *COGNITION AND EMOTION*, 24(2): 299-321.

Joy, Ph.D., J. (2015). *Is Punishment Ethical?* Concord: Thrive More Now.

Keeney, J., & Ilies, R. (2011). Positive Work--Family Dynamics. In K. S. Cameron, & G. M. Spreitzer (Eds.), *A Path Forward: Assessing Progress and Exploring Core Questions for the Future*

Kessler, R. C., Demler, O., Frank, R. G., Olfson, M., Pincus, H. A., Walters, E. E., et al. (2005). Prevalence and Treatment of Mental Disorders, 1990 to 2003. *The New England Journal of Mediine, 352*, 2515-2523.

Khansar, D. N., Murgo, A. J., & Faith, R. E. (1990). Effects of Stress on the Immune System. *Immunology Today, 11*, 170-176.

Kobylinska, D., & Karwowska, D. (2015, October 27). How automatic activation of emotion regulation influences experiencing negative emotins. (P. Kusev, Ed.) *Frontiers in psychology*, 1-4.

Koerner, N., Antony, M. M., Young, L., & McCabe, R. E. (2013, April). Changes in Beliefs about the Social Competence of Self and Others Following Group Cognitive Behavioral Therapy. *Cognitive Therapy Research, 37*(2), 256-265.

Koole, S. L. (2009). The psychology of emotion regulation: An integrative review. *Cognition and Emotion, 23*(1), 4-41.

Koran. (n.d.). http://www.forgottenbooks.com/readbook_text/The_Koran_or_Alcoran_of_Mohammed_100024313 3/639. (Chapter XC, p. 490 (639)) Retrieved 2015, from Forgotten Books: http://www.forgottenbooks.com/readbook_text/The_Koran_or_Alcoran_of_Mohammed_1000243133/639

Kudinova, A. Y., Owens, M., Burkhouse, K. L., Barretto, K. M., Bonanno, G. A., & Gibb, B. E. (2015, May). Differences in emotion modulation using cognitive reappraisal in individuals with and without suicidal ideation: An ERP study. *Cognitive Emotion, 15*, 1-9.

Kumar, S. (2016). Burnout and Doctors: Prevalence, Prevention, and Intervention. (P. A. Leggat, & D. R. Smith, Eds.) *Healthcare, 4*(37).

Kutluturkan, S., Sozeri, E., Uysal, N., & Bay, F. (2016). Resilience and burnout status among nurses working in oncology. *Anals of General Psychiatry, 15*(33), 1-9.

Kwong, J. Y., Wong, K. F., & Tang, S. K. (2013). Comparing predicted and actual affective responses to process versus outcome: An Emotion-as-feedback perspective. *Cognition, 129*, 42-50.

Lai JC, E. P. (2005). Optimism, positive affectivity, and salivary cortisol. *British Journal of Health Psychology*, 4:467-84.

Langer, E. J. (2009). *Counterclockwise: Mindful Health and the Power of Possibility*. New York: Random House.

Lansing, A. H., & Bert, C. A. (2014). Topical Review: Adolescent Self-Regulation as a Foundation for Chronic Illness Self-Management. *Journal of Pediatric Psychology, 39*(10), 1091-1096.

Larson, M. D., Norman, S. M., Hughes, L. W., & Avey, J. B. (2013). Psychological Capital: A New Lens for Understanding Employee Fit and Attitudes. *Internal Journal of Leadership Studies, 8*(1), 28-43.

Lashinger, H. K., Borgogni, L., Consiglio, C., & Read, E. (2015, June). The effects of authentic leadership, six areas of worklife, and occupational coping self-efficacy on new graduate nurses' burnout and mental health: A cross-sectional study. *international Journal Nursing Studies, 52*(6), 1080-1089.

Lazarus. (1991). *Cognition and Emotion*.

Leary, M. R., Schreindorfer, L. S., & Haupt, A. L. (1995, September). The Role of Low Self-Esteem in Emotional and Behavioral Problems: Why is Low Self-Esteem Dysfunctional? *Journal of Social and Clinical Psychology, 14*(3), 297-314.

Lee, MD, F. J., Brown, PhD, J. B., & Stewart, PhD, M. (2009). Exploring Family Physician Stress. *Canada Family Physician, 55*(3), 280-289.

Lemelle, C. J., & Seielzo, S. A. (2012). How You Feel About Yourself Can Affect How You Feel About Your Job: A Meta-Analysis Examing the Relationship of Core Self-Evaluations and Job Satisfaction. *Journal of Business Diversity, 12*(3), 116-133.

Lépine, J.-P., & Briley, M. (2011). The increasing burden of depression. *Neuropsychiatric Disorder Treatment, 7*(Suppl 1), 3-7.

Lewis, S. (2011). *Positive Psychology at Work: How Positive Leadership and Appreciative Inquiry Create Inspiring Organizations*. Wiley-Blackwell.

Li, X., Guan, L., Chang, H., & Zhang, B. (2014, December 26). Core Self-Evaluation and Burnout among Nurses: The Mediating Role of Coping Styles. *PLoS One*, 1-12.

Liberman, V., Anderson, N. R., & Ross, L. (2010). Achieving difficult agreements: Effects of Positive Expectations on negotiation processes and outcomes. *Journal of Experimental Social Psychology, 46*, 494-504.

Lipton, B. H., & Bhaerman, S. (2009). *Spontaneous Evolution: Our Positive Future (and a way to get there from here)*. Carlsbad: Hay House.

Livingston, J. S. (2003, January 1). Pygmalion in Management (HBR Classic). *Harvard Business Review*.

Lohmann, MS, LPC, R. C. (2013, June 27). *Teen Bullying: A CBT Approach to Addressing the Issue*. Retrieved from Psychology Today: https://www.psychologytoday.com/blog/teen-angst/201306/teen-bullying-cbt-approach-addressing-the-issue

Lopez, A., Sanderman, R., Smink, A., Zhang, Y., van Sonderen, E., Ranchor, A., et al. (2015). A Reconsideration of the Self-Compassion Scale's Total Score: Self-Compassion Versus Self-Criticism. *PLoS One*, 1-12.

Luken, M., & Sammons, A. (2016). Systematic Review of Mindfulness Practice for Reducing Job Burnout. *The American Journal of Occupational Therapy, 70*.

Luthans, F., Luthans, K. W., & Luthans, B. C. (2004, January-February). Positive psychological capital: Beyond human and social capital. *Business Horizons*, pp. 45-50.

Lyubomirsky, S., & Porta, M. D. ((in press)). Boosting Happiness and Buttressing Resilience: Results from Cognitive and Behavioral Interventions. In J. W. Reich, A. J. Zautra, & J. Hall (Eds.), *Handbook of adult resilience: Concepts, methods, and application*. New York, NY, USA: Guilford Press.

Lyubomirsky, S., King, L., & Diener, E. (2005). The Benefits of Frequent Positive Affect: Does Happiness Lead to Success? *Psychological Bulletin, 131*(6), 803-855.

Manzano-García, G., & Ayala, J.-C. (2017, April 7). Insufficiently studied factors related to burnout in nursing: Results from an e-Delphi study. *PLoS ONE, 12*(4).

Martin, R. C., & Dahlen, E. R. (2005). Cognitive emotion regulation in the prediction of depression, anxiety, stress, and anger. *Personality and Individual Differences*, 1249-1260.

Mason, W. A., January, S. A., Fleming, C. B., Thompson, R. W., Parra, G. R., Haggerty, K. P., et al. (2016, February). Parent Training to Reduce Problem Behaviors over the Transition to High School: Tests of Indirect Effects through Improved Emotion Regulation Skills. *Child Youth Services Review*, 176-183.

Mauss, I. B., & Gross, J. J. (2004). Emotional Suppression and cardiovascular disease Is hiding feelings bad for your heart? In I. Nyklíček, L. Temoshok, & A. Vingerhoets (Eds.), *Emotional Expression and Health* (pp. 62-81). New York, NY, United States of America: Brunner-Routledge, Taylor & Francis Group.

Mauss, I. B., Bunge, S. A., & Gross, J. J. (2007). Automatic Emotion Regulation. *Social and Personality Psychology Compass*, 146-167.

Mauss, I. B., Shallcross, A. J., Troy, A. S., John, O. P., Ferrer, E., Wilhelm, F. H., et al. (2011). Don't Hide Your Happiness! Positive Emotion Dissociation, Social Connectedness, and Psychological Functioning. *ournal of Personality and Social Psychology, 100*(4), 738-748.

McCarthy, B., & Casey, T. (2011). Get Happy! Positive Emotion, Depression and Juvenile Crime. *American Sociological Associaion Annual Meeting*. Las Vegas: UC Davis.

McGregor, B. A., Antoni, M. H., Boyers, A., Alfen, S. M., Blomberg, B. B., & Carver, C. S. (2004, January). Cognitive-Behavioral stress management increases benefit finding and immune function among women with early-stage breast cancer. *ournal of Psychosomatic Research, 56*(1), 1-8.

McHugh, R. K., Hearon, B. A., & Otto, M. W. (2010, September). Cognitive-Behavioral Therapy for Substance Use Disorders. *Psychiatric Clinics of North America, 33*(3), 511-525.

McLeod, S. A. (2009). *Emotion Focused Coping*. Retrieved 2017, from Simple Psychology: https://www.simplypsychology.org/stress-management.html

McManus, I. C., Keeling, A., & Paice, E. (2004). Stress, burnout and doctors' attitudes to work are determined by personality and learning style: A twelve year longitudinal study of UK medical graduates. *MBC Medicine*, 2-29.

Meissner, C., & Brigham, J. (2001). Thirty years of investigating the own-race bias in memory for faces. *Psychology, Public Policy, and Law 7*, 3 - 35.

Miller, F. E. (2001). Challenging and changing stress-producing thinking. *Western Journal of Medicine, 174*(1), 49-50.

Mohd, R. S. (2008, October). Life Event, Stress and Illness. *The Malaysian Journal of Medical Sciences, 15*(4), 9-18.

Montague, MD (neurologist), J. (n.d.). Why is the brain prone to florid forms of confabulation?

Montero-Marin, J., Demarzo, M. M., Stepinski, L., Gill, M., & Garcia-Campayo, J. (2014, June). Perceived Stress Latent Factors and the Burnout Subtypes: A Structural Model in Dental Students. *PLoS One, 9*(6).

Montero-Marin, J., Prado-Abril, J., Demarzo, M. M., Gascon, S., & Garcı́a-Campayo, J. (2014, February). Coping with Stress and Types of Burnout: Explanatory. *PLoS ONE, 9*(2).

Montero-Marin, J., Zubiaga, F., Cereceda, M., Demarzo, M. M., Trenc, P., & Garcia-Campayo, J. (2016, June 16). Burnout Subtypes and Absence of Self-Compassion in Primary Healthcare Professionals: A Cross-Sectional Study. *PLoS ONE*, 1-17.

Montgomery, J. (2012, May). *Cafe Mom*, Cancer Might be the best thing that ever happened to me. Retrieved 2012, from http://wwwthestir.cafemom.com/healthy_living/136851/cancer_might_be_the_best

Mroczek, D. K., & Spiro III, A. (2007, May). Personality Change Influences Mortality in Older Men. *Association for Psychological Science, 18*(5), 371-376.

Muris, P., & Petrocchi, N. (2016, February 19). Protection or Vulnerability? A Meta-Analysis of the Relations Between the Positive and Negative components of SElf-Compassion and Psychopathology. *Clinical Psychology Psychotherapy*, ePub.

Murphy, E. R., Barch, D. M., Pagliaccio, D., Luby, J. L., & Belden, A. C. (2015 (in press)). Functional connectivity of the amygdala and subgenual cingulate during cognitive reappraisal of emotions in children with MDD history is associated with rumination. *Developmental Cognitive Neuroscience*.

Murphy, R., Straebler, S., Cooper, Z., & Fairburn, C. G. (2010, September). Cognitive Behavioral Therapy for Eating Disorders. *The Psychiatric Clinics of North America*, 611-627.

Nadler, R. S. (2011). *Leading with emotional Intelligence: Hands-on strategies for building confident and collaborative star performers*. New York: McGraw Hill.

Neff, K. D., & Vonk, R. (2009, February). Self-compassion versus global self-esteem: two different ways of relating to oneself. *ournal of Personality, 77*(1), 23-50.

Nettles, R., & Balter, R. (Eds.). (2011). *Multiple Minority Identities*. New York, NY, USA: Springer Publishing Company.

NIH. (n.d.). *National Institute of Health*. Retrieved 2014, from http://www.nlm.nih.gov/medlineplus/magazine/issues/winter08/articles/winter08pg6b.html

Nisbett, R. E. (2003). *The Geography of Thought: How Asians and Westerners Think Differently...and Why*. New York: The Free Press.

Nubold, A., Muck, P. M., & Maier, G. W. (2013). A new substitute for leadership? Followers state core self-evaluations. *The Leadership Quarterly, 24*, 29-44.

October, T. W. (2015). Work-life balance is an illusion: replace guilt with acceptance. *frontiers in Pediatrics, 3*(76), ePub.

Okunda, M., Balán, I., Petry, N. M., Oquendo, M., & Blanco, C. (2009, December). Cognitive Behavioral Therapy for Pathological Gambling: Cultural Considerations. *American Journal of Psychiatry, 166*(12), 1325-1330.

Ong, A. D., Bergeman, C. S., Bisconti, T. L., & Wallace, K. A. (2006). Psychological Resilience, Postive Emotions, and Successful Adaptation to Stress in Later Life. *Journal of Personaltiy and Social Psychology 91*, 730-49.

Ong, A. D., Mroczek, D. K., & Riffin, C. (2011, August 1). The Health Significance of Positive Emotions in Adulthood and Later Life. *Social and Personality Psychology Compass, 5*(8), 538-551.

Ornstein, R. E. (1977). *The Psychology of Consciousness.* Harcourt Brace Jovanovich, Inc.

Orri, M., Revah-Levy, A., & Farges, O. (2015, November 24). Surgeons' Emotional Experience of Their Everyday Practice - A Qualitative Study. *PLoS ONE,* 1-15.

Papathanasiou, I. V. (2015). Work-related Mental Consequences: Implications of Burnout on Mental Health Status Among Health Care Providers. *ACTA Inform Med,* 22-28.

Parashar, F. (2015). *Optimism and Pessimism.* Retrieved from www.positivepsychology.org: www.positivepsychology.org

Parrott, W. G. (2001, September). Implications of dysfunctional emotions for understanding how emotions function. *Review of General Psychology, 5*(3), 180-186.

Parton, S. (2016, March 12). Complaining is Terrible for You, According to Science. (J. Stillman, Interviewer)

Pathways to Resilience: Maternal Nurturance as a Buffer Against the Effects of Childhood Poverty on Metabolic Syndrome at Midlife. (2011, September 24). *Association for Psychological Science.*

Paul, K. I., & Moser, K. (2009). Unemployment impairs mental health: Meta-Analysis. *Journal of Vocational Behavior, 74,* 264-282.

Peckham, C. (2015). *Burnout and Happiness in Physicians: 2013 vs 2015: Physician Burnout: It Just Keeps Getting Worse.*

Peckham, C. (2016). *Medscape Lifestyle Report 2016: Bias and Burnout.* Medcape.

Peil, K. T. (2014). Emotion: The Self-regulatory Sense. *Global Advances in Health and Medicine,* 80-108.

Peña-Sarrionandia, A., Mikolajczak, M., & Gross, J. J. (2015, February 24). Integrating emotion regulation and emotional intelligence traditions: a meta-analysis. *Frontiers in Psychology, 6*(160).

Peschke, I. (2015, 3 31). *Career Burnout? How to Relight Your Candle.* Retrieved 2017, from http://www.huffingtonpost.com/ingrid-peschke/career-burnout-how-to-relight-your-candle_b_6968966.html

Peterson, C. (2006). *A Primer in Positive Psychology.* Oxford, UK: Oxford University Press.

Petit, G., Luminet, O., Maurage, F., Tecco, J., Lechantre, S., Ferauge, M., et al. (2015, December). Emotion Regulation in Alcohol dependence. *ALCOHOLISM: CLINICAL AND EXPERIMENTAL RESEARCH, 39*(12).

Pugh, S. D., Groth, M., & Hennig-Thurau, T. (2011, March). Willing and able to fake emotions: a closer examination of the link between emotion. *Joural Applied Psychology, 96*(2), 377-390.

Pyszczynski, T., Greenberg, J., Solomon, S., Arndt, J., & Schimel, J. (2004). Why Do People Need Self-Esteem? A Theoretical and Empirical Review. *Psychological Bulletin, 130,* 435-468.

Rees, C. S., Heritage, B., Osseriran-Moisson, R., Chamberlain, D., Cusack, L., Anderson, J., et al. (2016, July 19). Can We Predict Burnout among Student Nurses? An Explorationof the ICWR-1 Model of Individual Psychological Resilience. *Frontiers in Psychology, 7*(1072), 1-11.

Ricard, M. (2003). *Happiness: A Guide to Developing Life's Most Important Skill.* Little, Brown and Company.

Riccomini, P. J., Bost, L. W., Katsiyannis, A., & Zhang, D. (2005). *Cognitive Behavioral Interventions: An Effective Approach to Help Students wtih Disabilities Stay in School.* National Dropout Prevention Center for Students with Disabilities (NDPC-SD), College of Health, Education, and Human Development - Clemson University. Clemson: Office of Special Education Programs of the U.S. Department of Education.

Richards, J. M., & Gross, J. J. (1999). Composure at Any Cost? The Cognitive Consequences of Emotional Suppression. *Personality and Social Psychology Bulletin,* 1033-1044.

Richards, J. M., & Gross, J. J. (2005). Personality and emotional memory: How regulating emotion impairs memory for emotional events. *Journal of Research in Personality,* xxx-xxx (in press).

Roberts, B. W., Lou, J., Briley, D. A., Chow, P. I., Su, R., & Hill, P. L. (2017, January). A Systematic Review of Personality Trait Change Through Intervention. *Psychological Bulletin*, online.

Robertson, S. M., Stanley, M. A., Cully, J. A., & Naik, A. D. (2012). Positive Emotional Health and Diabetes Care: Concepts, Measurement, and Clinical Implications. *Psychosomatics, 53*, 1-12.

Rogala, A., Shoji, K., Luszczynska, A., Kuna, A., Yeager, C., Benight, C. C., et al. (2016, January 8). From Exhaustion to Disengagement via Self-Efficacy Change: Findings from Two Longitudinal Studies among Human Service Workers. *Frontiers in Psychology, 6*.

Rollin, M., Bradley, R. T., & Atkinson, M. (2004). Electropsyciological Evidence of Intuition. Part 1: The Surprising Role of the Heart. *Journal of alternative and Complementary Medicine, 10*(1) pp. 133-143.

Romani, M., & Ashkar, K. (2014). Burnout among physicians. *Libyan Journal of Medicine*, 1-6.

Rosenberg, T. (2015, January 15). For Better Crime Prevention, a Dose of Science. *The New York Times*, p. The Opinion Pages.

Roth, T. L., Lubin, F. D., Funk, A. J., & Sweatt, J. D. (2009). Lasting Epigenetic Influence of Early-Life Adversity on the BDNF Gene. *Society of Biophysical Psychiatry*, 65:760–769.

Rubenstein, E. (1999). *An Awakening from the Trances of Everyday Life: A Journey to Empowerment*. Sages Way Press.

Salami, S. O. (2007). Management of Stress among Trainee-Teachers Through Cognitive-Behavioural Therapy. *Pakistan Journal of Social Sciences, 4*(2), 299-307.

Samson, A. C., & Gross, J. J. (2014). The Dark and Light Sides of Humor. In J. Gruber, & J. T. Moskowitz (Eds.), *Positive Emotion: Integrating the Light Sides and Dark Sides* (pp. 169-184). Oxford Scholarship Online.

Sani, F., Herrera, M., Wakefield, J. R., Boroch, O., & Gulyas, C. (2012). Comparing social contact and group identification as predictors of mental health. *The British Psychological Society, 51*, 781-790.

Sbarra, , D. A., Smith, H. L., & Mehl, M. R. (2001, September 21). Advice to divorcees: Go easy on yourself. *Association for Psychological Science*.

Schnall, S., Roper, J., & Fessler, D. M. (2010, February 3). Pay It Forward: Elevation Leads to Altruistic Behavior. *Psychological Science*.

Schneider, T. R. (2004). The role of neuroticism on psychological and physiological stress responses. *Journal of Experimental Social Psychology*, 795-804.

Schwarz, D. J. (1959 (2007)). *The Magic of Thinking BIG*. New York: Simon & Schuster.

Schwarzer, R., & Knoll, N. (2003). Positive Coping: Mastering demands and searching for meaning. In S. J. Lopez, & C. R. Snyder (Eds.), *Positive Psychological Assessment: Handbook of Models and Measures*. Washington, D.C., USA.

Schwingshackl, A. (2014). The fallacy of chasing after work-life balance. *frontiers in Pediatrics, 2*(26), ePub.

Scoglio, A. A., Rudat, D. A., Garvert, D., Jarmolowski, M., Jackson, C., & Herman, J. L. (2015, December 16). Self-Compassion and Responses to Trauma: The Role of Emotion Regulation. *Journal Interpersonal Violence*, Epub.

Seidman, L. J., & Nordentoft, M. (2015, April 29). New Targets for Prevention of Schizophrenia: Is it Time for Interventions in the Premorbid Phase? *Schizophrenia Bulletin, 41*(4), 795-800.

Seligman, M. (2011). *Flourish: A Visionary New Understanding of Happiness and Well-Being*. New York: Free Press.

Seligman, M. (n.d.). Berkeley-Oakland Study (ongoing). *Reported by Seligman in Flourish*.

Seligman,, M. (2006). *Learned Optimism* (Originally published 1991 ed.). New York: Simon & Schuster.

Seppala, E. M., Hutcherson, C. A., Nguyen, D. T., Doty, J. R., & Gross, J. J. (2014). Loving-Kindness meditation: a tool to improve healthcare provider compassion, resilience, and patient care. *Journal of Compassionate Health Care, 1*(5).

Shanafelt, T. D., Oreskovich, M. R., Dyrbye, L. N., Sataele, D. V., Hanks, J. B., Sloan, J. A., et al. (2012, April). Avoiding burnout: the personal health habits and wellness practices of US surgeons. *Annals of Surgery, 255*(4), 625-633.

Shatté, A., Perlman, A., Smith, B., & Lynch, W. D. (2017, February). The Positive Effect of Resilience on Stress and Business Outcomes in Difficult Work Environments. *JOEM, 59*(2).

Shenk, D. (2010). *The Genius in All of Us*. Doubleday.

Shenk, J. W. (2009, June 1). Writing about the Grant Study. *The Atlantic*. Writing in September 1938 [Arlie] Brock declared that medical research paid too much attention to sick people; that dividing the body up into symptoms and diseases--and viewing it through the lenses of a hundred micro-specialities--could never shed light: on the urgent quesion of how, on the whole, to live well.

Sheppes, G., & Gross, J. J. (2014). Emotion Generation and Emotion Regulaton: Moving Beyond Traditional Duel-Process Accounts. In J. W. Sherman, PhD, & B. Gawronski, PhD (Eds.), *Dual-Process Theories of the Social Mind* (pp. 483-496). New York, NY, United States of America: The Guilford Press, A Division of Guilford Publications, Inc.

Siemer, M. (2001). Mood-specific effects on appraisal and emotion judgements. *Cognition and Emotion, 15*(4), 453-485.

Siemer, M. (2005, Sept). Mood-congruent cognitions constitute mood experience. *Emotion, 5*(3), 296-308.

Siemer, M., Mauss, I., & Gross, J. J. (2007). Same Situation—Different Emotions: How Appraisals Shape Our Emotions. *Emotion, 7*(3), 592-600.

Spreitzer, G. M., & Porath, C. (2014). Self-Determination as a Nutriment for Thriving: Building an Integrative Model of Human Growth at Work. In M. Gagne (Ed.), *Oxford Handbook of Work Engagement, Motivation, and Self-Determination Theory* (pp. 245-258). New York, NY: Oxford University Press.

Srivastava, S., McGonigal, K. M., Richards, J. M., Butler, E. A., & Gross, J. J. (2006). Optimism in Close Relationships: How Seeing Things in a Positive Light Makes Them So. *Personality Processes and Individual Differences, 91*(1), 143-153.

Stangier, U. (2016, March). New Developments in Cognitive-Behavioral Therapy for Social Anxiety Disorder. *Current Psychiatry Reports, 18*(3), Epub.

Steptoe, A. W. (2005). Positive affect and health-related neuroendocrine, cardiovascular, and inflammatory responses. *Proceedings of the National Academy of Sciences*.

Strengths. (n.d.). Retrieved from https://en.wikipedia.org/wiki/Values_in_Action_Inventory_of_Strengths#cite_note-3

Stutzer, A., & Frey, B. S. (2006, April). Does marriage make people happy, or do happy people get married? *The Journal of Socio-Economics, 35*(2), 326-347.

Sullivan, P., & Buske, L. (1998). Results from CMA's huge 1998 physician survey point to a dispirited profession. *Canadian Medical Association, 159*(5), 525-528.

Suri, G., Whittaker, K., & Gross, J. J. (2015). Launching Reappraisal: It's Less Common Than You Might Think. *Emotion, 15*(1), 73-77.

Talbot, M. (1991). *The Holographic Universe*. New York: Harper Collins.

The American Institute for Cognitive Therapy. (2016). *Warning Signs of Too Much Stress*. Retrieved from cognitivetherapy.com: www.cognitivetherapy.com

The HeartMath Institute. (2012, November 11). *Coherence*. Retrieved from www.heartmath.com: www.heartmath.com

Treglown, L., Palaiou, K., Zarola, A., & Furnham, A. (2016, June 23). The Dark Side of Resilience and Burnout: A Moderation-Meditation Model. *PLOSone, 11*(6).

Troy, A. S., Shallcross, A. J., Davis, T. S., & Mauss, I. B. (2013, September 1). History of Mindfulness-Based Cognitive Therapy is Associated with Increased Cognitive Reappraisal Ability. *Mindfulness, 4*(3), 213-222.

Turiano, N. A., Pitzer, L., Armour, C., Arlamangla, A., Ryff, C. D., & Mroczek, D. K. (2012). Personality Trait Level and Change as Predictors of Health Outcomes: Findings From a National Study of.). *The Journals of Gerontology, Series B: Psychological Sciences and Social Sciences, 67*, 4-12.

University, O. S. (2012, May 23). Wearing two different hats. Moral decisions may depend on the situation.

Vaillant, G. E. (2012). *Triumphs of Experience: The Men of the Harvard Grant Study*.

van der Wal, R. A., Bucx, M. J., Hendriks, J. C., Scheffer, G. J., & Prins, J. B. (2016, March). Psychological distress, burnout and personality traits in Dutch anaesthesiologists: A survey. *European Journal of Anaesthesiology, 33*(3), 179-186.

van Mol, M. M., Kompanje, E. J., Benoit, D. D., Bakker, J., & Nijkamp, M. D. (2015). The Prevalence of Compassion Fatigue and Burnout among Healthcare Professionals in Intensive Care Units: A Systematic Review. *PLoS ONE.*

Vantiborgh, T., Bidee, J., Pepermans, R., Griep, Y., & Hofmans, J. (2016, May 12). Antecedents of Psychological Contract Breach: the Role of Job Demands, Job Resources, and Affect. *PLoS One.*

Veilleux, J. C., Skinner, K. D., Reese, E. D., & Shaver, J. A. (n.d.). *Negative affect intensity influences drinking to cope through facets of emotion dysregulation,.* University of Arkansas.

Voellmin, A., Entringer, S., Moog, N., Wadhwa, P. D., & Buss, C. (2013). Maternal positive affect over the course of pregnancy is associated with the length of gestation and reduced risk of preterm delivery. *Journal of Psychosomatic Research, 75*, 336-340.

Waddimba, A. C., Scribani, M., Hasbrouch, M. A., Krupa, N., Jenkins, P., & May, J. J. (2016, October). Resilience among Employed Physicians and Mid-Level Practitiners in Upstate New York. *Health Services Research, 51*(5), 706-734.

Weiner, E. L., Swain, G. R., Wolf, B., & Gottlieb, M. (2001). A qualitative study of physicians' own wellness-promotion practices. *Western Journal of Medicine, 174*(1), 19-23.

Werner, K. H., Jazaieri, H., Goldin, P. R., Ziv, M., Heimberg, R. G., & Gross, J. J. (2012). Self-Compassion and Social Anxiety Disorder. *Anxiety Stress Coping, 25*(5), 543-558.

West, C. P., Dyrbye, L. N., Satele, D. V., Sloan, J. A., & Shanafelt, T. D. (2012, November). Concurrent Validity of Single-Item Measures of Emotional Exhaustion and Depersonalization in Burnout Assessment. *Journal of General Internal Medicine, 27*(11), 1445-1452.

Westermann, S., Boden, M. T., Gross, J. J., & Lincoln, T. M. (2013). Maladaptive Cognitive Emotion Regulation Prospectively Predicts. *Cognitive Therapy Resarch, 37*, 881-885.

Whitney, D., & Trosten-Bloom, A. (2010). *The Power of Appreciative Inquiry: A Practical Guide to Positive Change* (2 ed.). NY: McGraw-Hill.

Wilcox, D. (2011). *The Source Field Investigations.* New York: Penguin Group.

Wingo, A. P., Ressler, K. J., & Bradley, B. (2014). Resilience characteristics mitigate tendency for harmful alcohol and illicit drug use in adults wiht a history of childhood abuse: A Cross-sectional study of 2024 inner-city men and women. *Journal of Psychiatric Research.*

Wong, E., Tschan, F., Messerli, L., & Semmer, N. K. (2013). Expressing and Amplifying Positive Emotions Facilitate Goal Attainment in Workplace Interactions. *Frontiers in Psychology,* 188.

Wood, J. V., Perunovic, W. E., & Lee, J. W. (2009). Positive Self-Statements Power for Some, Peril for Others. *Psychological Science, 20*, 860-866.

Yamaguchi, Y., Inoue, T., Harada, H., & Oike, M. (2016, December). Job control, work-family balance and nurses' intention to leave their profession and organization: A Comparative cross-sectional survey. *Internal Journal of Nursing Studies*, 52-62.

Zambrano, S. C., Chur-Hansen, A., & Crawford, G. B. (2014, August). The experiences, coping mechanisms, and impact of death and dying on palliative medicine specialists. *Palliative Support Care, 12*(4), 209316.

Zimmer-Gembeck, M. J., & Skinner, E. A. (2014). The Development of Coping: Implications for Psychopathology and Resilience. In D. Cicchetti (Ed.), *Developmental Psychopathology* (Vol. Resubmission #2, pp. 1-117). Oxford, England: Wiley & Sons.

Zuffiano, A., Alessandri, G., Gerbino, M., Kanacri, B. P., Di , Giunta, L., et al. (2013). Academic achievement: The unique contribution of self-efficacy beliefs in self-regulated learning beyond intelligence, personality traits, and self-esteem. *Learning and Individual Differences, 23*, 158-162.

Zyromski, B., & Joseph, A. E. (n.d.). *Utilizing Cognitive Behavioral Interventions to Positively Impact Achievement in Middle School Students.*

Zysberg, L., & Rubanov, A. (2010). Emotional Intelligence and Emotional Eating Patterns: A New Insight into the Antecedents of Eating Disorders? *Journal of nutrition Education and Behavior, 42*, 345-348.

Citations

---

[1] (Hall, 2017)
[2] (NIH)
[3] www.nimh.nih.gov
[4] The National Institute of Mental Illness
[5] www.nih.gov
[6] ((US), 2007)
[7] ((US), 2007)
[8] (The American Institute for Cognitive Therapy, 2016)
[9] (Beth Israel Deaconess Medical Center, 1989 era)
[10] (Hessler & Katz, 2010)
[11] (Baumeister R. F., Vohs, DeWall, & Zhang, 2007)
[12] (Peil, 2014)
[13] (Carver, Control Processes, Priority Management, and Affective Dynamics, 2015)
[14] (Baumeister R. F., Vohs, DeWall, & Zhang, 2007)
[15] (Peil, 2014)
[16] (Kwong, Wong, & Tang, 2013)
[17] (Carver, Control Processes, Priority Management, and Affective Dynamics, 2015)
[18] (Hopp, Troy, & Mauss, 2011)
[19] (Seligman M. , 2011)
[20] (Rubenstein, 1999)
[21] (Fredrickson B. L., Positivity, 2010)
[22] (Ekmund, 1992)
[23] (Talbot, 1991)
[24] (Peil, 2014)
[25] (Peil, 2014)
[26] (Baumeister R. F., Vohs, DeWall, & Zhang, 2007)
[27] (Peil, 2014)
[28] (Hopp, Troy, & Mauss, 2011)
[29] (Kwong, Wong, & Tang, 2013)
[30] (Carver, Control Processes, Priority Management, and Affective Dynamics, 2015)
[31] Peil Kauffman, 2015
[32] (Baumeister & Beck, Evil: Inside Human Violence and Cruelty, 1999)
[33] (McCarthy & Casey, 2011)
[34] (Joy, Ph.D., 2015)
[35] (Mauss, Bunge, & Gross, Automatic Emotion Regulation, 2007)
[36] (Siemer, Mauss, & Gross, Same Situation—Different Emotions: How Appraisals Shape Our Emotions, 2007)
[37] (Goldberg, 2002)
[38] (Broderick, 2012)
[39] (Rubenstein, 1999)
[40] (Talbot, 1991)
[41] (Ricard, 2003)

[42] (Eiser & Pahl, 2001)
[43] (Fredrickson B. L., The Science of Happiness, 2009) (Seligman,, 2006) (Seligman M., 2011)
(Achor, The Happiness Advantage: Seven Principles of Positive Psychology That Fuel Success and Performance at Work, 2010)
[44] (Peil, 2012)
[45] (Seligman, 2006)
[46] (Fredrickson B. L., The Science of Happiness, 2009) pp. 109
[47] (Parashar, 2015)
[48] (Westermann, Boden, Gross, & Lincoln, 2013)
[49] (Papathanasiou, 2015)
[50] (Seligman,, 2006)
[51] (Burnette, O'Boyle, VanEpps, Pollack, & Finkel, 2012 (in press))
[52] (Lipton & Bhaerman, 2009)
[53] (Seligman,, 2006)
[54] (McManus, Keeling, & Paice, 2004)
55 (Ricard, 2003)
[56] (Feldman, Tarr, & Lebrecht, 2012)
[57] (Schneider, 2004)
[58] (Goleman, 2006)
[59] (Wilcox, 2011)
[60] (APA, 2014)
[61] (Parton, 2016)
[62] (Haidt, 2006)
[63] (Haidt, 2006)
[64] (Seligman,, 2006)
[65] (Montague, MD (neurologist))
[66] (Parashar, 2015)
[67] (Armstrong, Galligan, & Critchley, 2011)
[68] (Kutluturkan, Sozeri, Uysal, & Bay, 2016)
[69] (van der Wal, Bucx, Hendriks, Scheffer, & Prins, 2016)
[70] (Waddimba, Scribani, Hasbrouch, Krupa, Jenkins, & May, 2016)
[71] (Jackson, Firtko, & Edenborough, 2007)
[72] (Jackson, Firtko, & Edenborough, 2007)
[73] (Peterson, 2006, pp. 115-116)
[74] (Srivastava, McGonigal, Richards, Butler, & Gross, 2006)
[75] (Srivastava, McGonigal, Richards, Butler, & Gross, 2006)
[76] (Shatté, Perlman, Smith, & Lynch, 2017, p. 139)
[77] (Seligman M., 2011)
[78] (Seligman M.)
[79] (Pathways to Resilience: Maternal Nurturance as a Buffer Against the Effects of Childhood Poverty on Metabolic Syndrome at Midlife, 2011)
[80] (Shenk D., 2010)
[81] (Romani & Ashkar, 2014)
[82] (Gross, The Extended Process Model of Emotion Regulation: Elaborations, Applications, and Future Directions, 2015)
[83] (Aspinwall, 2011)
[84] (APA, 2015)
[85] (Carmona, Buunk, Peiró, Rodríguez, & Bravo, 2006)
[86] (Rees, et al., 2016)

[87] (Siemer, Mood-specific effects on appraisal and emotion judgements, 2001)
[88] (Assagioli, 1965)
[89] (Folkman & Moskowitzz, 2004)
[90] (Schwarzer & Knoll, 2003)
[91] (Doerrfeld, 2012)
[92] (Peña-Sarrionandia, Mikolajczak, & Gross, 2015)
[93] (Nettles & Balter, 2011)
[94] (Hopp, Troy, & Mauss, 2011)
[95] (Shanafelt, et al., 2012)
[96] (John & Gross, 2004)
[97] (Montero-Marin, Demarzo, Stepinski, Gill, & Garcia-Campayo, 2014)
[98] (Samson & Gross, 2014)
[99] (Mason, et al., 2016)
[100] (Miller, 2001)
[101] (Weiner, Swain, Wolf, & Gottlieb, 2001)
[102] (Boden & Gross, An Emotion Regulation Perspective on Belief Change, 2013)
[103] (Boden & Gross, An Emotion Regulation Perspective on Belief Change, 2013)
[104] (Achor & Gielan, Make Yourself Immune to secondhand Stress, 2015)
[105] (Miller, 2001)
[106] (American Psychological Association (APA), 2010, p. 15)
[107] (Hopp, Troy, & Mauss, 2011)
[108] (Baumeister, Vohs, & Tice, The Strength Model of Self-Control, 2007, p. 351)
[109] (Hopp, Troy, & Mauss, 2011, p. 543)
[110] (Pugh, Groth, & Hennig-Thurau, 2011)
[111] (Carmona, Buunk, Peiró, Rodríguez, & Bravo, 2006)
[112] (Treglown, Palaiou, Zarola, & Furnham, 2016)
[113] (Treglown, Palaiou, Zarola, & Furnham, 2016)
[114] (Dalton, Mauté, Jaén, & Wilson, 2013)
[115] (Seligman,, 2006)
[116] (De Castella, Goldin, Jazaieri, Ziv, Dweck, & Gross, 2013)
[117] (Neff & Vonk, 2009)
[118] (Montero-Marin, Zubiaga, Cereceda, Demarzo, Trenc, & Garcia-Campayo, 2016)
[119] (Muris & Petrocchi, 2016)
[120] (Werner, Jazaieri, Goldin, Ziv, Heimberg, & Gross, 2012)
[121] (Lopez, et al., 2015)
[122] (Neff & Vonk, 2009)
[123] (Scoglio, Rudat, Garvert, Jarmolowski, Jackson, & Herman, 2015)
[124] (Sbarra, , Smith, & Mehl, 2001)
[125] 1925 January 28, The Marcellus Observer, Stick to the Finish, (Acknowledgement to Exchange), Quote Page 1, Column 7, Marcellus, New York. (Old Fulton)
[126] (Chang, 2011)
[127] (Livingston, 2003)
[128] (Bigman, Mauss, Gross, & Tamir, 2015)
[129] (Keeney & Ilies, 2011)
[130] (Romani & Ashkar, 2014)
[131] (Shanafelt, et al., 2012)
[132] (Fagley, 2012)
[133] (Srivastava, McGonigal, Richards, Butler, & Gross, 2006)
[134] (Nettles & Balter, 2011)
[135] (Peil, 2014)

[136] (Siemer, Mood-congruent cognitions constitute mood experience, 2005)
[137] (Hopp, Troy, & Mauss, 2011)
[138] (Hopp, Troy, & Mauss, 2011)
[139] (Hu, Zhang, Wang, Mistry, Ran, & Wang, 2014)
[140] (Hopp, Troy, & Mauss, 2011)
[141] (Diener & Chan, Happy People Live Longer: Subjective Well-Being Contributes to Health and Longevity, 2011)
[142] (Vaillant, 2012)
[143] (Berry, Chapple, Ginsberg, Gleichauf, Meyer, & Nagpal, 2014)
[144] (Berry, Chapple, Ginsberg, Gleichauf, Meyer, & Nagpal, 2014)
[145] (Boehm, 2012)
[146] (The HeartMath Institute, 2012)
[147] (Kumar, 2016)
[148] http://the-happy-manager.com/articles/characteristic-of-leadership/
[149] Source Edgar Schein in his book Organisational Culture and Leadership
[150] (Creswell, et al., 2005)
[151] (Wood, Perunovic, & Lee, 2009)
[152] (Bedynsa & Zolnierczyk-Zreda, 2015)
[153] (Heller, et al., 2013)
[154] (Strengths)
[155] (Gross & John, Individual differences in two emotion regulation processes: implications for affect, relationships, and well-being, 2003)
[156] (Sani, Herrera, Wakefield, Boroch, & Gulyas, 2012)
[157] (Jensen, RN PhD, Trollope-Kumar, MD PhD, Waters, MD CCFP, & Everson, MD CCFP FCFP, 2008)
[158] (Peckham, Burnout and Happiness in Physicians: 2013 vs 2015: Physician Burnout: It Just Keeps Getting Worse, 2015)
[159] (Seppala, Hutcherson, Nguyen, Doty, & Gross, 2014)
[160] (Doolittle & Windish, 2015)
[161] (Koole, 2009)
[162] (Suri, Whittaker, & Gross, 2015)
[163] (Seligman,, 2006)
[164] (Nettles & Balter, 2011)
[165] (Westermann, Boden, Gross, & Lincoln, 2013)
[166] (Seligman,, 2006)
[167] (Boyce, Wood, Daly, & Sedikides, 2015)
[168] (Dweck, Can Personality Be Changed? The Role of Beliefs in Personality and Change, 2008)
[169] (Hounkpatin, Wood, Boyce, & Dunn, 2015)
[170] (Mroczek & Spiro III, 2007)
[171] (Roberts, Lou, Briley, Chow, Su, & Hill, 2017)
[172] (Turiano, Pitzer, Armour, Arlamangla, Ryff, & Mroczek, 2012)
[173] (Gross & John, Individual differences in two emotion regulation processes: implications for affect, relationships, and well-being, 2003)
[174] (Richards & Gross, Personality and emotional memory: How regulating emotion impairs memory for emotional events, 2005)
[175] (Mauss & Gross, Emotional Suppression and cardiovascular disease Is hiding feelings bad for your heart?, 2004)
[176] (Parrott, 2001)
[177] (Westermann, Boden, Gross, & Lincoln, 2013)

[178] (Shenk D., 2010)
[179] (Langer, 2009)
[180] (Chang, 2011)
[181] (Glashouwer, de Jong, & Penninx, 2012)
[182] (Leary, Schreindorfer, & Haupt, 1995)
[183] (Pyszczynski, Greenberg, Solomon, Arndt, & Schimel, 2004)
[184] (Zuffiano, et al., 2013)
[185] (Rogala, et al., 2016)
[186] (Doolittle & Windish, 2015)
[187] (Treglown, Palaiou, Zarola, & Furnham, 2016)
[188] (Troy, Shallcross, Davis, & Mauss, 2013)
[189] (Cisler & Olatunji, 2012)
[190] (Armstrong, Galligan, & Critchley, 2011)
[191] (Kobylinska & Karwowska, 2015)
[192] (Zyromski & Joseph)
[193] ((US), 2007)
[194] (Hofmann, Asnaani, Vonk, Sawyer, & Fang, 2012)
[195] (Hu, Zhang, Wang, Mistry, Ran, & Wang, 2014)
[196] (Nettles & Balter, 2011)
[197] (Nettles & Balter, 2011)
[198] (Nettles & Balter, 2011)
[199] (Nettles & Balter, 2011)
[200] (Nettles & Balter, 2011)
[201] (Nettles & Balter, 2011)
[202] (Baumeister R. F., Vohs, DeWall, & Zhang, 2007)
[203] (Kwong, Wong, & Tang, 2013)
[204] (Peil, 2014)
[205] (Carver, Control Processes, Priority Management, and Affective Dynamics, 2015)
[206] (Spreitzer & Porath, 2014)
[207] (Spreitzer & Porath, 2014)
[208] (Peil, 2014)
[209] (Luken & Sammons, 2016)
[210] (Luken & Sammons, 2016)
[211] (October, 2015)
[212] (October, 2015)
[213] (Schwingshackl, 2014)
[214] (Kessler, et al., 2005)
[215] (Aufderheide, 2014)
[216] (NIH)
[217] (Danner, 2001)
[218] (Vaillant, 2012)
[219] (Lyubomirsky & Porta, Boosting Happiness and Buttressing Resilience: Results from Cognitive and Behavioral Interventions, (in press))
[220] (Lépine & Briley, 2011)
[221] (Lyubomirsky & Porta, Boosting Happiness and Buttressing Resilience: Results from Cognitive and Behavioral Interventions, (in press))
[222] (Rosenberg, 2015)
[223] (Riccomini, Bost, Katsiyannis, & Zhang, 2005)
[224] (Hopp, Troy, & Mauss, 2011)
[225] (Garland, Fredrickson, Kring, Johnson, Meyer, & Penn, 2010)

[226] (Boehm, 2012)
[227] (Mohd, 2008)
[228] (Lyubomirsky & Porta, Boosting Happiness and Buttressing Resilience: Results from Cognitive and Behavioral Interventions, (in press))
[229] (Garland, Fredrickson, Kring, Johnson, Meyer, & Penn, 2010)
[230] (Hopp, Troy, & Mauss, 2011)
[231] (Lyubomirsky & Porta, Boosting Happiness and Buttressing Resilience: Results from Cognitive and Behavioral Interventions, (in press))
[232] (Butler, Chapman, Forman, & Beck, 2006)
[233] (Hofmann, Asnaani, Vonk, Sawyer, & Fang, 2012)
[234] (Schnall, Roper, & Fessler, 2010)
[235] (McCarthy & Casey, 2011)
[236] (Rosenberg, 2015)
[237] (Hofmann, Asnaani, Vonk, Sawyer, & Fang, 2012)
[238] (Clark, 2010)
[239] (Baumeister & Beck, Evil: Inside Human Violence and Cruelty, 1999)
[240] (Lyubomirsky & Porta, Boosting Happiness and Buttressing Resilience: Results from Cognitive and Behavioral Interventions, (in press))
[241] (Lyubomirsky & Porta, Boosting Happiness and Buttressing Resilience: Results from Cognitive and Behavioral Interventions, (in press))
[242] (American Academy of Pediatrics, 2012)
[243] (Hofmann, Asnaani, Vonk, Sawyer, & Fang, 2012)
[244] (Okunda, Balán, Petry, Oquendo, & Blanco, 2009)
[245] (Stutzer & Frey, 2006)
[246] (Boehm, 2012)
[247] (Goodwin, Pagura, Spiwak, Lemeshow, & Sareen, 2011)
[248] (Armeli, O'Hare, Covault, Scott, & Tennen, 2016)
[249] (Veilleux, Skinner, Reese, & Shaver)
[250] (Petit, et al., 2015)
[251] (Wingo, Ressler, & Bradley, 2014)
[252] (Berking, Margraf, Ebert, Wupperman, Hofmann, & Junghanns, 2011)
[253] (Boehm, 2012)
[254] (Blechert, Goltsche, Herbert, & Wilhelm, 2014)
[255] (McHugh, Hearon, & Otto, 2010)
[256] (McHugh, Hearon, & Otto, 2010)
[257] (Hofmann, Asnaani, Vonk, Sawyer, & Fang, 2012)
[258] (Lyubomirsky & Porta, Boosting Happiness and Buttressing Resilience: Results from Cognitive and Behavioral Interventions, (in press))
[259] (Fredrickson B. L., 2005)
[260] (McCarthy & Casey, 2011)
[261] (Anderson & Taylor, 2011)
[262] (McGregor, Antoni, Boyers, Alfen, Blomberg, & Carver, 2004)
[263] (Boehm, 2012)
[264] (Mohd, 2008)
[265] (Hofmann, Asnaani, Vonk, Sawyer, & Fang, 2012)
[266] (Dissanayake & Bertouch, 2010)
[267] (Deechakawan, PhD, RN, Cain, PhD, Jarrett, PhD, RN, Burr, MSEE, PhD, & Heitkemper, PhD, RN, FAAN, 2012)
[268] (Lansing & Bert, 2014)
[269] (Voellmin, Entringer, Moog, Wadhwa, & Buss, 2013)

[270] (Roth, Lubin, Funk, & Sweatt, 2009)
[271] (Lohmann, MS, LPC, 2013)
[272] (Lyubomirsky & Porta, Boosting Happiness and Buttressing Resilience: Results from Cognitive and Behavioral Interventions, (in press))
[273] (Garland, Fredrickson, Kring, Johnson, Meyer, & Penn, 2010)
[274] (Hu, Zhang, Wang, Mistry, Ran, & Wang, 2014)
[275] (Murphy, Barch, Pagliaccio, Luby, & Belden, 2015 (in press))
[276] (McCarthy & Casey, 2011)
[277] (Hopp, Troy, & Mauss, 2011)
[278] (Armstrong, Galligan, & Critchley, 2011)
[279] (Butler, Chapman, Forman, & Beck, 2006)
[280] (Stangier, 2016)
[281] (Koerner, Antony, Young, & McCabe, 2013)
[282] (Hofmann, Asnaani, Vonk, Sawyer, & Fang, 2012)
[283] (Driessen & Hollon, 2010)
[284] (Bujoreanu, PhD, Benhayon, M.D., PhD, & Szigethy, M.D., PhD, 2011 November)
[285] (Kudinova, Owens, Burkhouse, Barretto, Bonanno, & Gibb, 2015)
[286] (Armstrong, Galligan, & Critchley, 2011)
[287] (Butler, Chapman, Forman, & Beck, 2006)
[288] (Butler, Chapman, Forman, & Beck, 2006)
[289] (Hofmann, Asnaani, Vonk, Sawyer, & Fang, 2012)
[290] (Armstrong, Galligan, & Critchley, 2011)
[291] (Driessen & Hollon, 2010)
[292] (Hofmann, Asnaani, Vonk, Sawyer, & Fang, 2012)
[293] (Hofmann, Asnaani, Vonk, Sawyer, & Fang, 2012)
[294] (Beck & Fernandez, 1998)
[295] (Hofmann, Asnaani, Vonk, Sawyer, & Fang, 2012)
[296] (Hofmann, Asnaani, Vonk, Sawyer, & Fang, 2012)
[297] (Hofmann, Asnaani, Vonk, Sawyer, & Fang, 2012)
[298] (Hofmann, Asnaani, Vonk, Sawyer, & Fang, 2012)
[299] (Murphy, Straebler, Cooper, & Fairburn, 2010)
[300] (Zysberg & Rubanov, 2010)
[301] (Driessen & Hollon, 2010)
[302] (Butler, Chapman, Forman, & Beck, 2006)
[303] (Hofmann, Asnaani, Vonk, Sawyer, & Fang, 2012)
[304] (Hofmann, Asnaani, Vonk, Sawyer, & Fang, 2012)
[305] (Hofmann, Asnaani, Vonk, Sawyer, & Fang, 2012)
[306] (Hofmann, Asnaani, Vonk, Sawyer, & Fang, 2012)
[307] (Butler, Chapman, Forman, & Beck, 2006)
[308] (Butler, Chapman, Forman, & Beck, 2006)
[309] (Hofmann, Asnaani, Vonk, Sawyer, & Fang, 2012)
[310] (Armstrong, Galligan, & Critchley, 2011)
[311] (Hu, Zhang, Wang, Mistry, Ran, & Wang, 2014)
[312] (Butler, Chapman, Forman, & Beck, 2006)
[313] (Lyubomirsky & Porta, Boosting Happiness and Buttressing Resilience: Results from Cognitive and Behavioral Interventions, (in press))
[314] (Lyubomirsky & Porta, Boosting Happiness and Buttressing Resilience: Results from Cognitive and Behavioral Interventions, (in press))
[315] (Garland, Fredrickson, Kring, Johnson, Meyer, & Penn, 2010)
[316] (Salami, 2007)

[317] (Alkadhi, 2013)
[318] (Nisbett, 2003)
[319] (McCarthy & Casey, 2011)
[320] (Barnet, 2008)
[321] (Daily, 2012)
[322] (Achor, The Happiness Advantage: Seven Principles of Positive Psychology That Fuel Success and Performance at Work, 2010)
[323] (Fredrickson B. L., The Science of Happiness, 2009)
[324] Bhagwath gita (Bg. 10.11).
[325] Śrīmad-Bhāgavatam" (SB 1.19.36).
[326] Laozi (2009-10-04). The Tao Teh King, or the Tao and its Characteristics
[327] Woodward, Frank Lee (2011-03-24). The Buddha's Path of Virtue A Translation of the Dhammapada
[5] The Koran (Al-Qur'an) (2005-02-01).
[329] Abraham, Chicago, IL on Saturday, September 18th, 2004
[330] (Abraham, 2004)

www.ingramcontent.com/pod-product-compliance
Lightning Source LLC
Chambersburg PA
CBHW051401070526
44584CB00023B/3242